STAY MINE FOREVER

LETTERS FROM NAM

THE STORY OF TONY & CLELLIE JOLLEY

Denise Jolley

STAY MINE FOREVER
Letters from Nam

The Story of Tony & Clellie Jolley

Denise Jolley

Published by Jolley's Journeys Publishing
Stay Mine Forever: Letters From Nam
Copyright 2021 Denise Jolley All rights reserved.

No part of this publication may be reproduced, stored in a retrieval system, or transmitted in any form by any means, electronic, mechanical, photocopying, recording, or by any information retrieval or storage system without the express written permission of the author except in the case of excerpts used for critical review.

For more information or to contact the author:
Email: JolleysJourneysPublishing@gmail.com
Book cover design: Ann Mathews & Denise Jolley
Book design & formatting: Ann Mathews
Book editing: Denise Jolley & Barbara Hollace, www.barbarahollace.com

ISBN: 978-0-578-92775-6
Printed in the United States of America

DEDICATION

Dedicated to Tony and Clellie Jolley and the many people who call them friends and family.

Much love to my husband Chad who is my biggest supporter, encourager, and motivator.

Special thanks to Ann Mathews and Barbara Hollace, without your help this would not have been possible. Thank you for making this labor of love a reality.

FOREWORD

A few years ago, I was gifted a bunch of tattered and discolored letters that had been stored in a cardboard box. They were not in any particular order, and much like the couple that wrote them, they were older and frail. I stored that mouse-chewed box in a trunk to be dealt with at a later time. Curiosity wouldn't keep me away long though. I needed to know what was so special about these letters. First, one letter, then another, and another…I couldn't put them down.

As I read the incredible account of a love story between my husband's parents, I realized it was a story that needed to be shared. They were more than just love letters; this collection was a part of American history. These letters were a treasure.

As a person born after the war, my knowledge of this time comes from what I've read in history books or seen in movies. Learning more about the Vietnam War, I am constantly amazed by the incredible people who so bravely and selflessly gave their lives to fight such a controversial battle. Tony didn't speak much about his experiences in Vietnam and Cambodia, so the insight brought by reading the words he wrote at the time was so precious. Many of the names were respectfully changed for their privacy.

It is my hope that this book would bring honor to all veterans and their families. I share Tony's story knowing it is the story of many others who have gone into battle.

Thank you to all of the military members who fight so bravely and with great courage. For those who have returned from war to face the unknown, and the ones who didn't whose memory lives on, we owe you everything. You have my respect, my gratitude, and my prayers continue for you and your family.

May the Lord protect and prosper you all of your days!

Denise Jolley

CONTENTS

Dedication 5
Foreword 7
Contents 9
Love Interrupted 12
Basic Training 15
Advanced Individual Training (AIT) 43
A Baby is Born 119
Non-Commissioned Officer (NCO) School 139
Time to Get a Job 177
Getting into Trouble 231
Time to Pay the Piper 255
Leaving for Ft. Hood, Texas 321
Thanksgiving! 353
Our Christmas Together 379
Leaving for Nam 423
Entering Cambodia 457
Hawaii and Returning Home 501
Freedom! 513

LOVE INTERRUPTED

Many people spend their entire lives searching for just the perfect person, but in all reality, it often catches you off guard when you least expect it. It disrupts any normalcy you thought you had but replaces it with a desire to live for more than just yourself. To love beyond depths you ever thought possible.

I was born in 1949 in Minico, Idaho. I met Clellie Graf at school and found it hard to believe she'd want to run with a guy like me. We were from two different worlds and I could only have dreamed to have caught her attention. Somehow, as fate would have it, I did just that and for a short period of time, we were inseparable.

I graduated in 1967 and we married just two years later. Clellie was a strong gal whose family life was very difficult. Her parents had recently separated and Clellie was living at home with her mom to help care for her younger sisters (Ann, Nancy, and Alice) while her brothers (Virgil and Steve) helped her father with farm work.

Before Nam, I was going back and forth between odd jobs, construction, and taking care of my parents, Wayne and Angeles, and looking after my brother Allan. I was raised in a traditional Catholic family with two sisters (Marie and Amanda), five brothers (Andrew, Barry, Leo, Rick, and Allan), and parents that believed in hard work and honoring your word.

Before I was drafted, all I knew was we were in Vietnam to fight for the freedoms of the people of Nam and end the tyranny of Communism. The VC (Viet Cong) had taken over a lot of Nam. All of the north was controlled by the Communist VC and now they wanted the south.

The day my draft number was called was the scariest but one of the happiest moments of my life. I was real happy because I knew I was going to be part of something big that was going to change one country, to free Nam from Communism.

I was sent to BT (Basic Training) in the spring of 1969. I was scared with the thought of leaving my family and wife behind. Clellie was pregnant with our first child and I did not want to miss such a special time or leave her to care for things on her own. Clellie and I were just 19 years old when we married in December of '68.

From the time I met Clellie, I knew she was the one for me. They say sometimes you just know, and I guess they are right. I just knew! But not all relationships are perfect, and distance takes a toll on relationships when you're so far away from the person you love. Nam changed me in many ways. It made me jealous, lonely, angry, and demanding but it could never take away the love I had for my Clellie…sometimes that was the only thing that got me through.

Things haven't been easy. In order to see our love at work, and what it was like to be in the middle of the war, I'm going to share with you letters that we wrote so long ago. I had just left for Basic Training and had no idea what to be prepared for. Some of our letters had to be tossed out but these are what we could save. Our love was interrupted by Vietnam, but we were determined to be together forever. I hope you enjoy our story.

Love,
Tony

BASIC TRAINING

✉ 21 Mar 1969

Dear Clellie,

I just woke up and am ready to run a mile before we eat. Just wrote this short note to let you know my address.

I miss and love you very much. I wish I had more time but the D. I. will be here in a short time, yelling his head off. Goodbye for now and remember I love you.

Love, Tony

Pvt. Anthony Jolley
H.H.C 5th Bn 1st Brig.
Ft. Ord, California 4th Plt 93941

✉ **24 Mar 1969**

Dear Clellie,

Well I'm at the Basic Training camp now. I just started this letter about a half-an-hour ago, and we were told to fall out, so I'm back to finish it now.

Boy, I sure am tired. Today is Saturday and we finally finished our outside training until Monday, but they sure have worked us hard so far. Yesterday we took a P.T. test. This is a physical exercise test to see how fit you are. Wow, I'm a hell-of-a lot in better shape than I thought I would be.

They put John Butler in a different barracks after we got here, and it sure is a bummer. John and I really got along great, and every time we see each other we really get a kick out of fooling around. The only good thing about this barracks is that Spear and Miller are in it too. Spear and I are both in the same squad too.

Oh, guess what, Clellie? The platoon I'm in is called the "Fat Forty." This is because a lot of the guys in it are very fat. Since we got all the fat ones, in our platoon, we're the last ones to eat and also they cut down on our food. This means that every time I go through the chow line, I have to fight and argue like hell to get enough to eat. Also we have to do a lot of extra exercises. We run a mile first thing in the morning before chow, and all day long.

Clellie, you really wouldn't believe the morale in this Army. Everybody is drafted and all they talk about is going A.W.O.L. One guy named Gib, completely cracked up. He's about 23 years old and went to college for 3 years. When he first came into the Army down at the reception station, he didn't act too bad. But when we got here to Basic, he started to get really nervous. He got so bad and all he did was jump continually. When the drill sergeants saw this they just harassed him and laughed at him and called him names until they finally took him to the hospital. He left the day before yesterday and we probably will never see him again. Of course, in a way he's kind of lucky because he gets to go home.

While we are at Basic we won't get leaves, and we work out every day except a few hours on Sunday. This is going to go on for 8 weeks. The reason for this is that by keeping us working all the time they'll win some more.

Boy, Clellie, I sure do miss you, and all I do all day long is think about you. I knew while I was gone I would miss you, but I didn't think a person was capable of missing someone as much as I do you. I've only been in this Army about a week and a half and it seems like three years. This life is so straight, strict, and uniform; I really don't see how I'm going to make the first 8 weeks, let alone 2 years.

The next letter you write to me, Clellie, I want you to send me a lot of pictures of you. Also tell me how much school you've missed, how many boys you hustled, and how much you go out. Clellie, if you see Carter some time, give him my address and tell him to write.

How are you feeling, Clellie? I wish I were there with you. I know it's not much consolation to you but maybe I could help. Ha! Ha! I hope you're all right because I'm so afraid that something is going to happen. I wouldn't know what to do. You might not believe it, but the time goes so slow because I can't get you and our baby off my mind.

Clellie, you should stay home at nights if you can stand it at all. This is because at 9:30 PM we have to be in bed. When I go to bed, all I can think about is you. And if you were home thinking about me (which I doubt) maybe, just maybe, our brain waves would meet somehow in the distance that separates us and it could be some consolation to me. I wish I were home with you right now, but I guess I'll have to face it out here. I miss you so much that I really can't see how I'll make it through this mess.

I better change the subject before I start repeating myself worse than I already have. Oh Juan Lopez is in my platoon again here in Basic and today he really caught hell again. The commanding officer tore his footlocker apart because it was all messed up. Juan is really lazy, Clellie, and he's also weaker than I thought. At the P.T. test yesterday I beat him in every event. I came in 3rd place in the mile run out of 44 men. I also came in 2nd on the hand bars.

Oh get this, Clellie, the Army tried to get me to sign up for six years. This is because out of 400 men I was in the top 20 on our written test and they were going to send us to a school to prep us for West Point. But I am married and couldn't do it. Then the Captain said if I signed up for 4 years I could go to any school that I wanted if they had openings. But I told them I wanted out in 2 years, and that was it.

Well, Clellie, I really hate to say goodbye to you, but I think I have rapped enough to you for one night. Also it's 8:30 PM and we have to mop and sweep the barracks by 9 PM, then we have to take a shower, and be in bed by 9:30 PM. I miss you, Clellie, (I'll say it again for the fifth time) and love you very much. I'll have to close for now but please keep loving me like I do you and write to me every day if not twice a day.

I love you and I'll say good-bye for now.

Love you lots, Tony

P.S. I'm sending you forty dollars with this letter. Pay for that phone call and then put the rest in the bank if you can. Because when I come home for leave we should have about a hundred dollars to goof around on. Use my savings account book. I love you, I love you, I love you.

P.P.S. Mushy letter. But I can't help it. Send pictures.

Pvt. Anthony Jolley
H.H.C 5th Bn 1st Brig.
Ft. Ord, California 4th Plt 93941

✉ **27 Mar 1969**

Dear Clellie,

I'm going to start off by asking you some questions that I want some answers to in the next letter I get from you.

Did you get the $40 I sent you? Where are my pictures of you? Send me some of you as you are now. Also send me some of you in the swimming suit when you were in the pageant if you have any.

Clellie, I do love you and I do wish I were with you. They really gave us hell today. We've been running all day. You ought to see some of the guys' feet in our barracks. Their feet are all swollen with big blisters on them. Then when they can't keep up, the whole company gets punished. Like tonight, we all had to fall out at 8:30 PM and go through P.T. for over an hour.

How do you feel, Clellie? Does our baby kick much? How was the trip to Mountain Home? I sure do miss you, Clellie. I think about you so much that I'm just about ready to go out of my mind. When we run our 2 miles before breakfast, the only way I make it is to take my mind off running and think about you. I haven't had anything to drink or any fun in so long I forgot how it is to be a civilian. But most of all, I miss you. I hope your kidneys don't bother you much, because I can't stand to think of you in pain.

I want to see you, and hold you, and kiss you so much that I can almost taste it. One of these days though I'll be through all this and be able to come home. I'd better close for now because we have to turn the lights out. Then we have to get up at 4:30 AM in the morning and do our little run. Please write often, Clellie? Write me twice a day if you don't have anything else to do. I love you very much. Be good and stay mine.

Love, Tony

P.S. Send me some stamps because you can't get change to buy any here and I only have 1 left. Also send me Carter's address. I love you, Clellie.

Pvt. Anthony Jolley
H.H.C 5th Bn 1st Brig.
Ft. Ord, California 4th Plt 93941

✉ **1 Apr 1969**

Dear Clellie,

Guess what? I finally got the letters that were in the envelope with the picture in it of you standing by the car. You really look nice. I also got the two other letters; one of them had a picture of you standing in the doorway at your house. You look so nice and inviting that you almost blew my mind.

How's Mitch & your mother? Tell them both hi for me.

What's all this shit about you seeing Angie Gibson? I really don't think she breaks her neck looking at you, but I'm glad you care enough about me to be a little jealous still. You can be assured, Clellie, that I did tell her that I thought we had the grooviest love & marriage of anyone else in the world. You know why I say this? Because we really do.

You say the baby stretches now. Wow, I bet that's really a neat feeling. You know something, Clellie? We're going to have the cutest kid that ever has been, or ever will be. I'm so proud of you and the way you're taking all this shit about me being drafted and all. The name Chad Wayne Jolley is really an out of sight name for a boy. I also dig the names for the girl you picked out, but I'm going to let you decide which one for sure. I got some pictures of me, and if I decide to put them in this letter, you'll probably already have seen them. If not, I probably won't send them. I looked really stupid though. I still want you to send me some pictures of you. Clellie, tell me what you think I should do with all your letters. We have to keep everything in order, and I really don't have any room to keep them.

Next time you go over to Mom and Dad's place tell them I'm fine, and say hi to all the kids, and tell them to write. Also what is this about Barry taking off, and is he back? If he's back, where did he go?

You know, Clellie, the Army is really easier for some people to adjust to than it is for other people. Matt Spear is always bitching about the Army, but he says it ain't really too bad. For me, the Army is about the worst thing that ever happened to me. When the D. I.s (Drill Instructors) will get some kid that's kind of stupid and can't march and start calling him names and beating him I really get burned up. It just really doesn't seem like people should treat each other like that. Of course when I get out of Basic I will probably treat trainees the same way. I'm getting now to where the exercises don't bother me as much as they used to. I'm not as stiff as I was. Tomorrow we have to take another P.T. test. I hope I get as good as I did last time. I'll actually probably do better.

I can't wait until I get to come home on leave, Clellie. If I get transferred to another base after Basic, Clellie, I will probably get to come home for 2 weeks. That would be around the 26th of May. If I get infantry, I'll probably get a 30-day leave around the 1st of July. I just hope the time goes fast and I get to come home to you soon. If I get infantry I'll go from home, after my leave, to Vietnam. The only guys that are guaranteed to get out of infantry are the guys that joined, or the ones that re-upped. I had the chance, but I just want to be in for 2 years, and then get out.

I really miss you, Clellie. I sure wish I could put my hand on your fat little tummy and feel him kick. I do miss you next to me at night, and I do sleep on the top bunk. Also if you could see me at night I'd be laying there with my eyes open, hands behind my head, staring at the ceiling, and thinking of you.

This letter probably seems kind of long to you but it seems that you are really close to me when I am writing to you. These are the only moments of the day I look forward to, along with reading your letters.

I'd better end for now because the D. I. is going to catch me here in the bathroom and start yelling. Of course every time he yells or says anything to me, I just smile and say, "Yes, Drill Sergeant." That's why my writing is so sloppy though, because I'm in the bathroom writing because the lights are out.

I do miss you, Clellie, and I want you to think of me whenever possible. I love, love, love you, Clellie, and I'm so lonely. I'll try to call you Sunday and wish you a Happy Easter if you are home.

Your loving husband,
Tony

P.S. I'm sorry I couldn't get you anything for Easter, but I couldn't get nothing at the P.X. I'll get you something when I get home though. I love you.

Pvt. Anthony Jolley
H.H.C 5th Bn 1st Brig.
Ft. Ord, California 4th Plt 93941

✉ **4 Apr 1969**

Dear Clellie,

How come I didn't get a letter from you tonight? I was really disappointed. I also haven't gotten a package from you. With this letter I'm sending some pictures. Keep the ones you want. That's the reason I bought them was for you. Give mother one of them in the folders. Then you can distribute the others to all my girlfriends. Chuckle! Chuckle! Ha! Ha!

They gave us another P.T. test yesterday. I got a 430. I was number 3 in our platoon again.

I don't have much time in this letter because we've got to clean up the barracks for tomorrow's inspection.

The Army's still a big drag. I'm getting lonelier and lonelier for you as the days go by. I love you very much, Clellie, and I'm longing for the day when I'll be able to come home and hug and kiss you. I miss you so much that I don't know if I'll be able to make it for 2 years without you. I have to go for now, but remember that whether you love me or not, you'll always be the one and only for me.

Your husband,
Tony

Send me some six-cent stamps. I love you so much!

Pvt. Anthony Jolley
H.H.C 5th Bn 1st Brig.
Ft. Ord, California 4th Plt 93941

✉ **5 Apr 1969**

Dear Clellie,

I just had to write tonight for some reason. I wrote you yesterday, and was going to send some pictures, but I forgot to put them in the letter. So I'm putting them in this one. They're really funny looking aren't they. Notice I tried to smile in one?

The Army really isn't very bad for some people, but I just can't adjust to it. Juan is really getting in a lot of trouble. He smarted off to the D. I. and for a punishment they made him carry this sign on his back. It's a wooden sign that tells what company we are and the people who screw up and make mistakes have to carry it. I really feel sorry for Juan. Today, while we were double-timing, he fell out so I grabbed him and helped him along. It was no use though, because the whole company started falling out and the ones that kept going had to hit the other guys with their rifle butts to keep them going. I ended up clean in the front with Spear & Miller. Juan has really changed. He always gets in line with me and follows me around. Spear keeps saying that Juan acts like he's married to me. I'll send you a picture of the whole platoon and I want you to keep it for me, ok? (Notice who's standing beside me) Send me Carter's address, Clellie. I sure do miss you, Clellie. Our baby's really getting big! God, I sure wish I could be with you. I want to put my arms around you so bad I can almost taste it. When I get home I'm going to sit around you all day. If I'm not kissing you, I'm going to just sit around and watch you.

We really had a good married life together didn't we, Clellie? When I get back we're going to have to start where we left off. I want you so bad. I've considered going AWOL and taking off to Mexico or Canada with you many times. I'm going to have to get all these ideas out of my head I guess, but sometimes I just can't help it.

I have to close for now. Just remember, Clellie, that I love you very much. I also miss your cooking very much. The chow around here is awful. Clellie, please wait for me.

Your loving husband,
Tony (the lonely)

Pvt. Anthony Jolley
H.H.C 5th Bn 1st Brig.
Ft. Ord, California 4th Plt 93941

8 Apr 1969

Dearest Clellie,

Well here it is Tuesday evening, 8:30 PM. We just got in from the rifle range, and boy, I sure am tired. They ran us back from the rifle range today. Out of 45 men, there were only about 10 of us left when we stopped. They kept running us in circles when someone fell out and we ended up running so far, that I almost didn't make it. (About 3 ½ miles)

After today, Clellie, I know that the Army is just not my bag. I sprained my ankle, when I was pushing this Peterson kid, and I can hardly walk. I was pushing him to keep him from falling out, but he ended up falling out anyway.

Boy, I'm in such a horrible state. My throat's so sore I can't swallow. All I do all day is blow my nose. Tomorrow the guys with hurt ankles and hung up feet get to be trucked up to the rifle range. I'm not going to get on the truck when they tell those guys to fall out though. I think I'll need all the shit they can throw at me because the way things look I'll end up in Vietnam, probably all of us will. Send me some Contac pills if you have the money. If you don't, or if they won't get here by Friday, forget it because I'll buy some down at the P.X. Friday night.

Ask Mother & Dad if they ever got my letter. Tell her to write me. Also tell Marie and the kids to write me if they have time. Also send me some of my civilian shorts & t-shirts, if I have any good t-shirts. Tell Carter, he'd better write me or when I get back I'll act like I don't know who he is.

Boy, Clellie, I sure do miss you. Last night I couldn't sleep because of my cold. To ease my mind, and make me feel better, I just laid there in bed and thought about all the good times we've had together. I wish it were summer and me and you were lying down, side by side, and I had my arm lying over your bare middle (because you had on your two-piece). Maybe if I had enough nerve and wasn't so shy I could even kiss and caress you. Man, when I get home we're going to spend 3 or 4 days in bed. The only time we'll get up, is to eat. The rest of the time I can catch up on my sleep and whatever else comes up…

I didn't think it was possible for me to miss you as much as I do. I love you so much that I just don't see how I can last 6-14 more weeks without you. Do you miss and love me as much as I do you? I sure hope you do. If you don't, I guess I'll have to let you go if you want to. I have to go for now, Clellie. Just remember to wait for me. I sure do wish you were here with me. I love you very much.

Your husband,
Tony (who is very, very lonely without you)

P.S. I LOVE YOU!

Pvt. Anthony Jolley
H.H.C 5th Bn 1st Brig.
Ft. Ord, California 4th Plt 93941

✉ **17 Apr 1969**   **Thursday**

Dear Sweet Clellie,

Guess what? I just wanted to write this letter and inform you that I just got out of the hospital. I'm sorry I didn't call you Monday, but they wouldn't let me out of traction.

What's this shit about you and Sue feeling bad about my knee? It wasn't Spear's fault. The thing that made my knee bad was afterwards when I was running I twisted it worse. Then I walked about 3 miles to the rifle range that evening, and I really banged it up.

I want you to take the $10 Carter gave you and give it back. Leave it on the cupboard or table, but give it back and I mean it, Clellie. I'll take it as a personal offense if he won't accept it.

I'm sending you some pictures. One of them is when a bunch of us were fooling around after a day's work. The other one is of me when I was in the hospital, pretty sad. The other one is a friend. I had to take it because he really digs me and wanted to give it to me. Do you understand? Put it somewhere. I really do miss you, Clellie. While I was laying there in the hospital I had a lot of time to think. If you ever decided to leave me, I don't know what I'd do. I really miss you, Clellie, and I want you forever.

I want you to tell the family to get on the ball and write me a few lines. What's wrong with Marie? I at least thought I'd get a letter from her.

I thought I was at the point in the Army that I was getting used to it, now it's worse. All I could think about in the hospital was coming home and seeing you. I love you and miss you, but I've got to go for now because everyone's yelling turn out the lights.

Your loving husband,
Tony

P.S. Who was in the house earlier to make your mother think someone was there with you?

P.P.S. I love you.

Pvt. Anthony Jolley
H.H.C 5th Bn 1st Brig.
Ft. Ord, California 4th Plt 93941

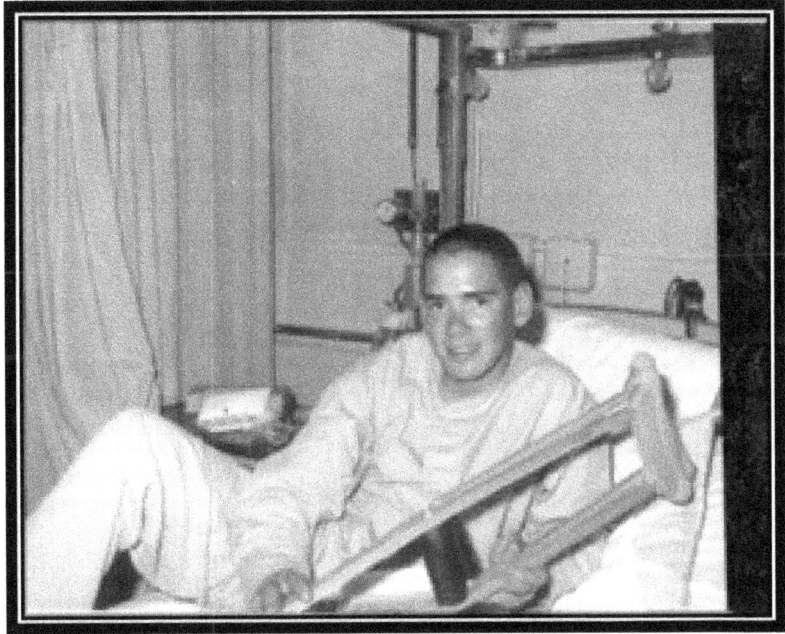

21 Apr 1969

Dear Clellie,

How are you? I'm fine. How is the weather? The weather here is fine. What are you doing at the moment? At the moment, I am writing you a letter. How do you like that for a typical starting of a letter? Really plastic, ain't it? You know, Clellie, there are a lot of things that I wish you could feel the way I do about them. I'll bet you don't really realize the deep and true way I love and miss you. I mean, really! You keep asking me if I read your letters. You act like I just glance at them then put them away. It seems you just don't realize how I look forward every day just to be able to receive one of your letters, then lie on my bunk and read it. I usually read the letter at least 3 or 4 times before I put it away. Your letters are my only contact with the one person who I love so much and who I had to leave.

You know it's really a bummer. I had a fairly good job, a very lovely wife, and a place for us to live. We had to give all this up just as a favor for the government. So I could serve in their Army. I'm sorry I'm writing like this. I know I owe these 2 years to my country but I just get pissed off. I can't get used to being away from you.

Well I had better change the subject. Guess what? Tomorrow morning we go out to the rifle range to qualify with our rifles. The other guys have had a week to practice the targets on the range. I don't even know what to expect. I wanted to get an expert rifle medal, but I guess I probably won't make it. I just hope I qualify.

You know what I only wish, Clellie? I wish that my next 12 weeks were over. I'd be at your house holding you. I guess it's better in some ways that we are separated. You know when we were together, Clellie, I appreciated you and loved you very much. Now that I'm away from you I realize that I only appreciated you half as much as I should have. I want so bad to be back there with you. I'd better close for now. Just remember Clellie, I love you and want you to stay mine.

Love, Tony

P.S. I LOVE YOU!

Pvt. Anthony Jolley
H.H.C 5th Bn 1st Brig.
Ft. Ord, California 4th Plt 93941

✉ **23 Apr 1969**

Dear Clellie,

I just read your letter and decided to answer some of your questions. I don't know what to think of Hope. If you babysit her kids why don't you have her bring the kids over to your house? But I definitely don't want you going anywhere with her.

About our baby I don't want it named after me. I thought that Chad Wayne Jolley was a beautiful name for the baby if it's a boy. If it's a girl, Clellie, any name you pick is all right with me. I do think that you have a lot of good names for girls. Why don't you think a little harder for more names for boys?

I hope you have given Carter back his money. What's this shit about living with the Carters when I get home on leave? You might as well not worry about it, Clellie. I sure am not going to move in with the Carters. I sincerely think we'll have considerably more privacy at your house.

I qualified with my rifle. I just missed the highest level by 3 points. That's really good considering it was the first time I shot at those targets. The other guys shot at them for a week. I still beat most of them.

Clellie in all sincerity, I want you to quit crying and depressing yourself. If you don't quit, you're going to end up hurting yourself and our baby. Don't worry about me. I'm all right. I hate the Army, but I guess I'll have to live with it. You know you don't have to worry about my love for you. If my love for you was any greater, it would be impossible to imagine. I love and miss you so much that I'm going out of my head.

Clellie, you are eating regular, aren't you? With big and well-balanced meals? I wish I were home right now and preparing to go to bed with you. Instead I'm sitting on my footlocker staring at my bunk, wishing you were here for just one night. Wow, the thought is so neat, it almost blows my mind.

I better close for now, Clellie, just remember to love and miss me as much as I do you. (If that's possible.) Good-bye for now.

Your loving husband,
Tony

I love you.

Pvt. Anthony Jolley
H.H.C 5th Bn 1st Brig.
Ft. Ord, California 4th Plt 93941

✉ **25 Apr 1969**

Dear Clellie,

Well, here it is Friday of my fifth week. Today we just finished another P.T. test. I went down a little on my score, but I still got a 426. Anybody that got over 400 didn't have to do extra P.T. So guess what? I was one of 15 guys that stayed in our barracks and watched the others do P.T. They also have to do P.T. tomorrow and Sunday. Boy, on the run, dodge and run, and the mile run I just about didn't make it because of my knee. Juan was out with the other guys doing P.T. I kind of feel sorry for him though, because he tried his best and got a 391.

I never did make it to the doctor's appointment the other day. The first sergeant really got pissed off at me because I didn't make it. He came up to me out on the field today and said the doctor called. He said I should have kept the appointment. I told him my knee really didn't bother me that much. Right now though, I wish I would have gone on sick call because it's really sore. They're probably going to make another appointment for me. I just don't want to get put on profile. I want to keep in shape, because I know I'll probably get infantry AIT and I'll need to keep in shape for my own good.

Clellie, I'll probably end up going to Vietnam after AIT. Just about all the guys in our company will do the same. I don't want to worry you because Vietnam isn't all that bad. It can be bad in spots. They tell us though that if you use your head and keep your cool you'll probably end up coming back from Vietnam at least alive.

Every minute, hour, and day, Clellie, I realize more and more just how much I do miss you. I want so bad to be able to come home and put my arms around you and kiss, kiss, kiss, and kiss you. I hope you love me as much as I do you. I don't know what I'll do without you, Clellie. You are undoubtedly the most lovable and wonderful person that could ever come into my life. I'd better get off this kick for a while because I have a few other things to say.

What's this about the Carters? Are they really getting along as bad as it sounded in your last letter? Is Denny going out with other girls? It really sounded like they aren't getting along very well. Oh yeah, you asked me awhile back about my cigarette smoking. I smoke about the same as I did before I came into the Army, if not a little bit more. Anyway I smoke a little over a pack a day.

I guess I had better end this letter, because we've got to clean the barracks. I just want to say again how much I do miss you. I love, love, and love you. I know I'll never be able to learn to live without you. I'll never get used to being away from you. I hope you'll wait for me to come home. Please stay mine forever, Clellie.

Your loving and lonesome husband,
Tony

P.S. I love you. I miss you. I cherish you. I adore you. I'm lonesome without you. I'm yours forever & forever. I hate the Army, because it took me away from you. I LOVE YOU!

Pvt. Anthony Jolley
H.H.C 5th Bn 1st Brig.
Ft. Ord, California 4th Plt 93941

✉ **1 May 1969**

Dear Clellie,

Well I just got back from bivouac. That's when you go out for 4 days and 3 nights. Man, it was really rough. All we did all night and day was run into ambushes and run patrols. I sure am tired, so don't mind if this letter is sloppy. The second night there I got gassed twice while I was sleeping in my tent. It was also colder than hell all the time we were there.

How about Chad Wayne Jolley for our baby, and Jeanette Marie Jolley, if it's a girl. The initials for the girl would be J.M.J. In the Catholic school, we used to put the initials J.M.J. at the top of our English papers. It stood for Jesus, Mary, and Joseph. The name just popped into my mind.

I'm really sorry to hear about your dad and mom going to court. I know how hard it is on you and your sisters. I think one of these days, your mother and father are going to get things all straightened out. I'll sure be glad when this happens.

Clellie, you asked me if I got all my stationery free. I don't. I pay for all my paper and envelopes. I got paid yesterday. I got $78. Out of this they took $13 for pictures, $8 for a (BCT) Basic Combat Training album, and $6 for extra laundry. It's really a bummer. They give you $50 and take back $49. Do you need any money? I'm going to send home probably $20 as soon as I can get a money order. Have you got a check from the Army? If you haven't, see who it says to contact on the papers you have and contact them.

Clellie, you don't really know how anxious I'm getting for our baby to be born. I really wonder what it'll be, a boy or a girl? I want so bad to be back home with you. Then I'll be there for sure when you have the baby. I know it would be better for both of us if I could be there with you.

I miss you, Clellie. I really missed your letters out on bivouac because they wouldn't give them to us while we were out there. I'd give anything to see your cute little smile. Trying to look innocent at times, all we wanted was to go to bed. I love you, Clellie, and want you to stay mine. I know our love will last for all eternity.

Your tired, but ever-loving husband,
Tony

Love, Caress, Tease!

P.S. I love you! Feel! Kiss! Kiss! Touch! Touch!

Pvt. Anthony Jolley
H.H.C 5th Bn 1st Brig.
Ft. Ord, California 4th Plt 93941

✉ **7 May 1969**

Dear Clellie,

I know this card is a couple of days early, but I just had to send it to you. This is the first Mother's Day card I ever have sent you. I hope you like it.

I really do love you, Clellie. I need you very much and I hope to be with you soon. Happy Mother's Day!

Love, Tony

P.S. I love you!

Honey, no one else...

Can fill your slippers!
Happy Mother's Day
With Love!

8 May 1969

Dear Clellie,

I want to start this letter, Clellie, by saying how much I love you. So I think I will. Clellie, I love you very much and I never want to leave you again after this is over.

I'm sending you a picture of me. I walked out of the barracks after taking a nap and Winston took my picture. I looked kind of sleepy. This picture was taken just before we got inspected for guard duty that night.

Guess what? I got my orders today. We got them after our final P.T. test. I got a 445 on it. It's really a bummer. Our Sgt. lied to us. He said that 26 were going infantry. About 70 of us ended up going. I go to AIT as 11 Bravo. Commonly known as light weapons infantry. I guess it's just the way the ball rolls. I think, personally that they're trying to screw me over, because I wouldn't re-up and go to their damn schools. Spear got infantry too. He was put in for M/P, and he didn't get it. You ought to see the stupid bastards that got artillery and cooks and clerks. You wouldn't believe it. There's guys in our company that don't know how to write English, and they got a clerk's job. I guess I should have put in for something else, but I didn't. I think now that I got infantry, I might go Airborne. Airborne might be a little harder, but you actually get more out of it.

Oh, yea before I forget to tell you, Butler got infantry too. We all take infantry right here at Ft. Ord. We probably won't get a leave after Basic. We'll more than likely graduate Friday and start AIT Monday. I want you to come down for graduation very bad. When you come down bring as many of my civilian clothes as you can. You'll have to get together with Spear's wife and get in touch with Perrin's wife in Boise. Find out about how much it will cost for gas. Also decide on how to get to Boise. With that $20 I sent you, you ought to buy you a new dress or outfit or something.

If the doctor doesn't want you to come, I don't think you better go against his orders. If something happened to you or the baby because you came down, I'd never be able to forgive myself. Clellie, write me and tell me if you're going to come down. I love you very much and I never want to lose you. I hope you can come down for graduation. I'd better close for now. Just remember I love you very much.

Your loving husband,
Tony

P.S. Don't worry about me getting infantry. It doesn't mean that I'll go to Vietnam. Wherever I go, I'll certainly see a lot of action though. I love, love, love, love, love, and miss you!

Pvt. Anthony Jolley
H.H.C 5th Bn 1st Brig.
Ft. Ord, California 4th Plt 93941

Clellie recalls visiting me in for BCT graduation at Fort Ord.

On Wednesday, May 14th, Sue Spear and I left to go to Boise. At Boise we got in touch with Carol Perrin. We all 3 were heading for Fort Ord, California to see our husbands graduate. We stayed Wednesday night at Carol's in-laws place. They were very nice people. At 4:00 AM on Thursday we got up and were on our way. We reached Salinas at about 5:30 PM. We went to the Down Towner Motel and put our junk in the room. We then headed for Fort Ord to see our husbands. Luckily we got to see them for about ½ an hour.

On Friday, the three of us went to Fort Ord at 11:30 AM. We looked around the base and then we ate. At 2:00 PM we went to see our husbands graduate. After it was over we went back to their barracks. At about 4:00 PM we were headed back to the motel with our husbands. After Tony and I got to our room, we changed our clothes and went for something to eat. It was really good to be with him again. At 9:00 PM we headed back to Fort Ord. The three of us girls went back to the motel at about 10:00 PM.

On Saturday, we were just preparing to check out of our rooms, when Matt called Sue and informed us that they got a 22-hour leave from about 2:00 PM. By 1:00 PM we were waiting at their barracks. At 2:00 PM our husbands were released. Tony looked so neat in his uniform. We got back to our rooms and changed clothes. At about 4:00 PM we went to a Laundromat to wash the men's clothes. We finally got done at 6:00 PM. We then dropped Sue and her husband off at the motel and the rest of us went to eat. After we ate we went back to the motel. Tony and I borrowed Perrin's car and went to the Auto Movie. The show was "Candy" and "Barbarella." We watched all of it except for about ¼ of "Candy" before we left. When we got back to the motel, we watched TV for a little while.

At 11:00 AM Sunday we headed back to Fort Ord. It was so sad to say goodbye. We all wanted so very much to stay. There will come a time when Tony and I will be together. I just can't wait.

✉ **May 19, 1969**   **12:15 PM**

Hi Hon,

Well here we are in Mountain Home. Sue has just gone in to get her ID card so I decided to start my letter to you. I love you, Tony, and I want so much to be with you. After we left you guys yesterday, we were all bawling. I saw you on the balcony. I wanted so much to jump out and run to you.

I forgot to tell you but on the way up to Salinas from Boise we saw 5 deer. Man, they were really close. They jumped over a fence right in front of us. You can imagine us. We were so darn excited. We also had a detour off the highway before San Francisco. We heard that a part of the freeway had sunk about 13 feet. Spooky! California is supposed to sink you know.

We got to Perrins' place at about 2:00 PM our time last night. Man, we were so bushed. You wouldn't believe it. This morning we got up at 10:00 AM and Mrs. Perrin fixed our breakfast. You wouldn't believe how sweet the Perrins are. I feel as though I've known them all my life. Mrs. Perrin told me that she would go there to stay even P. G. (pregnant). I want to so bad, I miss you so much. It seemed so very good to be with you again. I need you so very much. It does seem like only a dream. It was so neat, but so darn hard to leave you again.

                                                      2:00 PM

Man, you don't know how bad we're all wanting to come and live. It was so rough to leave you. It felt so neat to be secure in your arms again. Man, your old hanky was just soaked when I finished bawling. I can't wait until I'm with you again.

I'm writing while Sue's driving, and it's so rough. You ought to try it. It's warm here, no humidity, thank goodness! Well I hate to have such a short letter but it'll have to do for now. I want to get it mailed as soon as I can. I'll write another one tonight. I love you so very much, Tony. I can't wait to be with you forever & ever.

Your lonely wife,
Clellie

P.S. I love you very much. Hugs & Kisses, etc.

ADVANCED INDIVIDUAL TRAINING (AIT)

✉ **May 20, 1969**

Hi Hon,

How are you doing? I sure miss you so very much. Say if you can, will you go to the P.X. and get some postcards of some of the things you go through during Basic and send them to me? They would add a lot to my scrapbook. I got home today and started right in on my scrapbook. However Ashley came in and interrupted me. She wanted me to put Curl Free on her hair. So I did. I'm so bushed. When I got home I came up to my room. Wow, what a mess. My cousin Pat had brought me some baby stuff. She gave me her old walker, some undershirts, receiving blankets, little clothes for boys and girls, a mattress to a buggy, (I get the buggy soon), a new seater, and a diaper pail. I was so excited looking through it. I need to get some thank you cards, Downy to wash some of the baby's things, and some paint to paint the baby's dresser. Then I want to get it decorated cute. I'm really excited.

Mom told me that a lady plans on quitting this office job at a collection agency about August and all it is, is sort of reception work. It pays $225 a month. I'd get Saturdays and Sundays off. It would really work out groovy for me and the baby. Then I could pay off what little bills we have and get a car, and maybe a TV, and dress our baby neat. Never know though. Mom knows the woman there now and she said that she'd put in a good word for me.

I told you in my letter this morning that a piece of the freeway going to San Francisco sunk. Tony, what if some of California sinks? It really worries me with you there. The scientists are even expecting sinkage and an earthquake. Tony, I'm really worried.

I want so very much to come back down and live. Sue and Carol are. I want to be with you as much as I can. I do know though that I couldn't scrape up the money right now. If I can I want to come for even just a weekend. I wish the baby wasn't due so soon. Do you realize that we have less than 2 months to go? Maybe you can get a leave near the time that the baby's due. Ron Ibarra just went and told his Sgt. that his wife was due anytime, and it was their first, and she was sort of afraid being alone. His Sgt. gave him a week & a ½ leave. What do you think? I would like you home with me so much. By the way, I want your medal too.

Tony, when I was there do you think that things were the same between us, aside from me being a little bit big? I love you so very, very much, Tony. I tried so hard not to cry when we had to part 'cause I knew it would only make things harder for you, but I couldn't help it. I about bawled when we were in the car on the way to Fort Ord, but I did pretty good. Boy, when you walked away I felt like a fountain. Tears just gushed then I heard you whistle from the balcony. Tony, this being apart is no good and I do hate the Army. I never really believed that they'd take you away from me. Carol and Sue are leaving next Wed. so they'll be there for Memorial Day. I want so much to be with them. I'd just be a burden to them though 'cause I can't work. If you don't get a leave and I get some money saved I'm going to visit you one weekend. I really wish that the baby was here so I could go and work. I guess that's what we get for hanky panky.

Always yours,
Clellie

P.S. Hugs & Kisses, etc.

May 20, 1969   *10:30 PM*

Hi Hon,

I want you to know, Tony, that I love you so very much. Tony, I'm afraid that California's going to sink away. A lady (I think it's the same one who predicted all the other stuff) predicts that it'll be gone by the end of the summer. I'm really very worried.

Wayne told my mom that Marie and Amanda were so ashamed and sorry that they didn't come to the shower for me. They had forgotten all about it. I haven't gone to see them yet. I will real soon & tell them hi from you.

Today I got up and Mom and I went to town to get some things. I got some cute thank you cards to send to those who got our baby things. I got some beige enamel paint to paint the little dresser. I also got some Downy to wash the baby clothes my cousin gave me. Boy, she has some really cute things. Then I went to the Gold Strike Stamp Store to get a diaper bag. They were out. I barely had enough green stamps to get eight diapers, but they were out also. Ticked me off. If I get those diapers, I have four, so that would make a dozen. Sue is going to get a dozen for me I think, and so is Aunt Mabel hopefully, so I'll have 3 dozen, just enough! Then all I'll need is bibs, plastic pants, a diaper hanger, and a couple of nightgowns.

When I got home from town, the phone bill was here. Guess how much it cost me? Almost $35! It took almost my last penny. In June, the bill will have the 11th phone call on it. Tony, I want to hear from you still. I love to talk to you, but can you pay for the calls? If we limit the calls to less time talking, then they should be not as expensive. This bill had the two calls, that one Sunday and the one in the middle of the week. That's why it was so high. What do you think?

I painted the baby's dresser one coat today. I want to put another coat on it tomorrow. It looks kinda drab but better than it did. By the time I get my psychedelic flowers on it and the baby's clothes in it, it will be much, much better. I'm so excited. Tony, what if something happens to our baby? I'll just die. Oh well, it won't. It's so darn healthy.

Please write soon. Tony, your letters are so important to me. I love you and want you to always be mine. Tony, tell me how much you love me.

All my love forever,
Clellie

P.S. If you go to get those postcards for Basic Training, don't bother, 'cause the Army sent me a pamphlet on Basic Training with pictures. I can put it in my scrapbook.

✉ *May 21, 1969* *10:00 PM*

Dearest Hubby,

How's the Army been treating you? I love you very, very much. I enclosed an article of Vietnam so that you would know what's going on over there.

Bethany Meyer told me today that Mike McBride got home today on a leave. I sure wish that you were home too.

Today I finished painting the last coat of the baby's dresser. I'm not so sure I like that color. Maybe when it's fixed then it'll look better. What do you think? Course you can't say much until you see it. I ironed some of the baby's things that my cousin gave me. There's stuff for girls or boys. Boy, I can't imagine anything being so small. I've got receiving blankets galore. Wow! I sure can't wait.

I took Hope to the lawyers today. She has to file against her husband for not paying child support. Tough. I went to Thriftway and got a card for you at about 8:00 PM. Boy, I wanted so much to be with you today. It's so bad.

I can't believe how stiff I was today. Man, I can hardly move. My legs and back are so sore. I can't figure out why.

Tony, you know those pennies that we've been saving in that jar? I was thinking that when it gets full, we should put it in the bank for a savings account for our baby. What do you think?

I've decided that I want a Cougar for a car. Carol's car sold me on it. It does really good on gas, and man, it travels neat. What do you think?

I guess your mom is managing the Midway Bar for Ginger. She wants your dad to help but I don't know if he will. I still haven't really got to talk to them yet. I heard this from Aunt Mabel. Aunt Mabel thinks you look really sharp in your picture you sent me. You know, the one in the dress uniform? She saw it on our stereo.

I sure hope that you like the card I sent you. I thought it was really cute. I was going to buy you a plaque with a poem on it called sweetheart, but I didn't know where you'd put it. It was really nice. Oh well, the guys would probably make fun of it anyway.

How's your knee doing? Are you having any trouble with it at all? I should've kicked it before I left because then maybe you'd get it taken out and maybe you would get a medical deferment, or maybe you would get out of infantry.

Tony, I miss you very, very much! I love you, Tony, more than words can ever express. Take care and stay mine.

Your Lonely Loving Wife,
Clellie

P.S. Hugs & Kisses, etc.

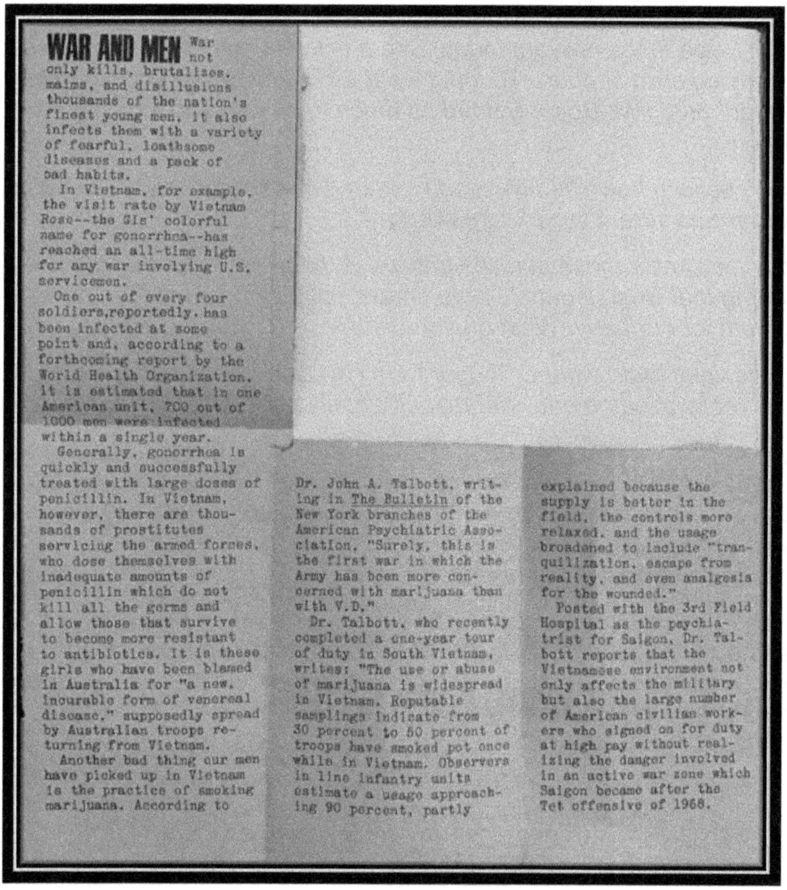

WAR AND MEN War not only kills, brutalizes, maims, and disillusions thousands of the nation's finest young men, it also infects them with a variety of fearful, loathsome diseases and a pack of bad habits.

In Vietnam, for example, the visit rate by Vietnam Rose—the GIs' colorful name for gonorrhea—has reached an all-time high for any war involving U.S. servicemen.

One out of every four soldiers, reportedly, has been infected at some point and, according to a forthcoming report by the World Health Organization, it is estimated that in one American unit, 700 out of 1000 men were infected within a single year.

Generally, gonorrhea is quickly and successfully treated with large doses of penicillin. In Vietnam, however, there are thousands of prostitutes servicing the armed forces, who dose themselves with inadequate amounts of penicillin which do not kill all the germs and allow those that survive to become more resistant to antibiotics. It is these girls who have been blamed in Australia for "a new, incurable form of venereal disease," supposedly spread by Australian troops returning from Vietnam.

Another bad thing our men have picked up in Vietnam is the practice of smoking marijuana. According to Dr. John A. Talbott, writing in The Bulletin of the New York branches of the American Psychiatric Association, "Surely, this is the first war in which the Army has been more concerned with marijuana than with V.D."

Dr. Talbott, who recently completed a one-year tour of duty in South Vietnam, writes: "The use or abuse of marijuana is widespread in Vietnam. Reputable samplings indicate from 30 percent to 50 percent of troops have smoked pot once while in Vietnam. Observers in line infantry units estimate a usage approaching 90 percent, partly explained because the supply is better in the field, the controls more relaxed, and the usage broadened to include "tranquilization, escape from reality, and even amalgesia for the wounded."

Posted with the 3rd Field Hospital as the psychiatrist for Saigon, Dr. Talbott reports that the Vietnamese environment not only affects the military but also the large number of American civilian workers who signed on for duty at high pay without realizing the danger involved in an active war zone which Saigon became after the Tet offensive of 1968.

✉ **May 22, 1969** *12:01 AM*

Dear Tony,

First of all I want to know one thing – Why haven't you written?!! Today for sure I thought I'd get a letter. Sue got one from Matt. How come?

Today I cleaned the car really good. I vacuumed it and scrubbed the floor and seats. Groovy. I got all the thank you cards sent out to the people who gave us things for the baby.

Nancy and Alice might come in for the weekend. Nancy's birthday is tomorrow. I'm going to bake her a cake. Can't afford a present. Oh well.

I babysat for Hope tonight while she went to a Jehovah Witness meeting. While I was babysitting, Sue called. Carol had called her last night and was wondering if we were still planning on going. Sue's borrowing $200 from her dad to go; she's so excited about going. I guess Carol is too. I wish so very much that I was going too. Oh, Tony, if you only knew how much I want to come down.

I love you, Tony, more than anything in this whole world. I could never bear losing you. Please take care of yourself and keep up the good spirits. It'll be over one of these days and we'll be together forever. Do you want that? Do you love me? Be good and stay mine always.

Your wondering but ever-loving wife,
Clellie

P.S. Hugs & Kisses, etc.

 **May 22, 1969**

Dear Tony,

I was so very much hoping that I would get a letter from you today. How come haven't I got one yet?

Tony, please help me find a way to get to come down. If I don't go, I'll have to wait 9 ½ more weeks. Oh, if only we were rich. It will mean so much to me. I want to see you so bad or even talk to you. After this, you'll be gone a whole year. Please think of something. I need you so very much.

Write Soon.

Love Forever,
Clellie

I love you! Hugs and Kisses

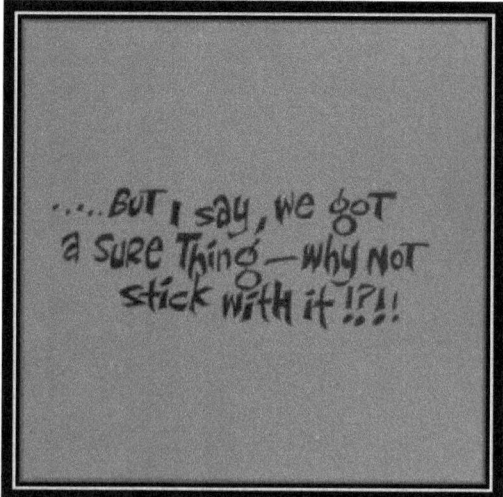

✉ **22 May 1969**

Dear Clellie,

I love you!

This is going to be a short letter, but lights are out and I don't have much time. I'm very sorry I haven't written you lately. To be honest, I haven't had any time. Everyone thought AIT would be easier than Basic. We found out though that they're training us for fighting in a war zone, and there's no fooling around. We started off by not looking good enough in our marches to the C.O. (Commanding Officer) so he took our smoking privileges completely away. We also ended up stopping every two feet we marched and dropped to do about 20 pushups with full field gear on.

Clellie, I love you and miss you very much. I wish you could come down with Spear and Perrin to live, but we can't afford it for one, and I want you to be with your mother and my family when the baby is born.

When you left Sunday, for two whole days, I just moped around. It's letting up a little, but I can't get the thought of you out of my head. You looked so tender and beautiful when you were down here. Your image just keeps running through my head. I don't know how I'll ever make it through a whole year away from you when I am overseas. You know when I close my eyes at night I think about you next to me in that motel room and I can almost feel your body next to mine.

The other night I had a dream that when you came down everything you said I argued with you. I called you a bunch of names and told you to get lost. Then I thought I had amnesia when I woke up and I tried to remember what happened. When I finally realized it was only a dream it relieved my conscience somewhat, but I could hardly bear the thought of being without you for another 9 weeks. You might not be able to understand this, but it was a mixed-up dream.

I want so bad to see you again (even if you are fat). I was so proud to walk next to such a beautiful pregnant girl as you are. I just know now and forever that I couldn't live without you. I love, love, love, love you, Clellie, and I want you to stay mine forever.

Your loving but lonesome husband,
Tony

P.S. It turned out to be a longer letter than expected but I couldn't quit writing.

I LOVE YOU! I MISS YOU! I WANT YOU!

Pvt. Anthony Jolley
H.H.C 1st Bn 2nd Brig.
Ft. Ord, California 2nd Plt 93941

May 23, 1969   *11:00 PM*

Dear Tony,

First of all, if you don't want to be depressed over a wife's angry letter you had better burn this one without reading very much further. Why is it an angry letter? Because this little wife hasn't received a letter from you! Why hasn't she got one yet? Good question. Hope you have a nice answer. I'm sorry about this ugly letter and I'm sorry for being so non-understanding, but it did tick me off. I just couldn't believe it.

Today I put the daisies on the baby's dresser. It looks quite cute now. I put its clothes in the drawers, I made its bed, and I got Nancy at school. She is staying the weekend. Alice couldn't come 'cause they're cutting potatoes. Fun and games. Right now Nancy's babysitting Hope's kids. I wanted to stay here in case you called. No such luck. Nancy and I took Hope to work with her kids. Fun.

Tony, I'll apologize again for this letter. Tomorrow I'll really regret writing it, but I have to let you know how I feel. It bugs me so very much not to hear from you. I love you, Tony, very much. I need you so very much.

All my love,
Clellie

P.S. I love you very much.

✉ *May 24, 1969*

Dear Hubby,

I just got your letter. It was sweet. I love you so much. A letter that good was worth waiting for. I'm so ashamed of my last letter I wrote. Tony, I'm very sorry for it. Please forgive me. I'll write you a longer letter tonight. I'm helping look for Nancy a dog. Fun.

Well I better close for now. I just want you to know that I love you so very much and I never ever want to lose you. Stay mine always. I love you so very much.

All my love.

Your dumb but loving wife,
Clellie

P.S. Hugs & Kisses. I love you.

May 24, 1969   *10:00 PM*

Dearest Tony,

I sure do love you and I miss you so very, very much. I can't wait until you get home. Tony, again, I'm sorry for writing that icky letter. I was so ashamed when I read your letter. I love you so much.

I have a piece of bad news. You ready? Remember how I didn't have any stretch marks on my stomach? Well I think I just got one, and a big one. Icky. I found one on my leg too. Boy, I can't believe it. I just keep growing. It's so hot here. I almost die in the heat. It got 87 degrees today. I keep drinking water and it doesn't all go out. My body is retaining. Now my stomach is bigger and my legs are too. I feel like I'm carrying a hundred extra pounds. Oh, Tony, that stretch mark is so ugly. I almost cry. I'll be so ugly when you get home.

Today Nancy and I went to find her a dog. We got a black one that is ½ Dachshund, and ½ Terrier. It's really cute. I got a diaper hanger too from Aunt Mabel. Sweet. Mom treated us to dinner. It was really nice. Hope fixed supper because I did last night. We had a "Cowboy Dinner" with ice cream and cake. If I do say so myself, it was good. Sure wish I were cooking for you instead of all these people.

Denny and Susan came over today. Denny wanted to know how he can get ahold of you by phone. I told him I'd ask you. He sure wishes that you were home. He really misses you. Susan and him want me to move in with them. This way Mom's not always around and what would I do if I had it when she's not here? I told them I just couldn't. Mom would be really hurt. Susan had mentioned me moving in before and I told her I couldn't and it wasn't right to move in on a newlywed couple. She doesn't care but I won't. I feel comfortable here at home. If I move anywhere, it would be to your place.

Tony, I feel so rotten. My veins are swollen and I'm swollen and I now have a stretch mark. I sure hope that I don't have to wait 1 ¾ months until it's born. My legs get so tired and I haven't been on them very much. I was so excited to get on my two-piece swimsuit. What a laugh! Ugly stretch marks! I'm a big boob, I just want so much for you to be proud of me, and I just get so depressed sometimes. One thing I can't wait for is our baby. I'm so excited. I hope I have everything prepared for it.

Boy, it sounds like AIT's going to be rough. What does it mean he took your smoking privileges away?

I love you, Tony, so much & don't you ever forget it. Stay mine.

Your pregnant loving wife,
Clellie

P.S. Hugs & Kisses, etc.

✉ **25 May 1969**

Dear Clellie,

I love you very much. I'm sorry I haven't been writing as often as I usually do. Today they finally gave us from 4 PM to 8 PM off. Last night we got post privileges and me and Butler and another kid went to Stilwell Hall. They had a band playing there and they were really good. Don't worry though, it's a club for Army personnel and there was not dancing or girls. I had a fairly good time though. I could have had a lot more fun if you were with me though.

We are really going to have to save a lot of money, Clellie, if you're going to come to Hawaii when I get my R&R from Nam. The Captain told us today that it would cost about $300, and do you want to know something? It's only a 5-day R&R. It hardly seems worth it. What do you think? What would we do about the baby? Would you bring it to Hawaii? Or would you leave it at home? I'd love to see my kid you know. Clellie, you mentioned in your letter that you wanted me to think of a way for you to come down here. As much as I want you to, there's just no way. I want you to stay at home where you're in good hands. I don't want anything to happen to you. That's why you've got to stay home, and be careful. You might think this is easy for me to say, but it's not. I'd love to have you here with me, but I think it's best if you don't. I just hope that the time will go by fast so I can come home and be with you again.

There's something else I've got to tell you. You know something, after AIT before we go to Vietnam we only get a 14-day leave. I guess the Army has completely knocked off the 30-day leaves. I think when I get my leave I just won't go back to the Army and we'll run off to Canada and live out the rest of our lives there.

Clellie, I love you very much and I just don't know how I'm going to leave you once I get home on leave. I miss you so much it's unbelievable. I know the Army will do me good in some ways, but I just wish there was some way that these next two years could be over. I want to come back home to you and take over our life together where we left off. I hope you feel the same way I do. The only thing I have to look forward to is coming back to you and it means the world to me. My only hope is that I get out of the Army all right and we can be back together forever and ever. I guess I'd better close for now, Clellie. I love you now and for eternity. Do you love me as much?

Your loving husband, Tony
P.S. I love, miss, and cherish you!!

P.P.S. Could you please send me my sandals, Clellie?

Pvt. Anthony Jolley
H.H.C 1st Bn 2nd Brig.
Ft. Ord, California 2nd Plt 93941

✉ **May 26, 1969** **1:30 AM**

Hi Hon,

I love you so very much. I hoped that you would call today, but I guess you decided not to. Are you going to call me on Sundays anymore?

Today wasn't very exciting. Hope fixed a dinner about 3:30 PM and we ate there. I didn't stay too long 'cause I wanted you to call. At about 7:30 PM, I decided you weren't going to call so I took Nancy home. It seemed funny to go inside that house again. The kids don't keep it up worth a darn. Dad seemed glad to see me and so was Faith, Cora, Tom, & Emma were really glad to see me too. It was really neat. Alice seems really out of it. Ann & Nancy are constantly picking at her. It's really sad. It made me so sick. I left Dad's about 10:30 PM and went to Faith's to drop Cora off. She rode with me. Boy, Tom & Cora think my car is so groovy. They invited me in. We all had a real nice talk. The kids went to bed about midnight and Faith and I talked till about 1:00 AM. It was really nice to talk with her. She's trying to help Alice, but Alice fights back at Ann & Nancy. Tony, I don't know what's going to happen to her. Nancy has really changed; either that or I've just lost all my patience with kids. She just would say dumb things to get me angry with her. I wanted to pound her.

Remember in the last letter when I told you I thought that I had a great big stretch mark on my stomach? Well this morning I woke up and it was gone. I don't know what it was but I'm glad it's gone.

Cora said that a lot of kids thought that you wouldn't make a good husband because you were too used to being free, but they were proved wrong. I told her that you were the best husband ever. No one could have a better one. She also said that Joyce Conklin talked about us a lot. She thought I was dumb. Cora said but look at her. McCall won't live with her even after her parents offered to buy him a house, or a new car. They had a little baby girl.

That dumb dog of Nancy's yelped all night last night. Boy, I was ticked. I had her put it and its box outside in my car with a crack in the window. It still yelped to beat the band…one sleepless night. It is really cute though. It's so little. Mom wants me to get this little Chihuahua. I wouldn't mind it. I don't know if I will. It's free.

Boy, it's so hot up here at night. It'll be rougher yet when you get here. I sure can't wait though…nine more weeks! It doesn't sound too long in weeks, but break it down to 60 some odd days and it's a long time.

Tony, I love you so very much. I can't wait to be with you again. It'll be so neat. Couples don't know how lucky they are to be together. I look at your picture so much. You're so handsome, and so grown-up looking, and so darn sexy looking! I love you so much.

Lovingly Forever,
Your Wife, Clellie
P.S. Hugs & Kisses, etc.

✉ **May 27, 1969**   **10:30 PM**

Dearest Tony,

I sure do love you gobs and gobs and I want so very much to be with you. I miss you so much.

Today I cleaned up the house and hung some clothes out. At about 2:15 PM I headed for Sue Spear's. On the way I saw Susan and she stopped me and wanted me to babysit the baby while her & Amy Pearson & Claudia Stevens went to a roommate's wedding in Idaho Falls. I offered yesterday so she came to take me up on it. It was really fun watching Justin. I can't wait till our own comes. Anyway I went over to Sue's and gave her the package for you. She was so excited. I almost cried. I wanted so much to be going with her. Oh, Tony, it's so miserable not being able to go. I want to see you so much. I've been holding back the tears all day and I can now let them out. It just doesn't seem fair. I love you so much and yet I can't be with you. She gave me some pictures. One is of your barracks now. It's a little picture. One is of you walking across the street toward me on the day you got that overnight leave. It's a big one and a little one. Then there's the one I sent you. Cute. I kept the bigger one and sent you the little one. I want to put them in my scrapbook of you. You can keep the one I sent you if you want to.

Tony, I wish you would come home. I need you so very much. Last night I had a real ugly dream. I dreamed that Sue, Carol, & I had gone down to live. We wanted to see you and some dumb thing was going on. Everyone was sitting on the ground. You were sitting in front of the Sgt. I was only about 4 people away from you. You asked Matt & Perrin where I was 'cause you couldn't see me. Your Sgt. told you to get up and sing a song and the other guys to harmonize. Perrin had to help you up and you were laughing. After you got about ¾'s up, you saw me. I smiled at you and you gave a real disgusted look. That's the entire dream. Tony, I love you so very much and I hope that I never see you look at me that way.

Lonely as ever.

Your wife,
Clellie

P.S. Hugs & Kisses, etc.

✉ *May 27, 1969*　　　　　　　　　　　　　　　　　　　　　　　*11:00 PM*

Dear Hubby,

How's Army life nowadays? How's your leg been doing? Well you only have 93 weeks left of the Army; 21 ½ months. I sure hope it goes fast. You have less than 9 weeks before you get a leave. I can't wait. I love you so very much.

Molly told me today that you called last night after 7:30 PM. I thought you weren't going to call. I'm so very sorry I missed it. I wanted so much to talk to you. I was hoping you'd call tonight but you probably couldn't.

Today Hope asked if I could run her to Twin, so Ashley could see the doctor. I told her I would. At about 1:00 PM Susan Carter came over and wanted me to fix her hair, so I did. I also made a goody box for you. Sue's bringing it up. I sure wish I could deliver it in person with a big sloppy kiss. I sure hope you enjoy it. Then at 4:00 PM Hope, Ashley, Andy, and I went to Twin. We had to sit in the Dr.'s office from 5:00 PM until 6:00 PM until she was called. The Dr. said she had pus in her urine, nose, and throat and something was causing it. He wants to take x-rays of her body and blood tests. We all think it's the cancer acting up again. It's really sad. We got home at about 7:30 PM. Then I went to Thriftway to get her prescription…poor little kid.

When you call me on Sundays please try to call early in the day. I know you never know when you'll call and if you can't call early in the day then anytime will be okay. It's just that it depresses me so much to sit alone in the house all day. I hate to even go outside for fear I'll miss your call. It makes time go a little faster when you call me. I miss you so very much and like they say, "It's the next best thing to being there."

Did some guys from your old platoon get a leave to come home? I thought I saw a Mexican in his dress uniform Sunday. It'll be neat to have you with me for a month though. You won't be able to get rid of me. I'll have to go everywhere you go; time's too precious to spend it apart. I can't wait to have you here with me again.

I know Denny's planning lots of things in his head. He's never said anything but among my other traits, I'm an expert mind reader. If you really want to go with him alone then I'll have to let you, but Tony, I don't want to be apart from you for one second, not even to go to the bathroom. Silly aren't I, but that's me. Love me forever, Tony, please. I love you so very, very much.

Lonely but lovingly,

Your wife,

Clellie

P.S. Hugs and Kisses, etc.

✉ May 28, 1969   *1:00 PM*

Dear Tony,

I just received your letter. It was so neat. I just sat and cried. I love you so much. Your letter was so sweet.

Opal Smith got married, but I don't know who to.

Tony, when I have the baby how can Mom get ahold of you to let you know? I know I'm asking you quite a little ahead of time but we'd like to know. You know, I thought you would call me Monday night and then you didn't. When Tuesday night came I waited up until 10:30 PM thinking you'd have to be in your barracks then because it'd be 9:30 PM there. I went to bed and just laid there thinking about you and all our neat times together. Then I heard the phone ring and the first thought that came to my mind was it was you. Then Mom came and told me it was you. I jumped out of bed and ran all the way down the stairs. I miss you so much and I just love to hear from you. Even for a short while. I love you, Tony, and you're the most important person that I've ever known or will know.

Well, I'll close until tonight.

                                                                      9:30 PM

I went over to your parents' place finally today and gave them your new address. I told them all the news about you too. Your mother told me to write you and tell you she was very sorry she hadn't written. Lately she's been busy all day and some of the nights trying to manage the Midway for Ginger. I showed her the pictures Sue gave me. Amanda showed me your letter and wanted me to read it. She wrote you another. Your mother thought it would have done me good to go live with you. She says she'll write you as soon as she can.

Tony, how dangerous is it to go Airborne? If you go to that school to be an officer for 12 weeks, can I live with you? Then what do you do for 9 more weeks and I can live with you then too, right? I really am afraid for you to do that. You'd have to go ahead of them all and check things out. I'm afraid! How many days would you get off in July if you did it? Have you decided for sure & would you be a lieutenant then? I thought that's what you said but I wasn't sure. I'm glad they gave you post privileges. It did you good I'll bet. I'm also glad that there were no girls. I get very jealous you know! I'm glad you had a good time though.

I know we need to save a lot of money so I can go to Hawaii. A lady who has six kids went over to Hawaii alone. It cost her $500 by the time they did a few things. Another one went to meet her husband for a week & she spent $600 so as much as we can get will be better. Yes, I think a week's worth that much just to be with you. I love you and I want to be with you gobs. If you would want me to bring our baby I would. It would limit things to do, but if you would want me to it would be fine. I love you, Tony, and I can't wait to be with you again.

I'm so disappointed in only a 15-day leave. I'd love to run off with you when you get home. I really would like to Tony. It's not fair to keep us apart. You're my whole life and I don't want to lose you ever!

All my love.

Forever & ever,
Clellie

P.S. Hugs & Kisses Forever!

May 29, 1969   11:30 PM

Dearest Tony,

I love you so very much. My days without you are not great. There's nothing to do. No one to look pretty for, no one to want to impress, I miss you so much. Tomorrow's Memorial Day, if I was there we'd be sharing it together. You'd be by my side with your arm around me and I'd just hold onto you forever. If you weren't in the Army maybe we'd go to Twin or Shoshone Falls. It doesn't do much good to dream, though, does it? Tony, I don't want you to leave me a whole year, but there's not much either of us can do about it is there?

Next month I'm going to start sending your mail by regular mail. It'll be a dollar less and you'll be getting one every day like you do now so it shouldn't make too much difference. As for you, I want you to keep airmail 'cause I don't get one every day and it'll speed the ones that you do write.

Today I cleaned the stove, washed the sheets on our bed, and straightened up the house a little. How's that for exciting? About 8:30 PM Susan came over and asked me to go to Oakley with her. She was taking the baby so Denny's parents could watch him for tonight and tomorrow. Denny and Susan are either going to Sun Valley or to Yellowstone Park. It'll do them good to go away alone for a while. It only makes me wish that you were here with me. I guess I'll have to get used to it though.

Our TV's gone on the blink. Man, I'll go nuts. It's the only thing that has been keeping me company since you've been gone. I depend on it so much. Oh well.

How's the Army? Not much better I'll bet. I wish I was with you so much. Tony, when the baby's born I only want you with me. Not my mother or your mother or anyone but you to hold my hand. I need you and as the time gets closer the more I want you here. I love you, Tony, like no one has ever loved or will love anyone.

They have the carnival at Shelby's. It looks really neat. I told Mom that I'd just take a couple of rides and the baby would be here in no time. She didn't seem to like my idea. The baby's still lively as ever. I can't wait till I have it. I want to see what it is. I really want it to be healthy. I hope it looks like you. In some ways I can tell it's a lot like you. It likes to keep me awake at night & it likes my attention, and boy, it kicks up a storm. I think it's already spoiled. What do you think?

I see Ford a lot in town anymore. He's usually always with Stewart.

Tony, I love you so very, very much. I'm very glad you're going to be the father to the children I have. I couldn't be any luckier. I'm here waiting with all my love till you get home to me.

Your lonely but loving wife,
Clellie

P.S. Do you want our baby baptized in the Catholic church? You'll be here to do it with me, won't you?

Hugs & Kisses, etc. (can't wait to collect)

May 30, 1969   *11:00 PM*

Dear Tony,

How's the greatest guy on earth been? I hope fine. Do you like your Sgt.?

Today Mom and I went to visit the graves. I remembered last year you showed me your grandparents' graves and I tried to find them but I couldn't and I didn't remember their names. I saw Grandpa and Grandma Graf's grave. We went to Grandma and Grandpa Chesley's graves. Man, it seemed weird to see my first name on a headstone. When we get a headstone when I die or you do, I want to get one like theirs. In the middle, it had a pair of hands like in a prayer. On one side of it, was like an open book with Grandma's name on it & her birth and death date. On the other side, was Grandpa's name & dates in another book. At the bottom, it had the date they were married. It was really nice. What a great subject to talk about. Afterwards Mom bought me a hamburger. When I got home, I set & combed Molly's hair. At about 5:30 PM, I took Hope and her kids up for a hamburger and came home at 6:30 PM. I went to her place to watch the movie. At 8:00 PM, Mom came over to watch it too. At 9 PM, Hope and I went to the 24 Flavors to buy us and Mom a banana split. Hope was carrying the banana splits to the car so I opened her door and shut it for her. When I looked up I saw Wayne Jolley & his wife looking at me from the stoplight. They looked at me really funny. I felt so dumb. When they drove by, his wife just kinda frowned at me. Oh well. When we got home, we saw Mitch at the gas station right by Hope's house in that phone booth & Mom was in the house talking to him. It looked so funny we about died laughing. We told Mom just to hang up and step outside to talk to him. She about died when she found out where he was. Dumb guy. Oh well.

You know what popped into my mind today? Remember how when we park by the river and you'd act like you were a monster and it used to terrify me so? I had to kind of laugh about it. I'll bet though if you'd still do it to me it would still terrify me. You looked so real when you would do it.

Do you know what I want to do one night when you get home (in between making love)? I want to put on a nice slim dress, iron my hair, and go to a dance.

Tony, you know 15 days doesn't seem like a very long time to have you with me. By then, I'll have waited 4 ½ months for you. I wish it were a longer time. I love you so very much I wanted so much to be with you again today. I want us to be like a married couple should be which is together. I miss you so much. It must be getting close to time for the baby because anytime I get alone anymore and think about you I cry. I was listening to records today and I bawled. You know, I haven't slept good like I did when you spent the night with me in that motel room since you left. I love you, Tony, and I want you here so much it's unbearable.

Your insecure but ever loving waiting wife, Clellie
P.S. Hugs & Kisses, etc.

✉ *May 31, 1969*   *11:30 PM*

Dearest Tony,

I sure do wish that you were here. I miss you so very, very much.

Guess what? I have a few stretch marks. Ugh! They are below my belly button though so if I'm lucky they'll all stay below it so I can wear my two piece swimsuit when you get home. I sure hate the thought of them though but oh well. Just as long as you still love me.

Boy, today I was so ambitious I couldn't believe it. I scrubbed down the bathroom and washed the stuff off in the utility room. I washed the dirty spots off the kitchen walls. I washed clothes, cleaned the fridge, and swept the floors. What do you think about that? Then I went uptown for a few groceries. At 5:30 PM, Mitch came and got Mom to go to work. At 6 PM, he came back and brought some stuff for him and Mom to have a picnic tomorrow at the river. I sat and listened to records until 15 to 8 PM. Things started getting me down like you not being here, and the baby coming pretty soon and I need you. I hate to be alone. I think so much about you and I remember so many neat times together. I even begin to hate other couples that are together. It doesn't seem at all fair. At 7:45 PM, I went over to Hope's and watched TV. It wouldn't be so bad here if the TV was fixed. At 9 PM, Mom called for me to come and get her at work, so I did and then dropped her uptown. I came back home and went to Hope's to watch TV again. At 10:15 PM, she wanted me to tell her fortune, so I did, twice. I got home at about 11:15 PM. How's that for a good account?

Guess who I saw today? Barry Jolley. I was walking out of Thriftway and he walked by me. He said hi, and I said hi.

How's Sue and Carol doing, or do you know? Have they got jobs and a place to live? What does Matt and Ken think about it? I'll bet they're happy.

Tony, I love you so very much. I started wondering today how our old apartment would've been during the summer if it would've been hot or cold. Silly of me. You don't know how much I wish we were still living there together, safe and sound. I want you home now but no matter how long it takes, I'll be waiting.

Yours forever and ever,
Clellie

P.S. Hugs and Kisses, etc.

✉ **June 1, 1969**   *10:30 PM*

Hi Hon,

I was so very pleased to hear from you today. I love so much to talk to you. I sure wish that it was in person though. I'd do more than just talk.

Molly's been gone to Buhl today and Mom went on a picnic with Mitch. She got home about 9:00 PM tonight and she told me that she shocked Mitch to death. She was really plastered and crying. She told me that she went swimming in the nude today in the Snake River. I couldn't believe it. Man, what's happened to her. I just hope no one saw her. Tony, please don't ever let her know you know. When she gets drunk, she goes haywire. I still can't believe it.

Is Wayne Jolley your cousin? Is his dad your dad's brother? I can't remember for sure and Molly was asking me.

You know Sarah Grace? She's got an older sister named Stacy. Well guess what? Her mother ran off with Stacy's husband. How's that for a great mother? They went to California.

You remember Anna Cole? Boy, I saw her today in Thriftway's and I couldn't believe my eyes. You know how she's always been chunky. Well now she's as skinny as I was before I got p.g. Shocked me. She really looks nice.

Today I did the ironing, cleaned up the kitchen, and then I waited for your call. At about 4:00 PM I went over to Hope's to watch TV. At 6:00 PM I came back home and then at about 7:30 PM I remembered that I had to mail your letter. Hope wanted to get her kids a Frosty so Hope and I and her kids went up to the Post Office, then to Thriftway, and then home. Hope invited me over to watch TV so I did. I know I'm spending a lot of time with her but I hate being alone especially without a TV to watch. I came home at about 10:15 PM. A car pulled up in front of her house and two guys came to her door. She knew them and let them in. I told her I had to go and abruptly left before they even got in the front door.

Tony, will you give this thank you card to Matt to give to Sue? She gave me some diapers and I don't have her address. You can look at it if you want to. It's really cute.

Tony, are you going to fly home when you get your leave? Where will you land if you do? I know it's awfully early but I'm so excited I can hardly stand it. I want you home so very bad and I can't wait to see your face when you look at our baby (if it's here). I love you so much and I want to be with you. It was so neat to talk to you. I miss you so very much.

All my love forever,
Clellie

P.S. Hugs & Kisses, etc.

✉ *June 2, 1969*　　　　　　　　　　　　　　　　　　　　　　　　　　*11:00 PM*

Hi Hon,

I'll bet that you're getting pretty upset with me for not sending your sandals. Well, I tried to send them without a box, but the post office wouldn't let me. They were all wrapped and stuff, but they said they might lose them like that. I would've put them in a box, but I had run out at our house and Hope's out of boxes too. As soon as I can get one, I'll send it to you. Please don't give up on me.

Kate Ashcroft got married Friday, but I don't know who to.

This morning I went with Auntie Em to pick up the artificial flowers she had placed on the graves. Sounds fun. I spent the rest of the day paying bills and such. Tonight I stayed home and listened to the radio for a change. More fun.

Do you know what I want to do? I want to go fishing. I haven't been for so long I don't think I'd know how. Maybe when you get home we can.

Well here's where all the money went this time. Listen good. $25 to the ring, $25 to the gas bill, $6 to your insurance, $1 to send your sandals, $4 for Bonnie and Bill's wedding present and card and wrapping paper. I got them a real nice set of bowls to cook with. It was the cheapest thing I could find. I don't know for sure when they'll get married but I wanted to be safe. $1.50 for cards for your dad, my dad, and Amanda. I'll sign the cards from both of us. Are you still going to get your father another card? $8 for the prescriptions on my refill of last month, $11.00 to the bank for the baby (Now I have $21.00 in there), $5 for stationery and stamps, .50 for miscellaneous. This leaves me with $13.00 for gas, and any activity or miscellaneous for the rest of the month. Not much. Oh well it'll due.

I got a statement from Dr. Petersen for $150. I went in today and told them that I had showed them my id card and that the Army was to pay for it. They said that yes they knew it and was sorry that they had billed me. She'd make a note of it so I wouldn't get any more bills.

I thought of some more boys' names. Pick out the ones you like if any and submit any suggestions of your own. Anthony Blair Jolley and call him Blair. Anthony Boyd Jolley and call him Boyd. Damon Anthony Jolley and call him Damon. Todd Anthony Jolley and call him Todd. Chad Wayne Jolley. I really would prefer one with your name in it.

Boy, do you know what popped into my head today? I all of a sudden remembered the first night we went all the way in that old pick-up in the park. I'm so happy it happened. Maybe I should be ashamed but I can't be. It led to me getting you for a husband and having our baby. Strange for it just to pop in my head. I love you so much.

Tony, be careful and don't get into too many fights. I don't want you ornery when you get home. I sure hope I have had the baby by then. I want you to see and hold it. I love you so very, very much.

Your lonely but loving wife,
Clellie

P.S. Hugs & Kisses, etc.

✉ *June 2, 1969*

Dear Tony,

I sure love you gobs. I've decided to start sending my letters regular mail, but I don't want any to lapse between the switch so I decided to send a card regular, and the letter air mail today so I can start regular mail. I know you can't follow this but it's okay. I sure do love you and I wish you were here with me.

Love Always,
Clellie

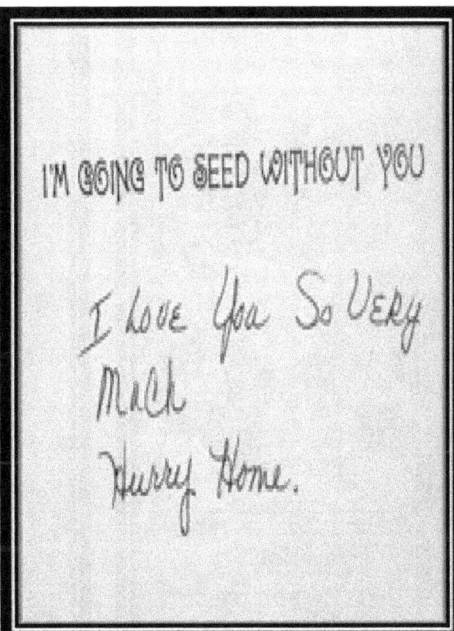

June 3, 1969　　　　　　　　　　　　　　　　　　　　　　**10:00 AM**

Dear Tony,

I saw this card yesterday and thought that you would really get a kick out of it. I thought it was cute.

I sure wish that you were home with me. I love you so very much and I miss you gobs and gobs. I think about you all the time. I can't wait until you're home forever 'cause I'm not ever going to let you out of my sight. Hurry home, Tony, and remember that I'll always love you.

Yours forever and ever,
Clellie

P.S. I love you!

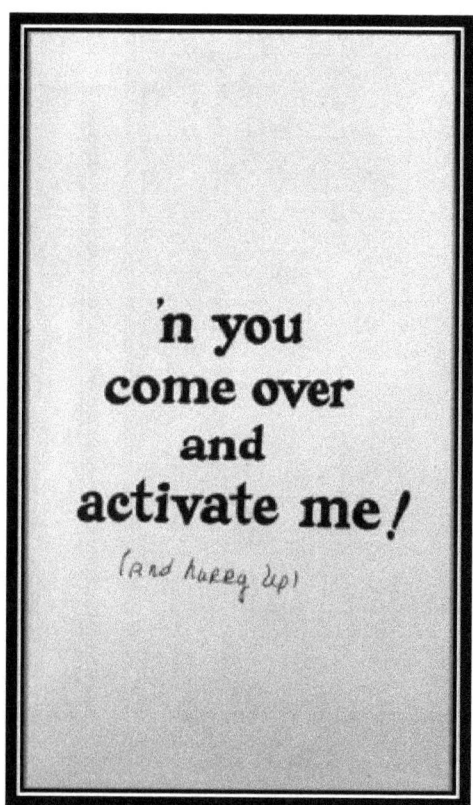

June 3, 1969   *10:30 PM*

Dear Handsome Hubby,

How have you been doing these days? How's your leg been doing? Fine, I hope.

Well I'm getting prepared for the baby. All's I need now is 5 more dollars in the bank to pay the hospital, and $7 to get a case of S.M.A. for it. I need plastic pants and some powder, oil, soap, swabs, lotion, diaper liners, and Vaseline. Susan told me not to buy any more stuff until she gets me the present from them. I hate to wait around though 'cause I feel so unprepared, but I don't have any money to get anything with anyway so I'll have to wait.

I got the invitation for Bill and Bonnie's wedding today. The reception will be on June 14th at 8:00 PM at the Mormon Church. I sure am glad I've got their present now. I hope they'll be happy. The invitation was addressed to Mr. & Mrs. Tony Jolley. I sure liked that. Kinda weird, aren't I? If they are half as happy as we were, they'll be doing great. Course it'll take a great husband like you to make a great marriage.

I finally got your sandals mailed today. Please tell me if you've gotten them. How did you like the box I put them in? At least I got them mailed to you.

I washed the inside of the windows today and Mom washed the outside. I also washed my car by hand so it would really be clean. Aren't you proud of me? I went over to Aunt Mabel's and she gave us a little meat. Some ham hocks, ribs, & stuff. We had fish for supper tonight. It was really good. One of Molly's boyfriends gave her some.

I hope you know that it will be a week tomorrow since I've gotten a letter from you. I know they keep you busy, but Tony, can't you write? I love you now and I will for all eternity.

All my love forever & ever,
Clellie

P.S. Hugs & Kisses, etc.

✉ **June 4, 1969** **11:00 PM**

Dear Tony,

I love you and can't wait until you get home. Time is going so slow. I sure do wish it would hurry up.

This morning I took Hope and Ashley to Twin. Hope had to take Ashley to the hospital for x-rays. Boy, you sure could hear poor old Ashley holler. They have to stick this little rubber hose up her and drain her bladder. Then they fill her system with a needle and syringe with iodine in order to make the x-rays. I'll bet it hurt her a lot. The one x-ray technician asked Hope if they suspected a mass growth in her. Hope told them she wasn't sure. I guess the technician can't tell her what he can see, only her dr. can. I'll have to take them back to see the dr. & get the results Friday. It doesn't look too good though, the poor little thing.

Do you know what I want to do when you get home also? I want to have a picnic at Shoshone Falls. It would be so neat just the two of us.

Tony, what are you going to do about birth control when you get home? It'll be the easiest time for me to get pregnant. I can't take birth control pills until a while after the baby. Do you have any suggestions?

Boy, it's so hot up here in the room. You can't sleep until 1:00 AM 'cause of the heat and with nothing on you and then about 5:00 AM you need the sheet. It was 92 degrees here today. Ugly. Boy, I sure hate the heat.

Tony, I'm getting a little afraid. I don't know if I can bear being in the hospital when the other husbands come to visit. I feel today like I used to before my monthly so I just might have it early. I can't wait. I hope so very much that it looks like you. I love and admire you so very much. You're so neat. Please hurry home.

All my love forever,
Clellie

P.S. Hugs & Kisses, etc.

✉ **4 June, 1969** **Wednesday**

Dear Clellie,

Here I am on fireguard. It's 3 o'clock in the morning. I'll pull fireguard until 3:30 AM and then I get to go to bed for a whole hour before we get up. I'm sorry I haven't written you, Clellie. They haven't given us any free time since the weekend. I was going to write you Sunday. When we got back to the barracks they were having a supper inspection for booze and marijuana. They tore everything apart, and we had to put everything together before we went to bed. Consequently, I didn't have time to write. I was going to be sure to write Monday, but we had an honor guard parade yesterday and we had to G.I. our boots and brass. Last night, which was Tuesday, we had to buff the floors for today. Some Lieutenant General is inspecting the company area. I didn't get to bed last night until 11 PM, and I had to get up at 2:30 AM till 3:30 AM on fireguard. We have to get up at 4:30 AM, so that means I'll get about 4 hours sleep and we have a big march tomorrow. Man, I'm so tired I can barely write. Everyone in the whole company is so tired and pissed off that it's pathetic.

They never give you time around this place to write letters or to be on your own time. I don't think they want you to think about the situation you're in, or you just might tell them to go to hell and go AWOL.

Today out on the range we used all kinds of explosives. We had to set our own charges and everything. You know the plastic explosives they use on "Mission Impossible"? We used a 1/4 lb. of that in one of our charges, and also some TNT.

Clellie, do you think you love me as much as you ever have? I just want to know because I find that the longer I'm away from you, the more I love and want you. A guy couldn't ask for anything more wonderful than you in one lifetime. Do you know that? The only day I'm looking forward to is the day I get a leave to come home to you. I hope you want me to come home as much as I want to come home, because it would take 100 horses to keep me away.

Clellie, I love you very, very much. No matter what happens between us, I know we'll never break apart. No one has a love that could even compare to 1/10th of what our love is. Anyway, that's my love for you.

Clellie, I have to close for now but I want you to love me forever and ever. I love you so much, Clellie, I can barely stand the thought of being away from you. Well I have to go wake up my fireguard relief.

Your loving husband,
Tony

P.S. Clellie, I love you, I want you, I need you, I LOVE YOU!!

You are beautiful!

Pvt. Anthony Jolley
H.H.C 1st Bn 2nd Brig.
Ft. Ord, California 2nd Plt 93941

✉ *June 5, 1969* *11:30 PM*

Hi Hon,

I got your letter today. Boy, it sure adds to my day. I was so very happy when I got it. It made me feel so neat. I just love your letters.

Today Mom went out to Price's and got her check and bought me dinner. Then we paid a few of her bills and that was the end of that money. I told her about them inspecting you guys for marijuana. She said you'd better be careful and for you to send it all to her. It'd be in good hands until you got home. I said, "Sure it would!" She just laughed.

Man, they plan on building a shopping mall here for sure. Rumors are that it will be 7 to 9 blocks long on Main Street where the Stinker Station is and on up. Sounds pretty good. They're starting to build in July.

They have a new grocery store here. It's called the Discount Warehouse. You have to be a member to shop there, but it only costs 50 cents a month to join it. That's not bad for the money you save. You save 20% to 30% on almost everything. On a carton of cigarettes you save about 35 cents. My aunt said she bought $27 worth of groceries and figured it up and had saved $7. The only catch is no stamps, no box boy, and you have to mark your own stuff. Not bad. It had another store in Twin or somewhere and had forced the other stores to lower their prices 'cause they had lost so much business.

Boy, Tony, it sure sounds like they are being awfully rough on you guys. How come? Will it let up after a while? 4 hours of sleep isn't good at all. Here they sent us their pamphlet and told us how great they were taking care of you guys. What a bunch of rubbish. Tony, it's okay that you couldn't write. They are keeping you awfully busy, but please write as often as you can. Your letters mean so very, very much to me. Do you like messing with explosives? Could you get hurt with them?

Tony, this separation made me realize just how much I depend on you and how much you mean to me. I knew before that you meant everything to me but the realization of it has really come with you gone. Now I want you home so I can just love and please you. I hate us being apart!

Well I'd better close, Tony. Take good care of yourself for me. Stay mine forever. I love you so much and want you to hurry home.

Love for eternities,
Clellie

P.S. Hugs & Kisses, etc.!

 **5 June, 1969**

Dear Clellie,

I love you very much, I'm in a very depressed mood today, Clellie, because I really do miss you. Also today we ran about 9 miles, and walked about 5 miles. I wish somehow you and I could be together. It just doesn't seem fair that other people get to be together and you and I have to be apart. Well, I'd better change the subject before I go AWOL and come home.

Those names you picked are all right if you like them better than Chad Wayne Jolley, but I guess I'm just partial to that name. I really think it's the best name.

I think that you ought to quit having those nasty little thoughts. I'm glad though that you don't regret going all the way that night in the park. At the time we thought that it was really a bad and awful thing that it happened. It actually turned out to be about the best and most wonderful thing that ever happened to me.

Clellie, I'm going to send your pictures back. Also I'm sending home $60 with this letter. I want you to put as much in the bank as possible. You'll probably have to send some back to me before the month is over. If you don't have to send me the money, I'll have to pay back the Army for the money because they're overpaying me. I only have 12 bucks left, but I'm going to do my damnedest to make it last for the rest of the month.

Clellie, do you really think you'll be able to wait for me for a whole year? I only hope to hell you'll be able to wait for me. If you end up not waiting for me, I'd stay in the Army. If you wrote me a "Dear John" letter, I'd re-up in Vietnam until I got killed over there. If you ever left me, I wouldn't have any reason to go back to civilian life.

I really do love you, Clellie. I want so much to be able to put my arms around your fat little stomach and kiss, kiss, and kiss you. I want you forever to be mine, Clellie, so please do. I'd better say goodbye for now. Write me and stay mine forever.

Your lonely loving husband,
Tony

P.S. I love you!

Pvt. Anthony Jolley
H.H.C 1st Bn 2nd Brig.
Ft. Ord, California 2nd Plt 93941

✉ *June 6, 1969* *10:00 PM*

Hi Hon,

Well, here I am being a good kid and babysitting for Hope. Sweet aren't I?

Today I took Ashley and Hope to Twin to see the doctor again. He got the results from the x-rays. She's got a growth where her last one was and it's bigger. The Dr. said that it's bigger than what it should be. They hate to operate so soon after the last one. There's a tumor clinic in Utah next week for Dr.'s and they come from all over to look at x-rays and decide what to do. Hope's Dr. is going to take Ashley's and see what other Drs. say. It sure doesn't look very promising. The poor kid and Hope. I don't think I could take it.

I cleaned the house up good today. I don't feel too good tonight, probably the ride to Twin. Also the 24-hour stomach flu is going around. Andy and Ashley had it. Then again, I might just be tired.

Angie Gibson's even bugging me subconsciously. I had a dream last night that I can't figure out why I dreamed it. Here it is. I dreamed I went over to your place to visit and Angie was there talking to Marie. She left when I came in. I asked Marie what she was there for and Marie said she was talking about you (Tony). She had written to you and you wrote back but you told her that there could never be anything between you two but friendship and you'd write to her as such. It hurt me so bad that you were writing to her anyway that I bawled. I ran out of the house crying and then I woke up 'cause I had to use the john. Dumb dream.

Boy, I think Ford lives up town. I always see him dragging Main, even at day.

I sure wish that our baby would come. I'm not quite ready with all its stuff yet, but the little bit I still have to get could be charged and paid when I get the check with the extra money for the baby. I wish Susan would get what she plans on 'cause then I'd know for sure what I need. It's getting awfully uncomfortable and hot. He's even moving down at the bottom. I'd sometimes swear he's going to crawl right out. He's going to be strong that's for sure.

Tony, I don't want you to go to Vietnam. I'd worry so much. Please hurry home, Tony. I can't wait until I see you again. I miss you so very, very much. Be good and stay mine forever.

Yours Eternally, Clellie

✉️ **June 6, 1969**

Dear Tony,

I love you, Tony, very much and I'm so happy that you're my husband. I couldn't ask for a better one. You're one of a kind, and I was the lucky one to get you. I love you so very much. I hope you enjoy your goodies. You're the greatest father-to-be that ever was or will be.

All my love,
Clellie

✉ *June 7, 1969*   *10:30 PM*

Dear Tony,

I love you so very, very much. I received your other letter today with the money and pictures. I read it almost 5 times today. It made me feel so very, very neat.

Today I took Steve over to Rupert so he could pay his Dr. bill and get his prescription. He's working at Simplot's on midnight shift. It's about to kill him off he says.

Virgil wrote me a letter and said to say hi to you for him, and he hopes everything's okay. He went to Mom and told her that he sure thought a lot of me. Makes me sad for all the bad times I've given him.

Nancy and Alice called tonight. They also said to say hi. Alice walked all the way into town from the farm. I guess Dad was quite upset.

I forgot about Amanda's birthday. I didn't even go over and wish her Happy Birthday. Boy, I really feel bad. I sure hope she's not mad at me. I'll have to go over next week. Did you wish her happy birthday?

My mom and dad didn't go to court when they were supposed to. It was cancelled until the 13th. My aunt told Mom that she wanted some money by the 10th. I don't know what's going to happen. I sure hope we don't have to move.

I got an invitation to a personal shower for Bonnie on the 11th. I just don't see how I can get her a present with trying to save money and the baby and all. I think that the gift for the reception, and my appearance at that should be sufficient. What do you think?

Carrie Conner called tonight. Dale's gone to summer camp and he'll be back Wednesday and then they might move to Utah. He's going to go ahead to look for a job, and if he finds one, they'll move. He won't know for sure about the schooling until the middle of July.

After I pay the phone bill (after I get it), I'll put the rest of the money in my account so if you need it I can draw it back out. I can't draw any out of your account 'cause it's just in your name.

Thank you for returning the pictures. I put them all in the scrapbook of you. I guess we'll name the baby, if it's a girl, Jeanette Marie Jolley, and if it's a boy, Chad Wayne Jolley.

Tony, do you realize that we have 7 more weeks to go before we are together? I wish time would go faster. Tony, don't worry about me waiting for you. I'll be right here waiting even for a whole year.

Your lovingly waiting wife,
Clellie

P.S. Hugs & Kisses, etc.
Hurry home!

June 8, 1969   *4:00 PM*

Dear Tony,

Man, I sure had a weird dream last night. I dreamed that you got to come home on a leave and you flew here. I went and picked you up and then we had to go to this motel. The Spears and Perrins were there too. They got to be with their husbands but I couldn't be with you until I went through this obstacle course. You could come with me, but you couldn't help me. It was really weird. There were so many funny things to go through. I finally made it through after a lot of work and I turned around and you were gone. It was really weird. I sure do love you.

Guess who just walked in. Curt and someone else to have Molly tell their fortune. I'm glad I'm up here. I hate him something awful. He's so weird.

Tony, I wish that you were here. We'd get away from this ugly place. I miss you so much. Well, I guess I'll sit up here and wait for your call. I love you, Tony, so very much.

12:30 AM

Hi Hon,

Mom and I've been sitting downstairs talking about ghosts and such. Do you know that 3 murderers from Seattle were being held in Twin Falls and they got out? They are armed. Great.

After you called tonight, Mom came home and we found a new way to tell fortunes. It was quite interesting. At about 9:30 PM we went and mailed your letter, and got a banana split. Mary dropped by to see me about 9:00 PM. She only stayed for a minute. It sure was good to see her. She said that she is going to have to have some tests done on her. She's been gaining weight rapidly and she doesn't eat hardly anything but salads. Her face has really been hard to control the pimples and her hair is falling out. At first they thought it was sugar diabetes, now they don't and want to find out. I sure hope it's nothing serious.

Boy, today was so very boring. All I could think about was you and it makes me sad. Sundays used to be my favorite day because I got to spend the whole day with you. Now it's the ugliest day there is, it was so good to talk to you. I just love it. Maybe it would be better for you to go to that U.C.O. School, the longer that you stay out of Vietnam the better.

Did you have a good time over the weekend? Did you kiddingly tell that kid you'd have to steal his wife? Tell me the truth. Is she really pretty? Blonde or brunette? Brown or blue eyes? Yes, I still have that ugly ole jealousy and it's getting worse. I can't even bear the thoughts of you looking at another girl. I guess I'm really getting bad, but I'm so afraid. I sure wish you were here with me tonight. Wow, we'd have so much fun even if I am fat and can't see my feet for my stomach. You helped put me in this shape you know, and I love it except now I want to see it. Well, write lots. Be good & stay only mine.

All my love forever,
Clellie

P.S. Hugs & Kisses, etc.!

June 9, 1969   10:30 PM

Hi Hon,

How's the great ole Army treating you? I hope okay 'cause I hate you being real unhappy.

Did you get your sandals? I sure hope you did.

Susan came over to see me today. Boy, that baby sure is growing. I can't believe it. She said that Denny's getting really anxious about you getting home, and that once you do get home Denny will never give us peace, and he'll be wanting to go places. I told her she'd better inform him that anywhere you go, I go. I'm going to stick to you like glue. Two weeks isn't too long to be with you and I plan on spending it all with you. Please let me know your plans.

I did some baking today. Mom went up town and got a couple beers. Then she came home and kept eating what I baked. Needless to say, she got sick. Told her it teaches her.

Dottie Dodson gave me 1 dozen & ½ diapers today, also three bottles and lots of little socks. It has to be a girl, they're girl's socks. So I have all of my diapers. Boy, I am glad to have them.

Tony, I mailed you a package or I will mail it tomorrow. I don't want you to open it 'til Sunday. I hope you like it. I would've sent fudge, but it takes 3 or 4 days before it gets to you and I was afraid it would melt. It's for a Father's Day present. I think you'll make the greatest father that ever was or will be.

I love you so, Tony. You're the most important thing in my life and I miss you so very much. Hurry home!!!

Your loving waiting wife,
Clellie

P.S. Hugs & Kisses, etc.

✉ *June 10, 1969*   *10:30 PM*

Dear Tony,

Boy, do I ever miss you! All day today I've been trying to figure a way out to come and live there.

I went over to your folk's place to visit. Barry has come back to live. I'm really very glad. I took some cookies over and before I left they were almost gone. I took Amanda a birthday card from you and I and told her that I was very sorry I was late getting it to her. Marie's still there, she doesn't know what to do. She's lost some weight too. We had a nice talk. Your mother and dad were at work.

I was thinking and do you know that the Carters have been married one whole year this month. It seems like yesterday we took the present over to their reception. Bill and Bonnie will marry six months and one day after we did. Around the 6th of July, Carrie and Dale will have been married 2 years already.

The baby sure is active. I sure wish it would hurry up and come. I still have a whole month to wait before it's due but I would like it early so I could get back into shape by the time you get home. I sure hope it does come early. I'm kinda anxious to see what it is.

I saw on TV the other night a show about high school kids that were worshipping the devil. They said they were tired of the fairy tales about God. He's dead. Sad, isn't it? It seems all that you hear about anymore is husbands and wives stepping out on each other. Tony, I love you and only you and I couldn't feel right if I went with anyone else. You're so very special to me and our love is special. I can't see how other people can do it. 'Course I forgot they don't have the kind of love we do.

I heard on the news where Nixon is pulling out 25,000 men from Vietnam immediately and more later, so maybe you won't have to go. I sure hope not. I want you safe. How has your knee been? It has to act up sooner or later with a broken cartilage. I love you so, Tony.

All my love forever,
Clellie

P.S. Hugs & Kisses, etc.

June 11, 1969   **10:30 PM**

Dear Handsome Hubby,

It seems to be getting worse all the time. Instead of getting used to you being away, I'm getting more and more depressed. You've been gone 3 months exactly today, and I hate you being away from me.

Well, first off Mom and I went to Aunt Mabel's and Uncle Carl's. Then we had to go to Rupert 'cause Dad paid most of the money he owes Mom. Mabel wanted to go so we took her too. I stopped in at Susan's and had a short visit. If Mom and I can find a two-bedroom apartment that's not too much I think we'll move. I told Susan to keep an eye out for one. Mom hates to move so close to time for the baby so I don't know. Then we came back over here and took Aunt Jane the rent money. Then we came home and I took Hope to work.

I broke Mom and Opal Morton's friendship up I guess for a while. It all started because last night Carol (Opal's daughter) called collect to anyone. We had had such a time collecting the money from Opal when Carol was in California and calling that we had decided not to accept the calls anymore. So Mom was gone last night and I simply told them that I couldn't accept it. This morning Mom went over Opal's, and Opal told her that I was really snotty to Carol on the phone & Mom and her were no longer friends. I was not snotty, Tony, honest, and I never meant to do it. I told Mom that maybe it was better because now maybe all the Mortons would stay away, but Mom said that Opal will really start telling lies around about all of us. Tony, I really don't think I can take her telling lies. I don't know what she'll say but she has a vicious tongue. I've been so close to tears all day. But that's not all that upset me. Mabel said Mitch made a snide remark the other day about me being p.g. It ticked her off. Also, all my Aunt Jane can do is find fault in our family. I'm so sick of this whole place it's not even funny. Also, I want so much to be with you, it's pathetic. All in all it's been a very tearful day. Curt Morton hasn't been over since Sunday. Mom told him quite a while ago that it didn't look good for him to come over with me here 'cause people would talk even if he comes just to see Molly who's his aunt. He kept away until last Sunday. I was upstairs when he came thank heavens. I didn't hear him ask her, but Molly said he asked where I was and she told him I was gone with Mom. His friend got on the phone once and talked for about 10 minutes. I got ticked off but I sat up here. I was waiting for your call. When he got on it the second time after he had just hung up I went downstairs and told them that I wished they would quit using the phone 'cause I was waiting on a long distance call from you. I then went into the bathroom and then directly back upstairs. They left within 10 minutes. I hope Curt stays away now and his friends. I really do hope we move, Tony. If I can find a two-room apartment after the baby and after your leave then I want to, Tony. This whole place stinks as far as I'm concerned.

I wanted a letter from you today so bad. I needed it to cheer me up. I didn't get one though. You know, Tony I resent other couples that are together. Every time I think about Bill and Bonnie getting married and being together I really get to dislike them. It doesn't seem fair. I remember how happy we used to be. Tony, I don't know what has gotten into me, but I resent everyone and everything. I don't think it's fair that I can't be there with you, and I don't think it's fair that they took you and not Bill & Denny. I'm a wicked ole witch today aren't I? I'm sorry that I write to you about all my troubles 'cause you've got enough on your own, but you're the only one I can turn to. You're all I have besides our baby. I love you so very much and I need you. Hurry Home!!

Your very depressed but ever-loving wife,
Clellie

✉ **11 Jun 1969**

Dear Clellie,

How is the most sweetest and most precious being alive? I really so love you, Clellie. If it wasn't for you, I really don't know what I'd be living for right now.

Guess what I had today? K.P.'s the answer. I never washed so many trays in my whole life. You really work your ass off on K.P. I'm so damn tired I'm about ready to fall over. All I could do was think about you today. I hope I don't have K.P. again. It doesn't keep your mind off home for one minute. I'm really making a lot of mistakes in this letter, but my fingers don't seem to want to do what I try to make them do.

I'm sending you some pictures with this letter. Four of them are of Butler and I. We're at the P.X. and we're pretty drunk. How do you like my different expressions in the four of me? I'm trying to look happy. The one I'm laughing in is because Spear stuck his hand through the curtain and hit me. Clellie, I love you. I don't know why I keep writing it in this letter. I guess it's because this last week and a half I just want to go AWOL and come home.

Tomorrow, and for the next week, we're going to shoot the M-60 machine gun. This Friday we have to qualify expert. Of course though, I'm going to.

Is the baby coming along all right, Clellie? I hope it's a girl and it looks just like you.

What's this shit about these dreams with Angie Gibson in them? Clellie, how many times do I have to tell you that there never was and never will be anything between me and Gibson? How could I possibly have room in my mind to love anyone else? It just isn't possible, Clellie. I want you to quit thinking about things like that. It isn't doing you or our baby any good. So please knock it off.

I'd better go for now, Clellie. Remember just how much I do love you. Also try to love me as much. I love you.

Your husband & father-to-be,
Tony

P.S I miss you very much.

P.P.S. Sorry for the raggedy pictures. Butler wanted the other 4 so we cut them.

Pvt. Anthony Jolley
H.H.C 1st Bn 2nd Brig.
Ft. Ord, California 2nd Plt 93941

June 12, 1969   **11:00 PM**

Dear Tony,

I miss you so very, very much. I can't believe how slow time has been going. It seems like it's taking forever to go by.

Our baby is doing fine. It's so full of life. It's always moving. I just wish it would stop growing. It's tearing my stomach to pieces. Every day it tears it more. All I had to do tonight after my bath was rub in some of that oil and I ripped some more. It's ugly.

Today, I washed the windows on the inside in the kitchen, our room, and Alice's old room. Then, I washed down the front room walls. As you can tell I was a pretty busy girl today.

Tony, when you write me again please tell me what your plans are as far as Denny is concerned when you get home. I know I've asked you that in a previous letter and if you answered it then don't answer it again. I really would like to know though.

Mom went with my aunts tonight to the hot springs in Oakley. She said that it was really nice.

We had the T.V. fixed tonight for a while. He told Mom that it would keep breaking 'cause the picture tube's about gone and the remote control system needs a whole new job. He said that it would cost anywhere from $70-100 to do it all. She's going to have it done. They're going to pick it up Monday. I hope they do a good job on it. It's needed it ever since we first got it.

Tony, I want you to know one very important thing and that is that I love you now and forever.

Your lonesome & loving wife,
Clellie

Hugs & Kisses forever!!!

✉ *June 13, 1969* *10:00 PM*

Hi my Handsome Husband,

How's things been going with you this day? I received your letter and pictures today. You look so cute in your pictures. You and Butler must be really good friends. I'm glad that you're with someone you can have fun with. When did you take the pictures? I thought you liked Coors and Olympia was for women. Did Butler change your opinion on beer as well as cigarettes? I'd never have believed it if he has.

Today I dusted real good and vacuumed the furniture and the front room real good. I want it to look really nice when you get home. I know that it's early but while I can I thought I'd do it. I just can't wait until you get home. I also went to town and bought some diaper liners for the baby and a pen to write with. I had to mail your letter too 'cause I forgot to put a stamp on your letter today so I had to go uptown to mail it. Smart, aren't I?

Guess what? A woman went to the hospital to have her baby. She took her purse with her with $140.00 in it. She had it in the delivery room and someone stole it. The only ones who could were nurses. Boy, I'm going to wait until after I leave the hospital to give them the $25.

Tomorrow night Susan's coming over to get me to go to Bill & Bonnie's reception. Denny's going out with that young kid 'cause he don't want to go to the reception. I've almost forgotten what it's like to go anywhere at night.

I was filling some things in our baby's book and I want to ask you what's your dad and mom's full names?

Tony, I was so pleased to get your letter today. I've read it about 5 times already. Say why did you have K.P. today? Isn't it a punishment for something? Your expressions in your pictures are cute. It looks just like you. I sure wish I had you in person though.

How did you do with the M-60 machine gun? Course I don't know why I ask. I should know that you're known as deadeye, Tony.

Boy, the baby is so lively. If it don't hurry up and come I think I'll be one mass of black & blues. My ribs are so sore. Usually with the baby dropped they don't bother your ribs so much. That's why I think it is really big probably 9 or 10 lbs. I sure hope not but we'll see. I hope it looks like you so I'll have something here that's a big reminder of you. I can't wait till it comes. It kept me awake for 1 ½ hours last night, and it's been raising a storm today.

Well, I guess that I had better close for now. I'm at Hope's babysitting. I don't mind 'cause there's nothing that I want to do without you here. I love you, Tony, so very much. I can't wait until you come home.

Your lonesome loving wife, Clellie

P.S. Hugs & Kisses, etc.

 **June 14, 1969**　　　　　　　　　　　　　　　　　　　　　　　　**11:45 PM**

Dear Tony,

We sure have had a lot of excitement around here today. First of all I took Steve and Ida uptown to do some shopping. When I got home I discovered that Dad had Ann call Mom and tell her that he was bringing them home because he had to pay Mom her $60. He made it sound as if it were all her fault. Then he called up and told Mom that he was bringing them home tomorrow. Nice guy! I finished putting all our boxes in the closet and I moved your clothes out of the chest-a-drawers into this big drawer in here. I moved a few of your shirts in here too. Your work shirts I boxed up and put in the closet. I put the baby's bed in here. (Makes the bedroom look junky) Mom told Molly that it'd be better for her to move but she wants to try to stay so we can put her boxes all together in a corner and I guess Alice can share the bedroom with her or Nancy. Ann and Nancy will take the other bedroom. I don't know where they'll hang all their clothes. It's really a mess. I don't think Molly will stay too long. We really don't have the room anyway. Ann told Mom that she knew her and I couldn't get along. She didn't want me bossing her. Mom practically told her I won't. So I said that I wouldn't worry about her as long as she didn't try and boss the kids too much. Also my car will not be used for her transportation everywhere. Hope said she doesn't want them for babysitters 'cause she's tired of her cigarettes being smoked & the kids' money being taken & her drawers gone through. Boy, they better stay out of our room, and our stuff. They're all snoopy and they'd better stay out of the pennies and the $7 in change I've saved for a case of formula for the baby. Also they better keep their hands off our letters. They just better stay out of here. The phone, you'll have a bit of trouble getting through on Sundays. I have a feeling I won't be here for very long because I won't take the stuff that was before and I don't want our baby in a surrounding of constant yelling. I'd like to help them but they don't listen so I just don't know, lots of troubles. I sure would like you home with me.

We (Susan and I) went to Bill & Bonnie's reception. They really looked nice. It was a very pretty reception. I sent you the napkin. Boy, I'll bet it cost a mint for the reception. Orchid flowers, chandeliers, 5 bridesmaids, matron of honor, you wouldn't believe it. They got quite a lot of stuff. Montana was there. He was the best man. He got your address from Bill. I told him that he should've come over and got it from me a long time ago. I sure wanted you to be here with me. It made me so sad 'cause I remembered how happy we were when we got married. It may not of been as exquisite but I liked ours better. For one thing, I had the best, handsomest man on earth as my husband.

Susan said that you owe Denny a letter. You wrote him once and then he wrote you.

Well, we have six more weeks before we are together. Tony, I wish so much that I was with you right now. I miss you so much.

Remember before you left you said that on your leave you'd take me to the villa. Are you still going to?

Tony, I'm afraid that we won't have too much privacy here now either with the kids, or our squeaky bed and all. I guess we'll manage though. I love you, Tony, so very much.

All my love forever,
Clellie

P.S. Hugs & Kisses, etc.

June 15, 1969   *9:00 PM*

Hi Hon,

I sure enjoyed talking to you. I love you so very much. After I write this letter I guess I'd better run my other letter up to the post office. I forgot all about it until now.

Mom wanted me to go visiting with her to Aunt Mabel's today but I wanted to wait for your call, so she went and got back about ½ hour before you called. She was only teasing me while I was on the phone. We've been getting along pretty well. She's forever buying me stuff to eat. As long as Mitch's away we get along fine, and she doesn't drink. She worries about you and is interested in how you're doing. She says that she ought to write you a letter, but I tell you all the news. She wanted me to go to the movie with her and Edna Jolley, but I didn't want to go. She gets worried about me staying home all the time. I told her that on the 25th of June I wanted to go to the show, "The Shoes of the Fisherman" so her and I might go. She gives me money for apples or any crazy thing I want.

I guess Dad's going to keep the kids out there for a while longer, probably till he gets mad again.

Denny Carter and Barry stopped by to ask how you were doing and when you'd be home. Naturally, I had to brag about you doing so well on your test. I'm so proud. He wants you to write and hurry home. He says he wishes he had gone with you 'cause he just can't settle down to marriage. He still might join after you get home so he says. He said maybe it would help him want to settle down more. Boy, Tony I'm so very happy I married you. I never did have a problem with you. I'm so very lucky to have you as my husband. You faced the fact we were married and didn't seem to mind it so bad but most guys resent it. I love you so much, Tony. I gave Denny your new address. Denny and Barry were here for only about 5 minutes.

12:00 AM

Mom came in and asked me if I wanted to go get a pizza with her and Alice so you know me about pizza, I went. Alice took us to Rupert to show us where she lived so if Mom wanted to visit she could. It's a nice little house. Then we got a pizza at Maxie's to go. We then came home and ate it. We sat around and Mom and her talked about how come they got their divorces and such and then Molly walked in and had to tell us about her weekend in Buhl. I'll send you your stamps in my letter tomorrow. I'm getting you 10 airmail stamps so you can write me letters and 7 regular stamps for anyone else.

When I got up this morning I had a couple of small spots of blood on my pants. This is a sign that I'm getting ready to have the baby. However, if any more shows up it can be a sign of hemorrhaging inside. I'm not worried though 'cause so far no more has shown up. Hope said that I had better keep off my feet more and not be doing so much work like I have or it can start hemorrhaging. I'll get lazy & fat!! I have my suitcase all packed just in case.

I love and miss you, Tony.

Your loving wife,
Clellie

P.S. Hugs & Kisses, etc.

June 16, 1969   **10:00 PM**

Dear good looking (alias Tony),

I sure do love you so very, very much. You mean so much to me. I can't wait until I have you here with me.

Today I went uptown and took Mom and Hope and her kids so they could do what they had to get done. Mom was just teasing and said she was going to have to spank me. Andy told her she couldn't and Mom said that she could. Andy popped up and said, "Not when Tony gets home 'cause he'll spank you!" (meaning Mom). It was so cute.

I told you that Sarah Grace's mother ran off with Sarah Grace's sister's husband. Well the reason was that Sarah Grace's mother was p.g. by her son-in-law. Great. Also, Sarah Grace's aunt Gertie Winkler of Declo was shot to death the other night. She divorced her husband because he was always drunk and stepping out. She was staying with her daughter and son-in-law. She was planning on marrying another guy. Her ex-husband walked in the house the other night and shot her with a shotgun. Then he said, "I'll make sure she doesn't marry again." Wow, it's really something. He's up for 1st degree murder. I couldn't believe something like that would happen around here.

I got you 10 airmail stamps to write letters to me and 7 regular stamps for anyone else. I figured that would keep you busy.

I had a dream last night that you got to come home for the Fourth of July. I was skinny and we had so much fun.

A girl that used to work at Simplot's with me had her baby 2 weeks ago and she came over to show it to me. It was quite cute. It was a boy. She said that when it was born it weighed 7lbs and now it weighs 8 lbs. It looked so big. I want a tiny one, but I guess it's most important for it to be healthy. She was in labor for 21 hours.

Tony, I can't wait until you get home. I'm so excited. I miss you so much.

Your lonesome loving wife,
Clellie

P.S. Hugs & Kisses, etc.

✉ *June 17, 1969*　　　　　　　　　　　　　　　　　　　　　　　*11:30 PM*

Hi Hon,

I sure do wish I was with you now. I miss you so very, very much. Tony, you'll never know just how much you mean to me. You can't begin to know because there's not the right words to express it.

Today I went to see the doctor and he had gone to a funeral so I have to wait until next Tuesday to see him. Too bad 'cause I wanted to see what he thought about me having the baby early. It's really growing and I seem to have run out of room in my stomach.

There's this woman who Molly and Mom know who predicts your future somewhat and she was the one who told Molly how to tell fortunes. Mom and Molly went to her yesterday and had their fortunes told. She asked Mom if she had a blonde-haired girl who isn't living with her, and Mom said yes. She also asked if she had a medium dark-haired daughter now living with her. Mom said yes. Mom said that she told her quite a lot. This was the first time Mom had met her. She also told her that she had 6 kids and one baby had died which was true because Mom had a miscarriage. Today I went with them to have mine told. They live in a shack and are like hillbillies, but are really nice. She told my fortune and at the end she just had me shuffle the cards and cut them once. When I did she started to shake and threw them down. She told me that she wouldn't tell me. I really got scared 'cause I thought of you. Mom and Molly were worried about the baby and me. She told them not to worry 'cause the baby and I would be fine. Then she looked at me and like she read my thoughts she said not to worry 'cause it didn't concern my husband, he was healthy as a horse. After Mom and I left, she told Molly that it had to do with Mom. When I first sat down for the fortune she asked me if my husband was real dark-complected. It was really weird and spooky.

Today Andy went to the dentist. He had four fillings and two abscessed teeth pulled in the back. He never cried a tear. That kid has got roots on his baby teeth even I can't believe it.

So far we haven't heard anymore from the kids. I don't know what Dad has decided.

Mom got dressed up today and went around to the stores to see about another job. She went down to Nelson's to call me to come and get her. She was waiting outside for me to come when your dad came up behind her and asked her if anyone had told her lately she had pretty legs. She said no, and he told her that she did. Sounds to me "like father, like son." But you better not be telling anyone else but me that! See!!

I saw Denise today and she said that Andrew was really disgusted 'cause he hadn't heard from the family and he'd like to hear from you. Do you want me to get his address for you?

Well, I guess I'll close for now. Always remember, Tony, that I love you so very, very much and I feel so very fortunate to be your wife, and the mother to your baby. You are so wonderful and I'm so lucky.

Clellie

P.S. Hugs & Kisses, etc.

✉ **17 June 1969**

Dear Clellie,

I miss you. I love you. I want you to be here with me. Clellie, I never meant this as much as I do now. I'm so anxious to get home and run up to you and hug and kiss you to death. I'd better change the subject again. Every letter lately I have to change the subject. Don't I? It's just that I really do miss you and I'm getting so sick and tired of being without you.

There's a picture of me in this envelope. It didn't cost me a cent. The Army took it of us. I look funny, don't I? We just got back from the M-16 range and I was very hot and sweaty. I wish we could have changed fatigues. My fatigues were just about soaking wet. The rifle in the picture is the M-16. That's the weapon we use here. We'll also use it in Vietnam. It looks almost like a toy doesn't it? But that little baby sure puts out the firepower. You can shoot it semi-automatic as fast as you can pull the trigger, or you can fire it fully automatic. One pull of the trigger and you shoot 500 to 600 rounds a minute. This weapon's one reason why I'm not too scared about going to Vietnam.

I'm also sending you an article that Miller gave me when I saw him at the bowling alley Sunday. It's about the 11 Bravos, that's the outfit I belong to. You know, Clellie, the more training I get as an infantryman the prouder I am to be infantry. All the other units of the Army wonder why the infantry has such spirit and ego. It's actually because we're training with guys that we'll probably end up fighting with. You really get to know these guys too. We really have teamwork. Like on the last P.T. test. Everybody in our company really knocked themselves out. We did twice as good as we did in Basic.

What's this about Butler changing my brand of cigarettes, and now my brand of beer? The only reason I had an Olympia beer in that picture is because Butler bought it for me, and he paid for the pictures of us. Butler and I get along really good, even if we do have little arguments and fights and cuss outs, he's really a groovy kid.

Clellie, will you love me forever? Will you love me as much as you do now? Will you ever step out on me? I don't think you will step out on me, but a year in Vietnam is going to be a long time you know.

Clellie, I just want to tell you I love you very much. If you ever leave me, I don't know what I'd do. I know that when I get home from the Army, you, the baby, and I are going to have the best family and home ever imaginable. I have to go for now, but please, Clellie, love me forever.

Your loving husband,
Tony

P.S. I love & miss you. I also want you very bad. LOVE!

Pvt. Anthony Jolley
H.H.C 1st Bn 2nd Brig.
Ft. Ord, California 2nd Plt 93941

✉ *June 18, 1969* *12:30 PM*

Dear Tony,

Well, the mailman has come and no letter. I guess I'll get one tomorrow.

Today I did all the washing and straightened up the house. I was going to go over to Susan's but she dropped in. She didn't stay very long but it was real nice to see her.

Tonight on My Three Sons it was a rerun of Kate (Rob's wife) when she had her triplets. It was so funny and cute. Robbie was away at an Army camp and when she went to the hospital they called the camp. He got to come home just as they were being born. Tony, I want you to be with me so very much, and the show made me realize again how much I wish you could be with me. I guess it's too bad though, I'll have to face it without you. I know my mom'll be there, but somehow it doesn't matter. I'm spoiled 'cause I only want you with me.

Tony, are you going to fly home? Where will I pick you up or do you know? My mind is always thinking about you. I hate being separated and it gets worse all the time.

I talked to Carrie Conner today. Dale has gone to Utah to find a job and a place for them to live. They think it'll be better to get away from relatives. I guess they're really serious about it.

Well I guess I had better close for now. I'll always be here waiting for you to come home, Tony. I love you now and for all eternity.

Yours Eternally,
Clellie

P.S. Hugs & Kisses, etc.

June 19, 1969 **11:30 PM**

Hi Hon,

I was so very, very, happy when I got your letter today. I loved that picture of you. You look so neat looking and yet it scared me to see a gun in your hands. I know you will be using it for real - soon. The picture was so real-looking that I can almost feel you next to me.

I went over to Susan's today for about two hours. I took your picture over to show her. She liked it too. All I ever do is talk about you and she listens. I don't think I told you this but on the night of Bill and Bonnie's reception we went to the Russet afterwards. We were remembering some of the good old times before you left and we got on the subject of how you could change people's minds and opinions to your way of thinking. I said, "Yeah, there's something very special about Tony." Susan said, "Yeah he's got a lot of charm in him." I told her I knew it. Got a big head now?

I saw Elise White and she broke up with Greg and is going with Mario Gomez. How about that? She thinks I should be with you too.

Guess who I saw today and waved at? Estelle Ford, with Charlie's brother. Boy, their girl sure is growing fast.

I read that article you sent me. It makes me feel very proud of you being in the infantry, but it also scares me. You know this whole thing seems like one endless nightmare. I can't believe you're carrying a machine gun getting ready to fight in a war. Tony, it terrifies me. Mom thinks you look so lonely in your picture. So do I but you look great anyway. The machine gun sounds like it's a real good gun. I'm glad that you'll have it with you. I'm also very glad that you're proud of being in the infantry. I'm very proud of you too, but I'd like it much better if you were home. Promise me one thing, Tony. Please just take care of yourself in Vietnam and don't be a hero. You're a hero to me already, and the baby and I need you so please don't take any more chances than you have to. Please Tony! For me, and the baby. Oh, Tony, I love you so very, very much and I couldn't bear losing you. Hurry Home!! I love you so much. Be good and stay mine!!

All my love eternally,
Clellie

P.S. Hugs & Kisses, etc.

✉ *June 20, 1969*   *11:30 PM*

Hi Hon,

How's the Army treating the best guy in the world? I sure love you, Tony, and I miss you so very, very much.

Today I took Hope to see Dr. Sutton in Burley. She has a cyst on her ovary and is going to have to go to the hospital, probably at the end of this month. She has to have it removed. She was really worried about what she'd do with Ashley, and Tony, I told her I would watch them for her except that I never know when the baby's going to come and then with Mom working I didn't know who would tend them. She finally got it worked out with Dottie so she'll take them. Boy, that Hope has more problems than most people do.

Mom and I went to town today. We paid the phone bill. It was only about $13.00 for ours. That's a lot better than $20-25. Of course one Sunday I was with you so it lacked one Sunday call. It paid for our calls up until last Sunday's call. I sure hope we can keep our bill down for July too. I love to talk to you so much though that I hate to hang up. It seems so good to talk to you. I took another dollar to buy a henna pack for my hair. The baby's taking all the life out of my hair. I want it to look neat when you get home again. It needs a little trim, but I'll wait. It's really grown. Mom bought me some really good cream rinse that cost $2 a bottle 'cause I said I needed some. She also bought 4 plastic pants for the baby and me a milkshake. Now, she's broke like me.

Iris Cole came over to see me today. It was really nice to see her. Rod (her brother) and his wife Stacy had a baby girl. Iris's been sick with the rheumatic flu.

The baby and I are doing just great. We're excited to see what each other looks like. Anyway, I want to see it. Tony, thank you for our baby! I can't wait to see it. Scared, yes! But I'm also tired of all this excess weight.

I put the change from the phone bill & henna pack in my account at the bank. We now have $67 in my account. Of course $25 of it goes to the hospital. In your account, you have about $35 I think. We're not doing bad at all really.

Tony, I love you so very, very much. I was remembering last night, just before I closed my eyes to sleep, the Christmas that I got the flu when I worked at Simplot's and you had to work on swing shift that night so I asked you to stop by after work. I was asleep on the couch and the Christmas tree lights were on. I opened my eyes just before you came in the door. It seemed so awful not to see you every night. Now I see how lucky I was 'cause I can't see you for weeks & months at a time. I love you so very, very much, Tony. Love me always.

Your loving lonely wife, Clellie

P.S. Hugs & Kisses, etc.

June 21, 1969   **11:00 PM**

Dear Hubby and Father-to-be,

First of all I have to tell you how very much I love you. I just got finished looking through our wedding book and the scrapbook of you. You know I think that you are the handsomest guy ever. I'm so lucky. We were really happy on the night of our reception weren't we? At least I was. I love you so very much.

Today I mopped, polished, dusted, vacuumed, and cleaned the rugs. Ambitious aren't I? It only runs in streaks naturally. I just want everything neat when you get home and I have an awful feeling they won't be. Mom bought me a hot berry turnover. We've really been getting along. Mitch's been working away from here for two weeks, since he's been gone Mom is so different. She's happy and we can really get along. When he gets back, she'll get depressed again.

Cora McCarthy and Ann came over to visit me today. It was really good to see them. They said to say hi. I showed them all the baby stuff and they thought my dresser for the baby is so darling. I also had to show them all the pictures of you. Cora said that she liked you better with your hair. How about that? Dad and Faith have been gone all day and will be back tomorrow. He won't let Alice come back in. Ann said that Alice is really learning to hate Dad and so is Nancy. She told Dad that it would be better for Alice in here, but he won't hear of it. So he'll ruin her. He's so pigheaded.

Molly had a date tonight and Mom had to work. We don't have a T.V., so Hope said I could watch hers. She went to work and her sister had the kids.

Virgil sent me a real sweet birthday card today, and he asked about you. I didn't think he would remember.

A year ago tonight except it was the 22nd, we went to a dance and you gave me that pretty little necklace, and also the stereo record player. I remember how sneaky you were about it.

Tony, I really do want to come see you. I miss you so much and time is so important. I keep hoping every night that I'll have the baby so I can get better and come to see you. It just doesn't seem fair. I love you so very much.

Yours eternally,
Mother-to-be, Clellie

✉ *June 22, 1969*   *11:30 PM*

Hi Hon,

How are things going with you? I sure do hope okay. Well here I am a whole 20 years old. I'm beginning to feel ancient. I was so very pleased to hear from you today. I miss you so much and I wish you were here. I thought for sure that you'd forgotten all about my birthday and I had already rationalized that you were so busy you didn't know what the date was. Thank you for remembering. You're so sweet. I love you so very, very much.

Tony, you'll get more than a five-day leave, won't you? If I can, I want to go with you when you go to NCO school. I hope you know I was crying most of the time we were talking today. Tony, I miss you so much and it gets worse instead of better.

Today I had an exciting birthday. About ½ an hour after you and I hung up, Ann called me to come over. Faith and Dad got into a fight and he hit her twice in the face then took her home and got Alice and Nancy. Ann was at a dance. When Ann and Cora got home, they took Faith to the hospital and found out that she possibly has a dislocated jaw. Sweet dad. She called the cops, but she wouldn't sign a complaint against him. Don't tell anyone about this because Dad would kill her if he knew she had talked to me. Ann wanted to come home with me and sneak out for the girls, and their clothes. I told her that I couldn't, it was not up to me. She said he's really been treating them bad especially Alice. He calls them names and accuses them of things. I told her I already knew how he was. Faith said he's worse and she's afraid he'll snap one of these days. He goes out of his head. He is capable of murder when he gets that way. It really worries me and I don't know what's going to happen to the girls. Mom doesn't know what to do. I sure hope things work out. I stayed at Faith's until about 6:00 PM and then I came home. I guess they thought I could do something, but I can't, and I can't get all mixed up in it. I'm tired of being in the middle. I couldn't help Ann because I'm not their guardian. I wish I could.

When I got home I went over and watched T.V. at Hope's until after the movie. Exciting birthday.

Hurry home, Tony, and love me.

Your loving lonely wife,
Clellie

June 23, 1969　　　　　　　　　　　　　　　　　　　　11:30 PM

Dear handsome husband of mine,

How's that for beginners? I can't wait to have you here with me. It seems so long since I've been with you and had your arms around me. Tony, I miss you so much.

Man today I'm in a real raunchy mood. Any little thing will set me off. I got upset at Mom over nothing and then again 'cause she's going back with Mitch. I told her she was such a more beautiful woman when he was away and he was no good, etc. She admits she don't love him, but can't leave. I told her that she was dumb to stick with him. He is lazy and irresponsible. I really got mad, and I shouldn't because it's her life, but I do hate him, Tony, so bad. Oh well.

Took Hope and her kids uptown so they could go shopping, real groovy afternoon. Then ole brainy me washed the clothes and hung them out on the line. Sure it was cloudy, but I (being such a great weatherman) decided it wouldn't rain. Well they were out about ½ hr. and I had to run and get them in, naturally it was raining. It's been raining here all day long.

Our T.V. won't be fixed until about Wednesday, and I'm about going nuts without it. Tonight I spent a joyful evening of solitaire. Then I popped some popcorn.

Guess what? I have three beautiful new stretch marks; side-by-side right up the middle of my stomach almost to the top. I have so many Tony you're going to think I'm ugly. Oh they are too! I won't be able to wear a two-piece if we go swimming, I don't think. They'll go away somewhat Mom says but they are ugly. Boy, that baby had better hurry. My insides will be shreds soon.

Well how's that for a cheerful letter? Not too good. I'll try to do better tomorrow. The only cheerful bit I have is that I love you, Tony, so much and I'll wait for you forever.

Your lonely but so very loving wife,
Clellie

P.S. I love you so very much.

✉ **23 June 1969**

Dearest Clellie,

I just received one of your letters today. It was the one that you told me you had received my pictures with the M-16. I think that letter is one of the best letters that you have written me. I really do love you, Clellie. I could never step out on you. Also I could never look at another girl without that girl reminding me of you. You are the most beautiful and wonderful thing that could ever happen to a guy.

Clellie, this is probably the only letter I'll be able to write to you this week. We got our schedule today and we're going to be out all this week from 10:30 PM-12:30 AM all week long. All of our training is where we have to patrol areas just like in Vietnam. Friday we'll have escape and evasion. If they capture us, they torture us and try to make us talk. This training will separate the men from the boys is what they tell us.

Clellie, I've been thinking. If I go to NCO school, I'm going to try and get you a place to come and live with me. I also want to go to jump school. I figure if I'm going to go to NCO school for 12 weeks, I might as well go to jump school for 3 more weeks, and get to jump from planes. I think I could really dig something like this. Also if I went to Vietnam, I would get extra pay for being in an Airborne division.

Clellie, you're always asking me if I'm going to Nam, as much as I hate to leave you for a year, I think we'll have to face the fact that I am going to Nam. It won't be as bad over in Vietnam as you think. Somebody's got to do it. It might as well be me as be somebody else. It's true that a lot of people get killed, and wounded, but a lot of people also make it back with not so much as a scratch. I think Vietnam will be an experience that will profit us in our future. It's something that both of us can be proud of.

Clellie, I just want you to realize how much I hate to think of leaving you. I love, need, and want you so bad that I just don't know how I'll be able to live without you for a year.

Well, Clellie, I guess I'd better go for now. I love you and I want you to be mine forever. Goodbye for now but please love me forever.

Your loving husband, and father-to-be,
Tony

P.S. We're going to have the best-looking kid that was ever born.

I love you!

Pvt. Anthony Jolley
H.H.C 1st Bn 2nd Brig.
Ft. Ord, California 2nd Plt 93941

June 24, 1969   **10:30 PM**

Hi Hon,

I sure wish I were with you now. I love you so much. You're so great. Do you know? I had a very ignorant dream last night. I shouldn't tell you 'cause you're supposed to think I never dream such things. It all started out that you and I met out in the woods. We hadn't been able to see each other for such an awful long time. We kissed and hugged and your hands roamed and pretty soon we wanted to go all the way. I was skinny and wearing my Levi's. We went to a big hollow tree and got inside of it. You removed my Levi's and was about to remove my underpants when I woke up. That was the end of the dream. I told you it was ignorant. Do you think I'm awful?

Today I went to the Dr. but he was in surgery. I waited an hour and they finally rescheduled me to go in this Thursday. I haven't seen him for 6 weeks. It'll be here before I get to see him. While I was in there a boy fell in love with me. He's about 2 years old. Him and his brother were sitting on the floor next to my chair. His mother was sitting next to me. The waiting room was full. He has big blue eyes and dark hair. He was so cute and little. He kept looking up at me and smiling. I'd smile at him. His mother finally got tired of waiting and got up to reschedule their appointment. She came back and took her boys by the hand and they were walking towards the door. He said good-bye to me and waved. I waved back. Then all of the sudden he broke loose from his mother and came running back saying, "Kiss, kiss." So he kissed me on the cheek, and ran after his mother. It really shocked me.

Ann and Cora came over today. They brought some of the kid's things in. Mom told Ann that she couldn't get them back unless she went to court and she didn't want to do that 'cause it would be a big scandal. If Dad will consent in letting them come back then it'd be fine, so Ann's talking to Dad tonight. I don't know what's going to happen but I imagine they'll be back in here before too long. Alice's really thrilled about it. Cora, Tom, and Emma had a little talk with Faith and told her that if she went back to Dad again they would leave her and go live with their dad 'cause they just couldn't take seeing their mother beat, and crying all the time. So I hope she stays away from him. He's not good enough for her anyway. We sure won't have any privacy here if the kids are back. We'll have to keep the door shut continuously, and our bed squeaks so bad. Oh well, we'll manage.

Well I guess that I'll close for now. I love you, Tony, so very, very much. Hurry home I'll be here waiting for you. Be good and stay ONLY mine.

All my love forever,
Clellie

P.S. Hugs and Kisses, etc.

✉ *June 25, 1969* *12:00 AM*

Dear Tony,

Boy, you sure wouldn't believe the weather we're having here. Here it is the last part of June and cold. Today the wind blew and it has been so cold so we had to turn the furnace on. It was so cold that we had to wear coats even to go outside. I think winter has returned.

Today Mom and I went uptown to pay some of her bills. We then went out to Shelby's for groceries. While I was there who did I bump into but Mr. Cutter from high school. He asked me how "the gabber" (meaning me) was doing and I said fine. Then he said that he saw our wedding picture in the paper and he also heard that you'd been drafted. I said yes you had and asked him how he knew, and he said that he kept tabs on me. Then he asked how long you'd been gone and I said about 4 months. He said that I'd have plenty of time to play around then. I said, "Oh no not me. I love Tony and I'll just stick to home." He said that I'd better say that or he'd paddle me. Then I said good-bye and Mom and I finished shopping. How's that for an interesting bit? Mom and I went to Aunt Jane's and got some elk meat. Then we went home.

At 8:30 PM I took Hope to work and then babysat for her until Susan came over at 9:30 PM. She wanted me to go to Twin with her so Mom watched the kids. I told Susan that I couldn't rod main. We left for Twin about 5 to 10 PM. I guess Denny was with Barry and that Fox kid smoking grass. We went to Twin and looked at the "Inn Club." We just drove in and back out. It looked pretty dodgy to me. Then we went by where their grandmother lives (Denny's). Then we drove by the "Villa." Then we headed for home. Oh yes, before we left Burley we put some gas in the car at a serve-yourself station. I got home at about 11:15 PM or 11:20 PM. I put Molly's hair up and went over to Hope's and put Mom's up. How's that for an exciting day? Denny and Susan has a 4 & 8 track stereo tape player hooked up in their car. Boy, it is really neat. It's got the most fabulous sound to it. Wow, it's nice.

Well I guess I've told you every little boring detail about today. It was nice to be with Susan for the short time though. I do wish you were here, Tony, or I could be with you. I miss you so very, very much. The 4th of July will be here soon and I dread it 'cause you're not here. Remember last year when I ripped the seat of my pants out trying to get in the scrambler? Boy, that was most embarrassing. I love you now and I will forever.

Lonely & Loving wife,
Clellie

P.S. Hugs & kisses, etc.

June 26, 1969   **10:30 PM**

Hi Hon,

I received your letter today and I just sat down and bawled. I miss you so very much and your letter was so darn sweet. When you said that you wanted me to be able to come and live with you while you go through that NCO school it made me feel so good. I want to be with you so very much and I don't plan on letting anything stand in my way from now on. I love you.

The only thing that worries me is the idea of you going Airborne. Tony, I don't care if you get paid $1,000 an hr., it scares me. They pay you more for going Airborne because it is so dangerous. You make a great target for the enemy parachuting. At least when you're on the ground you can find some protection, but you have none in the air. Yes, I'm selfish; I want you to come home to me and the baby. Tony, please reconsider it. I thought infantry would be the worst, but Airborne is even worse. I don't think God has it in His book for anything to happen to you yet. We've still got our lives ahead of us, but don't do anything like going Airborne. I've heard so much about it.

Well enough for that lecture. I saw Dr. Peterson today. He said that the baby was doing fine, and was in position to be born anytime. I asked him if he thought it would be early, and he said no one ever knows, when it's ready it'll come. He said though that its head was ready and down there so it could come anytime. I can't wait. I'm so excited for it to come. It's so special to me because it's yours. I love you, Tony.

It sounds like your schedule from now on will be pretty full. Boy, I'm glad I'm not you. I'd crack up. Take good care of yourself for me.

Today I fixed Mom and Molly's hair. Great fun. But it keeps me busy.

Mom was kind of depressed and was saying that she was so tired of not feeling good, she wished that she could die. Andy popped up and said, "If you do that you won't be able to see Clellie's pretty baby." It was so cute. Tonight Mom's with Mitch, and Molly went out.

I guess I'd better close for now. Tony, I love you so very, very much. I miss you and wish I could be with you so very much.

Your loving wife,
 Clellie

P.S. Hugs & Kisses, etc.

✉ *June 27, 1969*   *1:00 AM*

Hi Hon,

Well, here I am. I can't sleep for some reason. I laid there and thought about you and was remembering some of the beautiful memories you have given me. Mom came home and she was a little drunk. She wanted to make sure I was okay. She said that she ran into your mother and Marie and they asked about me. I haven't been over to see them for about two weeks. I was going to go over Wednesday but I didn't feel quite up to it. I guess I'll have to go over soon. I have to brag on you anyway to them.

You know, Tony, Mom still loves Dad. It's sad but true. She really thinks a lot of Mitch too. She said that he denies saying anything about me. I got kind of angry and told her that I wasn't supposed to know anything about it and that now Mitch would talk to your dad about it and I'd gotten everyone in Dutch, but she said that he wouldn't say anything. Well anyway if she wants to believe him then she can because it's her life. I told her if she wanted him, she should go ahead. I really feel sorry for her, Tony. I believe he isn't any good. I also told her that it wasn't my decision to make. You know, Tony, I'm so glad that I have you and your family. I'm so lucky to have you for my very own. You mean all the world to me.

✉ **June 28, 1969** **10:00 PM**

Here I am again. I took Hope to the doctor today. He told her that as soon as she has taken Ashley back to her doctor on the 30th then she was to call him so he can schedule her at the hospital. She is a little worried.

Today Molly wanted me to go with her to get her driver's license in Rupert so I went with her. I had to comb her and Mom's hair. When I got home, I took Hope and her kids up to the Burger Port to eat. Right now I'm babysitting while Hope's gone to work. Tomorrow's her last night at work. She's quitting. Molly has gone to Buhl again. Next week Mom wants to go to Ogden to get her back straightened out. She'd be gone for about three or four days but she's afraid 'cause she thinks I'll have the baby real soon. I told her to go ahead if she wants to. Your mother and sister are close by and so is Hope and Faith, if anything happened I'd be okay. Mitch's going to take her. I really dislike it when he's around. She hadn't been drunk like last night since he'd been gone. She's such a great person without him. At least she's not drunk out of her head. He really makes her change. Oh well, it's her life.

Boy, everyone is so excited about me having the baby. They keep expecting it any night. I keep telling them that it'll probably be a month. I'll probably still be pregnant when you get home and I dread that terribly. No hanky-panky or anything. I want so much to be up and thin, but you never can tell.

Tomorrow is supposed to be cool still. The high it's supposed to be 59°. It was about 60° today. It's so cool around here. I can't believe it.

Well I guess I better close for now. I miss you, Tony, so much. I can't wait until you get home. I'm going to ask you one more time, how are you going to come home? Plane or bus? Where will I meet you? Remember that I'm here waiting for you.

All my love for eternities,
Clellie

P.S. I love you!!!

Hugs and Kisses, etc.

✉ **June 29, 1969**   *1:30 AM*

Hi Hon,

How's the best-looking guy around? I hope you're okay. Has your leg been acting up? Do you still love me? How much? How long?

Today I cleaned the house real good. I also went to town and spent my last $2 on a big box of Kotex so I'll have it. Mom gave me $10 for groceries so I bought a few, sounds like a most enjoyable day.

Tonight Susan came over about 9 PM. I wanted to go to the show, so I borrowed $2 from the grocery money to go. I'll have to pay you back when I get my check. We went to the show Smith at about 9:30 PM and it was over about 15 to 12 AM. Then we got some gas and went to the Russet for a roll and milk. Fattening. You'll never guess who walked in, Dee Dee Mannor with a boy. She has long hair like mine and it looks in real nice shape. I don't think she saw me. She made me real nervous for some reason. I hate that feeling.

Have you written a letter to Denny yet? I know you're busy but they want me to ask you. They gave me a birthday card. Denny's birthday is Monday. They also gave me a towel, washcloth, and a rattle for the baby, three bibs, 4 plastic pants, baby soap, and little bottles of baby powder, lotion, and oil. Really nice of them. Now I won't have to get so much. Susan and I got home at about 10 to 1 AM and I told her fortune twice. I'm becoming a regular ole gypsy.

Tonight was the Jamboree in Rupert and I heard that the Bitter Ends played for it.

Well that's about all the news except it's still winter here. Boy, you just wouldn't believe it. It's so darn cold, period.

Tonight my stomach muscles were pushing on the baby I began to open up further at the bottom so I think my time is near. I wish you were here with me. I love you, Tony, now and forever.

Your loving and lonely wife,
Clellie

P.S. Hugs and Kisses, etc.

June 29, 1969   *11:00 PM*

My Dear Handsome Hubby,

How's that for starters? I don't know where I got hubby, but it's kind of cute, don't you think? Well I do!

I neglected to tell you that when Susan came over last night she told me that she bought her some cowboy boots. They cost her $14. She said that she thought they were like your old ones so I showed her them, she said that hers were exactly like yours. How about that? Now you'll be twins.

Mom left today for Ogden. She said that she'd be back Thursday. She called tonight and gave me her number just in case of the baby, and Molly's still in Buhl. I kinda like it this way 'cause the house stays a lot cleaner. It's lonely though. I miss you so much, Tony. I don't care if Mom and Molly go. It's just that you're not here.

I called Carrie last night and she said that Dale's home for the weekend and then he's going back to Utah. They really want to move. I guess he's not going to go to that school though. There're some big mix-up or some such.

Today I swept, mopped, and dusted our room. I washed all the bedding and all washable items in our room. I cleaned the bathroom, did my mending, did the ironing, swept the kitchen, straightened up Mom's room, front room, and kitchen, washed my hair, and just was busy. How's that for a great day? I just know my car will be dirty and the house will be by the time you get home because after the baby I won't feel like doing anything for about two weeks, and no one else cleans anything.

Tony, I'm sorry I cried on the phone to you this afternoon. I tried not to, but I want to be with you so very, very much and I miss and need you. Hurry home.

I went uptown at about 6 PM today and mailed a letter to you, then I went over to Hope's to watch TV until 9:30 PM, then I came home, and took a bath. Exciting evening.

I enjoyed talking to you this afternoon so much. I wish that we could be together now. It seems like such a long time since I've felt your arms around me. I miss you so very, very much, Tony.

Your loving wife, Clellie

P.S. Hugs and Kisses, etc.

✉ *June 30, 1969*   *11:00 PM*

Hi Hon,

Well June is over now. I only have about two and three-quarter weeks to wait for you, maybe? Then you'll be home with me and our baby. Tony, I miss you so very, very much.

This morning I got up and went over to your parents' place. I showed your family the pictures of you and Butler, and of you with your machine gun. I talked mostly with Marie. I guess that she's pretty set on not going back with Lance. She just doesn't want to take it anymore. Do you realize, Tony, if they get a divorce Marie won't get hardly anything because it's all in Lance's dad's name? Boy, that really is too bad. I guess Lance might buy a new car and sell the old one to Barry. It's not definite though. The kids asked when you would be home and I told them about three more weeks. They were quite excited. I helped your mother and Marie peel eggs to pickle them. Great fun. Your mother sells them at the Midway. All in all it was a nice day. I left about 3:30 PM and went uptown and paid Mom's bills for her.

Molly just got home. She had a pretty nice time she says. I really would rather be here alone. The house stays much nicer.

This morning at 4:30 AM I woke up out of a sound sleep and I was leaking water. It worried me because I thought I was bleeding, I wasn't. It was water. Not a whole lot just enough to make my pants wet. Messy. Well that's supposed to be a sign of the baby ready to be born. Well I never had any pains so I fell asleep again. Then this morning I went to your mother's, walked all over town paying Mom's bills, and straightened up the house. Hope had gone to Twin and when she got home she came over to see how I was. I told her fine. Later I went over to watch TV and I finally asked her about it. She about died. She said that I wasn't supposed to be on my feet very much at all and that the baby could've been born uptown when I was walking. I still have some water leakage. She said that I'm ready to have it and by all rights I should have it tonight. Don't worry though because if I do have it, you'll have already been informed. I am somewhat afraid though.

Well, Tony, I guess I better sign off. Remember that I love you so very, very much. I wish you were there with me, Tony. I wish you could be beside me while I have our baby. I need you so much. Hurry home.

All my love for eternity,
Clellie

30 June 1969

Dearest Clellie,

It was so good to talk to you today on the phone. I think as the days go by I love you more and more. You are the dearest and most precious creature God has ever created or will ever create. I hope you love and miss me as much as I do you.

I thought when I came into this Army there would be a lot of things I would miss. It turned out though that the only one I miss is you. Even as much as I loved and appreciated you in civilian life, I found out that I love and appreciate you more now.

Clellie, I wish I had never got drafted. I wish I could turn the clock back and we could have left for Canada. Just think we could live in a big log cabin. It would be cold outside. I'd go outside and put some logs on the fire. We could sit there by the fire under a bear fur and just kiss and make love all night. How would you like that? I know it could never be like that, but it would be so neat if it had happened.

Well we start our seventh week of infantry AIT. I'm just about a full-fledged infantryman. Will be out late tomorrow night, then we'll be camping out the rest of the week. Then we get a three-day pass for 4 July. I guess Butler, Kershaw, and I will go to San Francisco. I'd like to see the Golden Gate Bridge and also Disneyland. It depends on how much it will cost though. I wish I could be home with you for the fourth. We could go over to Mom's place and watch the fireworks, maybe I could even get drunker than hell.

On the Life magazine this month there's the pictures and names of 242 men that were killed over in Vietnam in one week. It's really pathetic. All those GIs dying for no reason at all. I don't want you to worry about me though, Clellie. I'm coming back just the way I'm going over. What I'll do is just hide in a hole all day. Ha ha

Just to think, Clellie, in three more weeks I'll be home. We're going to make up for a lot of lost time. We're not going to plan nothing. We're just going to wake up in the morning when we want, then whatever we want to do that day we just hop in the car and do it. I don't want to go to an NCO school now. I just want to go to Nam and get it over with. The sooner I can go to Nam the sooner I can get back to the States and have you live with me.

I was talking to an NCO here. He told me when he was in NCO school that there were a lot of married guys. They have their wives live off-base. They rented a trailer and it didn't cost very much at all. If for some reason my orders come through for an NCO school anyway, we'll have to find a way and a place for you to come live with me. I think we could really dig it. The only thing is that we might have a slight problem taking care of the baby.

Well, Clellie, I had better say goodbye for now. I do love you and wish you could love me as much as I do you. But that is impossible and we both know it. Well goodbye for now, Clellie.

Your loving husband,
Tony

I love you.

July 1, 1969   *10:30 PM*

Dear Handsome Hubby,

I received your letter today I was so very, very happy to get it. It made me feel very special. You know no one could ever have a husband so wonderful as you.

Guess who I saw today? Stephanie and Luke. I was going to Safeway when a car pulled up beside me and I heard someone say something. When I looked over, I saw them and said hi.

Susan just left. She came over to give me a piece of Denny's birthday cake. She also wanted to see how I was doing. Sweet of her. She was here about one hour.

Does Ford have a fake ID card or is he old enough to buy beer? He bought some beer at Williams' store. He had Stewart with him and some other boys.

Well I guess I'd better let you in on the latest news about me and our baby. When I woke up this morning I had some more water leak. I went to Dr. Peterson's office about 2 o'clock this afternoon and told the nurse to ask him about it. He told her to tell me to go home and go to bed for 2 days and then call him and tell him if it quit. I guess I'm dilating and my bag's about to break. If it all leaks out though, I'll have a dry birth which is really hard and painful. I've stayed off my feet, but I can't stay in bed. If I was sick I could, but I'm not. I worry about you coming home to a dirty car and house. I have been laying around downstairs though so I'm doing good. How would you like staying in bed? At any rate, it's close to coming. I have to call him Thursday. I really hope I have it before then. Honest, Tony, I'd like it now. By the time you get home I'd be okay and almost skinny again. I hate everyone making a big thing over me too. I'd like privacy once in a while. Oh well, all in all I'm just waiting, so hang on father-to-be.

I wish we had gone to Canada too. That sounds so neat about the log cabin. I only wish that it were possible. I'm so glad that you only miss me because I miss and love you so very much, Tony.

I hope that you get to go to Disneyland over the 4th of July and San Francisco. It would really do you good. Have fun, Tony. I'd like you to be here with me better but I can't have everything. I'll keep you with me when you get home. You'll never leave my sight.

Tony, I can't help but worry about you going to Nam. I am afraid. However, I also know that you're smart and can outwit them any day so it helps.

If you do go to NCO school, the trailer house sounds great, just so I'll be with you. I also want you to get Nam over with. Whatever happens I don't care just so I can be with you a while. Be good and stay mine forever.

*Eternally your wife,
Clellie*

P.S. Hugs and Kisses, etc.

A BABY IS BORN

July 4, 1969　　　　　　　　　　　　　　　　*11:00 PM*

Hi Hon,

This letter will not be very long I'm afraid because I can't sit too long. I want you to know that I love you very much and I miss you gobs.

I guess you got the scoop on how things went. Boy, I'll wait a while for our second, it hurt so bad! I remember telling Mom that you should be here. My bottom is so darn sore. I get to go home tomorrow. The baby has your nose. It's so little and cute. It has lots of hair. I just love it to death. It's very special you know. I'm somewhat skinnier too, and boy, it feels good. Your mom and dad brought me some flowers in a cute vase and so did my dad. Emmy Lou, Marie, Susan, Denny, Ann, Alice, Tommy, Cora, and Hope called me and congratulated me.

I can't wait until you get home. I miss you so very, very much. You're the most wonderful husband ever.

Well my head feels a little spinny. Hurry home, Tony. I get to go home tomorrow, nothing like spending my 4th of July in bed.

Love you eternally,
Mother Clellie

P.S. Hugs and Kisses, etc.

✉️ *July 5, 1969*   *12:01 PM*

Dear Handsome,

They told me to send this to you to give to your commanding officer so I'll get more money. So you give it to him. It's a copy. Aren't our baby's feet little? I left the hospital today at about 11 AM. Boy, I'm sore. The stitches hurt like heck. They gave me two extra cans of SMA for the baby because you're serving our country. Sweet.

I'm sorry about the letter situation. I'll try to get more regular but I feel pretty weak. When do you get to come home so I'll know about when to quit sending letters? The baby has your nose and long hair in the back. I'm so proud of him. We did a great job.

The hospital was pretty good. The food was real good. I didn't care for it too much when I first got there, but after it was all over it was okay. My roommate snored. We had to take a shower twice a day. It was real hard to walk around with these stitches. I have no hair and it seems weird there. All the nurses were really nice. I guess all in all it's okay after it's over. I'm glad it's over and I love our baby, he's dark-complected too.

Susan and Denny came to visit me yesterday. They had gone swimming. It was nice to see them. Denny's really excited about you getting home. Honey, I'm so afraid we won't have much time alone together. Will you explain it to Denny if he keeps coming around? I'm stingy, you know?

You know I'd close my eyes in the hospital and could see you come bounding in my room so plain. I miss you so much. I knew you couldn't come but yet I wanted you there. I guess I talked quite a bit about you in the labor room.

Well I had better go rest again. Hurry home, Tony, and write me lots. Be good and stay mine forever. I love you so much!!!

All my love forever,

P.S. Hugs and Kisses, etc.

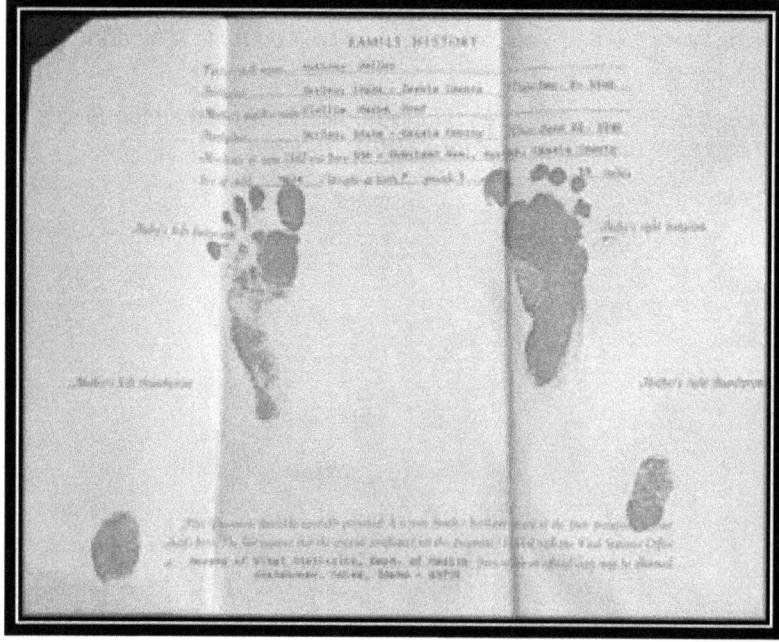

✉ *July 6, 1969*   *10:00 PM*

Hi Hon,

We just got through bathing your son. He's so cute. Mom thinks he looks so much like you in so many of his expressions. He even pops his ears like you said you used to. He's a pig. He gobbles down his food like it was going out of style. He's so cute and I'm so proud. He's so darn sweet. Mom saw your dad last night and I guess he's really proud. Mom said that he just beamed when she told him what we named him. Also it's the first grandchild that will carry on the Jolley name. I never realized that before.

I can't wait until you get home, Tony. I miss you so very much. We only have about 2 more weeks and I'm so excited. When I come and get you, wherever you are, I'm going to bring our baby. Tony, I love you so much more every day and do you know going through all that for the baby made me love you still more? I didn't think I could love you more but I do.

Our neighbor just came over to look at the baby and a little girl from across the street came over. Ann and her friends came also and everyone just loves it. I'm very proud. I'm sending you some pictures. They really don't do him justice and I'm not at my best but I thought you'd like them.

Mom was telling me today and I vaguely remember saying it that when I was in labor I told her that if you ever divorce me after this I would kill you.

Your parents didn't come over. I am quite disappointed. I was hoping they would come to look at him.

Tony, see if you can take the plane to Twin. I really am afraid to take the car to Pocatello, but I will if you can't make it to Twin. Also Hon, how are we going to pay the phone bill this month? I hate to bug you about it but I don't know how we'll pay for it.

Oh I can't wait to go pick you up. I'm so excited. It's not very long from now you know. It'll be so good to be in your arms again. I love you so much. Be good & stay mine forever.

Your loving wife,
Clellie

✉ **6 Jul 1969**

Dear Clellie,

How are you and the baby feeling? It's really going to be good to get back home with you. After 4 ½ months I get to come home for a few days. You can't imagine how good it will be to see you again. I miss you so much.

I just know you'll be in good shape when I get home. It'll be good to be able to put my arms around your middle again. It'll also be good to have it all over with. Just think, Clellie, you and I have a little baby boy. I know it'll turn out to be something we can both be proud of. What do you think?

Clellie, even though we have a baby now, I hope it won't make a difference in our relationship. I want you to love me as much as you always have. I know I'll love you as much as I ever have. Do you think you can love me as much now? I'm writing this letter on fireguard and I'm sleepy so it might not make much sense but I hope it does. Tomorrow's going to be a long day. In your letters, Clellie, I want you to tell me things you want to do when I get home on leave.

This next week of training is really going to be rough, but the way I look at it is they can have it as rough as they want because after 2 more weeks of it I can tell them to kiss my ass. Then it's home to see you and our baby. I'm sorry to cut this letter short, Clellie, but I've got to go wake up the other guy. I can't wait to see you and the baby. I love you, Clellie. Stay mine.

Your husband,
Tony

P.S. I love you!

✉️ **July 7, 1969**   *10:00 PM*

Hi Hon,

Well how was your day? I sure hope it hasn't been too rough. Tony, I want so much to come to your graduation. If only I could figure out a way. I was so proud of you at the last one. You looked so neat, and I know this one would be better. Do you have any ideas? Tony, I miss you so very much. Do you know I regret not naming the baby after you? I wish I would have. Maybe the next one will be a boy and we can then. However, it will be a little while before we try again.

When you get home do you want to sleep in Mom's room and shut that little door leading to the utility room, or would you rather sleep in our room? I'd rather our room but the bed does squeak.

Auntie Em, Aunt Mabel, and Cora McCarthy came to see the baby. They all just raved on how cute he is. Stephanie called and said congratulations. Sophia Meyer also called and said she'd be over tomorrow to see him. He's such a darling. He grabs my hair now and won't let it go when I lay him down. Daisy, Wyatt 6 yrs. old, & Celeste 2 yrs. old came over and gave me a cute sailor suit for him. It's so cute. I made an appointment for the Dr. to check him Saturday. My stitches are a little better but I still have a problem getting around.

Today I cashed the check from the government and took $15 from the bank. I took $10 from my check and the $15 from the bank and paid the hospital. I gave Mom her $25 and I'll have to pay my other bills when I can walk better. It'll take about $5 for stationery & stamps, $25 for rings, $6 for your insurance, $5.30 for a douche, $2 to the drug store, $2 for Playtex bottles, and $6 for oil for the car. Then it'll cost some money for gas for the car for the month and to come and see you and I'll have about $15 for that. How's that? I saved loose change, about $7 worth, and I have to buy SMA for the baby with it. I bought a case that should last a month. Well, that's been my very exciting day.

Hope went to the hospital today, she gets operated on tomorrow morning. Mom's going to go be there. She has a cyst on her ovary. She has more troubles than anyone I know. Molly went to Buhl over the 4th of July. She called today and said that she wanted Mom to get Lisa (a friend of hers) and come and get her at Buhl. Mom didn't want to leave me but she got Lisa. Molly had an epileptic fit down there and she couldn't drive her car home.

Your parents still haven't come over. I'm a little disappointed.

Well I guess I'll close for now. I love you, Tony, so very, very much and I'll wait for you forever.

Your loving wife,
Clellie

✉ *July 8, 1969* *10:15 PM*

Dear Tony,

I sure love you so very, very much. It seems so neat to look at our baby and see what a beautiful thing our love has created. Tony, we have such a beautiful and wonderful love. I don't want anything to ever spoil it. It's too bad that everyone can't have such a love as ours. God has been very good to me. He gave me the most wonderful husband in the entire world. I only wish we could be together forever. He also gave me a darling little baby boy that's a very big part of you. You sounded so different on the phone when I talked to you Sunday.

Today Daisy came over to see our baby. She thinks he's a doll too. Your parents still haven't come and looked at our baby. Maybe they will this weekend. It really makes me feel bad. Tony, I can't wait until you get home. The shows this month don't sound too great, but I guess we'll survive. I want to go swimming at least once if I can. Bill & Bonnie haven't been over to see our baby either.

Hope had her operation today. They had to remove one of her ovaries too because they were so infected. She's doing okay now though.

My stitches feel better today. I can walk somewhat better. I want to get so much done before you get home but first I have to get back my strength.

I had a dream last night. I dreamed that I was walking to see you with the baby. You were in a store. I was skinny again and I was wearing a pair of my shorts. It seemed so neat to be in my shorts again. About then the baby woke me up. I can't exercise until my stitches get better. I just have a little stomach and it's flabby. It's got quite a bit of blood yet to get rid of. When I can exercise, I'll get rid of it. I hope it's gone by the time you get here. It feels so neat to be able to feel my ribs and hips. Your baby's the best in the world. It doesn't get colic at all. It sleeps 4 hours and then eats, so it's on a 4-hour eating schedule which is very good. It's a pig too. It's now eating 3 ½ oz. Pretty good. He's so cuddly.

Well I guess it's time to go. Be good & stay mine forever.

Your loving wife eternally,
Clellie

P.S. Hugs & kisses, etc. forever!

July 9, 1969   **10:00 PM**

Hi Hon,

I sure wish I could be with you at graduation. Is Butler's wife going? If so, how is she getting down there? Time seems to be going so slow. I can't believe it. Maybe you'll be home in 9 or 10 more days and I'm so darn excited. Tony, I miss and love you so very, very much.

Emmy Lou came over today to see our baby. She thinks he's a doll, everyone does. She gave it an outfit that's really cute. It was nice to see her. Boy, Lou, sure is big. I can't believe it. Denise called and said she'd come over soon to see it. Uncle Roy and Uncle Virgil came over and saw him. Everyone just adores him. Sophia and Brandy Brooks and Chloe Bradford just left. They bought me some perfume. Sweet of them. Sophia said I looked really good. She said she expected me to look in rough shape but I really looked nice. How about that? They think Chad's a doll too. Brandy looked at your picture and said that she thinks you're really nice-looking. I told her that I thought so too. It was really neat to see them again.

I was so happy to get your letter today, Tony. I miss you so very, very much. The baby and I are fine. I can even walk pretty good now and it's not so hard to sit. Nice. I've began a few of my exercises but I've decided I'd better quit until I see the Dr. Saturday 'cause starting too early can be harmful. I sure hope I have my shape back by the time you get home. I want you to know I was flatter that almost all the girls at the hospital. When I lie down, I'm perfectly flat. It's just a poochy stomach at the bottom. I don't think I can get into any of my pants yet. I sure like being at least this skinny. It'll be neat to be able to make love and not worry about my stomach. Tony, our baby is and will be something for us to be proud of. He has to be. Just look at his great father. Tony, the baby won't make any difference in our relationship. I'll always love you as much as ever and more. He'll never come between us. You're still the very most important person in my life. At nights while your home, Mom said she'd watch the baby. I want you all to myself with no interruptions see? I've been thinking about going and getting you without the baby so we'll be alone but that's not fair to you.

When you get home, I mostly want to be alone with you. I want to go swimming, have a picnic at the falls, and go to the mountains, make love, and just be together. What are your plans? Tony, I'm not going to let you go anywhere without me. I've been waiting 4 ½ months and I want to spend all the time I can with you. I'm so excited to get you here with me. Take care, be good, and stay mine forever.

Lovingly your wife,
Clellie

✉ *July 10, 1969*   *10:15 PM*

Dearest Tony,

How's the greatest guy on earth been doing? I hope you're okay. I love you so very, very much.

Today I got up and bathed our son. He was really colicky all night long. He's such a good baby. He must've been pretty sick. After I bathed and fed our baby I decided to go to town and pay our few bills. We owe $100 more on the ring. I got 10 cans of oil. I want you to change the oil when you get home. In my account at the bank we have $52. In your account, we have $35 or something like that. How are we going to pay the phone bill this month?

I want so much to be with you alone when you get home. I am really debating about bringing our baby. I know you really want to see it but I also want to be able to kiss and hug you all the way home without any interruptions. Stingy aren't I? It's just that I want you all to myself.

Well I'm not doing too bad. I fit into my blue cut-offs now. I can't get into any of my other shorts yet though. Here I was so proud thinking I was so skinny again.

Dale and Carrie came to visit tonight. The baby was awake so I let him hold Chad. Dale's still staying in Utah. He doesn't have a job yet. He bought a 1967 red Datsun. It's real cute. He's put on some weight I think. Marie also came to visit. She thinks Chad's a doll. She fed him and he threw up. I felt so sorry for him. She said that they had some trouble Sunday and that's why your parents didn't get over. They are both working pretty hard and haven't been able to make it over. It was good to see Marie. She stayed about an hour to one and a half hours.

There's so much that I want to get done before you get home. It's been a week today since I had Chad. Tony, I love you so very much and I am so excited to get you home. I only have about eight or nine days more to wait and I'm so very excited.

All my love forever,
Clellie

P.S. Hugs and Kisses, etc.

July 11, 1969   **10:30 PM**

Hi Hon,

I'm getting so darn excited for you to get home. I miss you so very, very much. I can't wait.

Today Mom and I washed the windows. I also cleaned out a couple of drawers. I made the baby some formula today to last a couple of days. Boy, I'm getting so excited to see you again.

Bill and Ted came over tonight. I showed them our baby and they didn't say much about him. They stayed about 10 minutes. They want us to come and visit when you get home. My cousin Olivia came over and brought an outfit for the baby. Boy, if she hadn't given me what she has I'd be in sad shape. She is such a life saver.

Susan called tonight. She said that she really didn't think our baby looked like either of us. She said that he was the biggest baby in the nursery. Mom said that there was a couple every bit as big and everyone has said that he's got both of our looks. I think he's a doll and he looks like us. About a month ago I was talking about where you'd land. Someone had told me that it might be in Salt Lake City so I told Susan that her and Denny would probably have to take me if it was in Salt Lake 'cause I didn't trust my car that much. Tonight when she called I told her that you might land in Pocatello or Twin. She said you should land in Pocatello. I told her that I hated to drive that far. She asked me if I was going alone. I told her, why of course. You wanted me to come alone and I wanted to be alone with you. She said that Denny would be heartbroken. He really wanted to go get you. She said that he'd probably sit up all night until we get home. Hon, I know she's exaggerating a lot but I also know he hasn't had anyone to run with and he's got plans. Tony, I want to be alone with you as much as I can. Will you be able to tell him that you want to be with me alone if he is counting on things? I know that I'm crossing bridges before I get to them but I'm so afraid that we won't get too much time alone. It'll be so neat to have you here with me. I'm so darn excited.

Last night I did some more exercises like an idiot. No matter how many I do it'll take time for my stomach to get back in place. Anyway this morning I got up and blood just gushed. It's been coming pretty steady ever since, but I'm okay. I guess that doing them too early can 'cause hemorrhages. I wanted so bad to be totally flat when you get back.

Well I guess I'll close for now. I love you, Tony, now and for all eternity. I can't wait until you're home again.

All my love forever,
Clellie

P.S. Hugs and Kisses, etc.

✉ *July 12, 1969*　　　　　　　　　　　　　　　　　　　　　　　　　　*10:00 PM*

Hi Hon,

I love you so much. I'm so excited about you getting home, only six or seven more days. I can't believe it. It seems like I'm having a most beautiful dream and I'm going to wake up before you get home. The only trouble is that the days are going so slow. When I go to get you and we get in the car I'm not letting you even start up the motor until you hold me, kiss me lots, and tell me how much you really love me. It'll be so neat to have you next to me. I'm going to kiss you anytime I want and anywhere so you'd better be prepared. Oh, Tony, I just can't wait to see you again it's been such a long time.

Today I had to take Chad to the doctor for his 10-day check-up even though he's only nine days old. Doctor Peterson said he was doing great. He checked his arms and legs and everything. He now weighs 8 lbs. 1 oz. Doctor Peterson said that he was really good. I had to have Chad bare when Doctor Peterson checked him. Before Dr. Peterson got there Chad peed on me. Made me so mad. While I was bathing him this morning he did it then too. You've got to teach your son better manners you know. I wore an old culotte today that used to be too big. Now the bust is quite snug and so are the hips. I sure wish my figure would hurry and get back to normal. I don't mind the bust but I don't like my stomach. It's really not so big but I can't get into many of my clothes. Everyone told me that it usually takes a good six weeks or more to get back into shape.

I went to town today and got a little tub with stamps for Chad. He needs one. I also got him some cereal and a spoon; he'll need it soon. I need to buy some Tampax for in case we go swimming (if I look okay to you in my swimsuit). I'm not sure how much more I'll menstruate. Someone said for six weeks, ugh.

Well I guess I'll close for now. I love you so very, very much. I'm so excited. It'll be so neat to be together again.

Your excited loving wife,
Clellie

P.S. Hugs and Kisses, etc.!!

July 13, 1969   **12:00 AM**

Dear Tony,

We've been married seven months today. How about that? The Army has had you four of those months. Ticks me off!

Tony, about your parents coming over to see our baby, it is only proper that they come over to see it if they want to see it. I'm sure they could've come over today. Everyone asks me if your parents have been over to see it, when I say no they are real shocked. They are supposed to because for a week I couldn't get around too well and you shouldn't cart young babies all over. I haven't thanked them for the flowers yet but I was waiting for them to come over. I'm very upset, Tony. I'm angry and hurt. Even if I would take him over your parents are usually at work. It is their place to visit him first. Everyone else has come to see him. Why haven't they?

Stephanie came over tonight at 9:00 PM and stayed until 11:30 PM. She gave me a baby blanket that she made herself. It is so darn pretty. It was really nice. She also gave a rattle. She held Chad and fed him. She thinks he looks like you. However I think he's going to have blue eyes. He's so darling. Her and Luke are getting married on August 15. She's so excited. I'm very happy for her. Luke's working at Simplot's on swing shift right now. Bill had a bachelor's party right before he got married but he didn't until June. Brave isn't he? Listen to their bills; $60 a month for two years for their car, ring payments, sewing machine payments, and $85 or $90 rent. Lots.

Well I better close for now. I miss you very, very much, Tony. Be good and stay mine. I love you.

Yours eternally,
Clellie

P.S. Hugs and Kisses, etc.

✉ *July 14, 1969*   *2:30 PM*

Dear Tony,

I wanted to let you know that your mother just came to see our baby. She was very apologetic about not coming before now and she gave the baby a cute bank. She asked about when you'd be here and I told her. She also wanted to know if you knew your orders so I told her. Marie called wanting to know about you too.

Tony, if I could come down to your graduation could you come back with me on Friday? If Uncle Virgil would fly me down all I would pay would be for the gas. I'd like to know if you could when you call Wednesday or whenever.

Well I better close for now. I love you so much, Tony, be good and stay mine.

All my love,
Clellie

✉ **14 Jul 1969**

Dearest Clellie,

I'm really miserable tonight. Do you know why? It's because today seemed like a week. I want to come home so bad, that the time is just dragging by. I really am anxious to see what our son looks like. Most of all I want to see you again, in the flesh. I just want to be with you again. I want to be able to put my arms around you and all over. I do mean all over too.

I hope we can have a lot of fun. In your last letter you said you wanted to spend a lot of time in bed. I sure hope we can. Even if you can't go all the way, I'm sure we can think of something to do.

I'm sending you a picture of me. I just got back from bivouac. We marched the whole way back so I'm kind of dirty. I have dirt all over my face. How do you like all that gear? It might not look like much, but when you carry it for hours it does get a little heavy. Don't I look like a born killer? Ha ha!

Clellie, I was talking to all the NCOs around here and they say that it would really be a waste to have your wife come to Fort Benning. Sgt. Clark had his wife go live there. He said he never got much time off even after the six weeks. He said in about the seventh week she went back to Colorado, because it cost too much to live and he hardly ever got to see her. I guess Spear and Perrin aren't going to have their wives come to live there either. I don't know what we'll be able to do. Maybe it would be better if you didn't come to Georgia for the first 12 weeks. If I finish NCO school and get assigned to an AIT unit, I know you can live off post then. Then we can see each other for that nine weeks and then I'll get a 30-day leave before I ship to Nam. It's really a bummer. I want to have you come and live with me so bad while I go to NCO school. Well I don't know. We'll talk about it when I get home.

Clellie, I better go for now. Just think about six more days and I'll be home with you. I love you, Clellie, and I want you to love me no matter what happens.

Your husband,
Tony

P.S. When I get home, I'm not going to leave you alone for one minute.
I LOVE YOU!!!

Pvt. Anthony Jolley
H.H.C 1st Bn 2nd Brig.
Ft. Ord, California 2nd Plt 93941

July 15, 1969   *10:10 PM*

Hi Hon,

How are you doing this fine day? I guess this will be my last letter to you before you get home. You should get this one Friday. I can't wait until I have you here with me. I miss you so very bad.

About us going all the way. I sure hope I can. I can still feel that it is somewhat tender, but we'll see when you get here. I can't wait until I feel your touch again and your most welcome kiss. You're so tender and warm to me.

I saw Susan today. I had to take Hope to the doctor to get her stitches removed. Susan came out of the doctor's office. She had a coil put in her for her birth control. I'm not sure what it is but she said that it sure hurt. Susan and Denny are quite anxious about you getting home too. I really don't think Denny will be too big of a problem to us.

Today I bathed Chad and then fed him. He threw it up so I changed his clothes and washed him again. I waited about 15 minutes and fed him again and he threw it up again. I bathed him and waited for about 30 minutes and only fed him about 1 ½ oz. he kept it down this time. Last night he woke up at 11:30 PM and kept me awake until 1:30 AM. I could have pounded him. Oh well I still love him. His hair is a medium brown with a slight shine of red in it. He looks like he might have blue eyes, but no one can really tell yet. Susan now thinks he definitely resembles you and your family. I cleaned the little rugs today and my car rug. I straightened the house up somewhat too.

Molly got her in 1960 Pontiac today and left for American Falls. Mom left yesterday with Mitch to go to Lava Hot Springs so here I am alone except for the baby. You know I've cried twice today over you and you'd think I'd be so happy because you'll be home soon. It seems so long since you've been here that it's hard to believe you'll really be here. Tony, I miss you so very, very much. I have about four or five more days before you'll be here and I'm so excited. See you soon.

Yours eternally,
Clellie

P.S. Hugs and Kisses, etc.

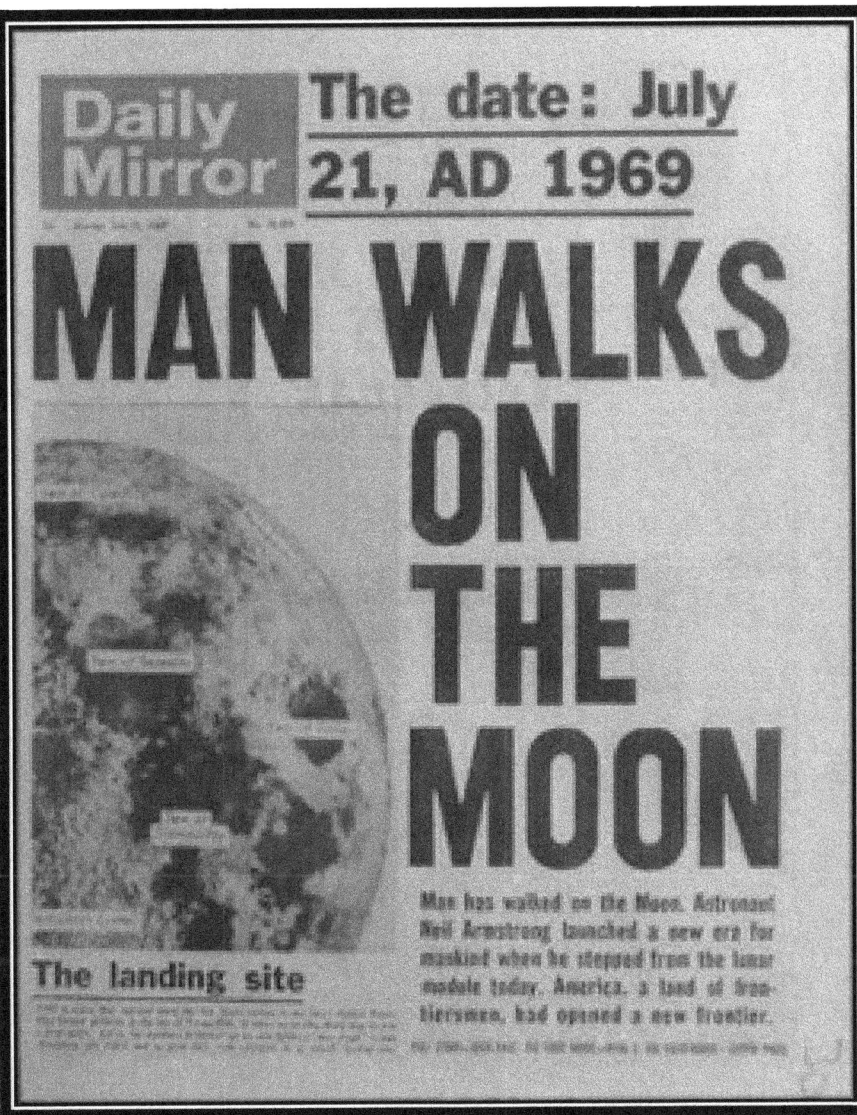

NON-COMMISSIONED OFFICER (NCO) SCHOOL

August 2, 1969   12 o'clock noon

Hi Hon,

Tony, I'm so miserable. Tony, I hate this so much. I must say I was proud of how I held up after you left. I had tears in my eyes when you took off and when we went back inside Sue and I both had tears. I slept most of the way home and held up real good. Aren't you proud of me? When I got home I started to feed the baby here and I just couldn't hold it back anymore. I just bawled, so I gave Mom the baby and here I am in our room on our bed where we were together not more than 13 hours ago. Tony, can you ever forgive me the awful way I was to you at times like when I took off for the ride? I thought Chad would make it easier to be away from you but so far no good. This room has so many reminders of you being here. I don't think I can take being away from you much more. Three months is a long time to be away from you. A year is even worse but I'm not worrying about it right now. Boy, our sheets are a mess. I guess that's what happens when you piddle around. I hated to see you board that jet. By the way, thanks for the hanky. It sure is getting a lot of use. Tony, you're the most precious person in the world. I love you more than you'll ever know and my love will never change. Take care and be good for me.

                                                                                     10:30 PM

Hi again. Boy, this day sure has been long. I miss you so very much, Tony. The baby has really been upset today too. He cries for no reason and he don't stop even when you hold him. I wonder if he knows you're gone? Mom said that when I held him I was feeding him and then I started to cry and gave him to her he wouldn't eat. She said he just cried as if he knew. It looks like we both need you very much.

I got our room cleaned up today. It was so hard to gather up your things and put them away. I have to get used to you not being here all over again. I have to get used to not kissing you good night, not feeling your touch, not having your arms around me, and not having you near me. I waited a long time for those two weeks and they went so fast. I hate the Army, Tony, for taking you away from me. I know it's good to get it over with but I wish it were over.

All my love eternally,
Clellie

P.S. I love you very, very much.

P.P.S. I got the check today from the government.

✉ *August 3, 1969*   *10:00 PM*

Hi Hon,

It's so lonely here without you. I hope you're as lonesome as I am. I hated to wake up this morning because you're not here. I wish I could fall asleep until you get here again.

Chad's been having colic. He can hardly sleep for very long at all, his stomach is so gassy.

I sat around today and watched TV. Sounds like a most exciting day. However, I did my exercises last night and this morning. I want you to be proud of my figure. I really don't mind not going places without you here. I'd rather stay home and wait. Everyone tried to tell me that after the baby was born I'd want to be gone constantly but I don't.

I had a dream about you in your uniform with me and some other guy was with us in uniform. The baby woke me up and I can't remember anything else about it.

How are you doing? Do you like it there? How's the weather? What is even going on so far?

I made another boo-boo. I soaked my yellow suit, new bra, and slip together and I got a few yellow stains on my bra and slip. It doesn't look too bad on my bra.

In about 12 weeks, it will be October 26. In about 21 weeks, it will be right on the weekend after Christmas. It seems such a long time off. I can't wait till a year and 7 ½ months are gone. Then we can be together again forever.

Chad is one month old today. It doesn't seem like it's been that long.

I miss you so much. Please don't worry about me, Tony. I'm a one-man woman and you are my one man. I'll always love you, Tony. Always remember that.

Your most loving wife,
Clellie

P.S. Hugs and Kisses, etc.

August 4, 1969   **10:00 PM**

Dear Handsome (alias Tony),

How's that for a great opening? To add to the opening I want you to know how much I love you.

Boy, the baby's face sure is broken out. I'm going to take him to the doctor as soon as I can. If it's eczema, maybe we can get it cleared up before it gets worse. It might not be but it looks like it. If it's not, at least my mind will be clear.

I went to the hospital today and got it straightened out again. I took the $5 Olivia gave me, and $7 from the check from the Army and got Chad a nice little highchair. I didn't want to get a real expensive one. I also took a book of stamps and got him a circus umbrella with animals on it to hang over his bed. I spent $7 on formula, cereal, and some baby vegetables. I got my oil changed and a new filter for $7. I paid $25 to our telephone bill, and $25 to Mom. I told Mom the highchair was from her and Olivia and now I don't have to pay her the $10 I borrowed. We are even. I paid Auntie Em the $5 I borrowed from her to go see you. So now I've paid everyone back. It sure feels good. I put $7 in my account in the bank, bought a book of stamps for $2, $1.19 for film, $4 for Stephanie and Luke's wedding gift, and $6 for your insurance. I have around $11-12 for gas for my car and spending money for me. You see now where the money goes. Wow.

Steve came over tonight and is watching T.V. He's been coming over every night since Saturday.

I got the cutest book from Flora. It's entitled "Recipe for our Friendship." It's really cute.

I'm faithfully doing my exercises still. I want so much for you to be proud of me. Tony, you looked so handsome in your uniform getting on that jet. I was so proud of you but I wish you were home for good.

I can't wait to hear from you again. I miss you so very, very much. Chad takes up some of my time, but he can't make up for the loneliness I have without you. I love you, Tony.

Your lonely yet ever so loving wife,
Clellie

P.S. Hugs and Kisses, etc.

✉ **4 Aug 1969**

Dear Clellie,

I found this card and I thought it was cute. It's actually a get-well card, but I thought it might cheer you up.

Clellie, I love you very much. I already miss you very much. I hear that we have to wait until the 12th before we start our 12 weeks. I hope that's not true, but it probably is. I've already made a few friends, and the way it sounds not very many of the guys here want to be here so maybe a lot of us will drop out.

Clellie, I love, love, love you and miss you gobs. I'll try to write as often as possible. Please stay mine. I love you.

Your loving husband,
Tony

P.S. Kiss and hug the baby for me.

P.P.S. I really do love you, Mrs. Jolley.

NCOC Tony Jolley
104 Co 10th Stu. Bn. 4th Plt
Fort Benning, Georgia 31905

August 5, 1969   10:30 PM

Dear Tony,

I sure do miss you. It was so neat to have you here with me. I wish it could last forever but the Army has first hold.

I saw Evelyn Whitmore today. She's got the cutest baby boy. Oh, it's a doll. Her husband is in Vietnam now. She's not working or anything. She said that's because he's in Vietnam and she gets around $300 allotment. How about that? She said that she lived with her husband while he was going to NCO school and she would never trade it for $1 million. She said they never had money to spend but at least they were together. They have saved up $1200 for the R&R and she never worked at all. She said that it also was worth it just to see him again. Tony, I want to be with you now. Please see if it's possible.

Have you turned in Chad's birth certificate? I took five pictures of him today; 2 were with him in his tub, one 1 was holding him, one was him bare on a blanket on his stomach, and one was face up with clothes. I've got three more pictures to take before I can get them developed. When I do, I'll send them to you when you can keep what you want if you want any and send the rest back. I want to get a little $13 dollar Instamatic camera if I can so I can take pictures inside too. I think I'll go to Mountain Home next month with Susan for baby food and maybe I can get one a little cheaper if I can afford it. Chad's getting fatter still and I think he's got eczema. I sure hope not. Is it okay if I get another camera? Please let me know.

I put on a turtleneck today and my gray and white hip hugger dress to go job hunting. The exercises have done some good. I didn't bulge. I looked flat. Great. I went job hunting today at all the stores. They don't need any help yet but I think they will when school starts so I'm going around again the 23rd.

Tony, I miss you so very much. You mean the world to me. I wish that I were with you now. I love you so much it's impossible to put into words.

Yours eternally,
Clellie

P.S. Hugs and Kisses, etc.

✉ **August 6, 1969**   *11:30 PM*

Hi Hubby,

I was so thrilled to get your card today. It is so cute and though you're writing was short it still made me feel neat. You know that you have such a way even in writing that makes me feel very special. I love you, Tony, with all my heart.

Chad kept me up most of the night last night. After I got to sleep he woke up at 12:30 AM, again at 3:30 AM, again at 5:30 AM, again at 7 AM, and he kept me awake from then until 10:00 AM this morning. Every time he woke me up I was up for about 45 minutes feeding and changing him. He's about to wear me out. He's so cute though.

Today I took the kids out and they got all their clothes from the farm. Ann was there and we chatted for a while. Dad was at work. I don't know what we're going to do about Molly, we are so crowded; Nancy doesn't have anywhere to put her clothes, she's sleeping with Mom, and Chad's in Alice's room. I want to get that big room. Mom's going to have to tell Molly, but she doesn't want to hurt her feelings. You'd think Molly would know without being told.

Carl and Mabel came over yesterday and told Mom that they saw Dad and he had told them that if Mom went to the lawyers anymore he'd bring a rifle in and shoot her. Sweet of him.

My cousin has a girl that's three years old, and she's not got enough of the girl hormones in her. Her lip where her vagina and pee hole (excuse me) is keeps trying to go shut to be more like a boy you know. One time the doctor had to cut it open because it was trying to go together and he's had them keep putting a salve around it in hopes it won't go shut. They also have to stick a long white stick with the pill on it up her and leave it there till it dissolves. They have to do this until she starts menstruating if she does. If she doesn't and the lip grows together, she'll never be able to live a normal life. She won't be boy or girl. I hope you can understand this. It's quite complicated and sad.

I went by Susan's on the way back here with the girls. They've got that little Corvair they were looking at. Susan really likes it.

When I was talking to Ann she asked me how much I'd sell my car for when I sell it and I said that I'd sell for around $275 or $300. She said that Dad wanted to get her car around the beginning of school. He was now looking at a Corvair for $400 but she wanted to buy mine if I wanted to sell it. She really likes it. I told her that I doubted I'd even consider selling it until the last of October when you'd be sent to Fort Ord and I'd go with you. I doubted if I'd sell even then and she said she hoped I would. Are you going to try and put a down payment on a car on your next leave or wait? You mentioned something about it when you were here.

Your card did cheer me up. I mailed all four letters to you today. I hope you get them soon enough, at least before Saturday. I sure hope that you start before the 12th you won't get out of it until the first part of November and I want you out sooner. Are you going to drop out? How is it? Have you met any guys that you think you'll get close to? Be good and stay mine forever.

Your loving lonely wife,
Clellie

P.S. Hugs and Kisses, etc.

✉ **August 7, 1969**　　　　　　　　　　　　　　　　　　　　　　　　　*10:00 AM*

Dear Tony,

Today Joshua, Allan, Leo, and Amanda came to visit. It was real nice to see them. They stayed about one hour. I gave your address to Allan but I'll have to give your mother it too so they'll be sure and have it. I took them home. I couldn't see them walking all that way. They asked me how you were and about when you'd be home.

Chad's face is clearing up somewhat. I don't think he's going to have eczema hardly at all. It doesn't look like Steve or Virgil's mom said. I sure am glad. Everyone makes the comment of how big he is for only a month old. He's growing so much. I can't wait till we go to the doctor for our six weeks and see how much he weighs. He's so cute. I just love him gobs, except I love his daddy more, and it's a different love.

Bonnie and Merl Webster came to see the baby. They think he's a doll and he looks like you. It was good to see them.

Auntie Em had a hamburger fry in her backyard today for us, her kids, their kids, and relatives. It was sort of a get-together. I took Chad and they all loved him. I'm so proud. We got back home at 9:15 PM and we went at 8 PM. Not too long.

Alice's going to Twin with Olivia for a week. Hope's asked me to go to the show for about three days now and I tell her I'm broke or I don't feel good. I guess I'm a hermit. I didn't want to go to Auntie Em's tonight either but Olivia and Molly came and got me. It's just not fun without you. I won't mind going out on weekends in around a month with Susan maybe. I hate to spend money on my fun when I can save it for us. That's why I only keep $15 a month for gas and odds and ends. I'm a real miser, aren't I?

Well I guess I'll close for now. Always remember, Tony, that I'll always love and need you!!!

All my love eternally,
Clellie

P.S. Hugs and Kisses, etc.

August 8, 1969   **10:00 PM**

Hi Hon,

Well a week ago tonight we were together making love for the last time before you left. It seems like such a long time ago. You were here for such a short while. I can almost feel your touch, your kiss. I miss you so very much. It seems almost like a most beautiful dream that lasted for almost 2 weeks. The only bad part was the arguments I picked with you. I'm so sorry, Tony. I love you so much and yet I fight with you. Will you always love me anyway?

Susan came over this morning, Denny and her went out to the hospital. She had to have a blood test to see what's the matter with her. She's been sickly. The doctor says it could be hepatitis or gallbladder trouble, either way it's not good. They won't know the results of the test until Monday.

I got an invitation to Luke and Stephanie's wedding on the 15th. It was addressed to you, Chad, and me. The first envelope was to Mr. and Mrs. Tony Jolley and family. Sounds weird but cool.

I've just got to get an instamatic camera. Chad was sleeping so cute today and I wanted the pictures so bad but I don't have a flash on my old one. Chad's so cute.

Dad went by tonight and Nancy hollered to him and waved. Do you know what he did? He looked at her and turned away. Ann said that he's really hurt and mad but it's his own fault.

Chad keeps me so busy that I don't have time for much of anything. I have to make his formula and wash his clothes every other day. Then he's awake most of the day with bathing, feeding, and playing. Do you know that he expected me to play with him at 5 o'clock this morning? Well I fed him and put him back to bed and he bawled for 15 minutes before he fell asleep.

Tony, I sure miss you. You'll be home again at about New Year's, right? I sure hope so, course I'll get to be with you a couple months before that. Right! I want to be with you as much as possible. How's school treating you? I love and miss you very, very much.

Your most adoring wife,
Clellie

P.S. Hugs and Kisses, etc.

✉ **8 Aug 1969** **Friday**

Dear Clellie,

I received your letters tonight, Clellie. I want to start off this letter by answering some of the questions you asked me. I think it would be all right if you buy that camera if you have the money. No, I haven't got the baby's birth certificate recorded yet. The reason is because we haven't even officially checked into the company yet. We haven't started our 12 weeks of training yet. We won't start until the 12th or 13th of August. Isn't that a real bummer? I could have been home for about two more weeks.

The weather down here is unbelievable. It's so humid that you're constantly sweating. Even this paper I'm writing on is damp. Everything is real sticky when you touch it.

All week long they put us on details. I've really been working my ass off. Today some new troops came in. Wow, they really started socking the harassment to us too. I got dropped two times in the chow line today. That means you have to do push-ups. Once for a button that was unbuttoned and the other time I had a thread hanging down on my pants. You have to keep everything spit-shined, and they check you all day long. We have to stay here training for at least three weeks. Then you can sign up to drop out. After the third week, they really start to kick a lot of guys out anyway. If these inspections keep up, I might go sign-up for dog school.

Guess what, Clellie? My MOS changed from 11B to 11F. That means we're still infantry but we deal in Recon patrols and Company intelligence. If we're good enough we could get a job at a base camp in Vietnam and just go on patrols and stuff like that. There is supposed to be a lot of bookwork in this course, and it's supposed to be pretty rough. Spear and I are the only ones from our company at Fort Ord in 11F. Perrin, Winston, and the rest of those guys are all still 11 Bravos.

Oh Clellie, notice that my address has changed from the 4th platoon to the 3rd platoon.

You know something, Clellie? Here in NCO school we have to take turns taking charge of the platoon. It feels kind of good to get in front of a platoon of men and give them commands. They think I do a pretty good job. Some of the guys in our platoon really screw up when they have to give commands, but a lot of us don't really do too bad for new candidates. By the way they call us candidates here. That NCOC in front of my name means "Non-Commissioned Officer Candidate."

Clellie, I've been trying to keep my mind off of just how much I miss you ever since I got here. I got to hold it off till the end of my letters or I never get anything else said. I do truly love and miss you, Clellie. It's twice as bad as it was before I came home on leave. That's one of the reasons why I might drop this course, so I can get home for a 30-day leave sooner and to get that long year over with.

I never thought I would miss you as much as I do. I miss Chad, too, but it couldn't compare to how I miss you, just you. When I got on that plane, I swear, I almost cried. I saw you standing on the sundeck, and I was going to jump off the plane and go AWOL. Well, Clellie, I better end this letter and get ready for tomorrow. Oh God, I love you so much. I wish I were there at home with you and Chad. Remember that I love you now Clellie, and I'll love you as long as there is anything that exists.

Your loving and faithful husband,
Tony

P.S. Give Chad a big hug and kiss for me. Could you send me some stamps, Clellie?

P.P.S. Oh yeah, we go 12 weeks to this school then we go another 12 weeks for on-the-job training. Also they don't send any 11Fs to Fort Ord.

P.P.P.S. It takes a lot of money to live here at Fort Benning, Clellie. We'd need a car if you came down too. If we could get enough money maybe we could have you come down, but I doubt it. I sure wish we could. How could we get your car down here?

I love you, Clellie!

NCOC Tony Jolley
104 Co 10th Stu. Bn. 3th Plt
Fort Benning, Georgia 31905

August 10, 1969 1 AM

Dearest Tony,

I love you so very, very much. How do you like our groovy picture? I think it's the best one that we've ever taken together, don't you? Do I get it back for our scrapbook?

Susan and I went to the show tonight. The name was "True Grit" with John Wayne. It sure was good. We didn't go until 9:30 PM and afterwards we went to the Ponderosa for pie. The Russet's closed because someone else is taking it over. Susan and Denny found a trailer house. Nice. So Susan has to work now.

Say, Tony, I want you to sit down and write me back because I'd like the answer to this question and I want to know whether you're going to keep that picture. Here's the question. Ready? How much or what of our sex life did you discuss with Denny? I'm just curious. I already know a little. Susan slipped. Will you tell me?

Guess who I saw working at the Ponderosa? Taylor Murphy. She said hi.

It was really sad when I went to the show tonight. So many couples happy together. I wanted you with me so bad. I love and miss you, Tony.

I was invited to a shower for Stephanie Monday but I can't get her a present for it so I guess I won't go. I have their wedding present. It's a set like our butter, sugar, and salt and pepper shakers, except it has vinegar and oil sets with it. It's really quite nice.

Boy, you should see Susan's glasses. They really don't do a thing for her. They are mod though.

Chad's been sleeping about 4 ½ hours between feedings at night. I'm going to have to break him pretty soon from his night feedings. How I dread that time. He's beginning to smile more, but not a lot. Do you know that he's almost as long as Susan's baby and almost as chubby. His legs are so chubby and he has a double chin, the little fatty.

Susan finally went into the Midway last night with Denny, but neither of your folks were there.

Guess who wants to work at Simplot? Sue Spear, she told Susan that! She wants more money. I guess I'll have to go talk to her.

Well, I guess I'll close for now. I love you, Tony, so very much. I'll wait forever for you.

Your ever-so-loving wife,
Clellie

P.S. I love you so very, very much, Mr. Tony Jolley!!!

✉ **August 11, 1969**   *12:30 AM*

Hi Hon,

I imagine you're wondering why I'm writing this letter so late. Susan called me up about 7:30 PM and wanted me to come over to her mom's and go with her to look at a trailer so I did. It was really nice. I got home at about 15 to 10:00 PM. However I didn't go over until 8:15 PM because I was doing dishes. Then I came home and watched the movie, "The Girl I Left Behind." It was about Basic Training at Fort Ord. It was really cool. I recognized some of the places in it. Then at 15 to midnight Chad woke up and I had to feed him. How's that?

When I went to Susan's her mom and I found a tarantula so I put him in a bottle and brought it home with me to show the girls and Mom. I've never seen one before. They sure are ugly.

Susan is planning on going to work at Simplot's on days if she can for six months so they can get a trailer house. How about that? She tried to get on everywhere else and no luck. I don't think I'd like a trailer house to live in.

Stephanie called today and wants me to come to the wedding. She also wants me to be over her guest book at the reception. How about that? I guess I will.

I had Chad drink water from a cup today. He's so cute. Do you know what? He's sleeping longer at nights. Last night he slept from 11:30 PM to 5 o'clock this morning. So far tonight he slept from 5:00 PM to 11:45 PM how's that?

I wrote letters to Pat in Florida today and took them up to mail with yours. Mom, Hope, and I went up for a Coke at the AC. I dropped Mom at Jefferson's and then went by Lance's place for Hope and came home. How's that for an eventful day?

Gary Lewis and the Playboys are going to be at CSI on the 22nd. I sure wish you were here and we could go.

Tony, I love you so very much. I can't wait until we're together forever. Be good and stay mine forever.

Yours eternally,
Clellie

P.S. Hugs and Kisses, etc.

August 11, 1969   **10:00 PM**

Dear Tony,

First of all, I want to thank you so much for your letter. I just loved it. I've read it four times now. I love you so very, very much. Did my other letters get to you? They were all addressed to the 4th Platoon. I hope so.

Today I cut Molly and Mom's hair. I also did the washing and washed my car.

You've been in the Army five months exactly today, 18 more months left. I can't wait until they are all gone. I want to be with you so much.

I guess Susan is going to take me to Mountain Home next month and stock us up on baby food for a month and formula. I sure hope I have enough money for a camera there too. If I get money for the baby, I'll have enough. Otherwise, I won't.

If you're not starting until the 12th or 13th why didn't you get to stay here longer?

Our weather hasn't been exactly dry. It got 100 degrees yesterday and today. I think it's bad here and from what I hear it's twice as bad there.

I think it's rotten of them to make you drop just because of a button and a string. That's really carrying it overboard, isn't it?

Do you think you'll drop out? I hate to see you do it if you have a chance at being at a base. I'd also like you to get it over with now. It's all up to you. Do you think you'll like being a sergeant?

I'm so glad to have you say that you love and miss me. That's the most important part of your letters. I love to know how and what you're doing, but I need to know how much you care. It's all I really live for.

I'll send you some stamps tomorrow. I might have to draw some money (one dollar) from the bank and use one of mine for you.

The carnival and rodeo are this weekend. I sure wish you were here. I guess I'll miss it this year.

Chad's been pretty good. He's really getting chubby. He's so cute. I don't know when I'll get that roll of film processed. I can't afford to do it right now. You know in a way I feel sorry for Chad. I love him very much and I know you do to, but when you're around I almost forget about him. Do you ever remember reading that story about a couple who have a baby but they were so wrapped up in each other they didn't give it all the attention it needed? Well I hope we're not that bad, but you are the most important person in my life. My love for you is so much greater. I need you and depend on you. I miss you so much. When you were on the plane I couldn't see in the plane. We could only see the hands when they waved. I hoped you'd see me. I wanted the plane to be broke or something so you wouldn't have to leave me. I hate these goodbyes. If I thought the car could make it, I'd drive there right now. I need you so much. I'll always love you.

Your loving wife eternally,
Clellie

P.S. Hugs and Kisses, etc.

August 12, 1969   **10:00 PM**

Hi Hon,

How's the best guy in this world doing? I love you so very, very much.

Mom, Nancy, Chad, and I went to Twin today to visit cousin Olivia. It was a very nice day. Olivia and I went uptown shopping. I found the perfect winter coat for $21. It's really nice. Maybe when I can afford it I'll get it. I need one desperately you know. We also went in the pawnshops. I found an Ansco Cadet camera with a flash for $6.50. I sure hope it's still there when I go down again. I'm sure I can afford it next month. It looks good enough. I don't need a real expensive one. When we got back to Olivia's place she told Mom I wasn't any fun because I don't flirt with boys. Mom said she knew it because whenever I'm driving along boys will wave and I just ignore them. I told them that was because I was perfectly happy being married to you and I am. I don't even notice other guys. They'd never be able to compete with you. You're too perfect and I love you too much. I hope that you don't care to flirt either. Olivia's husband has to work in Ketchum for two months starting in September. She wants me to come and stay while he's gone because she doesn't like to be alone. What do you think?

I saw Bill and Bonnie today. Ted was trying on coats, darn expensive ones too! They said to say hi. I guess Bill's supposed to be Luke's best man.

Mom called up Dad to see when he was going to pay. He's still behind. He said that he wasn't going to pay her, but he would the girls. Mom told him no deal, so he wasn't going to pay any. Besides he has custody of the girls till February and he won't bring them home. He denied saying to the girls they could come in to stay. He said that it would be like last summer when she wouldn't bring them home except reversed. He's just trying to get even. It makes me so sick. He keeps the girls in a constant uproar. I'm so glad we love each other so much and Chad will never have to live in a divorce. I love you.

Speaking of Chad. His eyes are growing somewhat darker and he's getting so big. I can't wait until I get his pictures processed. I hope they turn out. Did you get your stamps?

I want to be with you so much, Tony. It's so icky here without you. I pray to God, Tony, that you'll always love me with you. I don't want you ever to lose your love for me.

All my love forever,
Clellie

P.S. Hugs and Kisses, etc.

✉ **12 August 1969**   **Tuesday**

Dear Clellie,

How is Chad doing? Does he have eczema or not? Also how is the most beautiful, sweet, and most charming girl in the world? It might sound like I'm in a good mood, but I'm not. They jump in your shit so much around here, I don't know whether I'm coming or going. I sure wish I was back home with you. I really do miss you, Clellie, and I love you so very, very much.

Wow you won't believe the haircuts they give you here. They'll let you grow it two inches on top, but the sides have to be whitewall. Your head is bald almost to the top of your head, so you have to keep the top about a quarter of an inch long to make it look even. Pretty cool.

This course is really getting me down, Clellie. When they have inspections, they check everywhere for dirt. They give you a demerit if you have a wrinkle in your bedcovers. We just started the course yesterday, and I think I already want out of this bullshit. About 30% of the class is already going to drop out after they put in their three weeks. Then after the three weeks the sergeants start kicking guys out who screw up. The only reason I'm staying in for a while is because in about 6 to 8 weeks you should start getting $160 a month. You get $30 a month more because I'm getting the E4 pay (Cpl.). You'll also start getting $30 a month more for the baby. I got the papers all straightened out with the financing yesterday. They'll probably find out that they have been over paying me. I'll probably only get $40 a month for a while. Ha ha! You think it's pretty funny don't ya? I guess you'll be making all the money in the family.

13 August 1969　　　　　　　　　　　　　　　　　　　　**Wednesday**

Dear Clellie,

I bet your wondering why I'm still writing on this letter. Yesterday we had to fall out while I was writing the letter. The captain made us all get down and start pushing them out as soon as we formed up. He said it was because the barracks were dirty. But really the barracks were spotless. The reason is just for harassment and to keep us in line.

I got two letters tonight, Clellie. One of the letters you sent a picture, it was really nice, you look so beautiful. I wish I could just put my arms around you from behind and caress you. I'll send you this picture back Clellie, but I want you to send me that big graduation picture of you to put it in my locker. We're not supposed to, but I'll hide it when we have an inspection. When you send it wrap it up real good. Put it in one of those cardboard type folders that some magazines come in, tape it up real good, and send it to me, alright?

Clellie, what's this about me and Carter discussing our sex life? Only thing I can remember Carter and me talking about is he asked me if we could do it. I told him yes but you were real sore (that's right when I first got home). He also asked me once if I like it as much since I got back from the Army? I told him that it just seems like sometimes I couldn't get enough, but I did enjoy it as much. I want you to write me in your next letter just what Susan slipped and said. I want you to tell me everything she said and please don't lie or try to hold anything back.

Clellie, I've got to close for now. I sure wish I could call and talk with you. I also wish you could come down here and live. Maybe if we can get enough money you could come down.

Remember, Clellie, that I love you now, and I'll love you as long as anything that exists. Love me always too.

Your loving husband,
Tony

P.S. How much does Chad weigh now?

I love, love, love you.

　　　　　　　　　　　　　　　　　　　　NCOC Tony Jolley
　　　　　　　　　　　　　　　　　　　　104 Co 10th Stu. Bn. 3th Plt
　　　　　　　　　　　　　　　　　　　　Fort Benning, Georgia 31905

✉ *August 13, 1969*   *11:00 PM*

Dear Hubby,

Here it is the 13th. We've been married eight months today. The Army's had you for five of those months. Sweet people. I hate it this way.

I'm trying to break Chad from his two o'clock feeding now. He is old enough. Last night was the first night, and boy, he bawled. At 5 AM I got up and fed him and he really didn't want to eat, just to play and goo at me. So I had to put him to bed after he ate and let him bawl to sleep. This girl Raylee who used to work at the plant, her husband, and her baby came visiting tonight. Her baby is exactly one month older than ours and Chad is every bit as big as hers except he's not as fat. When Chad lays down in the little tub to bathe, his feet and head touch each end. He's really growing. It costs around five dollars to process film and I still have two more pictures to take on it. I have three dollars saved up so far from change.

Mom told Molly that she's going to have to move because we needed her room. Mom gave her about a month so she'll be gone soon. I kind of feel sorry for her.

Boy, I'm really awful. I haven't been over to see your folks since you've been gone. I think I'll take Alice and Nancy with Chad and me Sunday and we'll go. That way I'll get to see your parents for sure. I haven't given them your address even, except for Allan. I have to give it to Carters and call Butler's wife too.

The jamboree was tonight and I convinced Hope to accept a date from a guy who asked her. She shouldn't sit home all the time.

I love you, Tony, so very, very much. Be good and stay mine. Write often!!! Always love me please!!!

Your loving devoted wife,
Clellie

P.S. Hugs and Kisses, etc.

August 14, 1969　　　　　　　　　　　　　　　　　　　　　　　　　*10:00 PM*

Hi Hon,

Do you love me? How much? How long? I sure do love you. I miss you immensely.

I took Hope to town today to buy Ashley some bell-bottom pants. I took Chad with me and everyone had to see him. It was really neat.

Chad cried for quite a while last night. It's kind of hard to break babies of night feeding. He's been smiling more often now. His eyes are getting darker I think. I sure hope he has your color of eyes.

Most of our meals here have been fresh corn and potatoes. The guy who owns the garden next door has been giving us all we want of corn and red potatoes.

At about 7:30 PM I took Hope, her kids, Alice, and Nancy to the carnival. I only went on one ride. It was the octopus. It was really fun. I rode with Alice and Nancy. We really had a nice time on it. It was good to go with the girls for once. We're not together doing things too much anymore. We went through the exhibits too. We got home at around 9:10 PM.

Nancy said to say hi. I saw our insurance man and his wife tonight. He said I looked like a little girl again. I had my sides of my hair up in a little ponytail with a ribbon in it like I did on the way home from Indian Springs. My other hair went under. My hair is getting so long. I wish you were here with me and we could go to the carnival together. I didn't want to ride the scrambler tonight because I don't like it at all without you. I saw so many couples on it and it made me want you here even more. I guess I'll close. Always remember that I love and need you.

Your most lonely but loving wife,
Clellie

P.S. Hugs and Kisses, etc.

✉ *August 15, 1969*   *11:30 PM*

Dear Tony,

Today Raylee (used to work at the plant) came over with her baby and her camera. She took two of us so I'm sending them to you. If you want to keep them with you, you can, but if you don't then send them back. Do you like them?

I went to Stephanie and Luke's reception and wedding. You know, Tony, I guess I still have some belief in the Mormon Church. I can't believe it all but when the Bishop was talking about the Temple marriage it kind of worried me. What if they're right and I can't have you and Chad for all eternity? I want you forever, Tony. Stephanie gave me a corsage to wear while I watched the guestbook. It was a very beautiful wedding. They had quite a few come. They couldn't get Luke's ring on his finger either. It was real cute. Stephanie was a beautiful bride. It reminded me of our reception. They were so happy. When Stephanie and Luke looked at each other they looked so much in love. They looked almost as much as we are, but naturally no one can be as in love as we are. They really loved our gift. They saved a few gifts to open themselves and ours was one of the few. I said goodbye to Lucille Parker and she looked at me and I said, "Be happy forever." She said, "I hope our marriage won't be like yours, across the miles." I almost bawled. My eyes watered and I turned and walked away. Tony, I hate this across the miles junk.

Naomi Grant caught her husband Howard stepping out on her so she filed for divorce. He had the nerve to say that all his other friends stepped out on their wives and their wives still stayed with them so she should. He said he'll get it out of his system pretty soon. What a kook!

All of Stephanie's relatives came up to me tonight and told me how Stephanie had bragged on what a beautiful baby I had. Also Stephanie and her mother are forever bragging on me. How about that? I think Bonnie felt left out tonight because Stephanie didn't have her do anything.

Tony, do you get leaves yet?

Luke and Stephanie are going to live in Twin, Bill and Bonnie are too. Well, all of us are married now: Carrie and Dale, Bill and Bonnie, Luke and Stephanie, Susan and Denny, and you and me (the best ones). The only one left to go is Montana.

I guess I'll go for tonight. I love you, Tony, very much. Be good and stay mine.

All my love and devotion,
Forever, Clellie

P.S. Denny wrecked their little car. He ran into a bull and dented the side. I gave Susan your address to give to Denny.

P.P.S. I called Butler's wife and gave her your address. She's going to come over sometime to see Chad. She doesn't have John's address yet. He should call her tonight. He is still in the States and should leave for Germany tonight or tomorrow. Most important! I love you now and for all eternity!

Hugs and Kisses, etc.

✉️ **August 16, 1969**   *11:00 PM*

Dear Tony,

I just put Chad down to sleep tonight. He's been sleeping from about 10:30 PM or 11 PM until 6 AM so he's doing pretty good. He eats 2 ounces of cereal +5 ounces of milk at 10 AM and 6 PM. He has his bath at 5:30 PM and a sponge bath at 10 AM. He drinks about 2 ounces of water from the cup every time he has cereal. At 2:00 PM and 6:00 AM and 10:00 PM he drinks around 6 ounces of milk. He has a little bit of eczema but it's not serious. I've been using some salve on him that's keeping his skin pretty clear. I weighed and measured him today. He's about 22 inches long and he weighs approximately 12 pounds. He's really growing fast. Boy, it's going to run into money when I switch him from formula to milk, plus baby food and shoes. All in all, he's doing just great. I go to the doctor Tuesday for a check-up for him and me. He also gets two shots, one for polio.

Hon, I was so very happy when I received your letter. I needed and wanted one so bad. I think I would have really been in sad shape if I didn't get one. I love you so very, very much.

Denny and Susan asked if I'd watch their baby tonight so I did. It's good for them to go together once in a while. They wanted me to go with them to the rodeo but I told them I didn't like them very much but if you were here I'd go. I also made Denny promise he'd write you real soon.

Is it really tough there, Tony? Is it worse than AIT? You go to classes or what? It sounds like your haircuts aren't the best but you'd be handsome bald. Do you think you'll drop out? What are you, a corporal? They might not do anything to your pay if they find out they've been overpaying you. It's their mistake, course the Army don't look at it that way do they? I'll send you my graduation picture as soon as I can get a folder and some money. Let me know if you want the frame or not.

All Susan said was that you had told Denny the reason you were angry at me that night you took off in the car and ran into him was because I wouldn't give you any. That's all that was said. Please don't be angry at Denny or Susan. I guess he tells her things you say just like you tell me what he says. I just wanted to know if you talked about anymore. That's all, honest.

Oh, Tony, I wish you were here and in our little apartment again. We were so very happy. I'll wait for you forever, Tony. You're the greatest gift God's given me. You should be with your son as much as possible too. We both need you. Be good and stay mine.

Love eternally.

Your admiring wife,
Clellie

P.S. Hugs and Kisses, etc.

August 17, 1969   *9:00 PM*

Hi Hon,

I love you so very, very much. I wish I was with you right now kissing and hugging you.

You ought to write to your folks. I took Alice, Nancy, and Chad to visit them today. Your dad and Allan were over to the Midway cleaning it up. Your mother was taking a nap. Marie was getting ready to go to a wedding reception. We got there about 1 PM and were home at 2 PM. I visited with Marie for a while and then came home. I didn't want to disturb your mother. Marie is managing the Ponderosa. She starts tomorrow. She's still living with your folks and going out with Lance. She still doesn't know what to do.

After we got home from your folks home, I just dinked around. I washed the baby's diapers and clothes. I fed the baby too much and he threw up, the poor thing. Boy, he is about to wear me out. I go to bed usually around 11:30 PM or midnight and he wakes me up around 5 AM, from then on I have little peace. He's so cute though. He looks so much like you.

I'm going to send a roll of film off to be processed by mail. It'll cost around $2.80 for it, that's still better than five dollars like it is around here. I plan on sending it Wednesday. I can't wait to get them back. I hope they all turn out.

I'm sending a flyer of this groovy get-together happening now. I guess a bunch of bands and kids are all gathering back east for a music festival and it's huge. If you were here maybe we could have gone together.

I guess I'll close for now. I want you to know that I feel very fortunate and so proud to be your wife and to be the one who bore your baby. I love you, Tony, and with each day my love for you grows stronger. Look for a place for me to stay when you can. Be good and stay mine forever!

Eternally yours,
Clellie

P.S. I love you, Cpl. Tony Jolley!!!

Hugs and Kisses, etc.

17 Aug 1969   **Sunday**

Dearest Clellie,

Well how is the sweetest thing alive on this Sunday afternoon? Here it is Sunday and we are restricted to the company area. That means we can't leave the area around our barracks. It's going to be like this for three more weeks too.

I finished the first week of NCO school. I still think I want out. You wouldn't believe the PT they have around here. We have it sometimes two times a day, but I don't think it's half as hard as Basic or AIT at Fort Ord. We have some guys in our company that moan and groan all during the exercises like it's killing them. You'd think that once you've got to something like an NCO school all of the duds wouldn't be here. Most of the duds didn't make it, but we still have a few. You wouldn't believe how many guys are dropping this course after three weeks. I guess the academic standings here are fairly high. You're graded on your written tests as well as your leadership abilities.

Talking about leadership, I'm a team leader right now again. It's the second time in a row I've been picked by the sergeant. Wow, I get to wear a sergeant patch on my collar and everything. Big deal! Spear's on my fire team, we get along better than I thought we would. Here all the leadership positions change about every four days. That means everyone has to be a leader of some kind.

You know I really do miss some of the guys in AIT, like Butler, Kershaw, and Foster. By the way, I want you to call up Butler's wife and ask her for Butler's address, also ask her to tell Butler to give her Kershaw's address so you can send it to me. Kershaw left yesterday to go to Oakland where he'll be sent to Nam. I wonder what's going through his mind right now? I sure wish I was going with him. Well hell, I guess I'll get there soon enough.

Hey Clellie, when do you think you'd get about $400 saved up so you can come down here and live with me? Not really. What I hear is that it's very hard to find a place to live, if only we were rich, Clellie? I sure do miss having you near me though. Well who are you going out with now that you are all slim again? Are you still doing your exercises? How's Chad? Is he still growing? You said in one of your letters that you don't think we gave him enough attention when I was home. I think we did. I think by showing our love for each other around him we'll give him a good outlook on love when he gets older too.

Clellie, I better close for now. I want you to send me some goodies like fudge and brownies.

I love you, Clellie. I guess you're stuck with me forever, because I'm never going to let you go, unless you beat me over the head with a club and tell me to get lost. I miss and need you so much. I don't know what I'm going to do for 23 more weeks without you. I never want to lose you, Clellie, so please love me forever.

Your loving husband,
Tony

P.S. I want you here with me!

NCOC Tony Jolley
104 Co 10th Stu. Bn. 3th Plt
Fort Benning, Georgia 31905

✉ **August 18, 1969**   **11 AM**

Good morning Tony!

I put Chad back to bed after I sponged him, dressed him, and fed him. I also got breakfast over with. How's that?

After I wrote you last night I sat down and watch the movie, it was called "D.I." You know I've seen more pictures since you've been gone on Army and Marine training than I've seen in my whole life, this one showed the worst. The DI was so strict. Anytime one guy would make an error, the whole platoon got punished. It was as bad as you told me it is in the Army. I can see how some guys would crack. I couldn't take it. I don't think my brother Steve could take it and I doubt if Bill can. I just wish I were with you. I love you, Tony, and I'm proud to have you love me.

                                                         11:30 PM

Here I am again. Chad was crying so I had to leave. His stomach's been a little upset.

I went uptown today and helped Mom to pay her bills. I also got a picture folder for my graduation picture so you won't have to worry about breaking any glass. I bought a regular picture folder or mailer to mail it in also. You should be getting it soon. I'm mailing it tomorrow.

This morning I went out to the garden next door and dug some potatoes and picked some corn. A very eventful day, don't you agree?

Tomorrow I have to go to Doctor Peterson for my checkup and Chad's checkup and shot. If it wasn't for our child's shots, I think I wouldn't go. Oh, Tony, they're so embarrassing. I hate it so much. Oh well, this will be the last one until our next baby. It still doesn't make it less embarrassing. I really dread it. I want to ask him for birth control pills too. I kind of hate to take them because they do 'cause you to get a little fatter but there's no other way. I don't want to use a prophylactic, so you'll have to take me a little chunkier.

Ann called tonight and she wants to come in. Dad's been raising heck with her for quite a while, telling her how he's not letting her wind up pregnant like me, and how he should send Alice and her to Saint Anthony like you should've sent me. How about that? Do you know what else I found out? After he found out I was pregnant and before we got married he told Ann that he'd fix my wagon, but good. He was going to send me to a home for unwed mothers. Boy, it'd teach me. Isn't he great? There definitely is something wrong with him. I used to think he was so great but he is in sad shape mentally. He won't let anyone but me go and get Ann. Why? I'm so awful by his standards, oh well.

My mind keeps going back to school days when I first met you. I never dreamed that we'd end up married. I'm so glad. I also remember the day I was washing my bangs when you were here on leave and you decided you wanted to go all the way. I think it was the most remembered love *making of all. I love you so much, Tony. I want to be around you so much, to be able to touch you and know you're near. I miss you so very much. Always love me.*

*All my love forever,
Clellie*

P.S. Hugs and Kisses, etc.

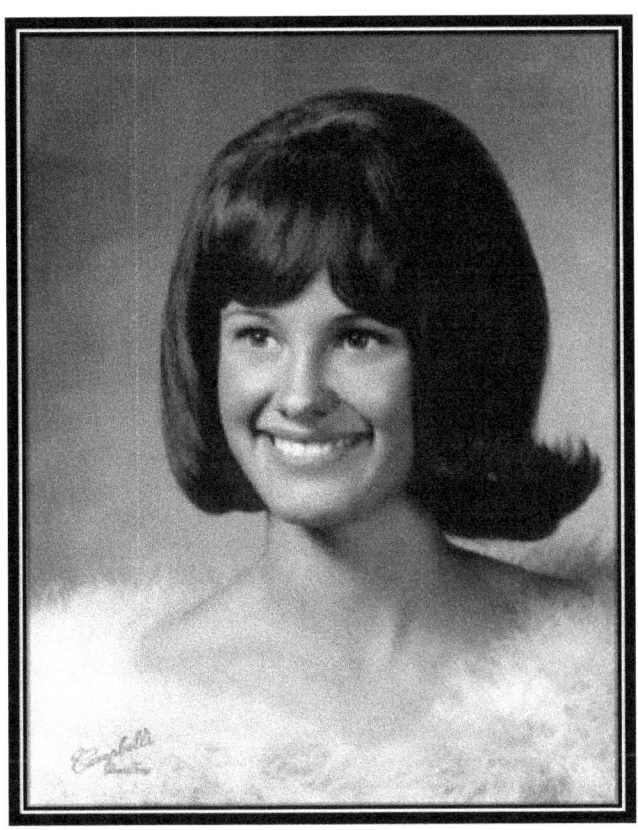

✉ **August 19, 1969**   *11:00 PM*

Dear Tony,

How's the Army treating the most handsome, charming, considerate, and ever so loving husband of mine?

Today I went to Doctor Peterson. They gave Chad a shot and he hasn't felt too good since. He's so cute. Everyone asked me how old he is and I tell them that he's six weeks and they about die. He's so big. He's not fat really either. He's just right. He weighs exactly 12 lbs. 8 oz. How about that? I have to start him on fruits and vegetables as soon as I get a check. More money! He (Doctor Peterson) checked me too and said I was going back like I should be. Things were getting back to normal. He gave me a sample of birth control pills to see how they affect me. If they're okay, then he'll give me a prescription. I can't take them until I start my menstruation. I sure hope they don't make me fat. I do have rh positive blood, but he told me not to worry about it. I do want to read up on it though.

I went out and got Ann today. I also stopped in at Faith's and said hi. I have to go get some more of the kids' stuff tomorrow so I'm taking some gas of his to put my tank on full again. It was full this morning. I mailed that film in finally today to get processed. I also sent my picture. Is it okay?

Ann and Alice told me that they hear requests to Denny all the time on the radio. Also Ann was riding around with some girls and Denny went by. One girl said, "Carter go home to your wife." He didn't hear them. They then discussed how they felt sorry for his wife and wondered who she was and how she could let him do this. It's really sad, isn't it? Oh, Tony, I'm so glad I can trust you and I know that our love for each other is so great and so special. You're the most wonderful guy in the whole world. You'll always love me, won't you? You'll never want anyone else. If only more women could be as lucky as I am to get the greatest man on earth. I'll always love you, Tony, and be thankful that I was so lucky to have you. You know, Tony, you're really mature for your age. You took it so good when we had to get married and you didn't resent me for it. We were so happy living together. At least I was. I'll be here waiting Tony, forever! Be good and always stay mine!!!

Your most admiring and ever loving yet lonely wife,
Clellie

P.S. Hugs and Kisses, etc.

✉ *August 20, 1969*   *10:00 PM*

Hi Hon,

Has Sue Spear quit her job or do you know? I never see her car in front of Penney's anymore. Is she going to go down there or do you know that?

I took Ann out to the farm again to get some more of her things. I took some of Dad's gas. He's supposed to bring them home, so if I have to go out and get them I'll take some gas.

I visited with Susan today for about two hours. We went to King's and saw Bonnie. Everyone I see says how Chad is getting to look more and more like you all the time. Denny's mom saw Chad for the first time today and remarked on how he looked like you. Poor Chad has not been feeling too well tonight, it's an after-effect of his shot yesterday.

Mom got the phone bill today and we owe $8 on it. I don't know how I'm going to pay it next month when I get the check unless I get $130 or if I only pay $20 on our rings. What do you think?

How's everything been going for you? Is it still really hot there? Does it stay really hot all year? When do you think that I can come and live with you? Pretty soon I hope!

I love you more than anything in all the universe. I want to be with you so much.

Yours eternally,
Clellie

P.S. Hugs and Kisses, etc.

August 21, 1969 10:00 PM

Hi Hon,

How's my most wonderful husband doing without his most lonely and miserable wife? I was so very happy to receive your letter. It was so sweet as usual. I love you, Tony, so very much.

Did I tell you that when I was over to Susan's we measured Chad and he is 24 inches long? Well he is. He's 12 lbs. 8 oz. and 24 inches long. I'll have you know that's a big baby for being only seven weeks old. He smiles so much now I can't believe it.

Today I washed our windows and the kids did cupboards. I also went to town and went shopping with Alice and Nancy. It took three hours to get Alice a pair of shoes and Nancy a skirt and blouse. Boy, I was so bushed.

Why were you guys restricted to the company area last Sunday? How come for three more weeks?

So you still have a few duds around there. They'll probably get kicked out though won't they? Are you planning on completing the course? I sure hope so. Like you say, you'll be going to Nam soon enough. Your sergeant must think you're a pretty good leader, doesn't he? How do you like being a leader? I'll bet you're so good...the Best!!

Alice said that she saw Juan Lopez at the carnival. How about that?

Denny stopped by tonight and Ann was outside. He asked Ann if she had seen Barry Jolley because he had a lid for him. How about that?

I have already given Butler's wife your address and she said she'd have him write you as soon as he could. She didn't have his address and she said it'd probably be a week before he could write her. Do you still want me to call again for the address? I know that you really miss all those guys but you'll find some more good buddies before you go to Nam. You have such an attracting personality.

Hon, would it really take $400 to come and live there? I want to get a job and save some money so I can come about the middle of October or November. We don't have to be rich. I'd even starve just to be with you. Are jobs hard to get there? Have you looked for a place yet? I'm not going with no one, slim or otherwise! I don't even care to go anywhere without you. Yes, I'm doing my exercises faithfully for a week now, and not eating too much, but I still have a small (but still there) tummy.

Hon, I'll try to send you some goodies soon. It may not be until next month because of lack of funds, but I'll try. You know Virgil wrote and asked for the same thing. How about that?

Tony, I'm not stuck with you, you're stuck with me, and I'll never let you go unless you prove to me that you don't love me. I hope and pray that you never do. I'd die without you. I'll always love and want you, Tony.

*Your loving wife,
Clellie*

P.S. Chad says Goo to you.

Hugs and Kisses, etc.

✉ **August 22, 1969**

Dear Handsome Hubby of mine!

How's that for an opening? Tony, I miss you so very much!!

Today Mom and I went around again checking for a job. I tried in Rupert and Burley again. I don't know how soon I'll get a job but I'll take any shift at any store just so I can earn money to get to you. King's at the shopping center still has my application. It's in a different folder than the others because I've worked for them before so I'll get one before most; there was about 10 - 15 others with mine. The Heyburn Food Store is going to lose two women the last of September so we're going to try there. Daisy (she works there) is going to put in a good word for us.

Chad's too big for his little bathtub now. I've been trying to get him on a schedule but he's stubborn too and he wants his own schedule. You think he'll get his way? I don't! He wants to go to bed at 7 PM, eat again at 3 AM, again at 6 AM, again at 9:30 AM, again at 2 PM, again at 5 PM. He only wants to take 3 ounces then wait an hour and drink another three. I want him to go to bed at 11 PM, eat at 6 AM, 10 AM, 2 PM, and 6 PM. He's so stubborn but he's going to have your charm. I see you in him more and more all the time. It makes me miss you more than ever. I'm so cranky I can't even talk decent to anyone. I'm also tired of people telling me what to do with Chad. I wish I was away from them all.

I saw Kevin Fortner's mother today. She said Kevin and Jackie had a baby boy on March 27. How about that? It's got blonde hair and blue eyes. It weighs 19 pounds. Mrs. Fortner said that she thinks he looks more like Jackie's brother, Lou. I saw Sue today. She's working at Shelby's.

Well I guess I'll close. I love you so very much, Tony, and I always will. Be good and write often!!!

Your loving wife,
Clellie

P.S. Hugs and Kisses, etc.

✉ **22 Aug 1969** **Friday**

Dear Clellie,

I'm sorry I haven't written to you sooner after my last letter. How's the most beautiful wife a guy could have? Also how's the best-looking and the toughest six-week-old boy in the world?

I got your graduation picture today. The guys that see it really think you're a knockout. I'm also keeping those two other pictures you sent me, the one of the baby and the baby and you. I have them taped to the side of my locker. Everyone also thinks I have a good-looking kid. I'm so proud of both of you, especially you.

You said that Susan told you the reason I was mad that night is because you wouldn't give me any? That's a goddamn lie! I think I'll write Denny a letter and call him a liar. I told him that the reason I was mad was because you got up in the middle of the night and took off. I said, "If she can do it, so can I." I don't know what he's trying to prove, but it makes me downright mad.

I'm glad that everything went all right for you and Chad at the doctor's office. If you take birth control pills, I don't want you getting too fat. Are you still doing your exercises? Is your chubby tummy gone yet? In the picture of Chad I could barely recognize him. He looks so big. He better not have eczema either. What did the doctor say about the eczema?

Clellie, I think you better tell Ann and her friends to keep their punk little noses out of Carter's affairs. I told you when I was home on leave I was pretty sure Carter would get caught stepping out with some little chick. I thought a couple of the talks we had, had made him change his mind. I guess I was wrong. I sure hope not though. I can't see how Carter could do that to a sweet girl like Susan. I could never ever step out on you, Clellie. I just love you too much. If I ever did step out on you, I could never live with myself afterwards. So please don't worry about me stepping out on you.

Clellie, did you ever get the letter I sent to you with the picture of me and you over at Carter's? You never did mention anything about it so I was wondering if you ever did.

You mentioned something in your last letter that you thought I took it pretty good when you turned up pregnant and we had to get married. I don't think it took much of me to take it. On the other hand though, you've never used that subject against me in any argument. We've never ever thrown it in each other's face in arguments, and I pray we never do.

Oh I forgot to mention, you'd never guess what happened to me. Of all the luck, I was climbing up the fire escape to the barracks yesterday, and a step in the ladder gave way. Well I fell all the way down and landed in a cement ditch on my right foot. They took me to the hospital last night and x-rayed my ankle, but found out there was no broken bones. I went back to the doctor today. He put a jillion casts on my foot and gave me a two-week profile. I don't think I'll use the whole profile, but for now I can't walk without my crutches. You wouldn't believe the size of my ankle. I couldn't even lace up my boots after I took them off last night.

Well, Clellie, I better go for now. I'd better not start another page or I'll never get the whole letter in the envelope.

Clellie, I love you so much. I wish that you could come down here and live with me. I sure do miss you. If we could only get enough money saved up. Goodbye for now, Clellie, but always love me.

Your loving husband,
Tony

P.S. Wouldn't you like to be here with me? On a weekend you could come and pick me up, then we could go to our little apartment and go to bed and then we could kiss and go to sleep. Ha ha! You thought I was going to be nasty.

NCOC Tony Jolley
104 Co 10th Stu. Bn. 3th Plt
Fort Benning, Georgia 31905

TIME TO GET A JOB

August 24, 1969   **12:30 AM**

Hi Hon,

How's the greatest lover God ever made? I love you so very much, Tony.

Our child sleeps from 8 PM to 5:30 AM so he's getting better. I still only get about six hours of sleep at night. I'm really cranky because of it. He's broke out all over his body now. I can't tell if it's heat rash yet or not, he just broke out last night.

I found a flash attachment to my camera. It costs $5.50 so it's better than buying a brand-new one. I haven't bought it yet though.

I told you I was cranky. Nancy had been sassing me a lot since she came in. I finally took all I could and I plowed into her. It was awful. I was so mad. I don't know what's gotten into me but it's sad. Guess what? Do you remember that $.25 Canadian piece you told me to keep? Well I had it in my jar and tonight it was gone with other money. Of course everyone denies taking it. I guess I'll have to take all my pennies and put them in an account for Chad. It's sad that I can't trust anyone.

I talked to Susan tonight and she's pretty down in the dumps about Denny, he's never home. Miriam Vargas and what's his name got married last night.

Well I got that roll of film back. I'll send you the best ones. If you can't keep them send them home. I want to get Chad a photo album. The only picture that didn't turn out was with you, me, and Chad.

Here I am among the workers. I now am an employee at Thriftway. I started today. I worked from 1 PM to 10:15 PM. It's really different. I worked everywhere. I have to switch shifts all the time; tomorrow I get off, and Monday and Tuesday I work from 8 AM to 5 PM. It's kind of fun but I have to get me some decent shoes. My feet just ache. After work Susan and I went to the Ponderosa to eat. I probably can't live with you at Fort Benning, but I'm going to when you get out of school.

Honey, I miss you so very much and I know that's why I'm so cranky. I want to be with you. I hate it here without you. I wish we could be together so much. It would be so great. I love you, Tony, more than you can ever imagine. Always love me. Write often!! Be good and stay mine forever.

Your loving wife eternally,
Clellie

P.S. Hugs and Kisses, etc.

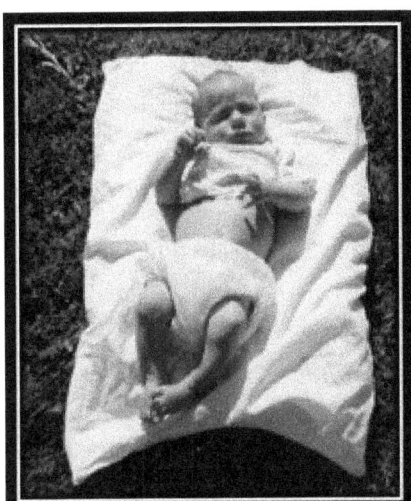

✉ **August 24, 1969**   **9:30 PM**

Hi Hon,

Here it is another lonely depressing Sunday. Boy, I sure hate them without you. I love you so very much. If we were together now I'd smother you with so many kisses.

Today it was so awfully hot and sultry. It still is hot in here. The last three days it's been extremely hot. It got to 101° in Rupert the other day. It doesn't cool down upstairs all night long.

There's supposed to be a real good pediatrician in Twin. He specializes in children and babies. He's dealt with quite a bit of eczema. Chad was clearing up real good until lately and now it's spreading on his neck and chest. It doesn't look real bad, but it's still ugly. His little bottom was really broke out too. His poop is a real weird green now and it shouldn't be. If I can get the eczema cleared up now it probably won't get too bad. Dr. Peterson really hasn't dealt too much with eczema so I've about decided to go to Twin and get him checked. It'll probably cost $25 plus a prescription, his stomach's really been upset too. What do you think? Should I get an appointment?

I hope you're happy now. I slaved over a hot stove and oven today just to get a box of goodies sent. I made fudge, cookies, and brownies. I'm afraid it'll all be melted by the time it gets to you because it's so hot, isn't it? Mom bought the ingredients for it all so thank her too. I made it, packed it, and paid for it being mailed.

I go to work tomorrow morning at 8 AM. I'm up front at the cash register from 8 AM to 10 AM until some more help comes. Boy, those cash registers are complicated. They have four and all of them are different. They had me switched all over yesterday. I was quite confused. I get $1.25 an hour start out pay, then 10% off on what I buy. At the end of 30 days I get 30% knocked off of anything I buy. On Sunday we work nine hours plus an hour for lunch. So when I work on Sundays, I'll be there 10 hours. All other days I work 8 hours plus one hour for lunch, every two hours I get 15-minute breaks. I switch shifts every week. Monday and Tuesday I work from 8 AM to 5 PM, what do you think? I missed Chad but if I save I'll be with you soon. I love you!

Well I guess I'll close for now. Always love only me, will you? You're the most wonderful thing God ever created! I'll love you forever! Be good and stay mine forever!!

Your loving wife,
Clellie

P.S. Hugs and Kisses, etc.

✉ **24 Aug 1969**   **Sunday**

Dear Sweet Clellie,

How's everything? How are you and Chad? It seems so long since I've been home. The time goes so slow here.

I still want to know if you ever received that letter with the picture of me and you in it. This humid weather makes the stamps wet before you put them on, sometimes they don't stick for shit.

My leg really hurts today. It's black and blue from my toes halfway up my knee. It really looks funny. It's also about twice as big as my other foot. It's got a cast on it, and boy, it sure makes my foot itch.

I talked to the CO (Company Officer) about my leg. I asked him if I would get kicked out or recycled because of it. He told me that if I wanted to stay he wouldn't let me go. He also put me on CQ that night. That's when I wrote that last letter to you. Now that I've hurt my leg and have to go around on crutches I've just about decided to drop the course. I want to go over to Nam and get it over with. I'm so damn sick and tired of training.

In your last letter you said you had a phone bill of $8. Maybe this $40 I'm sending you can pay for it. You won't start getting that $160 a month for about six weeks, Clellie. That's what they told me down at finance. I got an advanced pay of $60. That's where this $40 this from. They're still overpaying me. I should have only got $22 like Spear did. Of course when they look up my records to add the extra money on they'll find their mistake.

I better go for now, Clellie. I love you so much. I want you to come down here. I sure wish we could afford it. Love me forever. Clellie, never ever let anything come between the love you have for me and I have for you. I got a feeling something is going to go wrong before I get home. If anything ever happened that would change your love for me, Clellie, I'd never come back home. I'd put in for Vietnam and I'd stay over there, so love me forever, Clellie.

Your loving husband,
Tony

P.S. Use the extra money from the $40 to buy something nice for yourself, maybe something to wear.

P.P.S. You asked me in a letter if we're still restricted to the company area. Yes, we are. We still can't go anywhere.

                                                      NCOC Tony Jolley
                                       104 Co 10th Stu. Bn. 3th Plt
                                   Fort Benning, Georgia 31905

✉ **August 25, 1969**   9:30 PM

Hi Hon,

Each day I work brings in a day closer to living with you. I sure can't wait. I love you so much.

I fouled up a little at work today with the cash register. I guess it'll take me a while to get used to it. There's so much to know and so much to remember but I do like the work. I like working with the public. Tomorrow I go to work again at 8 AM, boy, it wears me out. I only get on the average five or six hours of sleep at night and work all day. Last night the baby was awake most of the night. I'm pretty bushed tonight. Mom's kind of worried about me because the whites of my eyes are going a little yellow. All I know is I'll keep going until I'm with you. I really don't feel so bad at all. I'm just kind of tired. Wednesday and Thursday I work from 10 AM to 7 PM. Friday and Saturday I work from 6 PM to 10 PM and if they need me I'll stay until 12 AM. I don't know what time I'll have to go in Sunday yet. I don't get a day off all week. Everyone else gets two. It's okay though because that'll be more money. It's good to be getting store experience too. It'll be easier to get jobs now.

I saw your mom today. I told her that I was working so I could go to you. The family went to Wagon Days over the weekend. I also saw Denise. Guess where she's working? Ore Ida midnight shift. Lot of good beauty college did her.

Everyone is really nice to me at work. It's so neat not to have everyone gossiping about everyone else.

Tony, do you think you were ready to get married or do you sometimes feel tied down? I love you so very much and I hope you'll always be happy with me. The only thing I regret is that we had to. I love you so much, and I love Chad, but it would have been better. I am glad that we got married when we did because we scraped it pretty close. If we hadn't of had to I would've missed all the wonderful times we had together. I'm so lucky. You're so very special and I'm the one who has you. I love you, Tony, and I always will.

Eternally your wife,
Clellie

P.S. Hugs and Kisses, etc.

✉ **August 26, 1969**   *10:00 PM*

Dear Tony,

Today is Susan's birthday so I got her a card from you and me.

If Chad's not better tomorrow then I'm calling the doctor in Twin. In his poop tonight he had a snotty substance with it. He kept me awake all night last night. I'm about beat.

Work was okay today. I saw Marie today. She came into Thriftway. I guess Andrew's probably not coming home. Rick tried to steal some sunglasses at Thriftway Sunday so I hear. He got caught so your mom made him buy them. Nothing else happened to him.

Alice lightened her hair. She's quite a bit like Ann. She's really snotty to everyone. It's kind of sad. Everyone notices it.

Well I guess I'll close for now. I. I miss you gobs. Stay mine forever.

Love eternally,
Clellie

P.S. Hugs and Kisses, etc.

August 27, 1969 *2:00 PM*

Hi Hon,

How's everything going for you? I'm now on my lunch break and decided to write you a short note.

Today I'm working in the drug section. It is really fun and I don't mind it at all. Hunter Hill came in for a prescription. He ran his finger into a saw at work. It sawed from the tip of his thumb to the end of his thumb, down the middle. He said to tell you hi and that they all wish you were still working there. They sure could use you. Also next time you get home try to get in touch with them.

10:00 PM

Here I am again. Work was fine today. I worked back in the pharmacy today and tomorrow. I really enjoy it. I count out pills and pour medicine in the bottles and gobs of stuff. If you were home I wouldn't like the hours too well, but now it doesn't bug me.

I get my first check Tuesday. Out of that will come shoes, hose, flash attachment, and bulbs. Then I can save the rest of the checks. I figure and hope if Chad doesn't need any doctor appointments or medicine that by November 2nd I'll have about $200 saved. I know it's not a lot but it's better than nothing. That's saving all my other checks.

Ann went to Wagon Days and met Will Sherwood. He said to say hi. He's going back to Vietnam now.

Today I came home from work at lunchtime. I found the card I was mailing to Susan all torn up. One of the kids must've gotten it. Boy, it made me mad. What I want to know is have you been getting all my letters? I've been writing every single day.

Well I guess I'll close for now. I really miss you!!! I love you very, very much. I can't wait until I am with you again.

Your loving but lonely wife,
Clellie

P.S. Hugs and Kisses, etc.

August 28, 1969   *2:00 PM*

Hi Hon,

Here I am again on my lunch break. I got both of your letters today. It was so neat to hear from you again. I love you so much. I also got the money from you. I'll pay the phone bill and put the rest in my account. I'll buy a new outfit just before I'm with you again. I don't have any desire to look nice for anyone else. You're all that's important to me.

By the way you said that I've got two letters a week ever since you've been gone. I only got one last week, but I'll forgive you. It was so nice to get the two today. Yes I got the letter with you and me at Susan's picture in it. I love that picture. It's hanging on my mirror.

Tony, don't ever worry about me changing. My love for you only grows. It's such a beautiful love. We're meant for each other. Really, Tony, I wouldn't be working if it wasn't going to give me money to live with you. You're all that's precious to me. I miss you terribly, Tony. I pray we'll last forever!! I guess I better get back to work. I'll write you later!

August 29, 1969 10:00 AM

Hi Handsome,

Last night I got home from work at 7:30 PM, then I fed the baby and myself. Marie dropped over and asked me if I wanted to go see the shop at the Ponderosa and I said yes. We went over there and she checked out the register. We then were going home and she asked if it would be all right to drive by the Midway to see if Ann was there. She was supposed to meet her there. So I said yes and we went there but Ann's car wasn't there so we were starting to drive away when I saw your dad outside so I said hi to him and he came over to the car and talked to us a few minutes. Then Ann drove up and talked to us for a few minutes. Marie asked if I wanted to go in or go home and I told her I'd rather go home. So she drove me home after she showed me where Kerry lived. Then we just sat in our driveway and talked. I guess your dad got angry at Barry and told him he hated him. It upset him pretty bad. I told you Rick tried to steal sunglasses at Thriftway, didn't I? Well your mother took him back and made him buy them and then she took him to Ted and told him to press charges if he wanted because she wanted it stopped now. Ted didn't press charges. Rick had told Ted f—k you when he got caught.

I'm glad you're proud of me, Tony, and our son. It makes me feel neat. I love you.

I figured it up again and with my job alone I should save about $375. I hope I'll have that much. I'm going to take that $40 I've decided and pay the phone bill and get me a coat for winter in Twin. Before I get to live with you I want to buy a pantsuit, a dress, two Levi's, and a pair of shoes. Thank you for the $40.

Honey, please don't write to Denny and cuss him out. I just wanted to know what was really said. I love you so much!

Yes, I'm still doing my exercises. I still have a small tummy. It makes me so mad. It'd better go down. Ticks me off so bad. Chad's eczema's gone again. It can't be bad. It's just a touch of it and he'll outgrow it. It's cold kind of now. It's getting winter so it should get better. I need to get a few winter clothes for him and some shoes. Babies cost so much you know but I'd never give him back because he's ours, with God's help our love created him. I love you, Tony, and my love will never die. Never. I know you wouldn't step out on me. I also know that you'll have lots of temptation. You're so good-looking that they'll always be someone after you. I'm glad we have the love we do.

Tony, I think your accident prone. Honestly, you're so lucky you didn't get hurt worse. Please be careful. I worry about you so much. How does it feel now? Are you going to finish the school?

I can't wait to be with you again. If I can get the stuff bought for me and the baby, I can save out of the checks when I start to get $160 a month. I should be able to save quite a bit.

You're ignorant. You put nasty thoughts on my mind. Boy, wouldn't I love to pick you up on the weekend and take you home with me.

Take care of your leg, Tony. You have such strong hairy legs. I don't want you banging them up. Take good care of my property. I love you, Tony, so much.

Your loving wife,
Clellie

P.S. Hugs and Kisses, etc.

August 30, 1969　　　　　　　　　　　　　　　*11:00 AM*

Hi Hon,

Guess who Hope went to breakfast with after work last night? Lance King! She told me quite a while ago that she heard they were getting a divorce and I said they planned on going off for a week by themselves to make sure. Well she asked Lance about it and he said that they were not. Boy, I'll bet Marie will be angry at me for telling Hope. Anyway Hope thinks Lance's really nice and good-looking. How about that? Lance came into the drugstore last night and I said hi to him.

I worked last night from 6 PM to 10:45 PM. Susan came over to see me. So did Denny and Barry. They were all there at the same time. After work, Susan and I went to the Russet. It's in new hands now and it's called the Kitchen Keeler. I was so hungry for a hamburger and a milkshake. Boy, they were luscious. I know I have to watch my weight, but I hadn't had one for so long. I paid for Susan's too 'cause she bought mine last Saturday. With two hamburgers, a large milk, and a milkshake it only came to $1.39. How's that? $.40 hamburgers are luscious.

Molly's been telling her friends that she wanted to leave here because I'd gotten too snotty and mean. It was horrible living here with me. Funny but Mom told her she had to move. Anyway she told them that I used to be so sweet and all of a sudden I changed. I said sure I have, I don't cook for her any more or wash her clothes, do her hair every day, and I don't like paying my share, and she bums off Mom. She never does a stick of work here. Well anyway she's moved, but she still wants to eat here until she gets her groceries.

Susan and Denny have to move. They were going to buy the trailer house so they gave their landlord notice and he has someone to rent it already. They went out to see if the trailer house was empty because they had already informed the guy who owned it that they were going to buy it. He sold it to someone else for cash. Ugly. Now they can't find anywhere else to move.

Chad's doing just fine, he is growing still, and he's so cute. He looks so much like you and I think he's getting spoiled a little too. Right now he's in bed crying. He goos and smiles quite a bit now. I can't wait until you see him and most important I can't wait till I see you. Oh, Tony, I miss you so very much. I love you, Tony, and I need you. Be good and stay mine forever.

Your loving and lonely wife,
Clellie

P.S. Hugs and Kisses, etc.

✉ **August 31, 1969**   **2:30 PM**

Dear Handsome Husband,

Sure love you so much. I wish that I could be with you.

I gave Chad a bath today and he splashed all over the table and floor. It's so cute. He just loves it. We're going to start putting him in the tub.

Well I have to be going to work I love you so much, Tony, and I can't wait until I'm with you. I miss you gobs and gobs.

11:35 PM

Here I am again. I worked from 6 PM to 11:05 PM. How about that? Tomorrow Sunday I work from 12 noon to 10 PM. Boy, it'll be a long day. I can feel it. Oh well more money to see you on. Oh, I'm so excited to be with you. I just can't wait. I love you so very much.

I have to buy my uniforms. I don't know how much yet, I have two. Boy, they're ugly yuck! They'll hold it out of my check. I have to charge anything I get there and they hold it out to subtract the percentage. I charged a flash attachment $5.50, two batteries at I think $.50 each, and some flashbulbs at $1.56. I don't know how big my check will be but at the end of August 31 I'll have put in around 59 hours. Then they hold out what I charge, and my uniforms. Not bad. I really don't mind working. It passes the time pretty good.

I cut Ann's hair today and I'm afraid I didn't do so hot. I tried to tell her I didn't want to cut it so short but you know Ann. We get along quite a bit better than we did.

Tony, I want you so much. I love you like never before. It's such a strong love. It keeps growing. I just thank God I have someone so special like you, someone who won't step out on me. I haven't worried about it for such a long time. Be good and stay mine!

All my love eternally,
Clellie

P.S. Hugs and Kisses, etc.

✉ **29 Aug 1969**   **Friday**

Dear Clellie,

I'm really sorry that I haven't written you, Clellie, but we have really been busy this last week. We've been on the go every day, and I've had to walk everywhere on crutches. I'm supposed to stay on them for another week and a half but I'm going to try and get off them.

I'm sending the pictures of you and the baby back to you. I'm keeping the one of me and the baby, because now I have one of the baby, you and the baby, and me and the baby.

Clellie, I've got to go now because I have a lot of studying to do. Our big land navigation test is tomorrow and it's really rough. Just remember, Clellie, that I love you now and forever. I love you very much, Clellie, and I never want to lose you.

Your loving husband,
Tony

P.S. I want you so bad.

                                                                    NCOC Tony Jolley
                                                            104 Co 10th Stu. Bn. 3th Plt
                                                          Fort Benning, Georgia 31905

✉ **August 31, 1969**　　　　　　　　　　　　　　　　　　　　*10:45 PM*

Hi Hon,

How's the Army been treating the best-looking guy in the world? You are you know.

This morning Susan called and asked me if I'd rent an apartment with her for a month. Shock. She said that they moved all of her stuff over to her mother's place. Her and Denny discussed it and decided it would be better to have a month separation. It makes me about sick. Susan said she just can't take it like this anymore. She'd like him to go into the service because she hopes that would straighten him up. I told her that I would like to but I couldn't afford half the rent, food, and utilities because I wanted to save as much as I possibly can so I can live with you. She said that she was going to get the apartment and she just wanted me to stay with her because she don't want to be alone. I told her I couldn't just stay with her without paying my share. I don't know what will happen. Maybe I'll ask her to stay here for that month and pay Mom a little for food and buy her own milk for Justin. I'm going to talk to her tomorrow. She doesn't want to stay with her mom. It just makes me sick how people love each other one day and are not sure the next. I guess they haven't found our kind of love.

I worked from noon to 10:15 PM tonight. Boy, I'm pooped. It's just been swamped all day. My feet are so sore and so are my legs. I need to wear support hose now. I finally get tomorrow off. It's way overdue. I believe Estelle Ford's going to try and get a job there.

Have you heard anything from Butler yet? Do you want me to call his wife for you and get his address?

Tony, I miss you so much. I'll always love you.

Your loving wife,
Clellie

P.S. About when do you think you'll graduate so I know about when I can be with you? Chad's so big and cute. I've seen so many babies that are three or four months old and they're smaller than him. I'm so proud of him.

September 1, 1969   10:30 PM

Dear Hon,

Here it is the beginning of another month. I sure do wish they'd go by faster than they are. They seem to go so slow. About 2 ½ months I'll be with you to hug and kiss you etc. It'll be so neat to feel your touch again. You're so good at that sort of thing.

I took Chad up to Thriftway today. Everyone thinks he's cute and big. They asked me what special food I was feeding him to make him so big. He's not fat just right and long. I gave him a bath in the big tub tonight and he gooed, laughed, and kicked. He's so darn cute. I can't wait until you see him again.

The family went up town today and we ate at the Arctic Circle. I spent one dollar for fries, cheeseburger, and a milkshake. I couldn't eat it all though. That's the only meal I had all day. I weigh around 116 or 117. My tummy is going down slowly but surely. How does that sound?

I have a store meeting tomorrow morning at 7 AM at Bryant's. They buy our breakfasts. But early! I should get paid tomorrow too. I hope so, the baby needs formula and food and I need some work shoes. I'm wearing support hose too. I don't want varicose veins.

Chad's eating 7 ounces of formula now before he goes to bed at 9 PM for the last time. Oh, he's so big.

I tried to get a hold of Susan today but no one was at her home. I hope to get a hold of her tomorrow. I work from 10 AM to 7 PM tomorrow.

Boy, I sure would like to go to a drive-in. I can't remember when we ever saw all of the show. You were so good at turning me on. I also adored just looking at you. You're so darn good-looking. I'll love you forever, Tony. Always be mine and love me.

Love eternally,
Clellie

P.S. Hugs and Kisses etc.

✉ **September 2, 1969**   9:15 PM

Hi Hon,

How's life been treating you? Fine I hope. I sure do love you.

I had to get up at 5:30 AM this morning to feed Chad and get ready for the meeting at 7 AM. It lasted until 8:30 AM. I won a prize of dusting powder. I worked from 10 AM to 7 PM, and I'm pretty tired.

I got paid today. I had to charge a flash attachment $5.50, batteries one dollar, and flashbulbs $1.56 plus money for rent of the uniform. Altogether it took $10.51 from my check. I had made $76. I have three hours overtime. After they took $10.51, and the taxes I have $55 left. I put $46 directly into the bank. I have about $9 for shoes. I also received the Army check. I went after work and got $12 worth of SMA and baby food. Quite a bit. I think the baby food should last more than a month, I hope so anyway. I'll pay the other bills as soon as I can. I'll write and tell you what I use it all for. In my account now I have $64. Pretty good start.

I called Susan tonight. She's doing real fine. She's decided to stay with her mom. Denny wants to save his money for a trailer house. He called her Sunday. She plans on going with her parents on a vacation to Canada for a week next week. I'm going to Twin Saturday to look for a coat. They're cheaper there right now than they are here. It's getting pretty chilly here now. Anyway I'm taking Mom, Susan, and Nancy.

Hope had me go over and look at the bottom of Ashley's feet. Her feet are slowly going white and losing their feeling. I'm afraid that it'll paralyze her. Some cancer does take away your feeling slowly.

You remember Fred Williams, the music teacher from Minico? He died from sugar diabetes.

Your record album by the Turtles with "She'd Rather Be With Me" you know? Anyway I grounded our stereo from the kids, and one day Alice decided she'd play it anyway while I was gone to work. Now the song "She'd Rather Be With Me" skips at the first. I could have killed her. It made me so mad. I'm so sick of them getting into my stuff!

Well I better close for tonight. I love you so much. I'm now $64 closer to you. I can't wait. I miss you so much.

Your loving and lonely wife,
Clellie

P.S. Hugs and Kisses, etc.

September 3, 1969 *9:00 PM*

Hi Hon,-

How's the greatest guy in the world doing? I want you to know I miss you so terribly. I'm so lonesome without you. Do you know what I dreamed last night? I dreamed that we were together and we would make out but just when we were about to undress and go all the way someone or something would interrupt us so we couldn't. I'll have you know that was the most frustrating thing I've known. Sad. In about two months, we'll be able to finish the job.

Chad's two months old today, and he goos pretty loud now. He's so darn cute. He has a horrible temper! When he wants something, he wants it now. Sort of like his dad don't you think? He was eating this morning and it sounded almost like he was calling for you, sort of like Daddy. Course it's probably a coincidence but it was cute.

I bought a pizza tonight for the family for babysitting for me. I'm saving about $30 a month when the kids and Mom watch him so I figured they're worth it. Don't you?

Work was okay today. Tomorrow I work from 9 AM to 6 PM and Friday the same. I work in the camera section. Do you know that Sunday some little kids stole 24 put-together planes at $.59 a piece without our knowing?

Almost all my nails are short now. After I pushed those keys on the cash register they've busted off.

How's your leg and foot been doing? Tony, I love you so very, very much. I can't wait to be with you.

All my love forever,
Clellie

P.S. Here's a letter from Juan that came today. I paid $25 on the ring. We only owe $75. I got some shoes for work. Boy, they are great!!! I love you so much!!!

✉ *September 3, 1969*

Dear Clellie,

How are you and Chad getting along? Is he getting mean yet?

I just got your letter today saying that you got the letters I sent you.

Clellie, I sure do miss you. You wouldn't believe all the things that have been going through my head. I want so much to embrace you and kiss you.

I've been having nasty dreams all the time now. There's always something to do with sex and every dream I've had for the last week. They're driving me crazy. Over the weekend we didn't get one night pass, but we did get to go on privileges. I went to about three NCO clubs and they're really nice. You have to be a corporal or above to get in. They serve beer and mixed drinks too. I really got loaded. I guess I got loaded so bad because I couldn't be with you and I was depressed. I drank about six dollars' worth of whiskey sours, Tom Collins, and Bloody Mary's.

Clellie, I wish I was with you. The thought of holding you drives me nuts. When I get home, Clellie, I'm never going to leave that beautiful body of yours alone. It might be the hot weather down here makes me so horny, but I sure am. Are you?

Well Clellie, I got to go now. I love you very, very much and I will forever. You'll never have to worry about me, because you're the only one for me. Love me. I'm going to love you in more than one way when I get home.

Your loving husband,
Tony

P.S. I sure do love you, Miss Clellie.

NCOC Tony Jolley
104 Co 10th Stu. Bn. 3th Plt
Fort Benning, Georgia 31905

September 4, 1969   **9 PM**

Dear Tony,

Here it is growing late again. It seems that all I do is work, bathe, and sleep. Sad life. At least I get sleep.

Are you getting pretty handy with your crutches yet? I'll bet it's pretty difficult to get around on them. Boy, that leg wouldn't be in the least bit handy to go to bed with, would it? Not that we do anything. Just piddle a little here and there.

How are your barracks? Are they nicer than your others? How's your weather there? It's getting quite chilly here. We're going to have to get some more fuel now.

What kind of studying are you doing? Do you go to regular classes? If you do, how many hours a day do you stay in class? How many are you out, and what do you do with the rest your day? What do you do in land navigation? I'm sorry about all these questions but I'm really curious as to what you have to do. Please do tell me.

Tony, you'd better use those crutches as much as you can to get completely better. We turned our furnace on tonight because it's getting so chilly.

Just think I'll be with you to celebrate Thanksgiving, your birthday, our first wedding anniversary, Christmas, and the New Year. We will be together again. That's the best celebration, the one where we'll be together as a family, like it was always meant to be.

At work there are some pots and pans on special. It's one fry pan, a 5-quart pan, 3-quart pan, and 2-quart pan with lids. They're Teflon. Real nice but the set would cost $25. They're on special. I'd like it real bad but I want to be with you more so I'll wait.

Work was pretty good today. I worked in the camera department. It's pretty fun. I will work there again tomorrow.

I can't wait to be with you, I wish time would go faster. It seems to be creeping by. Even with me working it doesn't go so fast. It just drags by. You've been gone to Georgia for a month and two days. I miss you terribly, Tony, and I want you so very much.

Your most loving wife,
Clellie

P.S. Hugs and Kisses, etc. forever

✉ **September 5, 1969** *2:00 PM*

Hi Hon,

I just received your letter today. I was so pleased. Made me feel so neat. I want you to know that you have the power to turn me on even in a letter. I had so many goose bumps that it was funny. I can almost feel your touch, and your kiss. I miss you so very much.

I want to explain why I dated one letter two different days. If you check the time on the letters, one was during my lunch break at work and one was after I got home from going to eat with Ashley. It was about 12:30 AM or so I think so it was the same night. Do you see?

Well I got to get back to work. I love you enormously. I will now and forever!!!

9:30 PM

Here I am again. I'll have you know that my mustache has gotten darker here lately. Talk about embarrassing! It's really not real bad but it is enough. Mom says it's because I have an imbalance of hormones. Sad.

Sandy Jefferson, you know the one who used to run with Flora with the funny glasses? She got married the day after we did. Anyway she's PG and due in October. She was in the store today. Her husband's going for a physical this month. She's afraid he's going to get drafted. She doesn't want to live at home if he does, so she asked if I'd share an apartment with her when he does. I told her I was going to go with you in November until about the last of January. She still wants me to when I get back. What do you think? She wants to be with someone who's waiting too. Manny Moore's in the Marines now. He's been away for about four or five months. His wife Dottie is also expecting. You know that she lost her first baby? Well she's sick again. She's got to be real careful. Also Ron Jefferson's writing every week to a girl named Janey. He wrote to Sophia Meyer and told her he didn't think he loved her anymore after she waited for him for almost 2 years, pretty sad.

Work was pretty good today. I'll bet I wrapped more presents than I have in my life. I'm working, or I worked today, in the camera section. It's pretty fun. I think he's going to ask me to be a plain cashier upfront, but I like being relief better so I don't know what will happen.

Boy, Chad goos louder every day, he gets his mouth full of food and goos. Food goes everywhere. He's so cute. He's on fruit now. He also drinks 7 ounces of milk five times a day, half a cup of cereal, three quarters jar of baby food, and about 2 ounces of water. He's mean just like his daddy.

I got the baby a photo album. It's really mod. You'll have to see it. It cost a dollar. I also got one dollar of different yarn ribbons for my hair, one pair of Wranglers at about $5.75, and a card for you. Fun.

You're a corporal now aren't you? You'd better watch drinking. You might stumble and hurt your other foot. Then what would you do? (chuckle, chuckle!) Yes, I'm what you say, horny! Bad! I want you so much. Wow! Your letter made me want you worse. I'm glad that I'm the only one for you because you're absolutely the only one for me. I love you so much I wish I could be with you now. It would be so neat. I love you so.

Your most loving wife,
Clellie

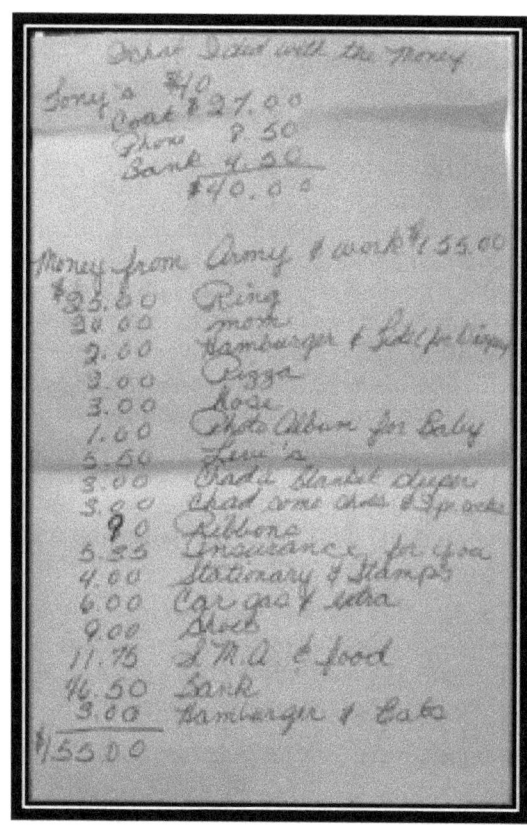

September 6, 1969　　　　　　　　　　　　　　　　　　　　　　　　　　**9:20 PM**

Hi Hon,

Here I am again. I guess you've looked over the list. I feel so ashamed to think I spent all that money. In fact it makes me down right ill. Don't hate me. I had to get a coat, and I tried for the cheapest I could get and the warmest. I think it's really neat. I got it at Sears. All the prices have gone up on coats. It's navy blue with white fur around the hood, down the middle, and around the cuffs. It goes to about 3 inches above my knees. It zips up with wooden buttons to snap. I'll take a picture with me in that. You know how bad I needed one. I was going to get one like Mom's, but they weren't as thick as Mom's or quite the same and they were $27. I went all over Twin and ended up with this one. I hope you like it. The phone bill was $8.50 with tax. I got some Tide for Chad's diapers and a little bit of hamburger for Mom watching Chad. Also I bought $2 of a $3 pizza for the kids babysitting and Mom. I got a little photo album for Chad for his pictures. I had to get him shoes and socks because it's getting colder. I bought him a blanket sleeper. It's some Thermo sleepers with feet. They're normally six dollars down here and I got it for $3 in Twin. He needed one for winter so I got it for him. I also bought me some ribbons of yarn for my hair. In the bank now we have $69. Oh Tony, I'm so ashamed for spending so much. I'm sorry.

Tomorrow I go to work from 2 PM to 12 AM. Ugh! But it's approximately 9 dollars closer to you.

Nancy bought Chad a rattle to set on his highchair. It sticks and he can hit it back and forth. Nice.

Susan, Mom, Nancy, Ashley, Chad, and I went to Twin today. We went to Cousin Pat's place and dropped Chad and Mom off then we went shopping. We got back to Pat's and she gave me a whole bunch of clothes for the baby again. Also she gave me a swing jumper for the baby. All it needs is a seat. I think I can someday get a combination of car seat and jumper seat for $5. She also gave me a stroller that needs a little work on the seat and shade. I could probably make a shade for it. She also gave me a bassinette. Nice. She gave me so much. It's really saved us quite a bit of money.

I want you to know that your son now weighs 15 pounds, and your wife weighs 116 pounds. How about that? Chad's not really fat either. He's just big. I can't believe it. No one else can either. Boy, when you created a baby you really did.

Minico and Burley played football last night. Minico beat 27 to 7. Pretty neat.

Susan wanted me to go to the show with her and her sister Carla from Utah. I told her I really didn't feel like it. I had a headache when I got home from Twin. Chad and work wear me out to where I don't feel like doing too much at all.

Tony, I love you so very, very much. I wish so much that we were together. Chad should be around you too. It's so neat to be your wife. I remember how much and for how long I wanted to get married. It seemed almost hopeless once, but here I am Mrs. Tony Jolley. We can legally go to bed and kiss and be real lovey. Oh honey, I want so much to be in your arms and feel your kiss and touch. It's been so terribly long. I love you so much.

Your loving wife,
Clellie

P.S. Hugs and Kisses, etc.

✉ *September 7, 1969* *12 midnight*

Hi Hon,

I love you so very, very much, Tony. I miss you so terribly.

I went to work today from 2 PM to 12 AM. Boy, I sure am bushed. The bosses are talking about putting me on steady as front cashier. I would work one-week 8 AM to 5 PM and the next 3 PM to midnight. I would get every other Sunday off, every Monday, and every other Tuesday. I don't want to take it though because from 11 PM to midnight I'd be alone except the pharmacist and so many drunks come in then. Just tonight (Sunday) there were quite a few. On this relief I get every third Sunday off, every third Saturday, every third Monday, and every third Tuesday and Monday. Like relief number one, I get Sunday off. Relief number two, I get Monday and Saturday, and relief number three, Monday and Tuesday. Every week I change reliefs. Also only every third week do I work late, and not very often to 12 AM. The only hang-up is I only get one Sunday out of three off.

Tony, after you get home and out of college, I don't want to work. I want to be able to enjoy our children, bake goodies, and take care of our own home. When I work I don't feel like doing any of them. What do you think?

Guess what? I've decided that when I come to live with you I'm getting a padlock for our bedroom door and putting all your clothes out of the big room, on my bed, and locking our door. I just can't trust the kids at all. Also when you get home on leave we're going through your clothes and taking out the ones that no longer fit because we might just as well give them away. Don't you agree?

Do you know that while Alice was living with Dad she went to a slumber party and the police raided it because there were boys? The only reason Alice didn't get caught was because she was outside. Also Alice wrote a letter to her friend. If she'd asked me for a stamp I would've given her one. Anyway I saw she had a stamp on her letter and I asked her where she got it. She said she bought it. Well last night I went to put one on your letter and one stamp was gone. The night before I had torn the corner off the stamp so I went and looked at Alice's letter and her stamp had the corner on it. I know a stamp's not much but she lied. Well this morning I asked her again about it and she said she bought it so I told her my proof. Then she said she found it in the drawer in the kitchen because she doesn't go in my room. I asked her four times and she still said she found it and she started to cry. I told her bawling doesn't make me believe it and I asked her again. She quit crying and just looked down, tugging at her skirt. Boy, those kids can lie looking you square in the eyes.

Hon, all I could think about today was you. I miss you so very much. I love you, Tony, and I'll never leave you.

Your passionate wife, Clellie

P.S. I love you, Daddy dear!! Hugs and Kisses, etc.!!!

September 8, 1969   **9:30 PM**

Hi Hon,

How's the handsomest Army man that ever was or ever will be? I sure wish I could be with you right now don't you? Boy, what I wouldn't do. Yesterday at work that girl whose husband's in Nam, and lives in the apartment where Susan used to live, came into Thriftway. She's all excited. She is leaving this weekend for Hawaii to meet her husband for his R&R. She was so excited she could hardly stand it. I was so happy for her. She only has five or six more months to wait.

Denny goes over and visits Susan every single night. Susan said that she didn't figure that was doing much good for their separation. The purpose of it was to see if he could settle down. He's not getting anything accomplished by going over and seeing her every night and then taking off. I don't know what's going to happen but I hope they can get together and make a go of it don't you? I hope Denny can make Susan happy and settle down. But that's a lot of hoping. If Denny could only be more like you, Susan wouldn't have a bit of trouble. You're such a wonderful husband and I love you so much for being like you are, faithful, understanding, sweet, and mature.

I got up this morning at 6 AM to feed Chad his bottle. At 7:30 AM Ann came and asked me to take her to school because her ride forgot her. Then when I got home I fed Chad his cereal, bathed him, and fed him his bottle. He just loves to bathe in the big tub. He goos and laughs and kicks his legs and hands. Water goes everywhere. He cries when you take him out. He's so cute. Then I started the washing, cleaned our bedroom, mopped it and washed the sheets, swept the kitchen, and did the dishes. Then I went to town and put all our pennies in an account for Chad. There was $14.50. So we now have an account for him. I fed Chad peaches at noon, and his bottle at two. I'm rather tired.

Mom got rid of Mitch thank goodness. He was telling everyone he was supporting her, the lazy thing, then he called her lazy when he never works. It made Steve so mad he told Mitch not to call Mom lazy around him or in this house. Mitch turned to Steve and said, "Well how about you, you're lazy." Mom got mad and really told him off and Steve told Mitch that he never knew him to work more than a day. It was kind of cute. Mom's going to court tomorrow. Faith called and said that Dad didn't want to go as long as he had Mom paid up on the 15th of each month. Mom still plans on taking him to court and get the money to come through the court. I don't know yet what will happen.

Did I tell you that Molly finally moved out? I'm so glad.

I informed Mom that I might live with another girl in an apartment when you go to Nam (if you do). I'm sick and tired of everyone borrowing and taking my things without my permission. Mom feels kind of bad but I just can't put up with it very much longer. It seemed so good when we were together to be able to leave money or whatever I wanted around and not *have to worry about having it swiped. I asked them what they were going to tell their friends when they asked them why I had a padlock on my door. I told them they'd better tell them the truth or I certainly would when I got back. Meany, aren't I? They're both grown-up girls now and shouldn't be stealing my things. Did I tell you that while Alice was down at Pat's she took a pack of cigarettes and put them in her suitcase? Well she did so when Pat told Mom, Mom told her if she wanted to smoke to buy her own pack and smoke in front of us all, but she won't.*

Well I guess I better be closing for now. Tony, love me forever, please? I need you so very, very much.

Eternally yours with buckets of love,
Clellie

P.S. Hugs and Kisses, etc.!!

How I'd like some etc. right now!!

 **8 Sept 1969**   **Monday**

Dear Clellie,

How's Chad, and everyone in Burley doing? How are you especially Clellie? Are you taking care of that ever so wanted body of yours? I sure hope so.

I just got your letter saying that you have received all my letters so far. I'm sure glad you got them all.

I received the goodies you sent me about 3 days ago. There was a great big hole in the box, and the brownies were a little stale, but I still thought they were delicious. I'm kinda glad that you're working too, Clellie, but in a way I wish you could stay with the baby. That's one reason why I love you, Clellie. You're always thinking of ways to help out like making money. You don't care how much discomfort it is for you. You just always think of everyone else before yourself. Boy, I sure do love you, Clellie.

I did mention all the pictures, Clellie. I told you the ones I was keeping and I sent the rest home to you.

You asked me what kind of studying I am doing. We're doing just about everything. We have land nav, communications, combat intelligence, radio intelligence, squads in the offense and defense, and about 30 more. You also asked me what I did with my spare time. Well I don't have any. We're doing work on all weekdays until 5:30 PM at night, then we have to clean the barracks, and we also have study hall. Sometimes we have night classes out in the field until 12:00 AM at night. I don't really study for any of my classes, Clellie. I can't seem to get interested in the course.

I'm off my crutches. I only used them for 4 days. That's because I couldn't put any weight on my foot at all. After hobbling around for another week, it doesn't really feel too bad. I went to the doctor about it today and he put me on profile again until the 15th, but I'm not going to use it. I was on profile last week, but I still did all my PT. During PT classes, now we have to teach the class. It's really different. But it is a good experience.

So Chad really has a temper? I hope he raises hell with you all the time. I'm sure you're exaggerating when you said that it sounds like he says Daddy. It sure was sweet of you to say it though.

Clellie, I really do love you. I can't seem to get used to the idea of being away from you. It seems that the longer I'm away from you, the more I want to be near you. You don't realize how much you mean to me. You're the most wonderful thing that could have ever happened to a guy.

I sure wish I was home and we could get in my '62 Chevy. We would go park on the Canal Bank. Then we can get in the back seat and make out like we used to. Wouldn't that be neat?

Clellie, I better go for now. Remember I'll love you forever. I have to love you, because I don't know what I'd do without you. Love and want me forever like I do you, Clellie. We've got a real original and unique love going for us, and I pray we'll always love each other like we do. (Anyway at least I do)

Your lonely, loving husband,
Tony

NCOC Tony Jolley
104 Co 10th Stu. Bn. 3th Plt
Fort Benning, Georgia 31905

September 9, 1969 **12 midnight**

Dear Tony,

How's my greatest guy ever doing? Fine I hope. I sure do love and miss you.

Well I had to buy Chad a new box of cereal today. He really gets a stomachache on the high-protein cereal, poor little thing. He sure is a doll though. He sleeps from 7 PM to 6 AM. That's pretty darn good for a baby. I started him on vegetables for tonight. I gave him carrots. Boy, does he love carrots!! I sure wish you could be around him. He's such a little doll and goos and smiles so cute. I'm really proud of him. It seemed so good to be able to be with him all day. I can't wait until we can be together as a family.

Susan and I went to the show. It was real neat. It was, "The Longest Day." It was about D-Day. Tony, I don't want you to be in war. I love you so very much and I worry about losing you. I know I shouldn't, but you're so special I can't help but worry.

Do you know what? At the show the manager turned on the air conditioner of all things and everyone there about froze to death. Well Susan and I finally got up and went to the manager and asked him to turn it off because everyone was freezing. So he said he'd turned it down which he never did. Finally about half an hour before it was over another girl went and asked him to turn off. Well he talked to her for about 15 minutes, and about five minutes before it was over he went and shut it off. Boy, ticked me off!! After the show we went to the Ponderosa and had cake then we came home. The show started at about 8:30 PM and it was a two hour and 45-minute show.

One of Ann's friends was telling her how a friend really liked Denny Carter. Ann asked her if she knew that he was married and she said sure but him and his wife were in the process of a divorce. It's really sad. Susan said that at the end of the month she's going to tell him that he has to stay home with her now every night or get a divorce. She said that she can't go on like this anymore and that she has given up. She said that her and Denny shove the fact that they had to get married in each other's face all the time. She said that he didn't want to get married as soon as they did and neither did she. I told her that I was so glad that we have never shoved it in each other's face and that I thought we both wanted to get married soon and it just sped it up a little. Oh Tony, I'm so very happy that I have you. I love you so much.

Hon, did you tell Denny when you were home that I was so sore I could barely walk? I told Susan that I thought Denny made up most of his stories. I just like to know this. I guess Susan told their old neighbors that too! Kind of made me a little angry at her. Oh well! Maybe I'm too modest. What do you think?

Tony, I love you so very, very much. I'll always need and want you. I depend on you so much. I can't wait until I can be with you.

Your loving wife,
Clellie

P.S. Hugs and Kisses, etc.

✉ **September 10, 1969**　　　　　　　　　　　　　　　　　　　　**11:30 PM**

Hi Hon,

Well just call me Ding-a-ling for putting the stamp and address upside down. Takes a real wizard, and boy, here I am! It's really my day. I guess you can tell by that that I'm a little sleepy. Really it's not so bad. Out of approximately 195 letters or more one upside down is a pretty good average don't you agree? You don't? Well ___ __! I was going to take the stamp off and try again, but I figure you have to love me through smartness (very rare), and dumbness. Boy, am I glad I'm rich or I'd be in sad shape when it comes to getting your love. Seriously Tony, I love you so very, very much and oh wow, what I wouldn't give to be with you right now with your arms securely around me.

Speaking of security… it's raining, lightning, and thundering something atrocious. Why don't you come on home and make me feel secure again? What if lightning would strike our house? Pretty darn spooky. If you were here and I was in your arms I wouldn't be afraid. In fact I probably wouldn't even notice the rain. This is the first rainstorm Chad's been in. I hope he doesn't get spooked.

Speaking of Chad. He is a spoiled little boy! When he wants something he wants it right now or he turns red in the face, bellers, and clutches his fist. Cute kid! Well you can bet his mommy just lets him lay there and throw his cute little tantrums. He's so darn cute and lovable when he's good. He threw up all over tonight. Everyone here's got the flu. I had the stomach flu yesterday and a little today. I'm afraid Chad will get something if he hasn't already.

I went to work today from 2 PM to 11 PM. Boy, it was a slow night. Tomorrow I go from 12 PM to 9 PM. This week I work four days of the late shift. One day for the cosmetics, tonight the camera, one for the prescriptions, and one as cashier. How about that? All I can say is it's closer to bringing me with you. You know there're so many things to learn about that store. I don't know whether I'll ever know it all but I'm slowly learning. The boss asked Helen the cashier who she'd like to train to be a cashier, and she told him that she'd like to train me but I don't want that shift because one week it's from 3 PM to midnight and the next is from 8 AM to 5 PM. I don't mind 8 AM to 5 PM but I don't want that late shift so much.

I sure do miss you loads! I love you very, very much forever.

Yours eternally, Clellie

P.S. Hugs and Kisses, etc.

✉️ **September 11, 1969** **10 PM**

Dear handsome hubby of mine,

How's that for a grand opening? How are things with you? I want to thank you for such a neat letter. It just made my whole day. I love you so very much, Tony, and I will till all eternity.

I went to work from 12 noon to 9 PM. I saw Ava Brooks. She got married just recently to that Ted guy who she used to go with. How about that? She claims that she hardly recognized me because I've changed so much, and I'm so much skinnier. I do weigh 116 pounds though. I don't have a small tummy yet, but it is quite small yet it's there. Also while I was at work this man came and yelled at Jim that we had a fire. Jim went outside and sure enough you could smell smoke. Well he went in and called the fire department. Two big fire trucks, two cop cars, and a big ole' truck was there in about three minutes. All the lights had been turned red. Boy, it was exciting. Take a guess at what it was. Just guess. Well we had a short in the light wiring. Boy, some firemen were a little upset. Funny.

I bought a little gift from us to Olivia Rose's baby. It cost about $4 to be taken out of my next check. She bought us one for Chad, or I mean she sent $5, which went on his highchair. Tomorrow I work from 3 to 12 midnight. Neat. Do you know that after working a month at Thriftway's you're supposed to get a $.30 raise which never happens? A girl's been working there six months and still has not got the raise. Everyone is making a stink over the hours, the money, and the holidays so I don't know what will happen. Thank heavens I only have about two months to go and I can quit to be with you.

That makes me mad about the brownies. They were my best ones I've ever made.

Boy, your courses sound pretty rough. You know I'm glad I'm a woman. I couldn't take the Army. I'm very proud of you, Tony.

I'm glad you're off your crutches but do you take care of your foot. Don't overdo anything. You know you're a pretty strong guy. I'd keep the crutches and the profile as long as I could. You're really something. But again do be careful.

Well you've been in the Army six whole months. I've got a quarter of the waiting over with. Boy, am I glad. At least I don't have two whole years ahead of me still. Then we can be together forever. Just thinking about two months I'll be in your arms. I can't wait.

Your loving lonely wife,
Clellie

P.S. I love you so very much, Tony Jolley! Hugs and Kisses, etc.

September 12, 1969   **12 midnight**

Hi Hon,

I just barely got off work. I went to work at 3 PM today. It wasn't so bad. Only one drunk came in. Tony, after you go to Nam do you want me to work at Thriftway? I'd like to know so when I quit to go live with you I can tell him if I'll be back. What do you think? I'm so excited Wayne Jolley and his wife came in tonight and asked about you. How's that?

Hope has gone out with Lance King twice now. She wants to know how you feel about it. She said that she don't want you to be angry about it. I told her not to worry about it because you don't care. It's not like you'd be mad. I think it's okay. Lance told Hope that he is absolutely not going back to Marie. He wants a homebody and Hope's a homebody. So they should get along fine.

I've had a lot of women compliment me on my wedding rings. How about that? They're gorgeous and I want to thank you for them but most important thank you for picking me to be your wife. I love you so very much.

Susan came over today and brought us some corn. She delivered it during my lunch break. She really figures Denny and her are through. She said she wants him back on her terms because she let him have his own way for so long and she's sure he will come back on those terms. Sad. It seems anymore that all the married people are getting a divorce or stepping out. Maybe I'm old-fashioned but I don't believe in either one. I could never divorce you because I love and need you too much. I couldn't step out on you 'cause there's no one that can halfway compare with you. You're too special and I love you too much to do anything that might 'cause me to lose you. Thank heavens that we have the love and trust we do. It's so special and important with us being apart. I'll always love you.

Well I hope you're proud of your wife. The boss came up to me and asked me to take cashier upfront regularly. He said that he'd inquired around to the girls and asked who they'd prefer and they said me because I was ambitious, intelligent, can handle my customers, and nice. How about that?

I love you so much. I will forever and ever, Tony. You'll never get rid of me. It'll be so neat to live with you. Be good and stay mine forever.

Love always,
Clellie

P.S. Hugs and Kisses, etc.

✉ **September 13, 1969** *11:58 PM*

Hi Hon,

Have you heard from Butler? If so how is he doing? How's Juan doing?

I saw Denise tonight and she said Andrew was planning on coming home in about January if he comes home. I hope he does because that's about when you'll be home and you two should see each other. Have you had time to write to him?

Guess who I saw at work tonight? Phyllis and Hank Ward. How about that? They looked very happy and very much in love. I think that it's so neat to see love like that.

I worked from 1 PM to 10:15 PM. When I got home Susan was here and wanted to go eat. We went to the Kitchen Keebler again and ate. It was pretty good. Before we got something to eat she went up to Safeway and turned around and went to the Kitchen Keebler. She wanted to see if Denny was in town. She is one very unhappy girl. Oh by the way did I tell you she cut her hair? It really looks darling on her. She looks 100% better. I told her that I thought if Denny kept going the way he is you and him won't have much in common when you get home. Do you mind that I said that?

Tomorrow I go to work from 9 AM to 7 PM – ugh! Oh well, it's money. Speaking of money. Monday and Tuesday at ID store in Burley they're taking 8 x 10 color pictures for $.99 plus $.50 handling, so I want to take Chad. I should get paid Monday.

Well today we've been married nine whole months. How about that? I love you very much even more than I did nine months ago.

I don't think I told you but we put the baby's bassinet in Mom's bedroom. You remember the wallpaper, don't you? It has a lot of little flowers on it. Anyway when I change his diapers he grins and goos at that wall more than he does anyone. It's so cute. He's kind of noticing his hands more and that's cute to watch. I must admit this, at times Chad's a really homely-looking baby and other times he's the cutest on earth. I just love him to pieces. Twice in the morning now after his 6 AM feeding I have to check his breathing to make sure he's okay because he sleeps so sound. It really kind of scares me.

I saw Mrs. Warren and Joshua today. They said to say hi and asked how you were doing.

Amy Pearson's fiancé is home, and they're getting married next week.

You know when I'm at work I think about you all the time, Tony. I miss you so much. I can remember our little apartment and how I used to get up in the morning and make breakfast (sometimes I was late) and when I used to take you to work. How I used to go in when you were taking a bath and how darling you looked in the tub trying to hide a very obvious part of your body. I also remember making love wow! How I remember. I want to thank you for being the guy you are, and I want you to know that I'll always need you. I'll be here forever as yours and only yours. I can't wait till we're together forever!!

*Your loving lonely wife,
Clellie*

P.S. Hugs and Kisses, etc.

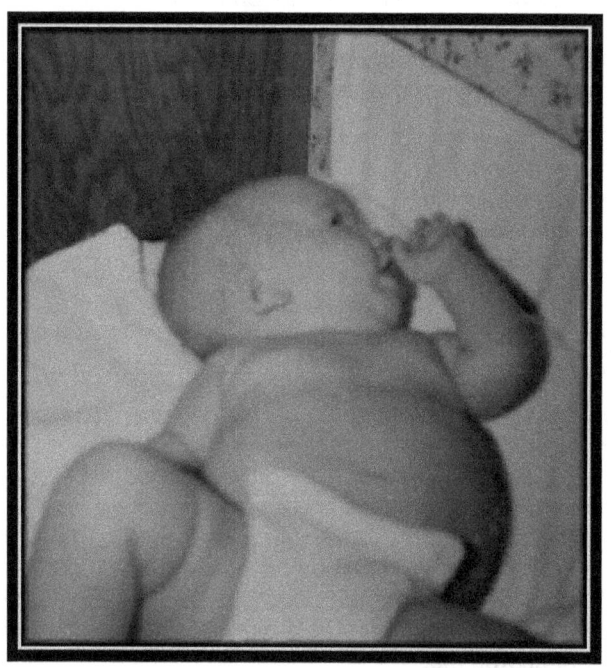

September 14, 1969   *9:00 PM*

Dear Tony,

I've been sitting here on the verge of tears. I want to talk to you so bad. Mom called and told me that you'd called. I can feel the tears coming to my eyes. I just kept blinking them back. Why haven't you called yet? Why didn't you call? Didn't you know how upset I'd be because I missed your call? I've been longing to hear your voice so long it's horrible. Why didn't you call at the store? I don't care about any old job when it comes to you, Tony. Tony, I miss and need you so bad. I know I'll cry myself to sleep tonight because here I am in the kitchen with tears in my eyes and I hate to cry in front of the family. I love you so much! Oh Tony, it's horrible. I'd like to pack up all my belongings now and go to you.

Well I guess I'd better change the subject. I seem to be sniffing quite a bit now. Chad goes to the doctor's Friday for another shot, poor little kid. I have to work all week except Monday and Tuesday from 8 AM to 5 PM. Sunday, I get off Sunday the 21st.

Last night I got the sum total of four hours of sleep because I got done writing your letter at 12:45 AM then I went upstairs to bed. At 4:50 AM Chad wanted to eat. Well I had to let him cry until 5:55 AM. He cried off and on. Then I fed him. Then I washed my hair, took a bath, dried my hair, and I got to work by 9 AM. I was so busy in the morning that I didn't get a break at all. I went to lunch from 1 PM to 2 PM. It was such a mess I worked until 7:10 PM tonight. I'm pretty worn out. This morning one tape on my register ran out so I changed it. The second one on the same one ran out so I changed registers because they were lining up fast. Finally a girl from the back came to help and she changed the other tape. About then mine ran out so we traded and she changed mine. They were really lined up by then and it was a plain old hectic day. By the end I had a horrible headache, which I haven't had for quite some time. All of my nails are ugly and broken off from hitting the keys on the register.

Chad is so cute. He's getting spoiled more and more all the time. You know most babies love bright colors, not Chad. He's a baby with his own mind. Mom's flowers on her wall excite him, and so does the dull dark couch in the front room. He goos and gurgles at it all the time. It's kind of cute. Boy, he sure digs vegetables. He thinks they're great.

Steve's over tonight teaching Nancy's dog "Tipper" tricks. He's got honey all over our freshly cleaned kitchen. Oh well that's a Graf for you.

I have my own name pin, and boy, you should see the people try to pronounce it. It's kind of funny.

How many more weeks do you have to go? By my count you have about seven more. Am I right or wrong? How's school and all?

Well I guess I'll go to bed. I don't feel too great and I'm so close to bursting in tears it's not funny. A good cry helps once in a while, don't you agree?

Well I better go. I'll always love you, Tony. Always love me too!!

Buckets and bushels of love,
Clellie

P.S. Hugs and Kisses, etc.

✉ **14 Sept 1969**

Dearest Clellie,

How are you and Chad doing this day? About 30 minutes ago I called you and you weren't home. I really wanted to talk to you. It's been a month and a half and I was really disappointed when you weren't there. Another reason I called was because I only got to write you one letter this week, and I'm very sorry about that.

By the time you get this letter you'll probably be really pissed off at me. You'll probably have also written me a dozen letters cussing me out. I'm really sorry, but we had squad tactics all last week and again this week.

Guess what? I was chosen as candidate of the week. I had to go before a board and answer a bunch of questions. Four other guys and I were chosen from the company. They choose one man every week from a platoon to be candidate of the week. Then those five guys answer questions from the board and the winner tries for candidate of the month. I don't know what the verdict of the board was yet. I just hope I didn't win because that means I'll have to go back to try for candidate of the month. Sgt. Boone also picked me to be platoon sergeant this week. Man I'm really going to be busy this week. You have to run the whole platoon. They give you sergeant E7 stripes to wear and the works. I might not have time to write you any letters at all this week, but I'm going to try.

Clellie, I wish you would've been home. I wanted to talk to you so bad. All the guys that dropped this course and the ones that got kicked out are going home on 30 to 40-day leaves and then on to Nam. I ought to just drop this course and come home in about 2 weeks for a 30-day leave. What do you think about it? I'm really in a down, down mood.

Why don't you send me Carter's address? I ought to write that guy and really cuss his ass out. I can't see why he can't settle down with Susan and grow up. Where's he living at? So he's got all of them young little girls Ann's age liking him. Well, I'll have to ask him to line me up with some of that young stuff. Ha Ha!

Clellie, what do you think of me getting a tattoo? Spear got one about a week ago. He told Sue today and I guess she really got mad at him. I won't get a very big one but I kind of want to get one.

Clellie, I really, really miss you. I feel like I don't have a damn thing to live for. It seems like I've hardly seen you. It's like I'm in prison and they won't let you in to see me. I lay on my bunk at nights listening to the radio. When a good song comes on I want to feel you next to me so bad I about go nuts.

I have dreams about you and me. Lately all of the dreams are me and you and we're up in the mountains or in great big grassy fields with big trees. We're always running and laughing. We're so happy because we're free and there's no one to bother us. Clellie, I'd better go for now. I won't write you nothing nasty, because it sounded like you got so horny last time. I'm kind of worried about you. Clellie, I love you now and forever. Please love me forever too.

Lonely restless husband,
Tony

P.S. I love you!

NCOC Tony Jolley
104 Co 10th Stu. Bn. 3th Plt
Fort Benning, Georgia 31905

✉ **September 15, 1969**

Hi Hon,

How's life been for you? For me it's miserable. I'm so lonely without you. I asked our insurance man what they would do when I left to go with you and he said that they would get an agent in the place where you're stationed to come to us. I can't wait until I'm with you.

Did I tell you that Friday night Marie and Lance came in together at the office? Hope's pretty shook up about it. Before she ever went out with Lance she asked him if he'd be going back to Marie and he said never. I think if they're going to get a divorce then they ought to go ahead and get it or go back together.

Last night after I wrote you that letter I went to bed and the phone rang. I ran half way downstairs and it was for Ann. It rang again and again I ran half way down the stairs, my heart pounding, hoping, but it was for Mom. I wish you'd have called. Are you going to call Sunday? I sure hope so.

Well today I washed the clothes, hung them out, and folded them. Exciting day don't you agree?

Hope's got a real cool sewing machine that she wants to sell. It cost her $70 plus $1.10 she won in a contest. She said I could have it for $50, anyone else she's going to get at least $70 out of it. I sure would like to have it but I told her to sell it if she could 'cause I wouldn't even attempt to buy it until you go overseas. I really like it though but I can wait for one. Susan has one that cost them $200. How about that? It's really sharp. I was going to get Chad a real cute ski outfit for $5 for him to be in when you first see him again. I showed Susan it and guess what she just bought for Justin? You're right! A ski outfit. Ticked me off! I still might get one for Chad or some other cute outfit. I told her that I knew you'd get a kick out of it 'cause you like skiing so well. I never let her know I was upset, but I am a little. I also found a little coat for Chad. She said I wouldn't need one for him, but Olivia gave me her old one for him. Well, Susan got one for Justin too. Oh well. She don't think there's anything wrong with it so I guess I should agree with it. I want Chad to be different from other ones. He's so cute.

You remember the Levi's that I didn't like of yours? The big legged ones? Well your wife has a pair of stretch ones like it. I tried to peg them but they were so big legged that they just didn't look right, And I look all the skinnier so I guess I'll leave them big legged. Everyone comments on how skinny I am. I really don't think I am so skinny. In fact I feel a little chunky still. Oh well, we'll see what you think.

I went over to see Susan today. Justin has pink eye she thinks.

Susan and I went uptown to the ID to get Chad and Justin's pictures taken. We got a big 8x10 color for $1.54 which you can't beat. I had to check one dollar out of the bank because I only had $.60 to my name. It kind of ticked me off though because he didn't take hardly any time at all with Chad to get him to smile and Chad's so cute when he smiles, but I guess I shouldn't gripe. It would cost about $20 or $15 for a professional picture. I sure hope it turns out cute. He took about seven poses and Chad wasn't in a real good mood.

I love you so much, Tony. I can't wait to be with you. I wish time would go faster. About how many more weeks do you have left to go in NCO school? I can't wait to crawl into our cozy little bed and _____. Well you just use your imagination. I get tomorrow off too. Pretty good. Well I had better close for now. I hadn't planned to write so much but I did. I love you, Tony, now and forever.

Your loving wife always,
Clellie

P.S. Hugs and Kisses, etc.!!!

September 16, 1969   *9:45 PM*

Dear handsome man of mine,

I love you so very, very much. I hope you know it, Tony. I don't want you ever to doubt it. You mean all the world to me.

Well today was a pretty boring day. I fed Chad at 6:30 AM and then put him to bed until he woke up again at 10:15 AM. I then got up and fed him his breakfast, bathed him, and fed him his bottle, and put him to bed at 11:40 AM. I grabbed a sandwich and then got dressed. At 12:15 PM I took Hope uptown for some shoes. We looked in at Thriftway, ID, Van England's, Mode O'day, King's, Penney's, and Ropers. Chad came with us. Boy, he sure is heavy. I got home at 1:20 PM and fed Chad some squash, potatoes, and pears. Then at 20 to 2 PM, Mom fed Chad the bottle and I went to Hope's. She trimmed my hair about three quarters of an inch. At 3 PM I fixed a ham. At 4:30 PM I put on the corn, fed Chad the applesauce and carrots. Mom and Ann dished up the food as well as fixed some squash. At 6 PM, I started to feed Chad his bottle then decided to go pick up my check so Mom fed him but guess what? They didn't have the checks made out yet. So I came home and finished feeding him. How's that for excitement?

At work since I've been there, three girls have quit. Two girls have given him two weeks' notice and so has one of the pharmacists. This happened all because of the lousy pay and hours and a rotten boss. Oh well I only have about eight more weeks so I'll live. It'll get me to you, which is very important. Just think we'll be together for about three months. I'm so excited. It'll seem so good.

Well tomorrow I go to work from 8 AM to 5 PM. I do all the rest of this week except for Sunday, which I get off. Then all next week I work from three to midnight ugh! On this job I have to take inventory, order candy, cigars, magazines, and food. I hear if I ordered too much the boss really yells. It kind of scares me a little... well actually a lot.

Do you know, I believe my bust is shrinking. Maybe it's the same size as it was before I was PG, but they seem small. I still wear the same size bra. I don't know maybe it's just me. By our scales here at home I weigh 114 pounds. I can fit into everything again. I want to get me a cute bellbottom slack outfit, cute shoes, cute dress, and a purse to come and live with you. Yet in a way I feel guilty spending that money on me. I'd like to be able to leave $100 here so we'd have something to begin with when we come back home again. It just depends on how much I can get saved up. I also want to send you $20 or $25 after you get transferred and find us a place to live so you can get things like milk, butter, eggs, soap, etc. Of course I'm counting my chickens before they hatch. I'll just have to wait but I'm so excited to be with you. I can't stand it.

Sometimes I can see you in school looking at my legs and how it would embarrass me. I can also remember the civic dance you took me to in your old black car and the snowflakes so big falling down. That's how I knew I loved you for you, because I don't just remember the sex. Remember last summer we went over to the park and goofed around and you told me that when you went into the Army those would be the most precious of times. Are they? Our bed times are very precious to and they strengthened my love for you. I'm also proud of you, Tony. I'm so fortunate to be able to say your mine. I depend on you so much. Always love and want me.

Your very loving and lonely wife,
Clellie

P.S. Hugs and Kisses, etc.

P.P.S. Tony, when we're together for good I want to move away. I don't want to live near relatives or such. There's no love here really.

✉ **September 17, 1969**   **9:00 AM**

Dear good-looking,

I received your letter today and I was very happy to get it. I miss you so much and your letters help me.

I went to work from 8 AM to 5 PM today. It was pretty good. I stocked the candy shelves and I put away the groceries. It went pretty fast.

Mom's got a job at Del Monte tomorrow. It's only going to go about one week more so in the meantime Hope will have to watch Chad during the day. I want to pay her one dollar a day but she doesn't want it so I guess I'll get her a gallon of milk and a loaf of bread maybe. I'll have to see. Out of the next check I want to get some deodorant, a spatula, measuring spoons and cups, and feminine hygiene deodorant all for when I come to live with you. Also a case of SMA, since I get a discount it'll be cheaper. I thought I'd take silverware, frying pan, and a sauce pan from here and ask your mom to borrow a couple of bowls, plates, and saucers, a couple of towels and wash rags. I'll bring our sheets and blankets if I can. It sounds like I have almost everything planned for November. Well I do! I'm so excited I can hardly believe it. I can't wait until November. I'll quit my job a couple of days before I leave. I want to get as much money as I can saved.

I got my check today and I made $108.01 so I put $99 in the bank. I took one of the $9 left and bought a half-gallon of milk and some toilet paper because we were completely out and Dad wasn't paying his money so we're broke. My car wouldn't start tonight. It's just as I thought, I had to get a new battery cable. It cost $1.50. I have $6.50 left. It'll take three dollars to fill my car with gas. I hope I can make it until October 2 on $3.50. I should be able to. Anyway most important we now have $167 in the bank. My next check won't be so big 'cause they'll deduct all the taxes from it and the stuff I will charge as I listed before, but we still should be able to have $400 by November sometime. Are you proud of me?

Chad and I are fine. Chad's so huge I can't believe it and he's so cute. I can't wait until we're all together again as it should be. See I haven't written you any letters cussing you out for not writing. I'm trying to be very understanding.

Hon, I'm so very proud of you for being chosen candidate of the week. I've always known you were the best that's why I chased you until I got you. What was the verdict on the board? Do you like Sgt. Boone? It sounds like he realizes how good you are too. How do you like being platoon sergeant for the week? Do you think you'll like being a sergeant? I'm so very proud of you, Hon, you're so very special.

Has Butler written you and did you get Juan's letter? Carter's mail will get to him just by sending it to Denny Carter, Oakley, Idaho. Susan told me it would get to him. He's staying with his parents. Don't you even suggest Denny lining you up with any girls or I'll hate you! See? Tony, do you wish you could go out with other girls? Denny and Susan are getting a divorce. Susan told me that if I heard anything to tell her because she wants to know and you'll probably hate me but Ann talked to Garth Bean's girlfriend and she was telling Ann about Garth and Denny coming to see her and her older sister who is a senior. He's been taking her sister to the city of rocks and out of way places. He told her Susan and him were in the process of a divorce. I told Susan this and she asked Denny. He sort of denied it, but Susan said she could tell. She thinks he's got a girl in Rexburg. Susan told him she wants a divorce and he wanted Justin three months out of the year but she won't let him go that long. I guess it's pretty final. She told me a couple weeks ago that she didn't love him hardly anymore because she's lost respect for him. I told her not to rush into getting a divorce but she said she wants it. It makes me so sick. Denny is so rotten. He's nice but so immature. He'll be sorry. Are you angry at me for butting in? Please don't be. If I were in her shoes I'd want to know but thank heavens I'm not. I love you too much and I'm so glad we don't rub it in each other's face about getting married, but I really believe we were both ready. I was anyway. I knew what I wanted, and it was you!

If you get a tattoo make sure it's little and on your bottom, chuckle chuckle. Not funny? I really hate tattoos. I think they're ugly but it's all up to you. If you really want one go-ahead but little. I'm glad you asked my opinion first. That means a lot to me. Thank you.

I need you so much and I can't wait until we're together again.

Your most miserable loving wife,
Clellie

P.S. Hugs and Kisses, etc.

✉ **17 Sept 1969**

Dear Clellie,

How's the most wonderful girl and the best-looking baby boy in the world? I love you both and I sure wish I were home with you right now. How's everything else doing in Burley? You don't know how much you miss a place until you go away from it.

Well I'm platoon sgt. still, in a couple more days I'll be graded on how I did and then I'll give it back to our platoon sergeant to give it to someone else.

We've been having all kinds of squad tactics out in the field these past two weeks. I've had to work late every night because I've been platoon sergeant and I had to get the schedule ready for the next day's training. Most of the guys in my platoon told the sergeant they thought I really had my shit squared away, so I think I'll probably get a good grade. We still don't know who got candidate of the week last week between the four guys that tried out. Boy, I sure hope I didn't get it.

No, I haven't heard from Butler, and I haven't had the chance to write to Lopez so I don't know how they're doing. Did you ever get Butler's address? If so, please send it to me.

Clellie, I sure do love you. You know if I go to dog school, I'll have to spend another 14 weeks right here at Fort Benning. If I'm going to spend all that time here, I can't see why I shouldn't have you come down here as soon as possible. What do you think?

I have to go now. I'm sorry for the short letter but I've got to go work on tomorrow's schedule.

I do love you Clellie, and I miss being next to your warm body at nighttime. I'm still having all kinds of neat dreams about us. Clellie, please love me forever and never ever quit. If you leave me, I don't know what I do. Goodbye for now and I'll try to write a good letter real soon.

Your loving husband,
Tony

P.S. I love you!

Here's a picture. It's taken far off but you can see the way the barracks are located.

NCOC Tony Jolley
104 Co 10th Stu. Bn. 3th Plt
Fort Benning, Georgia 31905

✉ **September 18, 1969**　　　　　　　　　　　　　　　　*10:15 PM*

Hi Hon,

Well I guess that you should know that my big mouth got me into a mess. Denny went over to Susan and told her that he knew where it was coming from and he said to tell Ann she better learn to keep her mouth shut and that he wasn't going to give Susan a divorce. He told her she wasn't about to ruin his life with a divorce. I called Denny's place because I wanted to have him yell at me now and I hated the thought of him hating you and me over it. He wasn't home but his mother talked to me and told me she wished I could do something to get them together. He just called and said he didn't hate Ann or I. I asked him if he thought he had done anything wrong and he said no. He had by the way taken her to the city rocks but with Garth and her sister. According to him there was nothing wrong with it. He said he loved Susan but he wasn't going to beg her. By the way, Susan's grounds for divorce is him never being home. I wish you were here. I get into so many of ugly messes. See? I told you I need you.

Well I'm learning more and more about the job and it's pretty interesting. They have so many sales, and boy, it sure is tempting, but I keep telling myself that I'll never get to you by spending the money. So I save. Today I saw Karen Higgins. She was happy for us being married. I see so many old classmates. It's pretty nice.

I had my car checked for antifreeze and it's good for 40 below. Is that okay? Right now it's raining.

Steve went to BYU today. He left early this morning.

I took Hope to work tonight. Someone told her that Lance said she's been chasing him. She's pretty upset. She watched Chad for me today. Speaking of Chad. Do you know what that stinker did? This morning I got up at 6:30 AM, got things ready for his bath, and ready to take to Hope's, I got ready for work, and finally at seven I had to wake him for his bath. Usually by then he's been awake for one hour. Ticked me off. He probably would've slept till eight. I think he misses me 'cause all day he acts upset with Mom and Hope until when I get home and feed him he goes to sleep and is just fine.

Tony I hope you don't hate me for butting in with Susan and Denny. This was just the last straw and I knew I'd want to know so I blabbed. I'm sorry. I love you so much and I don't want you to be angry with me. You mean too very much to me. From now on I'm not going to make a move without you okay, okay? I miss you so very, very much, and I can't wait to be with you. When I first see you I'm going to smother you with gobs of kisses.

Your most depressed loving wife,
Clellie

P.S. Hugs & Kisses, etc.

September 19, 1969   **11:00 PM**

Hi Hon,

I was so happy to get your letter. I wasn't really expecting another one, and boy, was I ever happy when I got it. Thank you so much for the picture. Even blurry, you're still the most handsome guy in the world. Your barracks look pretty nice and it looks pretty there, is it? I love you so very, very much, Tony.

Tonight I got home from work and I changed into shorts, took my hair down, and started to feed the baby. Ann had a couple of boyfriends here and after they left she was upset at me because I didn't put some makeup on and dress nice. I told her I wasn't trying to impress anyone except you, and you're not here so I'll save my makeup for you.

Today at work I had to take the box candy inventory, order some more, put more candy out, put away some school supplies, and mail the record stubs. I'm over the groceries, candy, magazines, books, and school supplies along with Helen. It keeps me busy. They have a book out on sex in marriage, and freedom of sex. It explains lots of things. I haven't read it, but it looks interesting. I got up at 5:30 AM, gave Chad a bath, fed him, got his things ready to take to Hope's, and got myself ready for work. I ran my legs off at work today.

I took Hope to work at 8:45 PM. Then I went to Susan's and we went uptown for a hamburger and I bought Mom one. We then came home and I told her fortune twice. I took her home and here I am. She said that Denny came over tonight and she asked him if he was going to still go out with Barry. He said that he probably would every other weekend and she told him that he wasn't going anywhere without her. She says that the only reason she wants to go back is because of Justin. She said that she'd lost respect for him a long time ago. I hope they can get back together again.

Tonight Chad had his hands around my pointer fingers and he was up against my knees and I was lifting him up by his arms and then kiss him. After about three times I quit and he tugged on my fingers and lifted his head up. Then when he wanted back he leaned backwards. It was really cute. He did about four times and Mom and the kids saw him. He's really strong. When he gets upset, he breaks out with eczema some.

I'll bet you're the best platoon sergeant ever. I'm really proud. You've got a great mind and a wonderful personality

Honey, I'll try to get a hold of Butler's wife and get his address. I thought he would have written by now.

Hon, are you going to dog school, and will it be 14 weeks after you get out of NCO school? Do you really want to take it? If you were going to take it, after it will you still have on-the-job training? Oh Tony, I want to be with you so much. As soon I can be with you I want to. I'd like to get a little more money so we have some and I'd have enough to get there and enough to get back home when you're done. Please answer my questions as soon as possible so we can get things underway so I can be down there by the 17th of October. I thought that would be a good time because by then I'll be taking my BC pills unless we can get things straightened out before then. It'll be so neat to be with you again. Could you find me a place to stay? I don't care if it's the cheapest, ugliest place just as long as I can be with you. I want to be with you now. So very wonderful and I want to be with you as soon as possible. Hon, the letter today was very good. Hurry and tell me my answer so we can get things underway if possible.

Your most admiring loving wife,
Clellie

P.S. Hugs and Kisses, etc.

✉️ **19 Sept 1969**

Dear Clellie,

You're the most beautiful girl in the whole world. You've got the best-looking baby son, and I'm the luckiest guy in the world to have both of you for my very own. I don't know how I ever lucked out, but I sure did.

Clellie, how come you keep writing in your letters that everyone keeps telling you that you're so skinny? Are you losing weight besides that chubby belly or something? You'd better not be or I'm going to be damn mad. You'd better eat a lot and keep in shape, because when I get back home you're going to need to be in shape.

What's this shit about Hope being upset because Lance and Marie came into the office together? Is she serious about Lance or something? When you told me about her going out with Lance I didn't really think much of it. When you told me that Lance said he'd never go back to Marie because he wanted a homebody I about shit. I know that Lance would go back to Marie if she would. I've seen them break up about 100 times. She leaves the house and goes to Mom's and tells him to stay away until he decides to do something about getting a bigger house. He says he never will, and the next day or night is over at the house honking his horn for Marie. She won't go out so he ends up coming in and sweet talks her into coming back out to the farm. I think the only reason Lance's going out with Hope is to get it. He surely has to know her reputation because he lives in Paul and she's worked there for a long time.

Clellie, when you ask me how long I have to go. This is the sixth week and I only have two days left in it. So after this week I'll be halfway through. I might be here for 14 more weeks after that though. If I go to dog school, I'll be stationed right here for that.

Spear's decided to go to dog school now too. I guess he told Sue to come down here and live. He tells me she'll be down here in about two weeks. He wants me to have you come down too. I told him I didn't think you should for a while. I don't want him getting the idea that you and Sue are going to rent an apartment together. Then me and him can go back to the apartment together. If I had to live around that dud I'd go nuts. Sometimes Spear's alright and other times the bastard makes me so mad I could kill him. All in all though he's a pretty good kid, but I sure wish he didn't have such an imagination.

Clellie, I would sure like you to come down now, but if you came down we'd need a car. If I could only get a hold of about $400-$500. I could buy a fairly cheap car down here and have you come live with me and everything would be just right.

I love you so much. You're the most beautiful and precious thing I could ever want. I don't know what I'd do if I lost you. I find myself thinking about you constantly. I'm so glad I have something like you to come back to.

I want you so bad I don't know possibly how I'm going to make it six more weeks without you.

I want to touch you on the most intimate places, and go to sleep completely satisfied.

Clellie, when I get with you, I want to try it the 69 way. You know why? It's because my roster numbers here at Benning is 96. We'll have to try a lot of ways too (if we can think of any more ways).

Well, Hon, baby Clel, I better go for now. It's going to be a long day tomorrow and I'd best get some sleep.

Your horny husband,
Tony

P.S. I want to love, love, love you. Be mine forever. I love you Clel!

NCOC Tony Jolley
104 Co 10th Stu. Bn. 3th Plt
Fort Benning, Georgia 31905

✉ **September 20, 1969** 9:00 PM

Hi Hon,

How's the most wonderful guy alive doing? I think you're the greatest. I want to be with you now. Oh, Tony, I'm so excited.

I saw Mrs. Bates and Irene today. Mrs. Bates said that when you come home again she wants us to go over and visit them and we are to bring our baby, so I said we would.

I saw Dana Sue today. She seems to be doing just great. I've seen quite a few of the kids we used to go to school with. I've seen Nancy, Taylor, Kerry Fergusen, David Carmen, and Renee Randall, and Karen Higgins so far.

I was being a Good Samaritan today at work. This old drunk Indian bought some cartridges for an ink filler and he wanted me to put it in his pen. So like a sweet kid I put it in the pen for him and the filler busted. Ink went everywhere. Boy, I was ticked. Permanent red yet! Oh well that's one of the many hazards of working in the store.

I got up this morning at 6:30 AM and fed Chad and got ready for work. I was late about two minutes 'cause our clock was off. I had to stock the candy shelves, and fix my department. I was sick today. I had a bad stomachache and I went to the bathroom three times at work. All I've eaten today is some cashew nuts and one piece of ham. Yesterday I ate a candy bar, milkshake, hamburger and fries. Great meals. But I'm in such a rush in the mornings and it's too early to eat, at noon I usually play or feed Chad and at night I don't feel like fixing anything. Usually the kids have supper ready except for the past two nights.

Chad's back is broken out and I don't know yet what he's allergic to. It's not real bad but I hate any eczema at all. I still might have to take him to a doctor yet. What do you think?

Honey, do you know how much it would cost me to fly to you? Or do you think I should take a bus or train? I want to know if you're sure you're going to go to dog school. I have to give two weeks' notice before I leave so I'd like to know soon. Oh I want to be with you now, Tony. I have so many things to get ready. How cold does it get down there in the winter? I'll have to bring a blanket to lay on the floor for Chad to lie on, and two blankets for our bed, plus sheets, frying skillet, one sauce pan etc. I don't know how I'm going to get it all in the suitcase. It'll be good for you to be around Chad too. You should be able to watch him grow and learn.

I miss you so very, very much. I want you to always love me.

Yours eternally,
Clellie

P.S. Hugs and Kisses, etc.

GETTING INTO TROUBLE

September 21, 1969 9:30 PM

Hi Hon,

I was so very happy to talk to you. I miss you so very much. I'm going to check and see if I can get to fly military standby. I can't remember who told me I could, but I'll find out for sure. You do want me to come down don't you? How many more weeks do you have of this NCO school? When do you think you'll find out if you're going to go to dog school? Honey, I'd rather you be in the company intelligence. It's not quite so dangerous. Chad and I need you!! It seemed so neat to hear your voice but I want you to know that I'll drop my job at Thriftway Drug just as soon as I can be with you. Money doesn't mean that much to me. You mean everything and I want to be with you as much as possible.

I called Butler's wife today to get his address, but she wasn't home. I left a message for her to call but so far she hasn't. Denny came over for about 10 minutes today to ask about you. I think Susan and him might go back together but I don't think it will last too long but at least I won't feel like I'm the one who caused it. I felt like I had been the one who's brought it about and I hated that. Denny said Susan told him he couldn't go out anymore without her. He asked what I thought. I told him that yes I thought she was right. It would be different if you went once in a great while if you had a good married friend but single guys and married guys don't mix. He said it would be hard to settle down and I told him if he truly wanted to he could and I thought Susan had been real good about his going out before. I wouldn't have been able to take it that long. I told him to write you and he said he would.

This morning Delah's (Alice's friend) mother called and asked for Alice. Mom was surprised because Alice was to stay the night with Delah. Well she didn't and she didn't come home and neither had one of her friends. We were all so worried. We waited from 7 PM to 9 PM before we called the cops. We had called a Randy Hatley who was supposed to have seen them last. He said he hadn't seen them since 11:30 PM last night. Well right after Ben Maxwell got here so did Mrs. Taylor with Alice and her friend. She said that she saw them out in the field. They had slept out in the field in a dugout. Randy and his buddy had kept going out and taking them blankets. Ben said that he was going to tell the swing and graveyard shifts to watch for them and if they were out after 10 PM they'd haul them in. And if they ran away anymore they would be sent up. Tony, I don't understand it. She lies with the truth staring her in the face, and she's so sneaky it makes me sick. There was another murder around here. Some Indians killed a guy and left him in a ditch and stole his car. They still haven't found them. There're so many transient laborers ugh! Anything could've happened to her.

I found out that the phone call today will cost about $8. I was so happy to talk to you. I'm so very lucky to be your wife. Tony, as soon as I can I want to be with you. I miss you so much.

All my love and more,
Clellie

P.S. Hugs and Kisses, etc.

September 22, 1969   *12 AM midnight*

Hi Hon,

I love you so very much. I wish I was with you right now. Tony, I want to get you a pair of dress pants so when you come home we can go to K's Supper Club again.

I was so happy to get your letter today. You're doing so marvelous about writing me letters. You don't know how much it makes me happy. Keep it up.

Marie stopped in to the store tonight and I told her about Lance taking out Hope. I really think she still loves him 'cause I could tell it. She said that you wrote them a letter saying that you didn't get a letter from anyone, and asked me what you meant. I told her that you meant the family because I've written every day. She said that her mother and her were going to stop in today, but my car was gone. I sure wish they would stop in.

Denny's mother called me during my lunch hour. Ann had been riding to Minico with Mrs. Matthews. She called Denny's mother (she's a relation to Denny) and told her that she was going to talk to Susan and make sure Denny and Susan never get back together and that I knew more about Denny and Susan's trouble than I was letting on. She also said that Ann had told her some things. Ann told Mrs. Carter that Mrs. Matthews told her the things and she agreed. I guess this Sandpedre girl's little sister went and told Mrs. Matthews about Denny taking her sister out and also a girl named Chris called her sister and told her to leave Denny alone because she's been going with him. If this is so, I hope he never gets with Susan. I'll hate him for doing this to her. I haven't told Susan anything about it and I told Mrs. Carter that I didn't know anything about anything. I feel sorry for Susan. She really lost out getting Denny. I'm so very thankful that I have you. I love you so much. I'm so thankful you're the person you are and I never have to worry about you. I love you, Tony, so much.

I just got off work. The 3 PM to 11 PM shift is a real killer. By the way, I've lost almost all of that chubby stomach, hooray!!

Hon, I love you too much to go without you. You remember that one night you and Ford were going out and you wanted to be away from me all night so I offered to go stay at Mom's? I was hoping you would want me to stay and you'd want to sleep with me. I didn't want to sleep one night without you I love you so much. Now I go so many nights without you and I can't do one thing about it. I'm coming down so count on it. I'm going to talk to Sue. Don't worry we won't get the same apartment. She's like me in a way. She wants to be alone with her husband too. I'd feel better with another girl going. To fly to Atlanta, Georgia it would cost me $123 +5% tax. To take a bus to Fort Benning it would be around $124.65 round-trip and $69.25 one-way. It would take 2 ½ days. By train it will take three *days and cost $72.69 one-way, and $131.68 round trip. So which would you prefer? I might wait until you find out for sure if you'll get dog school.*

I absolutely don't want you to go Airborne. Please!!!

We really wouldn't need a car if I come down would we? Couldn't we get a place near other guys so we have a ride out and back?

Well I did better end this book. I love you, Tony.

Your loving wife,
Clellie

P.S. Hugs and Kisses, etc.

✉ **22 Sept 1969**

Dearest Clellie,

I love you. Is Chad doing all right? I know he is. Of course, he's in the most loving, wonderful hands possible.

Here I am on CQ. It's real boring. This'll be the last time I have it in the cycle if I don't get restricted.

I'm sending you a picture Jones took of me while I was making that diagram for Sgt. Smith. It gives you an idea of how the barracks look on the inside. The desks and bunks are really nice; the barracks itself is so old it's falling apart.

If I don't forget to go to the barracks tomorrow morning and get some money, there will also be $40 in the letter. $20 of it I won playing poker. I was going to keep it to buy some threads (Bell bottoms and a sweater) but I want you to pay for the phone bill and buy you some nice clothes. I wouldn't send $40 to just anyone you know, Clellie. I don't know why, but I get such a kick out of giving you things. It's probably just because of that special look of surprise and joy you used to get in your eyes when I'd bring a present to you. You always have the attitude of "you shouldn't have done it, Tony." I'm really lucky to have such a beautiful but also sincere wife like you.

Clellie, I'm sure not very nice. Here I told you on the phone I got a tattoo and I was fibbing to you all the time. I know now beforehand how you would react if I did get a tattoo so I guess I'll have to go through life without one.

Clellie, I'm not mad because you butted into Denny and Susan's affairs by asking around about him, but I don't want you to do it again. You let her know that he was stepping out, but no more. Even if you do hear something accidentally about Carter, I don't want you to say anything about it to her. Let her find out for herself.

I sure hope they don't get a divorce. I really think they make a good couple. But in certain circumstances, it might be better if they did get a divorce. If they're going to fight all the time, it would be better if they weren't together.

Have you heard about all the hell breaking loose in Vietnam? I guess old Charlie is really starting to raise hell. They're trying to take over one of our main base camps. Maybe they'll fight it all out before I get over there. I sure hope not. I hope they save a few Vietnamese for me and the other guys I'm going over with. We all want them to save a few.

Clellie, I sure wish I could come home to be with you. We could go to bed and caress each other and make love all night.

I love you so much, Clellie. If you don't come down here soon, I'm going to go nuts. About you coming down in three weeks, I don't think you better plan on that. We really need a car and frankly I don't have the money.

On the phone, Clellie, don't even think, let alone say, that I don't want you down here. If you think I'm having a big ball down here and if you came it would spoil my fun you're wrong. I feel rotten that you're not here. I see all the guys with their wives and I can't even stand to watch them because I just want you here that much more.

Well Clellie I'd better go for now. I have to fill out some forms for the battalion CO. There's never a day's rest for a candidate NCO you know?

Clellie, if anyone makes a pass at you while you're working or anytime I want you to let me know. Promise me. (You just promised me I hope you know). So help me if you don't tell me and I find out from someone else I'll be mad at you. If someone does and you tell me, they better watch out when I get home. I'll jump right in the middle of their shit right? Right! Tough aren't I?

Clellie, always love me like I do you. It was so nice to talk to you today you really sounded good. Well goodbye for now.

Your horny lonesome husband,
Tony

NCOC Tony Jolley
104 Co 10th Stu. Bn. 3th Plt
Fort Benning, Georgia 31905

September 23, 1969   ***12 midnight***

Hi Hon,

I just barely got off work and my feet are killing me. I've been working a month now and I love day shift but night shift is an absolute bore. I had to get Chad a prescription for the rash on his bottom. It's diaper rash but anything we use he's allergic to and it won't go away. The prescription usually costs $2 and some but since I work there I get it for $1.95, which isn't bad.

Well I guess Susan and Denny are over for sure. Susan caught him red-handed. She was going past the AC when she saw him. She went around the block and parked a little ways from him. She could see a blonde girl in the car. He came over to Susan and she asked him who he had with him. He said that it was his cousin Gail. She told him to bring her over and he said she didn't want to. So when he went back to the car Susan followed him. She got in the car and asked the girl her name and she said that was Gail Carter. She told her to tell her the truth and she said she was. Susan told her she wasn't and to tell her who she was. She told Susan that it was not any of her business. Susan then asked her if she knew Denny and her were married and she said yes. Susan asked her if she knew they were getting a divorce and she said yes, doesn't everyone know? When Susan got out she told Denny she was going ahead with the divorce. Tony, I honestly think I hate Denny. I really hope you don't want to run around with him when you get home. But that's your decision.

Tony, do you wish you were free to go out with other girls? Do you feel pinned in? I know that you've told me the answer so much, but I'd like to hear it again. The rate things are going we'll be the only couple that's never been divorced. I want to be able to be as lovely as we are now when we celebrate our 50th anniversary together. It'll probably make headlines. I want Chad to know that there still is love that lasts and ours will.

Going to charge a book called, "Sex in the Marriage." It looks very good and interesting. It talks about sex during pregnancy, and such. This way when we get together again I can be more satisfying to you. I also want to try it other ways. I cannot wait to be with you. How does 17 October, or the last of October, or 3 November sound? You pick the date. I want to be with you. I want to be able to see you, touch you, and love you.

Well I better close and go to bed. I love you, Tony, so very, very much.

All my love eternally,
Clellie

P.S. Hugs and Kisses, etc.

✉ **23 Sept 1969** **Tuesday**

My beautiful girl Clellie,

You're mine, aren't you? I sure hope so. How is the kid? Is he as good looking as the old man? Wow I sure do love you.

I don't have much time to write this letter because in about 15 minutes they're going to turn the lights out, and have bed check. Everyone has to be in bed.

Tomorrow we start Ranger patrolling. Will be out every night until about 11:30 PM (2330 Army Time) except for Friday, Saturday, and Sunday. These three days we are going to stay all night and all day in the toolies. Right now it's still raining. It's been raining for three days, and is supposed to for another week. Undoubtedly we're going to get wet. You'll never guess what we will use to sleep in those three nights in the rain, one blanket and our ponchos, no sleeping bags, tents, or anything, survival for the fittest right?

Clellie on the phone you never did tell me about you calling up Carter. What do you mean you didn't want him to be mad at you? You said you thought Susan should know, so you shouldn't really care what Carter thought. How come he called you back? What's going on, Clellie? Is he crying on your shoulder or something? Has he come over since I've been gone? Does he ever come over or call you to ask you what he should do about the whole thing? I want these answers and truthful. You'd better.

Well, Clellie, I guess you think I'm cussing you out. I'm not, but I want to know these questions. If he's coming over and people see, you know there will be talk. None of it better get to me without you telling me first.

I love you, Clellie. I do sincerely want you to come down, but I think we better see what happens first. I might not get to go to dog school. If I don't go to dog school I'm not going to have you come down. No. If I go to dog school I don't go to OJT. That is my OJT.

Do you really love me, Clellie? I sure hope you do. I have to go for now but I'll try to write you this week. I'd sure like to be going to bed with you tonight. We could make love all night. Goodbye for now.

Your lonely loving husband,
Tony

P.S. I wish I was with you! I want and need you bad. I want to feel you next to me so bad I'm going nuts. I want to love you, Clellie.

NCOC Tony Jolley
104 Co 10th Stu. Bn. 3th Plt
Fort Benning, Georgia 31905

September 24, 1969   *12 midnight*

Hi Hon,

I want to thank you so much for the letter. It was so nice. You're doing so great about writing. Thank you. Hon, you should've got you some threads. You need them as bad if not worse than I do. You see I don't wear a dress anymore when you're not around. One of these Sundays I need to take Chad to church. Thank you for the $40. I want to get a dress, one pair of black shoes, and a Bellbottom suit. It was so sweet of you. I hope you know that you're the most wonderful husband in the world. Most husbands keep the money for themselves, but you're not at all like most. You're so special and I'm so lucky. I love you so much!!

The girl Denny was caught with is suspected to be Natalie Johnson. Real groovy girl. I hope he's happy with her. It's pretty good when a 21-year-old guy gets with 15, 16, and 17-year-olds. Real neat. Susan said she was smoking and really snotty. I hope Susan soaks him good. I know it's an awful way for me to feel but as far as I'm concerned he deserves all he gets. His mother calls me up when she's feeling low about it. She's called me three times now. Sad. Boy, it's an ugly mess.

At work I charged a book called "Sexual Freedom and Marriage." It looks quite interesting. It's five distinguished group of doctors, psychologists, and marriage counselors. It's got such topics as what happens during the sex act, how women really feel about orgasms, keeping sex alive in marriage, the wandering husband, and gobs more. When I get done do you want to read it?

I think I'll go to Twin Friday since it's my day off and get my clothes. There is such a bigger variety. You know I've gotten more new clothes since our marriage then I got in five years of living with Dad. It really feels nice to be given money and told to buy clothes. I want you to get some too.

How do you like this picture of Chad? He's exactly 2 months in it. Susan took it and the picture came with two little ones so I gave one to Mom and sending the other one to you.

Barry Jolley came in tonight and bought some candy. He's doing fine and is going to buy a car at a car lot. Fred Judd's little brother came in tonight. He had the top part of one of his fingers pulled off. Sad. He caught it in a machine at school.

Thank you for the picture too. It's really good of you. I love you so much and I miss you gobs. I wish I could kiss your neck and chest, etc. I also wish I could give you a big juicy French kiss. I love you so very much. I want you forever and ever. You must be a good poker player. I didn't know that. You learn something all the time.

You know what I do when you fib to me? Just you wait!! I told Marie you got a tattoo and the Carters. I'm glad you didn't get one. You have too great of complexion to ruin it. Thank you for thinking of me in your *decision, but I want you to be happy too so if you really want one, get one.*

Hon, I sure hope you don't go to Nam. Say did I tell you? Remember my cousin who was a pilot and got shot down in Nam? After three or four years of not knowing if he was alive or dead, my aunt and uncle got word that he's still alive. I'm so very glad.

Hon, would we absolutely need a car? Isn't there someone you know whose wife's there and has a car that we could live near? Please see if there is. I want to be with you and I've made up my mind that I'm coming down when you know for sure if you get dog school. I'd like to make it in time for graduation. I love you so much and I want to be with you as much as possible.

Hon, so far only that one guy said what I told you on the phone. Oh and one drunken Mexican asked me out almost 2 and half weeks ago. I told him no and that I was a happily married woman. He's left me alone since then. Oh I've had a couple of horn honks on the way to work and whistles, but I just simply ignore them. Don't worry about me. I can handle things. The only guy that exists is you. I love you to act jealous. It makes me feel neat.

Do any girls flirt with you? I want you to tell me about them too. Promise? I'll also pound them when I get there in no more than a month.

Well I better close for now. I love you so very, very much.

Your most admiring loving wife,
Clellie

P.S. Hugs and Kisses, etc.

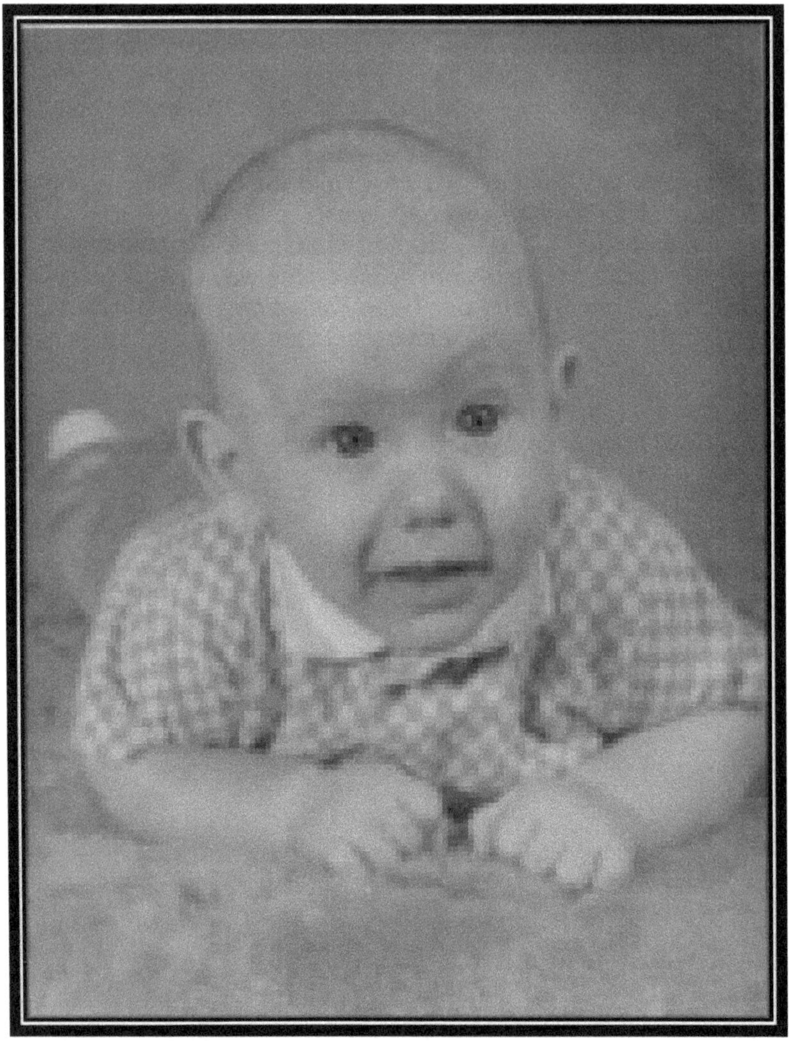

September 25, 1969 *12 midnight*

Dear Tony,

Well I just got off work. Boy, it seems like a long night. Thank heavens I have tomorrow off.

You know Tony, sometimes the fact that we're apart upsets me more than usual. I got off for tonight and on the way home I started to cry. I miss you so much and I want so much to be there with you. I'm so very happy that we're married. I was thinking tonight about us. What if we weren't married? I would have missed a lot of things with you and I couldn't even think about going down there to live.

Mom and I went to Shelby's to get her groceries and we saw Sue. She plans on going down around the same time I do. She says she wants to take $100 when she gets down there and buy an old junky car to get around in. Maybe we can do that too. Anyway don't worry about us getting one apartment to share. I don't want it and neither does Sue. Sue said that we can fly as student standby for about $80 so I guess I'll check it out. We won't be down until the last of October or 1 November whenever you get your orders. I might have to ship a few boxes of stuff by train. It depends. I'm not bringing very much if I can help it. I'm so excited. It's been such a long time. I want to feel your arms around me and you're so exciting to kiss. I can't wait!!

You know Frank Bean and that Margie his wife that went to beauty school with me? I guess they're divorced. He'd been stepping out on her. Oh it's such an ugly world. The only good thing is that I have the only faithful husband, good-looking and so considerate. I'm so lucky and Chad's very lucky to be your son. I hope he's just like you!!

I traded that book "Sex in Marriage" for another one called "The Marriage Art." It looks better. It's a famed physician's frank step-by-step guide to sexual joy and fulfillment for married couples.

I got a bill from the hospital today for $5 for the Pap test for the BC pills that I have to pay. Oh well at least I know that I don't have cancer.

We owe Jensen Jewelry $75 still and in October I'll pay $25 more and then I'll have to tell them that I'll pay the rest in about February and March. Or what do you suggest?

Tony, I miss you so much. I wish we were back in our apartment in Heyburn. It was so cool being your wife there. I want to be together so bad. And you know anyway I wish there was only you and I. Do you think that's awful of me? I'm stingy. I don't want to share your attentions with anyone even Chad. I'm awful. I'd never give Chad up now, but it would've been neat if we could've waited. Oh well we'll still be young when he's grown.

Well I better close. I love you, Tony, and I will forever.

Your loving wife, Clellie

September 26, 1969 10:30 PM

Hi Hon,

How are you doing? I hope real great. I love you so much.

I hope you know that I spent every cent of the $40 you sent me. I know you'll like what I bought. Susan took pictures of me in my coat, my dress, and my slacks. We went to Twin Falls today and I bought a cute pair of black shoes at Payless. They are black with little heels and a big gold buckle on top. I then bought a cute dark blue suit. The pants are tight except at the bottom where they sort of flare out. They are hip huggers. It had a vest with gold buttons that came to my hips. I got a scarf tie to wear with it. It all cost $15.51. Then I went to Penney's and bought a cool white shirt to go with my suit. It cost five dollars. I then got a cute dark blue suit with a V-neck and a red and white scarf as a tie. It cost $13.29. It took about two dollars for some gas. I hope you like the outfits. All I want to buy now is underpants and a cute outfit for Chad. I really don't need any more clothes because I don't go out that much and so I should wait till you're out of the Army to get more. Now you get some dress slacks, bellbottoms, and a sweater. It's so much to spend on clothes. I'll take eight dollars for the phone out of my second check from now. I'll send my pictures in for development 3 October. Then I'll send them to you.

You know that prescription I had filled for Chad for his bottom? Well it broke him out worse. I don't know what to do about it now.

Denny Carter's mom called me to talk to me today. She said that he told her he didn't take dope or marijuana and I told her that I didn't think he did. She asked him if he was going to change and he told her that he didn't see why. His wife doesn't love him, his parents don't care, and no one cares for him. I say why didn't he change before she caught him? He deserves everything he's getting. Susan's going to ask for $130 child support from him. She said that she wouldn't ask for the car if he wouldn't fight her on the child support. That's what her lawyer advised. Mrs. Carter told Denny that he'd be sorry when Justin doesn't know him and calls some other guy Daddy. I guess he cried about it. Mrs. Carter also gave him your letter.

Honey, I don't ever want to have to go through that. I want us to love each other always. I'll always love and respect you. You're too great of a guy to disrespect. I love you so many gobs. I can't wait until we're together again!! It'll mean so much to me and to Chad. He does almost say Daddy too. Really! He gets enthused when I asked him where Daddy is. Soon he'll get to see his daddy. I love you now and forever.

Your loving wife,
Clellie

P.S. Hugs and Kisses, etc.

P.P.S. Everyone here is getting worked up about Larry and the school kids are writing letters to the senators to get some of our prisoners of war home, and that we should have our rights as declared in the Geneva Convention like a list of who the prisoners are, and open communication. Neat. I love you so awfully much.

✉ **September 27, 1969**　　　　　　　　　　　　　　　　　*1:00 PM*

Hi Hon,

I just received your letter and I was so happy and surprised. This is the third one this week. It really makes me feel good. I love you so very much.

So far I've charged $16 worth of stuff at work. I'll get a discount on it though. I went up today and got measuring spoons, a measuring cup, demure mist spray for feminine hygiene, a case of SMA for Chad, some real cute black felt boots (cowboy) with a white strap around them, more ointment to try on his little bottom, a box of Tide, some Breck shampoo for Chad, and two boxes of D-con to put with our boxes to keep the mice out of them. I got the measuring spoons and cups for when I come to live with you.

I haven't got any white bellbottoms because they're out of season now. 'Sides I only need two pantsuits. That pink one I have and that real sharp one I bought yesterday.

Tony, I know it's not proper for me to say but I'd sure like to go to bed with you. I want to feel your touch and your kiss so much. I can't wait until we're together!

Well I better go and get dressed for work. Write you at midnight.

　　　　　　　　　　　　　　　　　　　　　　　　　　　12 midnight

Well I just barely got off work. You know I really feel sorry for some of those old drunks. They want to be important but they've goofed up their chances.

I went to lunch and Lena was minding the front. I guess some old drunk guy came in and bought a few things and came up to pay for them. Along with his stuff he got there he laid a new pair of pants down. Lena asked him where he had gotten them and he told her it was not any of her business, called her names, and everything so she told him that she didn't have to wait on him and he brought back his hand with a bottle of whiskey in it and was going to hit her. Frida tried to get out and call the cops but he shoved her back in and went on with his loudmouth. Finally he walked out. I felt sorry for Lena.

I have a girl under me now that I have to start training next week to help me in my department. I really don't know all I need to know yet but I'll try. I go to work tomorrow from two to midnight ugh!

Chad isn't as good looking as you, Tony. No one is or ever could be. I am your girl just as long as you want me to be. I want to thank you again for the letter. You're doing so great about writing!

Does it rain a lot there? Just how cold does it get in the winter there? (Just in case!) How soon will you know if you're going to dog school? I had the understanding that OJT you would be able to come home to me every night. Is that right? How often will you be able to come to me in dog *school? How soon will you know your orders? Will it be soon enough for me to come to graduation if I'm coming? What's ranger patrolling? How do you like school now?*

Honey, I'm sorry I didn't tell you on the phone about talking to Carter on the phone. I just couldn't talk about everything that I wanted and I knew that was in a letter. I didn't want him to be mad at me because 1. He's your friend 2. Most important, I was afraid he'd seek revenge. I was afraid that he'd try everything in his power to break us up to get even with me. Tony, it really scared me to think of him trying to split us up. I love you and I don't want anyone to try to bust us up. I need you so much and you're so important to me. I also had to know that I hadn't told Susan pure gossip. No Denny hasn't come over since you left except for that one Sunday you called and I already wrote you about that. He came into the drugstore last week looking for complexion soap and he talked to me about three minutes in which I told him to write you. I really think he's childish now and I could hate him for what he's done to Susan! Hon, I've told you everything. I always have! That's the only way we can trust each other isn't it? It's so important especially with you gone.

Honey, I want you to know how very, very much I love you. I want to be with you as soon as possible. Always love me and stay mine forever!

All my love eternally,
Clellie

P.S. Hugs and Kisses, etc.

✉ *September 28, 1969*   *12 midnight*

Hi Hon,

How's the greatest guy that ever was or ever will be? I sure do love and miss you so much. I can't wait until we're together.

I just barely got home from work. Boy, it was busy until about 10 PM and then it was so boring. I went to work at 2 PM until 12AM – ugh! Oh well its money, which we're going to need.

Boy, you know that book I got called "The Marriage Art?" It's pretty darn frank. I even blush. It talks about what turns the man and the woman on. I want to read it with you beside me so we can experiment.

Marie called this morning just to chitchat. She wants to catch Lance with another girl. Do you know that Denny Carter told Marie that they were getting a divorce but he didn't want it, the cause of it was a bunch of rumors! I think there's something wrong with Denny! He was caught and still says it's a rumor. He told Susan that he feels sorry for people and he was just trying to help her. By the way, Natalie Johnson's sister told Alice that Natalie has been going with Denny. Honey, it's such a mess. I hope that I never have to go through that and just as long as you always love me I know I won't.

Guess who I saw today? Russell Nelson and his wife, she's PG. She's not bad looking, not the best either. He asked how you were doing. It seems so funny to see our classmates married. I can't believe we're all grown up and beginning our own families. I'm glad we're as old as we are though 'cause if we just started going together when we were 15 years old, we'd be in sad shape. I couldn't have waited to have you for two or three years.

Today I came home for lunch and I was going back and I was out of the door talking to Mom when the Maselters (Susan, little sister, Mom and Dad) went by. Boy, they about broke their necks looking at me.

I saw Barry's daughter at work and she said that when you come home on your leave we are to come and visit her.

I remembered something today. The first time I worked midnight when I was still on relief shift a drunken Mexican asked me out. I told him that I was very happily married woman and he said oh. Really swinging. Also when Susan and I went to the Kitchen Keebler one night for a hamburger these two old buzzards came in and sat in the booth behind us. The one right behind Susan kept turning around and looking at us. Finally he comes up to Susan and asked her if we knew that we were cute. By then I was so ticked off, my face was burning. I said, "We're married women." He said, "What am I doing?" Susan said, "You're bugging us so turn around." He said, "You girls are cute." Susan said, "Shall we move?" And I said yes. Right then he turned around and left the salon. Old buzzards like that gripe me to death. Honey, I really don't see that it's necessary for me to tell you every time someone makes a pass at me. It'll just upset you and I don't want that. I'll take care of anything that arises. Now that you're away I have to learn to take care of stuff like that. If you still want me to tell you every time I will, but I want to know too!

Well I better go. I love you so very, very much. I only have about a month and then I can be with you. I can't wait! It'll be so neat to be with you. I love you, Tony.

Yours eternally,
Clellie

P.S. Hugs and Kisses, etc.

September 29, 1969 *11:30 PM*

Hi Hon,

Chad has found his fist now, and boy, oh boy, do they ever fascinate him, he goos at them and everything. It's so cute. I took him uptown today to go to the post office. I put a little blue hat on him and he looked so cute. I'm going to have to get a picture of him in it. He holds his head up real good now and he's a doll. Every kid goes through an ugly stage and a cute one off and on. Right now he's a little doll.

Tonight Susan and Nancy and I went to the Alfresco to the show, "West Side Story." Boy, we were all three just sobbing at the end but it was so good. It was car night and I was going to take Alice, Nancy, Ann, Susan, Mom, and I and we'd all chip in a little to get in. Well Mom went with Molly, and Ann didn't want to go with Alice and Nancy. As for Alice, yesterday while I was at work someone played our stereo and messed with our records. I could tell they have been played so I asked her again and she said no that I could ask Nancy. I asked Nancy and I told her to tell me the truth or she wouldn't go to the show either. She looked at Alice and then she told me yes Alice had played it. I then asked Alice again and she admitted it. I really got ticked and told her that she wasn't to ask me for anything or any favor and I wanted a dollar for the record that skips from last time she played it. I told her I was sick of her lying and she could forget about me ever believing her again. I know it's a little thing but it's the principle. I can't trust or believe her at all. I have one dollar missing that Ann gave me for Mom's gift, we're all chipping in one dollar for a simple gift for her birthday, and Nancy's missing $.50. I'm sick of it. I was so used to leaving my money and the letters from you around now I have to hide them. Someone went through my drawers. Guess what was in one of them? A prophylactic. The last one we had. I've hidden it now.

Well that's enough griping, don't you agree? Hon, that show upset me something awful tonight. It was so sad. The main guy's name was Tony and he got killed. Tony and Maria had such a special kind of love and he was taken away. It reminds me of our love. It's so special and so unique and you're the one who makes it that way. Tony, I never want to lose you. I simply couldn't take it. I can't wait until we're together. It'll be so very heavenly. I love you.

Your loving wife, Clellie

P.S. Hugs and Kisses, etc.

✉ **September 30, 1969** *10:00 PM*

Dear Handsome Hubby,

How's the greatest guy on earth doing?

Well, I had today and yesterday off this week. It sure felt good. It gave me two days to do all the washing, wash our bedding, and clean our room. I wanted to wash my filthy car but yesterday and today it's been raining, so that's out. Speaking of the car, I asked you in a previous letter if you thought my car has enough anti-freeze in it. Do you? It's good for 40 below zero?

This week I work from 8 AM to 5 PM and I'll get Sunday off. Pretty good. I plan on telling my boss that I'm quitting on the 1st of Nov. to be with you. Then I'll leave on the 3rd of Nov. 'cause I'll get the Army check and the one at work too.

I don't want to tell him until the 18th of Oct., which will give him a 2-week notice. They are thinking about changing the hours, on weekdays from 9 AM to 10 PM, and on Sundays from 9 AM to 6 PM. Sounds pretty good. They plan on changing them in a month. If they do change the hours I really don't think I'd mind going back after you leave. What do you think? No one can see how I've lasted so long 'cause no one likes the boss at all but he hasn't said too much to me yet. On my next check I want to charge some sparkly blush powder, a face pack, and some more film for my camera.

Boy, your little son is quite the ice cream eater. I got an ice cream today and gave him a couple of spoonfuls, and boy, he smacked it right down. Then he started to cry when I quit feeding it to him. He's so cute. He laughs more and more all the time. Almost giggles. I really love him. I can't wait until you can see him.

Around next Monday, October 5th you should be getting your October care package. I sent it yesterday. I hope you like it and get a big kick out of it. I love you, Tony, and I do wish that I could be there with you so very much.

This book I charged tells the best way to break virginity which is having a doctor break it. I do not like that. I'm glad we did it the way we did. It also tells of different positions and such. As far as I've read in it we have done them all. It also tells what effect each one has and such. It's really pretty interesting.

There was a car wreck last Saturday or Friday night. A Schaefer boy, who attends Minico, was taking out a girl named Dawn Warren, the sophomore secretary. He ran a stop sign and a car of Mexicans ran into them. Dawn and him were in a VW. She was thrown from the car and her throat was cut. They found pieces of hair and scalp in the VW. She bled to death. It took the ambulance 20 minutes to get there and just as they're putting her in the ambulance she died. The boy is in rough shape. I guess it was really sad at Minico.

Susan said Denny comes over almost every night and she gives him Justin to visit then walks away. He gets all mad because she won't talk to him but Susan said that after she saw him with another girl she could never take him back. Sad.

Boy, I've been in a dumb mood today. I cried about three times. One time Chad made a face that reminded me so much of you. Oh Tony, I want to be with you so much. By the time you get this letter you'll only have four more weeks to go at that school and then we can be together. I can't wait. I love you, Tony.

Your lonely loving wife,
Clellie

P.S. Hugs and Kisses, etc.

✉ **October 1, 1969**   9:30 PM

Hi Hon,

How are you doing today? I hope you're just fine.

Boy, I was sure busy at work today. I had to go to work at eight, and boy, it was sure sad. I still was sleepy. I had to talk to two candy men and tell them what to order. I had to stock the shelves with the groceries and the candy shelves. I also had to take inventory on magazines.

I got my check tonight. It took $20.38 for stuff I had charged. I sent the slips of what I had charged to you so you could see. We're supposed to be getting 30% off on everything we charge. Well I charged around $21.89 worth and they subtracted one dollar and some odd, nowhere near even 10%. Ticked me off! No wonder everyone quits. I got $111.58. $20.38 taken out for my account, and around $47.81 went for taxes. Boy, how sickening. Next check I'm only going to get some film, a facial, and a box of Tide. Anyway with this check all in the bank I'll have $210 in the bank. Then if I get $190 from the Army I'll put hundred or so in the bank. I'll pay Dr. Peterson $10 for Chad's shots and my Pap test. I owe the hospital $5 for Pap tests. The Army paid all the rest.

I talked to Susan tonight and she has signed the final papers for the divorce. Now they have to deliver them to him.

Do you know that there's another Clellie around here? I'm serious. Ann and Alice said that last night there was a request for Clellie B. I sure would like to see her. I really can't quite believe it. Mom said that there was a couple besides Grandma with the name Clellie, some cousins or something. It kind of makes me mad. Here all my life I believed I was the only one besides Grandma with my name. I hope that I can find out who she is.

How's things for the most wonderful guy in the ugly old Army? Do you think that you'll get to go to dog school?

Hon, I sure hope that I can have $400 by the time I go to live with you. Do you still have $100 at the credit union? Could we use it to start out when we get back home for the leave? Or are you saving it for something else? If you are, I want to be able to save about $30 here at least.

Chad is really growing and he's getting cuter all the time.

Tomorrow Hope has to take Ashley to the doctor in Twin. They want to put her in the hospital sometime this week. She needs a few tests and her tonsils out. Boy, her and little Tony sure are spoiled. They get on my nerves quite a bit lately.

Tony, how much longer will I have to wait until I know whether I can come there or not? My sensible mind tells me I should wait until 3 November so I'll get the Army check too and have $130 extra, but my whole heart and body wants to come as soon as possible! I miss you so much.

All my love forever,
Clellie

P.S. Hugs and Kisses, etc.

TIME TO PAY THE PIPER

✉ **1 Oct 1969**

My Dearest Lovely Clellie,

How's Chad and the most charming little lady ever created getting along?

I'm really sorry for not writing for about the past five days, but I couldn't help it. We just got off Ranger week, and the last 2 days we've been preparing for an inspection.

I just got your letter. I'm really glad that you got yourself a bunch of new clothes. About me getting some new threads, I kind of doubt if I can afford it. You've probably looked at the pink slip I have enclosed with this letter. You guessed it. I finally got the money situation straightened out with finance. You know all that money they've been paying me extra since I came in the Army, well they're starting to take it back. In case you can't remember, the reason they're taking all this money out of my check, it's because they always sent you your allotment, but they never took it out of my check. I guess I'm going to get two more checks like this one then it will all be paid. It's better I got it straightened up now, rather than wait longer and have to pay them back just that much more.

I sure hate to have to start paying it back now though. You know you're not going to be able to come down now don't you? I was going to send you enough money to pay off that ring bill. I guess I won't be able to now though. Well, Clellie, it looks like you're going to have to start supporting me now. That's a real bummer. You get $130.00, and I get $23.00. No, I'm not bitching, I'm just really in a bad mood. I ought to go out and jump off the bridge. That way you would get about $15,000 and you could get you a nice rich guy that wouldn't have to come in the Army and could buy you anything you want. I sure wish I could buy you things, Clellie. You really deserve a lot of things you haven't got. You know? I really don't know what in the hell I'm going to do. $23 a month isn't even enough to pay my laundry. Another thing, how in the hell am I going to come home? I won't even have enough to buy a ticket. Well enough said for that. I'll just sit here in the barracks and listen to records on the weekends.

Clellie, I sure do love you. I want to hold your firm body in my arms and press up against you. Then I'll kiss all along your neck 'til you got goose bumps. That's the only thing I can offer you now Clellie, my love, that is.

Clellie, no matter how poor or penniless I get you'll still love me, won't you? You know the only reason I don't have enough money is because I'm drafted and can't help it, right? I always worked when I was home, and we always had enough money to get us by. Well I'll get out of this damn Army one of these days and things will be just like they always were.

Clellie, I have to go now but remember to love me like I was before the Army got ahold of me, because I don't quite know what it's doing to me. I love you Clellie Graf (Jolley).

Your loving penniless husband,

Tony

I love you! I think I'll go AWOL!

NCOC Tony Jolley
104 Co 10th Stu. Bn. 3th Plt
Fort Benning, Georgia 31905

✉ **October 2, 1969** 9:30 PM

Hon,

I love you so much. I miss and need you so very, very much. You're the most wonderful guy in the whole universe. Oh Tony, I want to be with you so much.

Honey, would you please check on whether I'll be getting the money for the baby by next check? I expected it this month but I only got $100. I'm hoping to be able to put some of it in the bank. I thought I'd get $130 for this month plus $60 for the last two months. He's three months old now. Shouldn't I have got $190? I would've been able to put $100 in the bank. I'm so perturbed! You said it would take about six weeks and so it should've been this month, 'course leave it to the charming Army. If I get it I should get $220. $130 for the month of October and $90 for Chad's back pay. If so, it'll be nice and helpful for me and you when I go live with you. What do you think?

Mom called the airport today for me to find out if I can get student rates. They said yes I can. It'll cost $68.25 for a one-way ticket from Salt Lake to Columbus, South Carolina. Is that the closest town? It'll cost $136.50 for a round trip ticket. I have to pay $3 or $5 for a student ticket. Isn't that neat? It'll cost $22.25 to freight by train 100 pounds of stuff like dishes, bedding, etc. This includes insurance. Pretty neat. I can't wait!

Honey, when do you think I should plan on coming down? After the next check? Around November 3? What do you think? I'll have to start packing soon. I know I have a month yet but I'm so excited. I love and miss you so. Would you be able to meet Chad and I at the airport? Maybe if Sue and I fly together you and Matt can get there. What do you think? I guess when I go in to pay on the ring this month I'll tell them that I'm going to go to you and that I'll get them paid after we get back. We'll owe them $50.

Tony, I was let down today because of no letter. I know you've been busy but please write. Please Hon, I need your letter so much.

Boy, I was busy again today. I had to stock the candy shelves, talk to the candy and tobacco man, stock the school supplies, stock the tobacco, take inventory on the magazines, put magazines and books away, and fixed the candy shelves downstairs plus take care of the cash register part-time. We were short one girl.

Well I guess I'll close for now. Tony, I love you so much. I can't wait until I'm with you again.

Your lonely excited loving wife,
Clellie

P.S. Hugs and Kisses, etc.

✉ *October 3, 1969*   *12 midnight*

Hi Hon,

Well we now have $210 in the bank. Pretty good. I was going to put this $7 in the bank from the $100 from the Army, but I decided that you need it worse. Have a little fun on it if you can. I know it's not much but it's all I can do right now. I love you and I want you to have a good time but no girls! I'm glad I sent you that package anyway. Enclosed is what I've charged last paycheck at Thriftway. Also enclosed is a list of things I've paid with the government check and what I'm going to pay.

Work was pretty good today. They kept me pretty busy and then after work I went around trying to pay my stuff off.

Little Chad is exactly 3 months old today and he is 25 inches long and 18 pounds. Boy, if you don't think he's heavy! He dribbles now too. He sure is a living doll just like his papa.

Boy, that's ugly they caught up with you. It's their error. They should pay for it! I know the Army never pays for its mistakes. Ticked me off. Well you had better jump on them for not paying me all that I'm entitled to. Also Sue said that we were supposed to get a $30 raise because you're a corporal. Is that right? If so, boy, I should get gobs next month. Back pay for Chad, plus $130 for October, plus $30 dollars for you being a corporal.

Honey, thanks for the letter. You really sounded pretty down and out. Just think if we weren't married you could get more money. I don't care about money all I care about is that you love me. Honey, I'm coming down or I'll quit my job! All I have worked for is for us to be a family together! I don't care how poor we are as long as we're together. Please? Don't even talk about jumping off a bridge or such! Do you love me? Then don't even say such a thing!

Sue came over tonight and we're trying to work things out so we can get to you guys. Susan, Sue, and I went to grab a bite to eat and I told Susan's fortune. Great life.

Tony, you bought me enough! You're the greatest husband anyone could wish for. You've also given me things that you can't buy… your love and faith! That's more important! Honey, please don't worry about money. We'll work it out. I'll always love you. It's not your fault you're drafted and the Army's such a bummer! I love you now and forever!

All my love eternally, Clellie

✉ **3 Oct 1969**

Dear Clellie,

Do you still love me? Well I sure do love you. Is Chad doing alright? What's this about Chad being good-looking part of the time and homely the rest of the time? I think you're trying to tell me you don't think Chad is as good-looking as you let on. How about it?

What do you think about these goofy pictures I'm sending you? I really didn't want them, but I already signed for them. They only cost me a few bucks though. Notice how they make you take off all the brass off the uniform? Also they made us where our cunt caps. I know I look pretty ridiculous, but I thought I'd send them anyway. (They didn't even let us press our uniforms.) Give one to the folks and one to Marie if she wants it. I don't really care what you do with them, but if you're going to throw them away, burn them.

Clellie, this course is really starting to piss me off again. They're starting to treat us like we're in our first week again. I'm also broke. Just think, three more months with $23 a month. Well I'm not even going to think about it if I can help it.

Clellie, I don't see how you're possibly going to be able to come down now, do you? I also want you to pay off that ring instead of letting it wait until February or March.

I'm going to cut this letter short because I'm tired and very pissed off.

Clellie, the only thing I want or will ever want in this world is you. Please love me forever. Also please don't blame me or even mention to me in a letter about me not having you come down because I don't want you to. Because you know that I truly want you down here. (See I'm so tired I don't even seem to make sense. You understand though don't you?)

Clellie, I'll try and write you a decent letter in a couple of days. Maybe we can figure out some way to get you down here. Maybe right after Christmas or maybe we'll have to wait until I come home on leave. I love you, Clellie, and I always will.

Your husband,
Tony

NCOC Tony Jolley
104 Co 10th Stu. Bn. 3th Plt
Fort Benning, Georgia 31905

October 4, 1969   *11:30 PM*

Hi Hon,

I love you so much! I miss you so bad.

Boy, today at work Halloween candy came by the cases and I had to put it all out. I'm really drug out. I was on the go constantly at work today. What a drag.

Tonight, Susan and I went to the show in Rupert called, "Young Billy Young." It was really good. I picked Susan up at 5 to 8 PM. We got out at about 10:15 PM. We then came over here to Thriftway so I could show her some stuff; cosmetics, rings, and earrings. While I was there the girl got the tape stuck in the machine so I had to fix it. Great. I also ran into Denise. She said that Andrew wants to know when you get your leave because he wants to try and get one when you get yours. What should I tell her to tell him? Tony, you really need to write Andrew yourself. You never told him about Chad did you? I know he probably knows, but it's your place to tell him. He's not getting letters from your folks either so you two ought to communicate. What should I tell Denise about your leave?

After we left Thriftway as we came home and I showed her my makeup I use. I need to get some blusher. I'm going to order some. It's that sparkly stuff and it cost $3.50. After I showed her my makeup, I took her home.

Did you get the package I sent you yet and the money? Please let me know.

Ann dates now. She gets to stay out until 1am. Pretty good. Too bad I couldn't have the same privileges at her age. I am glad I was raised as I was though. I'd never traded it for Ann's.

Why can't I live with you just 'cause you're getting low pay? I've been thinking all day and it's bugged me so bad. I love you, Tony. You're everything to me and if Chad isn't around you some of the time you're both really going to feel like strangers. I love you so much. You don't know how much I've been counting on being with you! I miss you so much. All I want is to be with you, have your arms around me, and you telling me you love me.

Well I better close! I love you so much!

Your loving lonely rich wife, Clellie

P.S. Hugs and Kisses, etc.

✉ **October 5, 1969** *10:00 PM*

Hi Hon,

My cousin Pat gave me her old car seat that goes to a swinging jump set for Chad. I put him in it today. I made it swing and bounce. It looked so cute. He giggled! He's so cute and he talks a mile a minute.

Honey, if I can get away with it I don't want to have to work too much there because I'm afraid to leave Chad with someone I don't know. I've heard too many people leaving their kids and babies with a supposedly good babysitter and the baby winds up in the hospital from being beat.

I forgot to tell you in last night's letter, Bill and Bonnie seem to be getting along great. They dropped by last night to see Chad and me and ask about you. Do you want Bill's address? I can get it for you. They really treat each other good. It was nice to see them. They said Luke and Stephanie are getting along great. Stephanie's not working yet. Boy, Bonnie sure had a darling outfit on. She made it herself. It was so darling. It was a poncho over a skirt and top of the same material. I guess you know that as soon as I can I'm getting me a sewing machine. I have to learn to be a good seamstress. Then you can be proud of what I make.

It sure has been cold here now. Friday night it got to 25°. The mountains have snow on them. I don't know how cold it was today or yesterday, but it's so cold! Winter is here for sure. Well guess what? Saturday our furnace quit on us in the morning! Great. Everyone went hunting over the weekend and so no one could fix it. We had this guy who was supposed to clean it out, well it was so dirty it quit on us. So it is so thick on the walls, it's sickening. Ticked us off so bad! So here we sit freezing, coats on, and blankets. Chad's had on thermal sleepers most of the day. It wasn't so bad as long as the sun was coming in the windows, but it's getting cold now. Someone's supposed to come tomorrow.

Today I went and mailed your letter and bought some bubble bath for when I'm with you. I also went to the AC for us all a hamburger. We each paid for our own. Ann went out tonight. She's going with a Shawn Lynch who runs with Tyson Mason.

Well I better close for now. Tony, please say it's okay for me to come! I should get a big check from the Army next month and I know we can make it! Well I better go. Remember Tony that I'll always love and need you. I need you so much!

All my love and body eternally,
Clellie

P.S. Hugs and Kisses, etc.!!

✉ **5 Oct 1969** **Sunday**

My sweet Clellie,

How are you and our son on this Sunday? Here it is 10 o'clock at night here, and it's only 8 PM there. I'll be going to bed in about an hour or so, and the night will be just beginning back there. I sure wish I could be back there with you. Wow some of the things we could do.

I went and saw Jimi Hendrix this weekend in Atlanta. He's really great. It didn't cost me a thing either. This Thompson dude owed me five bucks, so he offered to take me. There was only about 15,000 people there. Some crowd. A lot of them were heads. They were selling acid and grass or anything you want to get. I sure wish I would've had some money. That's life though. After another 1 1/3 years of this goddamn Army, I can just get stoned and make love to you any damn time I want.

Clellie, what's this about Denny's mom asking if he took dope? Did she read my letter I sent him or something? The way it sounded she asked him about taking dope, then she gave him my letter. Wow man, she must be something if she read that letter. You'd better tell that asshole Carter to write, or when I get home I'll act like I don't even know him.

Yes, Clellie, I want you to keep telling me anything that happens. If some guy makes the least little pass at you I want you to tell me. I don't care if it makes me mad or not. The guy just better not be around when I get there.

I still want some pictures of you and those outfits you bought, Clellie. I bet you look good enough to have for dinner. By the way I am getting a little bit of an appetite for some. I guess I'll have to save that dessert for when I get home though.

Why hasn't Marie written me yet? She told me she would write this time. If you see her, you can tell her for me, but no matter what when I get home I'm not taking to her anywhere with us unless she gets her ass on the ball and writes me, I won't either.

Well Clellie, do you still love me? You haven't found anyone better have you? (Of course that would be damn hard ha ha!) I sure do love you, Clellie.

Clellie, I have to go for now. I don't know what I'd do without you and your love, so please don't ever leave me.

Your most loving husband,
Tony

I want you so much! I love you!

NCOC Tony Jolley
104 Co 10th Stu. Bn. 3th Plt
Fort Benning, Georgia 31905

✉ **October 6, 1969** *12 midnight*

Dear handsome hubby of mine,

Well I'm on the midnight shift this week ugh! It wouldn't be so bad if the drunk people would stay away. It was so slow. They're going to change the hours supposedly to 10 AM to 8 PM on Sundays, and 9 AM to 10 PM on weekdays. That won't be so bad. My boss came and talked to me and told me I was doing real well with my department. He asked me who I'd like to have work with me and I told him that it really didn't matter. He told this one lady that he thought he had a real good team of girls and he hopes he can keep us. How about that? I charged some film for my camera ($1.25), and some other ointment for Chad's baby rash ($.50). I'm about to give up. Do you know a Tony Lowe? He is the stockman. He was married the same day and year we were. He's a friend of John Butler's. He seems pretty nice. By the way I can't ever get Butler's wife at home to get his address. I'll keep trying.

Remember when I wrote and told you that I took Chad in for a picture at the ID? Well I got a card today saying their film is defective so I have to go in again Thursday to take them over. Boy, ticked me off. It's been three weeks ago.

Sue called me today and told me she wasn't going down there because Matt doesn't think she should. They seem not to be able to afford it either. I might as well warn you now that I'm in a disappointed, disgusted, let down, hurt mood. So please bear with me.

I had three women at the store go on and on about how beautiful they think my hair is. It's so long, pretty color, and shiny. Also Sue really digs it too.

I got your letter today and it made me quite heartbroken to be truthful. I must tell you that I love your pictures and so does Mom and the girls. It is very good and I'm proud of you. Mom wants one and if I ever get over to your mom's or see her I'll give her one and Marie one. I haven't been over but once since you've been gone and then your mother was asleep. I'm usually busy on my days off or they're working. I've seen them go by here a dozen times and they never stop.

Chad is a very good-looking baby. He just got out of an ugly stage. Ask anyone if they don't go through those stages. He's a big doll. I love him to pieces.

Carrie and Dale moved to Utah so I hear.

Honey, I'll pay the ring off with my next check. Also Chad and I are going to be with you at least from November 20 to January 2 and that matters closed. No matter where you are we're coming. The only reason I took a job was so we could be together. I don't enjoy being away from Chad all the time. Tony, money is not half as important as being with you. If you think otherwise, then I've failed as a wife. If you're going to be gone a whole year then we should be together as much as possible now. I boo booed once by not going with Sue and Carol but I won't again. If you're not around Chad more you won't even feel like his father when you get home. Besides I think we should be together on Thanksgiving, your birthday, our anniversary, Christmas, and New Year's as a family. If I have to starve I'm still coming around November 20. Tony, I've been counting on it so much. I don't see a problem or am I blind?

All my love forever,
Clellie

P.S. Hugs and Kisses, etc.

✉ **6 Oct 1969**

Dear Clellie,

Well here it is, 9 ½ weeks of the 12 weeks over. Benning, Georgia is really starting to get on my nerves. I've just about decided not to go to dog school now. The school would mean 12 more weeks here at Fort Benning, and I don't think I could do that at all.

Since the Army cut my checks so short, guess what I think I'll do, Clellie? How does it sound to you if I told you I might have a chance to go to Fort Carson, Colorado? In the school I still wouldn't have to be at a desk either. They train you for reconnaissance teams in Nam. When you get over to Nam, you're usually in long-range patrols or recon platoons. These are 6 to 10-man teams to go out in front of friendly lines and find out where the enemy is and what they're doing. Sounds exciting. I think I could really dig that. Also I'd probably be able to come home for a short Christmas vacation, and there's all kinds of skiing there, most of all though, I could have you and Chad maybe come and live with me. If the government's still cutting my checks, I could probably have you just come down for a week anyway. I want you with me as much as possible though. I better not count my chickens before they hatch or I'll probably end up getting something that would be the royal shits for both of us. Anyway I'll see what I can do.

Thanks for the money, Clellie. I used it to get my fatigues out of the laundry. I spend about six bucks a week on just laundry.

Clellie, you don't have to send me all your charge slips and lists of what you do with your money. I realize you're a big girl and I know I can trust you. You act as if you don't think I believe what you do with your money. I'm sending you your slips back. Please don't send me anymore unless there's something real important that you want me to see.

By the way Clellie, I still haven't received the package you said you sent me. I also can't figure out why you didn't get the money for Chad this paycheck. They told me it would be from 6 to 8 weeks so you should have gotten it. Don't plan on that money for anything though, Clellie. The Army is way behind on their financial records. There are still guys in my barracks that are trying to get finance to straighten out their records. Their wives haven't even received one check yet. Pretty good.

Clellie, I have to go now. Maybe in about five weeks we can be together for a couple of days. Then maybe for about three months before I go to Nam we can be together. I sure hope so, because all that time we're together I'm going to make use of you to the fullest extent.

I love, love, love you, Clellie, and I will forever. Love me too.

Your most lonely husband,
Tony

P.S. Send me some stamps if you would, Clellie?

NCOC Tony Jolley
104 Co 10th Stu. Bn. 3th Plt
Fort Benning, Georgia 31905

✉ **October 7, 1969**　　　　　　　　　　　　　　　　　　　　　*12:30 PM*

Hi Hon,

Well I'm really getting me an apartment or I'm coming there. I've had my fill! Mom volunteered me to comb Molly's hair Sunday, which ticks me off. So I told her today, and I also told her that she was gone too much again and the kids were getting the same as before. Well that did it and wham! She said everyone thought I was snotty and rotten since you left. Oh well I'll get over it.

Midnight

Boy, I sure am tuckered out. I had seven boxes of bag candy to put away, magazines to sort and put away, binders to put up, and lots. Sad. Then from 10 PM to 12 AM I didn't do anything but get bored.

How's the Army life? I hope it's okay. Or should I say as okay as can be. I miss you Tony so much and I want to be with you immensely! It would be so cool.

Susan came in to work to see me tonight. Did I ever tell you that she cut her hair? Well she did. Their divorce trial day is October 20, sad.

Ann got a job on the back of the harvester. I wonder how long that will last, don't you? Alice's bleached her hair almost blonde ugh.

Honey, do you think that I can plan on coming to you on November 25th? I want to be there for Thanksgiving-Christmas as a family. Who knows maybe next year you'll be out of the United States and we can't be together for the holidays.

I charged a five-minute pack at Thriftway. It was $.99 and I need it for my face. Remember when I told you in last night's letter that I bought a $.50 tube of ointment to see if it helps Chad's diaper rash? Well I tried it and it really turned it a beet red. Poor kid. So I burned some cornstarch and we're trying it. Cross your fingers. Boy, he sure loves his swing. He's so cute. He giggles so cute. You can see his giggle from his little stomach, and boy, he's going to be a little talker, he goos a mile a minute. He's so cute. When he is sobbing it sounds like he's saying Daddy and ow! Really! He gets upset and he just frowns so horrible before he cries. It's really cute.

I love you, Tony, more than you'll ever know you're so very special and I miss you so much. I can't wait until I'm with you. Always love me.

Yours eternally,
Clellie (Mrs. Tony Jolley)

P.S. Hugs and Kisses, etc.

October 8, 1969   *12 midnight*

Hi Hon,

How's my big Army lover doing? I sure do love you so much. I miss you gobs. Boy, it's a good thing you think things out beforehand. It would cost gobs to live there I guess. But don't you think that I could come to you for at least a month? I'd like to come in November around the 20th and stay until January 2. But if you don't think I should then how about December 3 through January 3? I'm sorry that I was so raunchy in my last few letters, forgive me? I just don't think too much, right? Right! I just want so much to be with you. I was so disappointed to think I couldn't.

I made an appointment with Dr. Katz in Twin for Chad. He's a pediatrician. Half of the time Chad bawls for no reason when we try to feed him his cereal or his vegetables and fruit. He also always has a lot of gas on his stomach. Also I want that rash on his bottom checked. I sure hope it doesn't cost too much, but I kept putting it off and now I'd better.

Well if people keep telling me how cute I am I'm going to get a swollen head. A teacher from the junior high said I was cute, and this woman who works there said her husband thought I was a living doll. How about that? It really made me feel neat.

I got these pictures back today. How do you like them? How do you like my outfits? They look better in real life. Isn't Chad a real knockout? He's so precious. Speaking of Chad. I know you're not going to believe me but I have witnesses to it, for quite some time Chad's been trying to say Daddy. When he gets mad at me, he scowls and tries to call you by saying da. Anyway when I came home from work for lunch Mom told me he'd said Daddy. I figured she was exaggerating and was fixing a sandwich when just as plain as day Chad said Daddy. It was so cute! Really! I about died. We've been saying Daddy to him all the time and finally he's doing it. He's so young. No one believes it but it's true! He tries so hard to form words with his tongue and mouth. It's so darn cute.

Well it's getting late so I better close. Tony, I love you so much and I do want to be with you. Who knows maybe I'll be able to save at least $200 for when you come home on leave.

Your lonely loving wife, Clellie

P.S. Hugs & Kisses, etc.

P.P.S. I'm sending half of the pictures tonight and half tomorrow night.

October 9, 1969   *12 midnight*

Hi Hon,

I sure do miss you. I wish so much I could be there with you. I'm so very lonely without you. It seems like such an awful long time since I've been with you. You're the best-looking guy in the world!

Do you know what October 8th was? It was an anniversary. Do you remember? You were a little plastered. You came over. I do believe it was about 11 o'clock and asked me if we could go park. You wanted to go all the way. I wanted to also, so I got a blanket, and we went out to your old blue pickup. I remember thinking that you'd probably decide not to at the last moment like you always had before. I wanted so much to be a part of you and finally I was. I also remember the next day, just two years ago today, I was so afraid you wouldn't love me anymore. You'd been so strong and I had practically raped you so many times. It was so neat when you dropped by after work to tell me you still loved me. I love you so much, Tony, and I think you're extra special. I'll always love you. Never can I change my feelings nor will I ever want to.

Well I ran my legs off again today at work. When I got to work at 3 PM, Melba only had half the books done, none of the tobacco done, part of the groceries, and she was working herself to death running back and forth from the cash register to her work. You see there were two other girls upfront working in the cosmetics. Well this gal named Carol is so lazy. She was just piddling around and the other girl was Ginger (the relief girl) she wanted to help but Carol told her she wasn't supposed to (a lie). So I got Melba and we went to finish the groceries. Pretty soon Carol yelled at me and said that one of us was to watch the cash register. I told Melba to ignore her and we went on with our work. One girl quit because of Carol a week ago, and one quit tonight because of the lazy thing. Ginger had missed a break because of Carol today. Anyway pretty soon Ginger came over and wanted one of us to come and watch the register because she had to count out her drawer. I asked her why Carol didn't and she said because Carol told her to come and get one of us. Boy, ticked! I told Jimmy about it tonight and he told me to come in tomorrow and tell Grant and he'd back me up because he'd been watching it all day. Man I am. I don't mind doing my share but she'd better get off her bottom too!

I saw Barry Jolley tonight driving an orange Mustang, first alone, then with some guys. That must be the car he bought. Pretty sharp. It's a fastback.

I'm sending you the rest of the pictures. How do you like them?

I got your letter today!

That sounds cool that you got to see Jimi Hendrix. I'm glad. Didn't see any neat girls did you?

I took Chad in for his retakes of his picture and I know they'll be darling. I can't wait!

I don't think Denny's mom read your letter. Mrs. Matthews was supposed to have told her. I never see Denny so I can't tell him to write. I really hope I never run into him again. I shouldn't be that way should I?

I don't know why Marie hasn't written Tony. Has your mother yet? Tony, it really kind of ticks me off. I can't see how come they can't write at least once a month. I work, take care of Chad, and everything, and I still get you a letter every day! I just can't understand it. Yet they expect you to call them the minute you get home. I imagine they'll write maybe a letter two weeks before you get home. I'm really kind of ticked off today. I don't know when I'll see them. I think they should stop once in a great while to see Chad. I'm kind of hurt. I've seen your mom go up town several times and she never stops, same with your dad. I'm sorry, Tony, but it gets to me. Oh well, I'll survive.

Well I better close for now. I need and want you forever. Be good and always love me.

Yours eternally,
Clellie

P.S. Hugs and Kisses, etc.

✉ **October 10, 1969**　　　　　　　　　　　　　　　　　　*12 midnight*

Dear handsome hubby,

I want some pictures of you. I miss you so very, very much. I was so pleased when I received your letter today. Boy, two in a row. I was so happy and they were so nice.

Gossip section: I heard that Tom Ford and his wife are getting a divorce, end of the gossip.

Today Alice and her friend walked over to your house for a while. Tonight Nikki, Joshua, and a friend of Barry's came over with Barry and took Alice and Nancy skating. By the way, it is Barry's car. It's a '66 fastback, orange Mustang. It's really sharp.

Well today was my day off and I spent all day tending to Chad, washing and ironing, washing my hair, and being slightly ill with cramps. Boy, I sure was glad that I got today off.

Susan and I spent a very impressive evening tonight. I went over and got her and we came over here to watch TV. Then at 10 o'clock we went to the Ponderosa and had a sundae. It was good. Then I took her home. On the way home after dropping her off the song "Shangri-La" came on and I just started to cry. I miss you so much and I want to be with you. Well I didn't want to be crying when I came into the house so I sat in the car for a moment and the song, "16 reasons why I love you" came on. Well then I really cried. About that time Alice and Nancy got home and came to see why I was crying. All I could do was sob and shrug my shoulders. I felt so dumb. Then on top of it all Mom came out. I asked them all just to leave me alone so they did. Tony, I kept it inside for quite a while and I finally broke tonight. I miss and love you so much. At about 11:40 PM I came in the house. I'm a boob.

I'm sorry I sent all those ugly slips and all that about what I do with the money but I figured if I showed you what I do with it you'd know because I forget what I do with it. So never ask me where the money goes because I can't remember that much. I won't send them again.

In your next letter please tell me when you graduate. Or how much longer you have to go. In your letter today you said something to the effect that maybe in about five weeks we can be together for couple of days. Does that mean that you might be able to come home after the school for a couple days?

If you want to go to Fort Carson, Colorado I hope you can go. It's really dangerous in the reconnaissance teams isn't it? For Chad and my sake I'd rather you'd be behind a desk. What are your chances to go to Colorado? A desk really sounds safer. I'd like it better but it's up to you. If you go to Colorado it'd be less expensive for me to get to you and we are going to be together for at least December and I hope Thanksgiving. We'll have to see what your orders are.

I was hoping you could use the money for a party. I'm sorry I couldn't send more to you. Also it ticks me off that you still don't have the package I sent you. He said that it'd take one week at the most!

Well I better go. I love you, Tony, so much.

Your loving wife,
Clellie

P.S. Hugs and Kisses, etc.

✉ **October 11, 1969**　　　　　　　　　　　　　　　　　　*12 midnight*

Hi Hon,

Well this is my last night at midnight shift. Great. They changed the hours at work. The store hours are Monday through Friday 9 AM to 10 PM, Sunday 11 AM to 9 PM. How about that?

Well you've been in the Army seven months now and it's been the loneliest seven months ever!

I had to push Barry in his new car today. About 11:30 PM Allan came over and asked if I'd go push his car to get it to start. So I did. Barry said that his starter has gone haywire. There I did my good deed for the week.

Honey, have you gotten the package yet?

Boy, almost a year of the Army is over with and am I ever so happy. I really am glad we're getting it over with aren't you? It used to bug me so much to know that I had two years ahead of me to be away from you. I'm glad that we have it almost licked. I miss you so very much.

You know, Tony, the only thing about that job that really bugs me is the old drunks and now that they've changed the hours maybe we won't have so many. You'd be surprised how many Playboy magazines we sell, gobs! And paper to wrap cigarettes. Speaking of marijuana, there was this kid who got picked up for pushing and possession of marijuana. When they tested it, you'll never guess what they found. It wasn't marijuana at all. It was simply weeds, so they booked him for selling under false pretenses. Poor kid.

Susan and I decided that we'd go get some more of that "weed" (oregano) we gave to you and Carter and sell it. What do you think? Ha ha!

Well I better close for now and retire. I love you so very much, Tony.

Your loving wife,
Clellie

P.S. Hugs and Kisses, etc.

✉ **October 12, 1969** 9:00 PM

Dear good-looking,

How's the big bad Army treating my wonderful husband?

Well work wasn't too bad today. I was kept so busy that the time really went fast, and boy, was I glad for that. There were so many people who were there today and it sure felt good to put in only eight hours instead of 10.

Denny came into the store today and bought something. I told him to get on the stick and write you because you told me to. He said he would and that there has been such a bunch of junk lately that he really hasn't been able to.

Tomorrow I take Chad to Dr. Katz's in Twin. I am glad I'll finally know for sure what is on his bottom.

All of us kids are pitching in one dollar and you and I put in 1 ½ dollars to buy Mom a birthday present. They already gave me their dollar and so I'm using two dollars of it for gas to take Chad to Twin, and $1 for Kotex. Excitement. Mom's birthday is October 26.

Honey for Christmas I've informed my family that we're not getting any Christmas gifts because of no money. All of the money's going for us to be together, don't you agree?

Tomorrow I go to work at 9 AM. I told them I'd stay until 15 till 2 PM because I had to take Chad to Dr. Katz so I guess I will.

Since Saturday at 5 PM until 1:00 PM today I waited on 479 people. Quite a few. Cash register keeps track, fun.

Guess who called me at work? My church teacher, she wanted me to go to a church fireside. I told her that I couldn't make it by 8 PM because I worked till 7 PM. I have a feeling that I'm going to be getting such phone calls from now on quite often. I wonder she knows that I'm married to a Catholic. What do you think?

Mom went with Molly and Edna Jolley today to American Falls. Sounds good.

Ann was supposed to have gone to work today but it had snowed a little out of Paul, Idaho. It also snowed in Oakley. It got 24° last night. Cold. I do believe it is winter at last.

Guess what's on TV now? It's "Fantastic Voyage." You know the one with the people going inside a person's body.

Do you think you will get a couple of extra days traveling time if you get transferred so you can stop by? If you can and you know what days they will be let me know so I can get them off. I miss you so much.

Well I guess I better go for now. I miss you so much.

Yours forever,
Clellie

P.S. Hugs and Kisses, etc.

October 13, 1969   *10:00 PM*

Hi Hon,

How's everything been going with you? I sure do miss and love you so much.

Guess who Gaylen is hooked on? Debbie Hill from Paul. Ann runs around with her. I guess Gaylen plans on marrying her when she gets out of school. He should be home on leave in February.

Well I took Chad to Dr. Katz in Twin today. It cost $7 which I'll pay out of my next check at work. Boy, he sure is blunt. He told me that I was trying to grow Chad up too fast, feeding him too many things all at once, and he was a very healthy baby. He weighs 15 pounds and is 24 ½ inches long by his scales. He had a small temperature of 100°. He told me to take them off of all baby food, and start him on carrots and applesauce for a week then give him a different vegetable for a week, and fruit, and keep doing it until I find out what he is allergic to. So I have to take the baby food back and exchange them. I'm going to feed him a jar of vegetables at noon and a jar of fruit at night. He told me not to get anything with egg, milk, or wheat in it until he is a little older. I'm supposed to keep him on SMA for a while. He said that he does have a little bit of eczema but it's very light and he'll grow out of it. He said that it's nothing to worry about. I have to get some diaperene rinse for his diapers, no plastic pants on him except at night, or if I have to take him somewhere until his bottom gets better. Also when he is napping undo his diaper and put it under him so his bottom will be exposed to the air. How about that for $7? Oh well I'm glad I found out for sure that he's healthy and okay. He has to go get one more shot at Dr. Peterson's the 25th and then he'll be all done.

I worked for five straight hours today. We got a shipment on candy that was old so I made the guy take them back today. Tough aren't I? I used up all the old candy downstairs and had to order a whole gob and wrote the date on them so I'd know how old they are. I get tomorrow off. Chad's been waking up at 6 AM and 3 AM sometimes again and it's about to get me down. I go around half asleep all the time.

Well we've been married 10 months today. We're getting right up there. Almost one whole year!

We went to put on Chad's little boots today and guess what? Chad has a big foot! He has outgrown his other shoes too. He's a big little man. He's so cute.

It's supposed to snow here tonight. Great. It's really been cold! It snowed in Pocatello already. It's supposed to be the worst winter and the longest we've ever had since 1948. Boy, am I ever glad that I have that big heavy warm coat since you're not here.

I wish that you'd hurry and find out your orders so I can make plans one way or the other. Be good and stay mine forever.

Your loving wife eternally,
Clellie

P.S. I love you so very, very much and will forever! Hugs and Kisses, etc.

✉ **13 Oct 1969**

Dear Clellie,

I miss you so much, Clellie. Last night at the NCO club I saw this girl that really reminded me of you. First when I saw her she didn't look much like you. As time went on, and I got a little drunker, she would smile and it would look just like your smile. I ended up leaving and taking a nice long walk in the cool night air.

Clellie, sometimes it seems that I can't remember what you look like or how it was to have you. Then other times I'll see us together and it's so real that I can almost feel your body next to mine. I almost go crazy some of the time and I feel that I just can't wait any longer to see you.

Well I better get off that subject.

How's Chad? Is his rash any better? I sure hope he doesn't have any skin problems when he gets older. How is everyone in the family? I hope everything is going okay. What's this about you saying you're going to get an apartment? Are the girls starting to get on your nerves? If they are just slap the shit out of them ha ha. Don't worry, Clellie, I'll be out of this Army before very long and we'll be doing our own little thing again.

Clellie, who is this dude that's the stock boy at Thriftway? You said his name was Tony Lowe or something. Has he been trying to make any passes at you? I want the truth. I want to know every little conversation you have with him. Go ahead and laugh Clellie, you're damn right I'm jealous. You know I trust you, but I sure as hell don't trust no stock boy that's been divorced especially when he knows you're married and your husband is away in the Army.

Clellie, you still haven't sent me any pictures of you in your new outfits. You better hurry up and send them. Also as soon as you get this letter I want you to send those pictures of me and you when we were at Banberry, also the ones when I had my mustache. I'll probably send them back, but I've been thinking of starting a scrapbook. I want those pictures though because everyone else has pictures of them before they were in the Army.

Clellie, I sure wanted to call you today. I was going to, but I don't have any money to send you and also I thought you would probably be at work. I think I'll call you next Sunday and let you pay for the call. What do you think about that?

Well I better say goodbye for now. Clellie, always love me as much as I do you, and we'll get along forever. Clellie, I love you very much.

Your faithful husband,
Tony

P.S. I love you.

P.P.S. Do you remember Perrin? Well I told you he wouldn't make it through NCO school. I guess he quit after his second week. Then he got his orders for Nam. Also Winston broke his leg and guess where he got stationed. He got stationed permanent party here at Fort Benning. That means he'll never see Nam.

October 14, 1969   *10:00 PM*

Dear handsome husband of mine,

I went over to your folks place today with Chad to give them the pictures of you, but no one was home. Mom wanted to borrow that jumper from Marie for Chad so she called her and told her that we'd been over. I guess she works every day except Monday and Wednesday. Her and Lance are still apart.

I took Chad's boots back and traded them for some Vaseline, swabs, and envelopes. Fun.

Well I washed windows, helped with the washing, folded diapers, went to town, and fixed some barbecue spare ribs. I tried giving Chad just vegetables for dinner but it just didn't fill him up so for supper I gave him vegetables and pudding. I am going to wait until 1 November to start him all over on carrots because I have all this baby food. He really isn't broke out so bad except his bottom and we went all day without plastic pants. Of course at the end of the day I didn't have the best of smells, but I think it'll clear him up. I changed him every hour. Lots of diapers. He's such a big cute boy! I love him gobs however, it can't compare to the love I have for you!

I got a letter from Bonnie Webster today. It seemed good to hear from her again. She loves BYU College and she misses Lance! How about that for summing up a letter?

Mom's supposed to go to work for King's in Burley around 1 November for the Christmas rush. I sure hope that she can. It would be really good for her and give her the experience she needs.

Boy, the Ramada Inn they're building here sure looks neat. It's not quite done but it sure won't take them too much longer.

Do you know it got 4° above in Colorado last night? Well it did. You'd freeze to death there.

You know when you get home sometime I want to spend one night in a motel just you and me. How does that sound to you?

Susan bought her a $24 birthstone ring this month. She doesn't wear her wedding ring. You know I sometimes wonder if I could live with my parents if they were like hers. I mean I like them and all that, but do you know what her dad came out and told me last Friday when she was going to come over and watch TV? He told me to take care of her and make sure she doesn't get too cold, and make sure she gets home early. He was really serious too! Oh well you never know do you?

Well with my job I'm learning a few things about cigars and pipes and tobacco. I still think cigars stink. They just about gag me and some old guys blow it right in my face. Pew what a smell! I also learned how to tell if a pipe has a filter or not. Boy, I'm getting smarter all the time.

Tony, I miss you! I can't seem to ever quit thinking about you. I'm forever remembering dumb things you used to do or precious moments. I love you!

Yours eternally,
Clellie

P.S. Hugs & Kisses, etc.

October 15, 1969 10:30 PM

Hi Hon,

I was so very happy to get your letter today. It was so neat. I love you, Tony, so much.

Boy, I sure was tired today. I can't hardly sleep at nights anymore. I wish I could be with you. I sleep light and usually wake up two or three times at night and you're all I think about. Other than me going around half dazed I'm just fine. I had to talk to a Roi Tan businessman and order some cigars. Boy, I'm big. Guess what? The girl that works part-time at Thriftway was talking to Susan and asked her when I was leaving to be with you and she told her about the last of November, and she said, "Boy, the boss isn't going to like that. He wanted to keep her because she's the best little worker he's seen." How about that? Now I'm getting a big head.

Susan and I went to a concert by the 3-D's. It was really cool. They were really good. Man we all sang the song "Give said the Little Stream." I thought I'd forgotten it, but I hadn't. We got in as students. It was at the Burley High so I guess I still look young. They didn't even ask us what our age was for an activity card. They bore their testimonies and sang at the end, Come Come Ye Saints. It was so cool but I guess it's not your sort of thing, but I think you'd of liked it. I'm on the songs they sang "Wendy", "Stormy", "I want to be Free", "Born Free." I really enjoyed myself. Then Susan brought me home. You know I kind of miss teaching primary kids the songs. I'd kind of like Chad to learn them and go to primary when he's old enough, but I guess we won't worry about it now. I do know I haven't lost all of the feeling for religion yet. Oh well.

You didn't talk to that girl at the service club did you? I don't care who she looks like. Unless it's me definitely no talking, see!

Chad's fine. Yes the kids are getting on my nerves and I imagine that I'm getting on theirs. I hope I can take one year and five months more of this.

Honey, don't worry about Tony Lowe. He's happily married and so am I. I'm sorry if I told you he's divorced because he's not. His wife's nice too and they are expecting their baby in April. He is a real good friend of Butler's and Bruce Graf. No he's not been making any passes. Promise! It was neat to know that you still get jealous. Honey, don't worry.

Have you got the package with the pictures? Please tell me if you haven't already.

I get off this Sunday the 18th and I want you to call. I miss you and I want to hear your voice so much. I hope you get this letter and my card in time!

Honey, I don't want you to go to Nam at all! I need you here with me.

Your most loving wife,
Clellie

P.S. Hugs and Kisses, etc.

✉ **October 16, 1969**　　　　　　　　　　　　　　　　　　9:30 PM

Dear good-looking,

Enclosed is $10 for you. I hope you will enjoy it. Do try to have some fun on it. Except no girls! I love you and I hate the thought of you with no money. Let me know if that helps brighten your day.

Well we now are minus of one payment. My wedding ring is now mine. Boy, does it feel so good. I had to get five cans of oil. Two of which went in my car. How about that?

Chad's getting better on his bottom already. Man, Tony, I think that we're going to have a kid with a horrible temper. Boy, if he gets mad at you he really lets you know and he will even take his bottle from you. If you look at him, he'll bawl. Spoiled? Heck no! Boy, when he starts to crawl he's really going to move! He tries so hard now, but he just can't quite get it yet. He really is a doll. Of course he gets his good looks from Daddy. He hasn't said Daddy for quite some time now. He's got beautiful blue eyes and he does have ears that stick out somewhat, but not really bad. I think he's such a little doll.

Well Ginger, a girl I'm training to help me, and I straightened up the magazines. They were in poor shape. They were so mixed up.

Sue called today and told Mom to tell me that she called. She wanted me to go to lunch with her today. I sure wish that I could have. Oh well I'll see her sometime.

Weather report: today we have showers all day long ugh! It was kind of warm though.

Sports: what do you think about the Mets winning the World Series? Did you make any bets on it?

Do you know that now it worked they have a schedule for our breaks? No kidding. Mine are at 11 AM sharp and 4 PM sharp. If I don't take them right then I'll miss out on them. Kind of ticks me off because half the time I'm ordering stuff from the salesman or putting stuff away. Oh well I'll just tell them to order it themselves 'cause I have to go on a break.

You remember Monica H. who married that McCrumbs? Well she works in Jensen's now. Her and her husband are buying a trailer house. She said they've got four years to pay on it.

Hope is back with Lance again. I can hardly see her anymore. She's being dumb, I think, about Lance. He goes with other girls for the night and only comes to see Hope about once a week at about 5 AM in the morning. Oh well it's her life.

So far our car has been starting okay in the mornings. Thank goodness. I'm so afraid that one of these mornings when I go to start it to go to work it won't start.

Honey, I love you so very, very much. Be good and stay mine!

Lovingly your wife,
Clellie

Hugs and Kisses, etc.

✉ **16 Oct 1969**

Dear Clellie,

How is everything back home in the world? How's Chad feeling?

I really dig those pictures of you and Chad. Chad is really growing isn't he? Man I hardly recognized him. You look beautiful in those outfits. You must really dig blue for a color. It looks to me like all your outfits were blue. I like them, don't misunderstand me. I think they're really cute.

You asked me if I got your box of goodies you sent me. Yes about three weeks after you sent the box, I got it. You think you're really cute don't you. Sending me a Roadrunner book and a perfumed bar of soap. You have some very comical things in it, and some things (like the candy and gum) that I really enjoyed. The thing I really dig and appreciate the most though is that back scratcher. Wow that thing scratches spots that haven't been touched since I left home for Fort Benning. It was really sweet of you to send them, Clellie.

Guess what? There's supposed to be 16 inches of snow on the ground already at Fort Carson, Colorado. It's also supposed to be colder than hell. If we can arrange it so you can come live with me you're really going to have to bundle up, Clellie. I don't mind though. That just means we have to cuddle up to keep warm.

What's this about you telling Carter to write? I thought you told me that you didn't want me to hang around with him when I got home. If you don't want me to hang around with him, don't tell him to write. Anyway Clellie, he shouldn't have to be told to write. If you can't write to me just for the simple reason because we're friends and because he should answer my letter, I just as soon not have him write. I don't know if I'm going to hang around with him or not. If he's hanging around with a bunch of high school punks, I'm sure as hell not going to. I guess we'll have to see what happens when I get home. I've changed quite a bit and I really don't know what I'm going to do and who I'm going to hang around with. I'd like to be alone I think once in a while to think things out. It'd really be something to be able to be alone. You know, Clellie, I don't think I've been alone ever since I got drafted. The only time I've been in company that I've truly enjoyed though is when you and me have been together all alone.

Well I better go for now, Clellie. Friday we have an operations test that accounts for 1/3 of our entire grade and it's supposed to be real rough.

I hope we can be together for Christmas, Clellie. I'll probably graduate November 4, but I won't get any leave. Not even a couple of days. They give you one or two days to get to Colorado.

Clellie, I love you very much, and I want you to remain the sweet, kind, and beautiful person you are. Always love me, Clellie, as much as I do you, and we'll never fall apart.

Your loving lonely husband,
Tony

I want you, Clellie!

NCOC Tony Jolley
104 Co 10th Stu. Bn. 3th Plt
Fort Benning, Georgia 31905

✉ **October 17, 1969**   9:00 PM

Hi Hon,

Tom Ford and Estelle are getting a divorce. Ann talked to Tom and his friend. He said that he felt really bad but she didn't like him going out. He also told Ann that he thought I was a real straight chick. I'm not sure whether it's supposed to be an insult or a compliment. He said that you and him used to be really good friends.

I was going through Alice's coat to find something and guess what? I found a pack of L and M's. Her and Nancy smoke them all the time. Mom and I told her that if she was going to smoke she'd better do it in front of all of us.

Work was pretty busy today, two candy man's orders came in. Boy, there was candy everywhere. It took me the entire day to get rid of it. My fingers are so scratched up and sore from the boxes. My nails are all broken off. My hands look a mess! Oh well you love me anyway.

Gossip of the day: I hear Val and Monica are getting a divorce. He wants to leave her now and go straight to California.

Chad's little bottom seems to be getting a lot better. Now he acts like a little angel, almost! Other than he has his own mind, and a great set of lungs he's a little doll. At most times he's so darn adorable.

Wow I'm so tired tonight. I think I worked for 10 days. It made the time go by fast though. I was walking to work from the car when a pickup load of boys whistled at me. I naturally ignored them. Other than that it was a normal day.

Ann's gone to a game, Alice went skating, Nancy's babysitting, Mom's with Molly, and so that leaves Chad and me here, Chad's in bed. Tony, I'm so lonesome without you. I miss you so much.

Mom got rid of Mitch. He still calls but she just hangs up.

Tony, when do you graduate? Do you know yet where you're going? I miss you so much it's sickening. I'm so lucky to have you, Tony. I want to always have you for my own. Be good and stay mine forever!

Your loving wife, Clellie

P.S. Hugs & Kisses, etc.

October 18, 1969   *10:00 PM*

Dear wonderful good-looking husband of mine,

How do you like that title? Pretty groovy.

I received your letter today and I was so very pleased! I sure hope that you call me tomorrow. I'm so excited!

I got the phone bill today. I had to call Twin to get Chad's appointment so it's on there too. Altogether I owe $9.05 which I will take out of my next check.

Do you want to hear about my wonderful day? Well like it or not here it goes. At 1 AM Chad woke me up groaning. At 3:30 AM he woke me up crying. At 4 AM, he woke me up bawling. He has a cold and his nose was all stuffed up and he had an upset stomach. I gave him some Pepto-Bismol and 2 ounces warm water plus I blew his nose. Sweet aren't I? He went to sleep and woke up at 6 AM and wanted his bottle. At 8 AM I got up and got ready for work. At 15 to 9 AM I went out and tried to start my car. Guess what? It wouldn't start so I footed it to work. At noon Mom tried to start it, still no go! At 5 PM, I footed it home. At 7 PM, I went back to work because we were short a girl and they needed me. I stayed till 9:30 PM and Daisy came to get me because Alice had to go babysit. Needless to say I'm tired (bloodshot eyes)! I want to make as much money as fast as I can! As soon as I get $400 I'm going to you. So far I have $250. Guess what Sue told me? I can claim you, Chad, and me as dependents. Right now I'm not claiming anyone. So when I get my tax returns we'll get gobs back. Good.

My Uncle Louie is going to come over and check my car Monday to see if he can find out what's the matter with it and how much it'll cost to fix it. Ticks me off. Footing it is for the birds, 'sides I'm skinny enough!

Those pictures of me weren't so good but thanks anyway! Yes, I love blue. It seemed any other color just didn't look so good. Really. Even Mom and Susan liked it the best. They're cuter in real life, and boy, that coat is so warm. I'm so glad.

I'm glad you liked the box I sent you. I was hoping you'd get a kick out of it! I love you so much! Is the back scratcher as good as me?

Tony, one thing for sure, when I get $400 saved I'm coming or at least by December 3rd. I'm going to be your birthday, and our anniversary present. We're going to spend December at least together. At the least I want to be with you from December 3rd to January 3rd. I'm going to too, and Thanksgiving if possible!

Honey, you told me to tell Carter to write so I told him. I really don't want you running with him. I hope you don't, Tony. I just don't trust him at all! I agree with you. He should write because you're friends not because he was told. I think I shouldn't tell your folks to write. They should because you're their son. Also I haven't told Marie to write or you'd never take her

anywhere with us because I figure she should just because you're her brother. Do you think I'm wrong? Please tell me if you do.

How did you do on your operations test? I'll bet you did real great.

Honey, do you think you've changed that much? I think your wanting to be alone, it's natural.

Well I better close. I'm about asleep. Tony, I love you so much! I love you so much.

Your wife eternally,
Clellie

P.S. Hugs & Kisses, etc.

October 19, 1969   9:30 PM

Hi Hon,

Honey, how long does it usually take my letters to get to you? I want to know so I'll know when to stop writing letters if you get transferred. When do you graduate?

I'm so happy your mother wrote to you. Did you tell Andrew about when you would get a leave for home? Has Marie wrote yet? I still have not been able to give them your picture yet. I'll try to real soon.

Boy, it sure seems like today went by fast. I attended Chad, did my ironing, washed our sheets, blankets, my work clothes, and my nighty. Hung them out (it took the whole day to dry). I cleaned our room up. Now I go eight days before I get another day off. I need to catch up on sleep but Chad and getting things done don't do any good. Chad's got quite a little cold. I wish you could see him. He's so darn cute. I love him more all the time. The only trouble is that I am a selfish person. I don't want to share you with anyone even Chad. Pretty bad, aren't I?

Carrie called today. Her and Dale moved to Tooile, Utah. She said that it's not too bad. It's like a desert and she's not going to work unless she can get a part-time job. I really can't blame her. I wouldn't work now except I want to be with you. She said to tell you hi from her and Dale.

Boy, everyone's going deer hunting. We sold completely out of deer tags and so did everyone else around here.

Susan called today. She goes to court tomorrow. She's asking for $120 a month. Natalie Johnson's in the hospital or was. Why? Well the gossip was: 1. One of her ovaries had fallen 2. She had to have her tubes tied (this her sister Gail was telling). Well anyway Denny was visiting her every night. Denny started you a letter and dropped it on the floor in the bathroom at his parents so Mrs. Carter was telling Susan. He told you in it not to believe all this you've been hearing because they're lies. So he might give you quite a snow job. If they are lies then I am the liar right? But I've told you all I know about it.

Guess what? Yesterday the money at work, the money from drawers B1 and B2 was missing about $300. We don't know where it's going. Someone had to have taken it within a half hour. It also had to be someone who knew where the money's kept. No one knows or even has an idea who did it.

This guy Mom's going with built Nancy's dog a doghouse. He works good and he's nice. He's kind of homely. He gave me $20 to go buy Mom a birthday present. He wants to marry Mom but I don't know what will happen. Mitch keeps calling to tell her how hard he'll work, but she tells him nothing doing. He's already proven himself.

I saw Karen Steiner yesterday. She told me that Flora's really hooked on this one guy in Utah. She really loves him and he seems to really dig her. How about that?

Well I better go for now! Love you forever!

Yours eternally,
Clellie

P.S. Hugs & Kisses, etc.

✉ **19 Oct 1969**

Dearest Clellie,

I sure did love talking to you on the phone today. The only thing I hate about talking to you on the phone is the bit when we have to hang up.

Chad really sounds like he's grown a lot since I left. That's pretty good when a father has to leave his son who can't even see yet, then the next time he communicates with his own son the kid can almost talk already. I might not make much sense, but I have a reason. Moltz came back to the barracks about an hour ago with a fifth of Southern Comfort. We're not supposed to have liquor in the barracks, so about three of us killed it. I guess I didn't make it the whole weekend without drinking. At least I didn't have to spend any of my own money though. This Calhoun dude (a soul brother) brought back a lid of weed and he said he'll turn me on this week. Groovy.

Starting tomorrow will be our 11th week. If I decide to make Sgt., I'm really going to have to hit the books to prepare for our "operations" test Saturday. Will have two-hour study halls every night this week because we have a lot of material on this test, and it's real rough.

Is Carter's and Susan's divorce final? Do they actually have the divorce yet, or are they waiting to go to court? Does Carter go over to see Susan or Juan at all? I hope that dude gets his head set right, goes back with her, and tries to start over. Have you seen him at all since he came in the store? I really don't know if Carter and I will have much in common when I get home.

Clellie, I don't want you to cry like that anymore on the phone. You really put me in a raunchy mood when you do. The next time you do, I'm going to go AWOL and head home to you. Then they'll catch me and put me on the stockade for six months of hard labor and then I'll have to finish my whole term over again.

I'm not sure when we can be together, but we will be together as soon as possible. I miss you too darn much to be away from you. I not only miss the sex part of our relationship, I miss all of it. Like you waking me up in the morning, and almost dragging me out of bed to eat breakfast because I wouldn't wake up.

Clellie, it seems so long since we've been together. I miss the talks we used to have. Remember all the times we would talk about getting married? You'd always accuse me of not wanting to marry you because all I would do was talk about it and not do it. I sure proved you wrong didn't I, funny face?

Well Clel, I better go for now. I love you gobs and I always will. I can't wait until we're together again in a nice cozy bed playing nice cozy games. Always love me.

Your loving husband,
Tony

P.S. I'm enclosing those pictures. Everyone really thinks you're a knockout. I want you, Clel!

NCOC Tony Jolley
104 Co 10th Stu. Bn. 3th Plt
Fort Benning, Georgia 31905

October 21, 1969   *10:15 PM*

Hi good-looking,

How's everything been going with you? I hope real good. I miss you so very, very much, Tony. I can't wait to be with you.

Well a car of boys tried for about three minutes to get my attention, but I wouldn't even look. A guy came in to Thriftway's and kiddingly asked if I wouldn't like to go home with him. I told him that I'd like to go home to my husband, how's that?

Susan and Denny went to court today. Susan had it stated in the divorce papers that Denny couldn't see Justin if he was under the influence of dope or alcohol. Well guess what the lawyer got the divorce on? Denny being a dope addict. They put him on the stand and he ended up having to admit it. Sad. Well the court gave no divorce grant yet. They have to make a few decisions. I'd say they're going to check up on Denny. Anyway for the time being he has to give Susan $100 a month. Susan came up to the store and was feeling pretty bad. Denny came down here to see me and Uncle Louie was checking my car. I needed a distributor cap and a rotor. Well Denny volunteered to put it in and get it. He came to the store and looked pretty sad and mad. He told me that by Susan he was a dope addict. I told him not to take it so hard. Then he asked me what year my car was so I told him. After he left I called Mom to see who had checked my car and who was fixing it. I told her to pay Denny the cost of the stuff and I'd pay her when I get my next check. Mom came up a lunch break to get me. It starts really good now. Mom told me that Denny's mother called to talk to me too. You know I'm going to start my own column in the paper called "Dear Clellie." What do you think? I feel so two-faced, Tony. I don't trust Denny, and I am angry at how he treated Susan, yet I feel sorry for him. I think he's not really right. What do I do?

It cost about $5 to fix the car. Not bad. Boy, I was worried.

Kenny Albertson and that girl he was going with got married recently in the LDS Temple.

I charged some baby aspirin at Thriftway's for Chad. He's got quite a little cold.

Boy, Ann sure has been knocking me lately at my skinniness and my long hair. I guess I'll have to knock her about her chubbiness and short hair. Everyone tells her that she better stop eating. She's getting chunky. I really think that I'm the same way as I was before I got PG. I am not so worried. Those dumb uniforms we have to wear make me look skinny that's all. Everyone compliments me on how neat they think my hair looks so I'm not worried.

Well enough of my problems, I love you so much, Tony. Be good and stay mine forever.

Your loving wife, Clellie

✉ **October 21, 1969**　　　　　　　　　　　　　　　　　　　　　*10:00 PM*

Hi Hon,

How's the most wonderful guy in the whole world doing? I love you, Tony, and I always will! Never decide you don't love me!

Alice's been babysitting Dottie's kids off and on for the weekends. Well last weekend she blew it. She went through all her drawers, emptied the $8 bottle of her perfume, and had boys over. She finally admitted it so Mom called Dottie and told her not to worry about paying her. Sad. I just can't believe these kids. I'm glad though that I haven't had to go through what they have.

Guess what? Susan called me this morning and told me that Mrs. Carter might call and ask me if you're on anything. Mrs. Carter blames everyone but Denny for his faults. Anyway she called Susan and asked her if you were on anything. Susan told her that she didn't know. Mrs. Carter then asked Susan how she knew that you and Denny weren't stepping out on Susan and I and when you were running with Denny. Susan said that we always knew where you were and what you were doing and we usually always ended up with you guys. Then she asked Susan why she didn't make Denny stay home with her instead of letting him go with you all the time (as if you drug Denny out of his house). She told Mrs. Carter that if Denny had wanted to be with her he could've stayed. Boy, I was so ticked. If she calls and brings you into it, I'll tell her to leave you out of it. Denny is a big boy and he's the one who's ruined his own life. No one else! If she only knew how good you kept Denny when you were here! Boy, I'm ticked.

This lady came in tonight and asked if I used to go to Beauty College. I told her yes. She said that she had been one of the instructors that went to the other school just before I started. She said that she'd heard so much about me from everyone that she always wondered who I was. How about that? She said that she was happy to meet me!

Well work was a big tussle today. The girl that was supposed to help me had to leave before I got there because her kids were sick. So I ended up putting all the magazines and books away and that was tiring. Then from about 8 PM to 10 PM I had to be at the checkstand alone because the other girl got sick. This week I work from 2 PM to 10 PM. I don't get a day off until next Tuesday.

Chad still has a cold. He has a little runny nose and is stuffed up. You know when these kids argue and fight he cries and is so upset that he won't take his bottle even for about 15 or 20 minutes after they're done. I'm afraid that it's going to make a very nervous child out of him. I hope not.

Well I guess I better close. I'm pretty bushed. I love you, Tony, and I will eternally.

Your most loving wife,
Clellie

P.S. Hugs & Kisses, etc.

✉️ **October 22, 1969** *10:20 PM*

Hi Hon,

I love you good-looking hubby of mine!

Say I got a $25 savings bond today from the Army. Where did you get the money for it? Course it's from September. What should I do with it? Put it in the bank or hide it here? Pretty cute, aren't you? Why didn't you ever tell me that you got it?

Tony, do you mind me sending you money? If so, why? Do you care if I send you $10 next paycheck? Please let me know. I hate the thought of you not having any money. It seems so unfair. I love you and I don't want you unhappy, Tony.

Man, my back and sides sure ache. They really bugged me today at work. I can't miss any work though 'cause I need as much as I can save to get to you. I'm quite bushed though. I still have to work five more days before I get a day off. I hope I can take it. It's good that we only work eight hours with an hour lunch a day.

Marie came in to Thriftway's today at about 1 PM. Naturally this week I don't go to work until 2 PM. She asked what time I came in and they told her but she never stopped off here. Oh well.

Chad still has his cold. It seems to be a little better though. I give him half an aspirin (baby) three times a day. His little bottom looks much better. It's all cleared up except a spot so I'm glad. He's still growing. He's going to be a big boy now and there's no stopping him!

I think for Christmas we'll get him a stuffed animal and an outfit. What do you think?

Dad's moved off the farm to someplace else. We don't know where except that it's in Rupert. He rented the house again.

I didn't do too much of anything today before I went to work. I ironed my uniform, did the dishes, fixed Chad's formula, took a bath, gave Chad a bath, ate, and fed Chad. Real neat exciting day.

I'm yours eternally, Tony! Be good and stay mine!

Your loving wife,
Clellie

P.S. Hugs & Kisses, etc.

✉ **22 Oct 1969**

Dear Clellie,

How are you and the baby? I sure hope you're just fine.

I'm in study hall and I only have time for a short letter, which will probably be the last one I write this week. We have to have two hours of study hall every night this week to study for our final exam Saturday. They're continually going through study hall making sure you're not writing letters or doing anything but studying and intelligence. Man, there're so much junk to know for that test you just couldn't believe it. We had a couple more guys get kicked out of the course today. It sure is a bummer, two of the best guys in the whole course just for signing their names and putting the peace sign behind it. A lot of us did it but only two got caught. Spear really is a pain in the ass. He's going around saying how stupid the demonstrations are and everything else. That's only because he's afraid to do anything about them, because he might get kicked out of the course. I'm sure glad he's going to dog school, and I decided not to go. We got drunk the other night and we had it out. Now we're getting along pretty good but he's such a baby he just plainly gets on my nerves.

Clellie, if by any chance we can't to get together by the third, I don't want you to be too disappointed. So don't plan on it. If we could wait until Christmas, I'd probably get a two-week leave and I could come home for the holidays. Then when I went back after that, I'd only be gone about four more weeks, then I'd be home on the 30-day leave before going to Nam. Think about this.

Clellie, I love you so much. The only thing I want is for us to be together. You have to believe that. As long as you love me we will always be together, because my love could never die for you. Always love me, Clellie. I want you with me so bad.

Your loving husband,
Tony

I love you, Clellie! You're still mine, aren't you?

NCOC Tony Jolley
104 Co 10th Stu. Bn. 3th Plt
Fort Benning, Georgia 31905

October 23, 1969   *10:15 PM*

Hi good-looking,

How's everything going with you? Fine, I hope.

Chad's doing okay, he goos quite a bit now, and smiles for almost everyone. He's rapidly growing. He's wearing a size 2 baby shoe and clothes that most babies can't wear until they're at least six months. Don't get me wrong. He's not real fat. He's big all over. He's so darn cute. His cold is much better.

Boy, you wouldn't believe all the compliments I've had on the wedding ring. Everyone loves it. I've also had a lot of compliments on my hair especially today for some reason. I don't think it's all that great, but I am proud of it. This old duffer came in tonight and showed me a cover girl on a magazine and told me I looked a lot like the girl. One guy even agrees with you that I look like "that girl" sometimes. I'll bet you think I'm getting conceited. Well as long as I stay away from a mirror I am conceited.

Mitch got back into town today. Mom went for a ride to tell him to get lost today at about 11:30 AM or 12 noon, well she didn't get back until 8:30 PM or so. If she wants to stick with him that's fine but she just needs to decide. This Red built Nancy's dog the dog house and is buying Mom a $17 pair of slacks and a $10 pair of shoes for her birthday. Pretty nice.

Tony, I was so happy to get your letter. I only wish that we were together instead of talking in letters. I miss you terribly!

Tony, what if you get caught with some weed? What then?

How did you do on your test? If you make a Sgt. when will it be?

The way that I understand things after so many more days if Denny doesn't contest the divorce it's final. I think his days are up. He goes and sees Justin quite a bit I guess. He wants custody of him for a few months out of the year and Susan doesn't want to let him. You know in a way she seems to be pretty bitter. I don't really blame her. Denny came in yesterday to buy some cough drops, but I didn't talk to him much. I told him thanks for fixing my car again. That's about it. I doubt if you and Denny have much in common when you get home either. You're so different, so special, and so great compared to Denny. You're so much better-looking and groovy! I think Denny's head's set crooked forever. One day he'll be sorry though.

I am sorry I cried on the phone. I didn't want to. I tried not to because I knew it would make you feel rotten. It's really bad though, Tony. Everything reminds me of you, of us! I miss you so much. Like tonight at work. The radio was playing the requests and on came "Keep your hands off my baby." Remember when Shirley Hutchins requested that to Denise for me? I almost laughed to remember that. Tony, I miss you so much and I want so bad to be with you.

You know, when we were going together and we used to talk about getting married? I knew most of the time that you wanted to marry me, but something was stopping you and I couldn't pinpoint it. Then other times I regretted going all the way because I figured if we hadn't, you'd marry me sooner. The only thing I regret is that we didn't get married sooner! I must admit it took everything I could muster up to get up and fix your breakfast in the mornings. I always want to fix your breakfast, Tony. I don't want one morning to go by without you eating ever. A couple of times I missed fixing it, didn't I? I love bedtime, bath time, mealtime, just every time. See you soon prayerfully!

Your loving lonely wife,
Clellie

P.S. Hugs & Kisses, etc.

✉ **October 24, 1969** **10:45 PM**

Hi Hon,

I didn't get off work until 10:15 PM because there were so many people in the store. Pheasant season opens tomorrow. Fun. Just from 5 PM till 10:15 PM I waited on 190 people. Not bad. We close down at 10 PM but it was 10:12 PM before everyone had left.

I went and saw Marie at the shop today and we went to lunch together. She said that she's going to have to write you real soon. I said yes that you figured she had a real badly broken arm. She thinks Chad's cute. Everyone does. They say he looks like both of us. How about that?

Tony, I received your letter today. It made me so sad. I about bawled. It was sweet, but the part about me not being disappointed if we can't be together by the third really clouded my day! Tony, why can't I? Is there a reason? Please tell me! I've been disappointed so many times now and it's frustrating. I wanted to be with you October 15th, then I changed it to the last of October, then to 1st of November, then to the 15th, then to the 26th, then to third of December. Tony, can't you understand that I want to be with you now! Since I can't now then as soon as possible. I've not been working for nothing! Chad needs me at home too. He's not going to even know which one of us is his mother. Since you get to come home for Christmas then I'm going to go to you by the 20th of November until you get to come home for vacation. Then I'll come back with you. What do you think? I do know one thing, if I quit Thriftway's he'll never hire me again because everyone's told me that once you quit he will not take you back. I'd rather be home with Chad until you get back anyway. Then I can get a job to help us. What do you think?

How did you do on your exam? How are you doing? So Spear really bugs you? You're both so different! You're so neat and he's kind of funny. I love you so much.

I have $250 in the bank now. Christmas is two months from tonight. That's so long!

I keep thinking that I'll run out of tears but they keep coming. I need you, Tony, so bad. I hate the Army so bad for this. I hope we can be together soon. Tony, please!

Yours eternally, Clellie

P.S. Hugs and Kisses, etc.

✉ **October 25, 1969**   **10:40 PM**

Hi Hon,

How's your day been lately? I hope A-OK!

Well I worked until 10:20 PM. Great. Boy, I'm tired. We were so busy! Town was crowded. Do you know there's not a vacant place here or Rupert? Even the Ramada Inn opened up 60 units and they were taken! How about that? It's just swamped with people! Enough for the local scene.

Weather: it's been pretty nice for the past two days. Thank goodness.

Chad's had this cold now for about a week. He's got a pretty bad cough with it to. Tonight I didn't have anyone to watch Chad. Mom went out, Ann went out, Alice went babysitting, and Nancy was watching Hope's kids so I took him to Hope's. I sure hope he doesn't get worse.

I changed shifts for tomorrow with Lena so I work 11 AM to 7 PM. I like that shift the best anyway.

Do you know what I want to do when you get home after we've spent quite a bit of time in bed? I want to go to a dance. Maybe the Villa in Twin.

I saw Dad and Faith today. They came into Thriftway's to buy a paper. Great. Dad didn't say much but Faith was chit-chatty. Oh well I am a no good in his eyes anyway.

Your dad got interviewed to be manager of the Ramada Inn bar. We don't know who got it yet. I hope he does. I heard he was having a little trouble with your car.

Tomorrow's Mom's birthday. Marie invited me over tomorrow because she was having a small party for Bradley but I have to call her and tell her I can't make it because of work. Mom said that she saw your mom a couple of days ago. She asked about Chad and I and was real apologetic about not being over to see him. Sometimes I believe that I'm acting like a baby because they never come to see him. Guess I have some growing up to do yet.

Well our time is changing tonight. We set our clocks back an hour.

I guess I better close. I'll bet tomorrow will be a real rough day. I love you, Tony, and I will forever.

Your wife eternally, Clellie

P.S. Hugs and Kisses, etc.

✉ **October 26, 1969**   **8:00 PM**

Hi Hon,

Boy, for some reason I'm in a very ticked-off mood. Nancy has some friends here and I've been cussing Nancy out all night. I'm so sick of this junk. I feel so ashamed of myself. I want to be with you so very, very much. I can't take it like this much more.

Work was so rough I'm about dead. Most of the time I was upfront alone. Talk about a line! I'm really beat!

Marie came into the store today and she looked pretty nice.

I went to work from 11 AM to 7 PM. From 5:00 PM Saturday night to 5 PM today I waited on 450 people. I was so busy. I think I've developed a hate for Sundays. It's always so busy I am bushed. Well enough for work complaints.

This one old duffer that said that I looked like the girl on the front page of the magazine. Well he came in today twice and was telling people about it. I was embarrassed…enough for my conceit section.

We gave Mom her present today. She's 43 now. She said to tell you thanks too. She's gone right now with Molly.

Susan has gone to Mountain Home for a couple of weeks. She's going to stay with her sister. I think it'll do her good. She needs to get away.

Tonight I took one of Nancy's friends home and on the way back home I saw Barry Jolley's car coming down Main. So when I was passing they honked and I looked over. Guess who was driving it? Denny Carter. He runs around with young enough kids. I hear that Natalie Johnson has his ring. How about that? She says that they're going to get married. Of course this is only gossip. I think it's a real sad deal.

Tony, I miss you so desperately. Please say that we can be together soon. I'll always love you!

Your most loving wife,
Clellie

P.S. Hugs and Kisses, etc.

October 27, 1969　　　　　　　　　　　　　　　　　　　　　　　　　　　*10:45 PM*

Hi Hon,

Work was pretty good today. I'm on the 9-to-5 shift again. I can't decide what shifts I like better. Today I ordered candy, straightened the magazines after yesterday, ordered tobacco, Ginger and I cleaned the freezer out, stocked the candy and tobacco shelves, dated the candy downstairs, and put them on their shelves, and watched my till. Sounds like one big ball. It was exciting. Tomorrow is my day off. Thank, heavens. I'm really beat. Seven days straight about kills you off. I shouldn't complain. I have it easier than you.

Well if one of these fine days I write and tell you of me getting a black eye don't be surprised. You see Nancy and her friend Janet were riding home on their bike around 7 PM when Pam Martin and about seven other girls jumped them and pushed them around, wrecked the bike, and scared them half to death. When Nancy and her friend got home they were bawling. Mom's at American Falls, she's been there since Sunday. Well I called the cops and reported them. Janet's mother called the cops and told them that she wanted them picked up because she wanted to talk to them. I called Pam's father to tell him and he was real snotty. Ticked me off. Nancy, Janet, Janet's mother, and I went to the police station and talked to the girls. They got picked up for having beer too. Two of the girls I felt really sorry for. The other two I wanted to throw the book at. Snotty! Four of them got completely away. Anyway Ann says that Pam pounds boys even. She does look strong, so do her friends. Ann said that she'd probably seek revenge on her and me. Oh well! We dropped the charges and one of the girls I felt sorry for told us to tell Nancy and Janet that they were sorry for scaring them or hurting them. How about that for excitement? Boy, if I don't get into messes. Never a dull moment agreed?

Well I better be going. Tony, I love you so very, very much. You're so special!

Eternally yours, Clellie

P.S. Hugs and Kisses, etc.

✉ **27 Oct 1969**

Dear Clellie,

How was the most charming, best-looking girl in Burley, Idaho doing on this Sunday? Also how's the best-looking kid? I sure hope you're all right. I really miss you. I really want you too.

Guess what? I just finished my 11th week yesterday. We also had our last big test for this course too. It really feels good to be almost done. One more week and we'll be through. We have our graduation party Saturday, and then on 4 November we graduate. I guess I won't be able to come home at all after this course. It makes me so damn mad. When they give us our orders for OJT they only give us about 24 hours to get there. That won't give me any time at all to go home. I sure wish I could though. I'll have to figure out some way for us to be together as soon as possible.

Clellie, the only thing I miss back home is you. You're the only reason I was hoping I would get a little time off. I want to see and hold you so bad.

I'm getting kind of nervous about OJT. I know that I don't want to be in an office or something. In this job and in an office, you're responsible for a lot of lives. You have to call in artillery support for the troops in the field and everything. If you made one little mistake on your coordinates, the rounds would land right in the laps of the American troops instead of the enemy. I think I could dig it better out in the boonies on recon looking for Charlie. You would be with four or five guys who really knew what it was all about, and they could teach you everything they know, and before long you'd also be ready to lead a patrol yourself.

No matter what I do in Nam, Clellie, I just want to go over there and get it over with. Then I can come home for good to the only person who matters to me in the whole world.

Clellie, we're going to have to get together real soon. I'll go nuts if we don't. I better go for now, but I do love you Clellie. I'll always love you. Will you me?

Your loving husband,
Tony

NCOC Tony Jolley
104 Co 10th Stu. Bn. 3th Plt
Fort Benning, Georgia 31905

October 28, 1969   *9:00 PM*

Hi most wonderful hubby of mine,

I was pretty busy today. I gave Chad a bath, did the washing, did the dishes, and straightened up the house. Chad's getting so grown up it seems and he takes a great deal of my time. I really miss not being with him. He seems to change every single day. He's a doll. He digs himself quite a bit. I try to keep his nails really short but he still seems to be able to dig. Ticks me off so bad. I got him a vaporizer today for his cold. I sure hope it helps him. He has quite a little hack and runny nose. Oh by the way he's to the slobbery stage now. He'll be cutting teeth pretty soon I imagine. He's a very tough little boy too. He's so darling. I'm very proud of him. This lady told me today that he resembles both of us. Like Mom says though you and I look quite a bit alike anyway.

You know I think I must be getting ancient or out of it. Ann showed me this kid she likes. No kidding him and another kid has hair past their shoulders. I can't take it. That May kid has long hair too. Almost every boy here does. Really Tony I can't see boys wanting hair longer than their girlfriends. Am I wrong? I like hair that's long in the front and stuff. I liked it like you used to wear yours. Do you think I'm an old fogey? Honest?

Tony, when we get together I want to go to a dance.

Hon, sometimes I get so depressed because I give up on us ever being together before you go overseas. Like that's all I've been working towards, having us all three together. It means so much to me yet I know that if you get a Christmas leave for two weeks, we'll need the money for a place to stay and you'll want money to go skiing. I also realize that we'll need money to get a place from your 30-day leave. Tony, I can't help it, I want to be with you, and I don't want you to have to work on your leaves. What are we going to do?

It was really chilly today. Leaves all over everywhere! Always love me! Please!

Your loving lonely wife,
Clellie

P.S. Hugs and Kisses, etc.

✉ **October 29, 1969**　　　　　　　　　　　　　　　　　　　　　　*9:00 PM*

Hi Hon,

Well October is almost over. I wish that the time would go faster. I miss you so very, very much. You're so very special! You don't know how bad I want to be with you!

Tony, what would you say to me putting your picture and a statement on how much you've accomplished in the paper? They have a place in the local paper for news of the area servicemen. I'd really like to and keep the clipping in our scrapbook. I'd be so proud. Tonight they had a clipping in the paper about some kid who had just completed Basic Training.

Work was pretty good today. I met two more salesmen. Man I thought I was just getting the hang of things, and they have to foul me up with two more salesmen. One's a gum man, and ones another tobacco man. Then I had to put the groceries up. I had to take inventory on candy again, make a list for the candy man tomorrow, and I ordered some candy today from another candy man.

Did you used to write notes to the girls at Ore-Ida who used to stitch boxes & sign it Jolley? I was told that today. I'm just curious.

Ann's going with that Billy May sort of again, ugly old creep he is, long old hair like a girl. I didn't even say as much is hi. He gives me the heebie-jeebies!

I met Kathy Harris today. She seems pretty nice. What do you think of her or do you know her?

I took Hope to work tonight. Exciting.

I saw your dad today. He walked by the store and I happened to see him through the window.

I saw a car tonight at Riverside drive-in on the way to take Hope to work. It was empty and it looked just like Barry's Mustang except the front was smashed in. I wonder if it was.

Well I got my car safety inspected today. I'm glad I have that over with. Now all I have to wait for is for the license plates. I can't wait until I get it over with for another year.

Chad holds up his head real well now. He's so cute. We put him on the floor and he tries so hard to crawl. He gets his little legs and bottom moving but his top just lays there. He actually tries to walk. He doesn't use his knees, he uses his feet. He gets his little rear right up in the air.

I love you so very much, Tony. I hope I can see you soon.

Your loving wife eternally,
Clellie

P.S. Hugs and Kisses, etc.

October 30, 1969 *9:00 PM*

Hi Hon,

How's my great guy? I think you're so neat. I love you so very much.

Man I was so busy today at work. The meat, candy, magazines, and tobacco all came in at one time. Everyone pitched in and helped me thank goodness. They're putting the overhead all over the store and starting the Christmas supplies to be brought up and put away. It's getting me in the Christmas mood already.

Alice, Jenny, and I made some popcorn balls tonight for Halloween tomorrow night. Fun.

Ticked me off! I got this card in the mail Monday telling me to come Thursday at 12 PM to 1 PM to see Chad's pictures and see which one I want to be an 8 x 10. So I went there and they told me it had got lost between Burley and Boise so they were sending a tracer on them. I'm supposed to check tomorrow. Ticks me off. Six weeks ago I have a picture taken, then later they have them taking over because the film had been defective, now this! Ticks me off!

Do you want me to send you some money? I want to if you don't mind.

Honey, I want you behind a desk. There's not quite as much danger in it. It's still dangerous but I wouldn't worry quite as much. Tony, Chad and I need you forever. Please think of us! It's a lot of responsibility, but I know you can do it. You're good at anything you want to be good at. Tony, I pray that you get an office job.

I told you Ann's going with Billy May, well I meant Billy Russell!

Today at 5 PM Nancy called and asked if I wanted Chad fed. Mom had left at about 4 PM. I could hear Chad bawling. Ticked me off. When I got home at 5:20 PM he still hadn't eaten. I'm not going to worry about him getting fed. I'm not working while you're over in Nam. I want to raise him my way. What do you think?

Honey, as soon as possible we are going to be together. I need you so desperately. I'll always love you.

Yours eternally,
Clellie

P.S. Hugs and Kisses, etc.

✉ **October 31, 1969** 9:15 PM

Hi Hon,

How's my favorite and only guy doing?

Did you get the $10 I sent you? You never did tell me. Say you only sent back half of the pictures of Chad and I that I sent you. What are you going to do with rest? What are you going to do with our wedding pictures and the pictures of us at Banbury?

Well this will be my last letter to you until I get your new address. How about that? I'll keep writing a letter every night but I'll wait to send them until I get your new address so hurry and send it. In one of your letters you were supposed to tell me how long it takes my letters to get to you, but you never said so I figure it'll take three or four days so it should be to you by Tuesday or Wednesday.

Work was pretty good today. I got a gob more candy in today. We finally got a new girl to take over when one of us are sick or needs a day off.

I had 42 popcorn balls when I left. When I got home we had about 25 left. Everyone had one or two and so did their friends. Needless to say we had to buy some more candy.

Steve came home tonight. I had to take him to Roy's and the streets were almost bare. Kind of spooky. How was your Halloween day?

Your dad came in today and planted a great big kiss on my cheek. He asked me how you were, how I was, and how Chad's doing? Nice. It sure was nice to see him.

Guess what? Our little darling boy talks in his sleep-well actually he goos. It's so cute. Last night I was just going to bed and all of a sudden-goooooooo for about 30 seconds. No kidding. Then he turned his head and was silent, then returned it back again and gooooo again for about 30 seconds. It's so darn cute! I know that you're going to be so proud of him. I sure am. He is almost as darling as a certain Tony Jolley whom I truly admire!

Well I better go take a bath for work tomorrow. It sure would be nice if you were here to keep me company while I'm bathing. I love you so very, very much!

Your loving wife, Clellie

P.S. Hugs and Kisses, etc.

November 1, 1969   **12:00 midnight**

Hi Hon,

How's everyone been treating the best guy in the world? Oh Tony, if you only knew how very much I want to be with you.

I just got back from taking Carrie over to Granny's, Dale and her came up for the weekend. Dale went out with Nusgen, he's home for his leave before he goes to Nam. Carrie's sister-in-law dropped her off at about 9 PM and we just sat here and visited until 25 till 12 AM then I took her over there. Groovy. Very unexciting.

Do you know what I figured out? Denise still is after you because she hasn't been over to see Chad since you've gone, and she never came over before you came home on leave. I think that she's still crazy about you. Of course I can see why. I love you, Tony, so much.

Guess what? A con artist came into the store today, and gypped me out of $20. He was so fast and I guess I'm so dumb. Everyone told me that they had similar things happen to them. I was so sick! 20 bucks and here I've been so good at being right at the cash register. I'll bet it took the sum total of one minute. I can see where I gave him an extra $10 but not $20. You see he bought something and paid for it. Then he turned around and asked if I'd give him a $10 bill for a $5 and 5 $1 bills so I said yes. He gave me the money and I gave him the $10 bill. Well he was short a dollar so I told him. He took the money and I started to count them he said "well here, give me two $20 bills for two $10 bills, one $5 bill, and 5 one dollar bills." So he counted out and I gave him two $20 bills. I knew it wasn't right so I told him to hold it but he quickly told me a whole bunch of jibber until he got out of the door then I knew – so I told Grant and when I checked my drawer out we added up when I had to what I was supposed to and Bam $-20 was gone. Sick? Boy, was I ever! Mad yes! Stupid dumb me! You better know it!! See you what a smart little wife you married! Great. Grant didn't get mad at me thank goodness.

Boy, you should've seen the streets and windows this morning. What a mess. I guess they threw about 15 kids in jail. The kids busted the windows in the fire truck, threw eggs at the cops, and all kinds of goodies. They had the firemen on duty, policeman on duty, and student policemen from Twin on duty. Ann didn't get home until 2:30 AM this morning but that's okay. She gets her way all the time. Am I being catty? Not me! Never!

Well I better close for tonight. I love you, Tony, so very, very much!!! I hope and pray we can be together soon.

Always your wife, Clellie

P.S. Hugs and Kisses, etc.

✉ **November 2, 1969**　　　　　　　　　　　　　　　　　　　　　　　　　　**10:00 PM**

Hi Hon,

I love you so very, very much.

Do you know by the time you get this letter we will have already been together, but I know how you like gobs of letters.

While I'm thinking of it, Tony, there's one thing about what you said on the phone today that's been bugging me. You told me not to go to Salt Lake if it cost me my job. Please tell me what you really think, Tony! Don't you want me to quit and be with Chad while I can? Does money mean more to you than us being together?! I know this is a rotten thing to ask you and I know you're going to be really ticked off at me, but I really need to know for myself. You've never told me how you feel. I know you want us together as bad as I do, but why did you say that? Hon, I'm sorry, I'm just upset I guess.

Mom and this Red guy are getting married 20 November. I think he'll be good for the girls. I hope they do.

I went over to your parents finally today, and told them all the news about you! It was good to visit with them again.

Sue has got her back allotments already. She got them Saturday. What's holding mine up?

I'm going to put your name in the paper as soon as I get back from Salt Lake. You have done so good, and I'm so proud of you. I just decided I'd let everyone else see what a great guy I married. I love you, Sgt. Jolley, so very, very much!!!

Yours eternally,
Clellie

P.S. Hugs and Kisses, etc.

✉️ **November 3, 1969**　　　　　　　　　　　　　　　　　　*11:00 PM*

Hi Hon,

Well tomorrow night by this time I'll be safe in your arms. I love you so very much and I'm so very excited! It'll be so heavenly to make love! Wow!

Susan got home from Mountain Home today. She's all excited for me too. She had a pretty nice time evidently, however Justin got a little homesick.

Tonight at lunchtime I walked into the house and Chad was drinking his bottle so I walked on by him. Well he started to bawl so I picked him up. Usually when I walk into the house I immediately grab him. Anyway when he stopped crying I gave him to Nancy to feed and he started to cry, then turn red, and he was mad. He wouldn't take his bottle so I took him again, shut him up, and fed him his bottle that he drank happily. Spoiled thing! He tries to grab the spoon now when I feed him his vegetables and fruit. He helps me shovel it in too. He also tries to hold his bottle. He's so cute.

Sue came in tonight at Thriftway. She's really excited about going down too. She may not leave till 6 PM though. I want to leave before that, at about 3 PM. It's a good deal she's going to leave later though in case my car breaks down.

By the time you get this letter we will have already been together and apart again. I hate the thoughts of goodbyes but I hate the thought of not being able to say hello worse.

I went over to your mother's after work and she gave me $20 to give to you to buy some dress pants or whatever you want. Neat.

Do you want to hear how cool my boss is? Today I went to work to ask him if I could go to Utah to be with you. He told me he doubted it and that it wouldn't be good for me to go see you, and I told him I thought it would do me a lot of good to see you. Ticked me off! He was serious. Then I asked him again, and he said that he would think about it. A little while after that Zena came up and asked me when you were getting in. I asked her how she knew and she told me not to tell anyone because she wasn't supposed to know, but this lady came in and told her she was taking over for me while I go to you. Well Grant came up and I asked him again and he said he still was thinking. Then before I could get to him again he had left for home. He never did tell me. I guess he figured I'd call him at home to find out. I haven't. If he can be that way I don't give two hoots about that ugly old job. I'm coming no matter what! When I have to call a boss at home to ask him it's tough. I wouldn't give him the satisfaction.

But I guess I better close for now! I love you so much. I have to dry my hair still.

Yours eternally,
Clellie

P.S. Hugs and Kisses, etc.

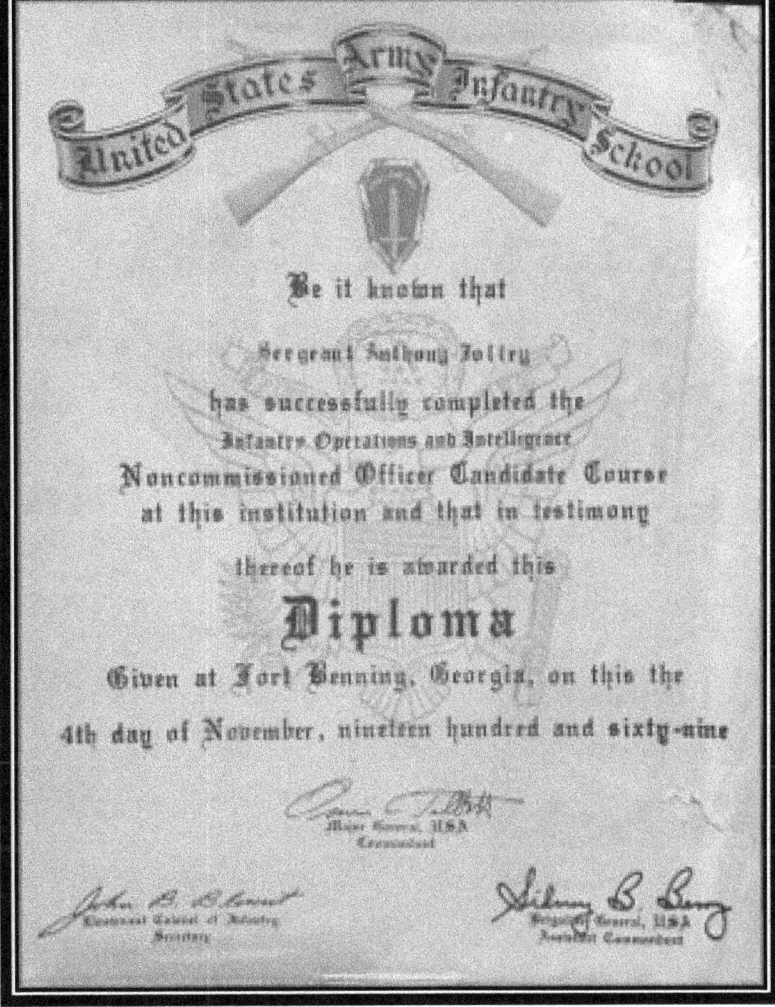

LEAVING FOR FT. HOOD, TEXAS

November 6, 1969   9:45 PM

Hi Hon,

I love you so much, Tony!

I thought I saw you look back at me just before you boarded the plane. Did you see me? I was crying so hard. I wanted to be on the plane with you. While I was up on the deck watching you get on the plane and crying, a stranger came up to me and put her arm on my shoulder and said, "He'll be back soon, don't cry. I went through this about two months ago." She was really sweet. Then she started to talk to me and it sure helped. I hated to see that jet lift off the ground!

I got here about 8 PM. A guy almost smashed into us and I just about turned the car over but we made it okay. I love you so much.

As soon as I walked into the airport after you left, I saw Mom sitting there. She said that she had been waiting for about five minutes.

I called this lady Zena at work and asked her if she had heard whether I was fired or not. She said that she hadn't heard but everyone was so rolled up about him doing that to me. He had told this girl that was to take my place not to tell anyone especially Clellie! Boy, he's quite a card! She said that no one hardly talked to him. I don't care if I am fired if he's so rotten. He must've thought I'd still go to work instead of go to you. I do believe he likes me, Tony. Maybe I'm wrong!

I wrote a letter to the allotments department of the Army about not getting my money. Now you start on your end. I hope we get it straightened out so we'll have the money for your 30-day leave.

Tony, I love you so very, very much. I want you for mine forever!

Your lonely, loving wife,
Clellie

P.S. Hugs and Kisses, etc.!!!

✉ *November 7, 1969* *10:25 PM*

Hi Hon,

I just completed one full busy day of work. It's getting so busy and junky. If it's like this now I sure dread Christmas. Ugh! Mr. Fillmore, my boss, asked me if I had a nice time as if nothing had happened. Then he embarrassed me at break time by saying that here I was feeling like a young bride again all happy and content. I really can't wait to quit.

I counted it up and we have about 47 more days until Christmas. It seems like such a long way off.

Alice got herself suspended from school while we were away. She was caught off the school grounds.

I checked five dollars out of the bank today. I had an extra five dollars left so I sent $9.95 for that bust builder deal. I can't wait to get it. I want to have a shape that you can't resist.

It's really been raining here today, all day long. How's that for a forecast?

Susan came into the store tonight. I guess their divorce isn't final after all. Denny's got a lawyer to fight the $100 child support. Susan says that he's been calling quite often lately. I don't know what's going to happen. She told Denny that if she could think of any more of his friends who were smoking grass she was going to report them. He asked her if she was going to turn you in and she said no. He asked her why? Is Tony better than the rest of us? Susan told him, "Yes, Tony is." How about that?

I got a letter from Sophia Meyer. It sure was nice to hear from her.

Mom went out so at 6 PM I had to take Chad over to Hope's where Nancy was babysitting. I sure hope he doesn't catch another cold.

Tony, what's the chance of us getting a place there? Or should I just forget it? Honey, I want to be with you as much as I can. I want to feel happy and secure like when we were together this week.

Your loving wife,
Clellie

P.S. I love you so very, very much, Sgt. Jolley!! Hugs and Kisses, etc.

November 8, 1969   *10:20 PM*

Hi Hon,

How's my greatest man doing? I sure do love you so much! I can't wait until Christmas!

Well Mom got married today. How about that? She really is. She got married at 2:30 PM.

Denny came into the store and asked if I had a nice time. I told him yes I did even though I was with you about 1 ¾ days. Susan told him that you'll be home for Christmas. I'm going to get us a little place by ourselves and no one's going to know where it is so we won't be disturbed unless you want to be. What do you think of that Sgt. Jolley? I miss you so much, Honey!

Speaking of Christmas are we going to worry about gifts for our families? I don't think we should until you get out of the Army. I've informed this family not to expect anything and we don't want anything either.

Susan came into the store tonight and visited for a few minutes. She didn't have much to say.

Ann pierced her ears. Nancy and Alice might too. I'm too big of a chicken! A boob.

Honey, do you want me to cut my hair? Don't tell me whatever I want because I want to please you and only you!

Say there's something I've been wanting to ask you for quite a little while so please answer it. How did you feel the night before we got married? Did you want to run away? Were you nervous? Did you feel unsure? Please be honest. I'm really very curious.

I saw Diane Webb tonight. She came into the store. She's getting married around December 6th. She's really excited about it! She seems really happy. It was nice to see her again.

Honey, I want to be with you so very, very much!

Your loving lonely wife,
Clellie

P.S. Hugs and Kisses, etc.

✉ **November 9, 1969**　　　　　　　　　　　　　　　　　　　*8:05 PM*

Dear Good-looking,

How's Fort Hood? Do you think that you're going to like it. How are they even treating you? Do you like Texas?

I'm going to put five dollars down on a stroller for Chad? The one my cousin gave us is all banged up.

My cousin Pat came down from Twin today and brought with her a baby crib. It's in real nice condition except for the mattress. It's got a few tape spots but it will be covered with sheets so it will be just great. That saves us from getting one. I'll take Marie's back after your 30-day leave. It's easier to move around.

Red went out to the farm and brought the girls their furniture. Finally. Pretty good.

Boy, work was so darn busy today. I'm so tired! I have to work from 11 until 7 and I'm really dead. Sundays we only have half of the girls we need.

Guess what my nice boss did? He's a real puck. This lady Zena wanted today off so she could take her boyfriend to Pocatello for a physical. He has heart trouble so she wanted to go with him. She asked Brenda (a relief girl) to take her place and Brenda said okay. So Zena went to Grant and asked him at about 2:30 PM. He told her no because Brenda was going to work anyway. At 3 PM he called Brenda and told her to come to work Sunday. That ugly old man him.

Alice told me that when school lets out Red wants to move us to Rupert. None of us like the idea too well. Mom said that I can probably quit paying the $25 a month. Even so I'd like to pay about $10 a month for food. What do you think?

Fred Judd was in the store today and was asking about you. Denny Carter came in today and said hi. He also said to tell you that he'll get the letter sent to you as soon as he gets your new address. I never asked him about writing you either. Honey, I hope that you don't run with him too much. It's up to you though.

Do you think that you'll get home on Christmas Eve or the day before? Oh Tony, I miss you so very much! I wish we could be together for Thanksgiving. I also would like to be together for our first anniversary. One whole year!

Well I'm starting my birth control pills December 1st when I start again because it should be okay. I don't need them this month because I won't be with you so I'll wait. It'll be about a month of taking them by the time you get home.

I guess that I'd better close for tonight. I love you so very, very much!!

Your loving wife,
Clellie

P.S. Hugs and Kisses, etc.

✉ **November 10, 1969** 9:25 PM

Hi Hon,

I've decided to go to bed early again tonight. Man I'm really tuckered out anymore. I got sick at work today but I stuck it out. We need the money.

How's the Army been treating you? I hope just fine.

Do you know this girl at work says she's been trying to get PG for six months? She quit taking the pill, but no luck. She's not telling her husband now 'cause he doesn't want any more children for a while. They only have one girl but she's six years old.

Susan came to Thriftway at noon and we went to the ID store and finally got the pictures of Chad and Justin. It's an 8 x 10 of Chad. It's so cute. I got a frame for it tonight. Everyone likes it. I guess it was worth waiting for. Sure took a long time for them to get them to us.

Tomorrow's my day off. I need to take Chad to get his last shot for a year, poor little guy. By the way I weighed him and he weighs 17 pounds, and is 26 inches long.

I got three shipments of candy in today and Ginger and I had to get it put away. Also some gift sets came in. I put the Bell wholesale candy away and we had most of the Russell Stover candy away by the time I got off work. I can't believe it, the closer we get to Christmas the more junk we get in and the more people come. My back hurts so bad Ugh!

By the time you get home for Christmas I want a small tree decorated in a cute little apartment. I want things so special just for you. I can't wait. Things have to be special because you're so special. You know what I like most of all? I'd like a cute little cabin in the hills with the nice warm fire going and just you and I. I love you so much!

Susan sort of wanted to go out tonight but I told her I was broke. I really am worn out and I don't feel like doing much of anything but sleeping.

Say if I get time before you get your apartment would you like me to make some fudge and brownies for Christmas in our apartment? I'm going to quit a couple of days before you get home so I can get things just so. By the way, I know it's really early but where will you want me to pick you up at?

Mom and Red (his real name is Nolan McKesson) seem to be really happy. In a way it seems really good to have a man who seems like a dad around. I am happy for them. He doesn't give me a creepy feeling either. The girls get along real well so far with him.

Well Honey, I guess I'll close. By the way, Alice asked me if I told you about her getting suspended and I told her yes and she felt pretty bad so I told her I'd explain to you how they left the grounds 'cause the food was so crappy, so don't say anything about it when you get home. I love you so very, very much!!

*All my love eternally,
Clellie*

P.S. They are decorating the town for Christmas already! Hugs and Kisses, etc.

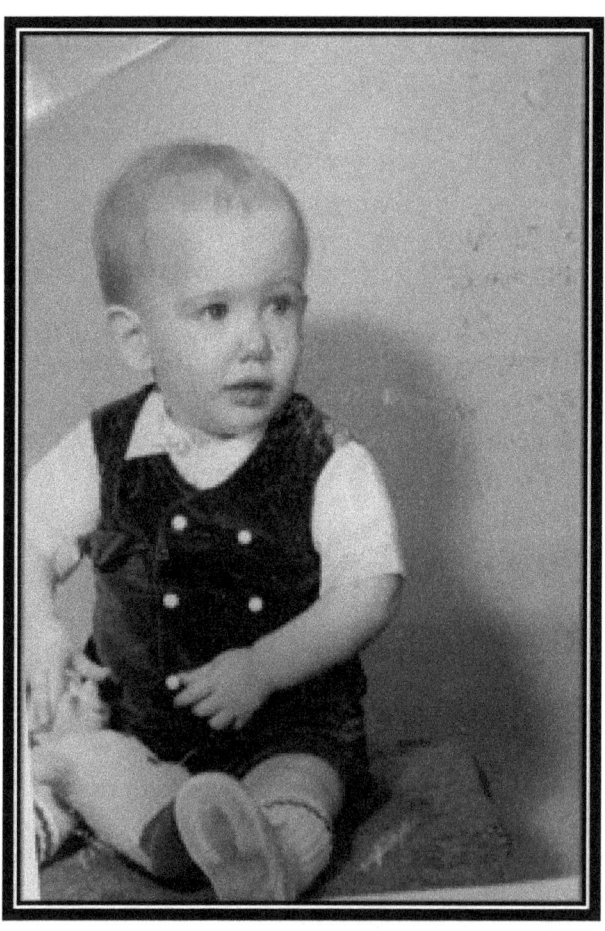

November 11, 1969   *10:15 PM*

Dear Good looking,

Did my great hubby get Veteran's Day off? I sure think you should. Do you realize that you've been in the Army 8 months today? That takes quite a little chunk out of the 2 years, don't you agree? I can't wait until the other year and ¼ is gone. How about you? I just want to be together forever like we should.

Well I got today off. I did my washing, cleaned our room, set up Chad's new crib, and changed the room around a little. I polished my shoes, cleaned out Chad's dresser, put away the things that are too little for him. The rest of the day I tended Chad, which is a chore itself. I think he's trying to cut teeth, and boy, is he ever cranky, poor little boy. I guess I'll buy him some teething wafers that he can chew on. I feel so sorry for him, but I didn't feel too good today either so my temper was quite impatient.

I went to bed last night right after I got your letter done. I started thinking of you, what we were going to do when you get home, when to quit my job, and money and what to do about gifts for Christmas. I tossed and turned all night. Alice got home from baby-sitting at about 1:30 AM - 2:00AM and I was still tossing and turning.

I didn't start up the car at all today. I sure hope it starts up tomorrow.

Marriage has been real good for Mom. She cooks supper, cleans the house, does the ironing, does the washing, and is happy.

Today the phone rang twice and both times Mom answered but no one answered when she said hi. The third time I answered I could hear someone breathing and trying to muffle the phone. I sat it down for 2 minutes, picked it up, and they were still on it. I think it might have been Mitch, he's still bugging Mom.

I guess I'll close. I love you, Tony, so much. One week ago tonight I was safe in your arms in our motel. I wish we were still together.

Your most loving proud wife,
Clellie

P.S. Hugs & Kisses etc.

November 12, 1969 9:40 PM

Hi Hon,

How's the best-looking greatest guy in the whole world? How do you like being a Sgt.?

Well, I got a check from the Army today airmail. It was $61.20. It's back pay for you being a Sgt. Now all they need to send me is $60 for July and August for Chad and then we'll be all straightened out. I'm going to put it in the bank so we'll have gobs of money. How are you doing for money? Could you use $5 or $10?

I guess I'll lay away a stroller for Chad for Christmas with my paycheck. What do you think?

Boy, I had a rough day at work today. I had candy, tobacco, magazines to put away, groceries to put away, and gobs of junk. It keeps me quite busy.

Say for Christmas what do you think about us buying maybe one game for your family and one for mine?

Hey guess whose picture I saw in the paper? Why it was right under the article called "news of the area servicemen." The name under the picture was Sgt. Tony Jolley. How about that? They had an article about you. Yes, I gave them your picture and the information they needed for the article. How does that make you feel? I'm so very proud of you! Anyway I bought the paper so I can put the article in our scrapbook.

What do you think about me renting a motel with a kitchenette in it for the two weeks you're here?

Susan called tonight. I guess Denny called her and asked her if he went to court if she would get on the stand and say he takes dope. She told him yes. He told her that he'd get on the stand and say a few things about her too. She said to go ahead. He doesn't date just Natalie either. I guess there's a couple of more. He says he's been so good to Susan and she's treating him rotten. Poor guy! He also called her and asked her what kind of coat she wanted. She told him she'd already laid one away. He called her again and said he's taking out insurance on her & Justin. How about that?

Tony, I pray to God that I never lose you! It would make me awfully bitter! You're too very important to me.

All my love eternally, Clellie

P.S. Hugs & Kisses etc.

SGT. TONY JOLLEY

Jolley Finishes Officers School

Tony Jolley, son of Mr. and Mrs. Wayne Jolley of Heyburn, graduated from non-commissioned officers school on Nov. 4, attaining the rank of sergeant.

Sgt. Jolley has been transferred to Fort Hood, Tex. for on-the-job training as a sergeant for 10 weeks.

Jolley, whose wife is Clellie Jolley, graduated from basic training at Ford Ord, Calif May 16, 1969, and gr from AIT on July 18 Ord.

November 13, 1969   **10:00 PM**

Dear handsome hubby of mine,

Gee just think 11 months ago to this very day we were married. One more month and it'll be our first anniversary. How about that? It doesn't seem like we've been married a whole year does it?

Man I was late for work after lunch today because I just had to wait for the mail to see if I got a letter from you. When it came and no letter I almost cried. I miss you so very much and it's been such a long time since I've heard from you. One week ago today I saw your jet go out of sight. Oh, Tony, I miss you so very, very much.

Work was not too bad. I only got in 20 cases of candy, talked to three tobacco salesman, two candy men, sorted out magazines and books, and goofed around. It was quite a bit easier today. Grant said that we would only get in 2 more shipments of candy. Thank goodness.

I saw Mrs. Bates today. She said that she heard your picture was in the paper, but she hadn't been able to see it.

Honey, do you want me to wait until you get home to get the Christmas tree, decorations, and stuff? I'd like you to help me pick it out and decorate it. It would mean so much to me.

Chad's been eating in his highchair now. He tries so hard to grab the spoon and feed himself. He's really cute! He stands on the floor pretty good now as long as you hold his shirt. He still doesn't crawl, but he sure tries. If he was in water, he could really move.

Tony, I want your love forever! I hope you'll still love me on our 50th anniversary! I can't wait until you get the rest of the Army over with. I'm so very proud of you, but I wish we were together.

Yours eternally,
Clellie

P.S. Hugs and Kisses, etc.

✉ **13 Nov 1969**

Dearest Clellie,

I'm sure sorry it took so long to write, but you wouldn't believe the hassle down here. They kept us at a replacement center for three days, then the holiday came up, and we couldn't get assigned to the unit until after it was over. I just got my address figured out, I sure hope they don't transfer me, or I'll really be messed up.

Morton and I missed our flight in Dallas, and ended up about three hours late. We got here at 15 after 3 AM in the morning. When we were waiting on the next flight out of Dallas, you should've seen Morton. He was swearing so bad I thought he'd go nuts before the plane got there. He got pissed off at me because I laughed and said we couldn't do anything about it and fell asleep.

He got assigned to the second division. I haven't seen him since I've been here. The first night I got in I thought I might catch hell. It was so late, they just gave me a couple of blankets and told me to go find a bed in one of the barracks.

They assigned me to the 2/46 infantry (another big unit). Of course this infantry unit might not be so bad because it's mechanized. They told me I'd be going to Nam around 10 February. I don't like this unit at all. Most of the guys in my barracks are Spec 4's. They've been to Nam and back, and they kind of resent the idea of a shake and bake like me being over them. Yesterday's training was canceled because they had to get enough Vietnam Veterans together for a parade. There were about 30 guys left in the platoon after I got through picking out the parade guys. The First Sgt. decided the rest of the platoon needed to be drilled, so he had me and another sergeant from Benning split the platoon and drill them. Most of the guys did real good, and cooperated fine, but there were these two soul brothers that kept cutting up the formation. I let them cut up quite a bit without saying a word, then I halted the formation and called one of them out. I got pissed off and told him I didn't like doing this anymore than he did and he got heated. I told him he better knock off the bullshit and get back in formation or I could see what I can do about finding him a little extra detail over the weekend instead of letting him go on pass. It's surprised the shit out of him according to the look on his face, but he didn't say anything and he did real good for the rest of the time out there.

I gave more blood today, that's why I'm writing this letter because I got the rest of the day off. The First Sergeant put me in charge of a group of guys and told me to march them down to the dispensary. So when I got down I decided I'd give some blood and get the rest of the day off.

You wouldn't believe how the First Sergeants and Second Lieutenants treat us new sergeants. They really think we know our shit. There're only two of us in my platoon. We're both assigned to Battalion 53, but we spent most of the time around the company. Man the guys around here are treated like trainees, they still have to do KP and all kinds of details, but I don't so I don't care.

Clellie, I sure did have a wonderful time at Salt Lake with you. It was so neat to be near you, and to sleep with you, and make love to you. I already miss you so much. I sure wish you could come down here, but there are guys that have their wives down here and can't find an apartment so they're staying in a motel.

Clellie, I love you very much and I already want to be with you. I already want to make love again. It was so good those few times we did it. I can see you still in your panties and bra and it makes me want you so bad. I better close for now, but remember that I love you, Clellie, now and forever. Send me your letters 'cause I want to hear from you so bad. I love you, Clellie.

Your loving husband,
Tony

P.S. I want to make love to you.

Sgt. Tony Jolley
HHC 2/46 Inf. (Mech)
1st armor division
Fort Hood, Texas 76545

✉ *November 14, 1969*　　　　　　　　　　　　　　　　　　*10:00 PM*

Hi Hon,

I was so very disappointed today. I came home from work and checked the mail. No letter from Tony. At first I was ticked off, hurt, and very upset which I took out a smidge on the girls. I tried not to talk to anyone. Now I'm just hurt. I know there's a good reason for you not writing. I try going over every possible reason that sounds legit. However, if it's because you didn't have your address yet I will be ticked because you still could write me. Honey, I miss you so very much. I'd like to talk to you, to feel you hold me, touch me, and tell me you still love and want me.

Work wasn't too bad today. I got the Whitman's candy in today. I only have one more big shipment of candy to come in before Christmas. Then the weekly Idaho candy came in today, and I got halfway with straightening out our paperback books. Other than that it was a nice day. My side hurts so bad from lifting so much. I'm very tired tonight. After I got home, changed clothes, changed Chad's clothes, gave him his bottle, ate, and played with Chad, Mom and I went to Shelby's to buy groceries.

Hon, don't tell anyone. Mom said that she really doesn't love Red. I think that she's trying to blame me and Hope for her getting married. I told her that yes I told her it would be good for her and the girls, but that she should decide for herself. Naturally it's everyone else's fault. Yes, I'll take some of the blame, but she's not a baby, she has a mind of her own.

Susan really does want to move to Provo, Utah and she wants me to move with her. What do you think? I love Utah and I wouldn't mind staying a month or so, but not to live. The only place that I want to live is with you.

Sid Poulton came in to the Thriftway today and asked me about you and whether you joined or were drafted.

Ann likes this Danny Kloer now. Boy, she changes her mind enough. She's sort of running with Sarah Grace and Ethel Hawn.

Well I guess I'll close. Chad says Goo. I have to sew my bra. It gave way on me at work. Tony, I can't wait until we can be together. I miss you so very, very much.

Your loving wife, Clellie

P.S. Hugs and Kisses, etc.

November 15, 1969   **12:30 AM**

Hi Hon,

I received your letter today and I was so happy to get it. I was late for work because I hurried and wrote the address on the other 12 letters and mailed them. It was so neat to hear from you. I love and miss you so much!

The weather here has been pretty nice lately. No snow and not really cold yet.

Tonight Susan and I went to the show. It was a double feature. "The Return of the Magnificent Seven" and "Death Rides a Horse." They were really good. We went about 8:45 PM because I had to comb her hair first. We got out at about 11:30 PM and then we went to the Ponderosa to eat. Boy, I'll never get a hamburger there again! Hard things in it and sweet pickles ugh! Then we came home. It was nice for a change. Only one thing is wrong. My sides are acting up again like when I was PG. They hurt really bad at work, but I didn't go home. Then after work Hope gave me a couple of pills for kidney infection, which helped a little bit. I sure hope they don't get worse. I still don't know what causes it. I go to the bathroom all the time!

Remember in the one letter when I told you about someone calling here and yet not answering? Well they've been calling everyday two or three times a day and only listening not answering. If it happens again, we're going to get it traced and find out who it is. It's kind of spooky!

How do you like giving orders? How did you and Morton miss your flight in Dallas?

When will you get to come home for Christmas and for how long? When do you get your 30-day leave before Nam? I didn't figure you would go to Nam until March.

Honey, I had such a neat time in Salt Lake too. It was so neat, just you and I! I want you forever!

Work was really slow today and I sure felt miserable. No matter how bad I get to feel I want to work until around December 20. We can use as much money as we can get right?

Chad's doing really great! He's still cute!

Tony, I miss and need you so very, very much. Please write often.

Yours eternally, Clellie

P.S. Hugs and Kisses, etc.

✉ **November 16, 1969**   9:45 PM

Dear best-looking guy ever,

How's everything been going for you?

Today I washed my hair, washed my work clothes and Chad's bedding, and I took a bath. I made five pumpkin pies for dinner. I went over to your folks' place and talked to your mother and Barry. I forgot to take your address with me so she said that she'd pick it up soon. Marie bought her a short blond wig. Really it's white. Your mother says she really looks nice in that. I was over to your parents' place for 1 1/2 hours. Then I came home and we ate. A friend of Red's and Mom's ate with us plus Hope and her kids. After we ate Aunt Virginia and her tribe came over. Then Paul, Mabel, and a friend of theirs came over. Man I couldn't take it. Paul, Mabel, and their friend were drunk so I took Chad and went over to Hope's until about 7:30 PM.

I forgot to tell you in last night's letter, but Carrie Connor came into the store yesterday to see me. She wanted to know when you'll get home on leave for Christmas. I told her that I didn't know, but I would probably know before too long. She might take a part-time job as a beautician there. She said that Dale was buying her a horse for Christmas. She doesn't like to ride horses but Dale's going to buy it anyway.

By the way your brother Barry thinks Chad has your ears and looks like you. He did wreck his car, but it wasn't his fault. This old lady decided to turn in front of him so she got cited for failure to yield.

I guess Andrew's going to be home sometime around the middle of January. You should get to see each other then.

Hope gave me some pills for my kidneys you know and my urine is really ugly. It's sort of orange and it's stained two pair of my panties. It has seemed to help though.

Honey, when do you think you'll get home for Christmas? Do you want to help me pick out the tree and decorate it? I'm so excited for you and I to be together. We'll celebrate our first anniversary. I can't wait. I miss you so very much.

I guess that I'll take Chad to the doctor tomorrow for his third and last shot for the year.

Your mother said that your dad's hearing is pretty bad. This hearing aid helps him quite a bit. He quit the Pilots Club and is waiting for the Ramada to open. It was supposed to Saturday, but it didn't so it's supposed open next Saturday.

I love you gobs.
Your loving wife ETERNALLY,
Clellie

P.S. Hugs and Kisses, etc.!!!

November 17, 1969　　　　　　　　　　　　　　　　　　　　10:15 PM

Hi Hon,

It sure is cold today. I about froze going to work and stuff. The wind was blowing and you sure could tell it was winter.

I sent you a Thanksgiving package today by airmail. I sure hope it gets to you in time. If it gets there earlier no opening!!! You have to wait until Thanksgiving. I hope you like it.

I don't know what I'm going to do with our car. I got off work tonight I went out to start it. Guess what? It wouldn't start. It sounded like my battery was dead. It's probably the other battery cable! If it's not one thing it's another. The pharmacist Jimmy (the old guy) brought me home. There it sits on Main Street. I'm so mad. That car is so undependable!

I heard a rumor at work today (from a pretty reliable source) that we are going to go back to the old schedule. 8 PM to 12 AM. I hate that ugly shift. Course I've only got a month or so left to work. It's supposed to change soon though.

It was real slow at work today. The time went so fast, ha ha! One time we're so busy we can't see straight, and the next time it's so slow it's sickening!

I went to take Chad to get his shot today, but the nurse wasn't there! All in all it's been one of those days.

Alice might be getting the mumps. Her glands are swelling. That's all we need! Poor Chad. I've only had the mumps on one side too.

I don't like the idea of our cars sitting up there all night. People who see it and know it's mine might start wondering. I hate to get Red out of bed though. Oh well people don't matter!

What have you decided about my hair? Do you want me to cut it or not?

How do you like being a sergeant? Do the guys mind you pretty good? For some reason or another I can't imagine you giving orders to people. It just doesn't sound like you. There's no chance that you'll get sent to someplace besides Nam? I keep hoping that you won't have to go, but I guess it's useless.

Hon, I love you so very much! I can't wait until we're together for Christmas.

Your wife eternally! Clellie

P.S. Hugs and Kisses, etc.

✉ **17 Nov 1969**

Dear Clellie,

How is the best-looking, best-built, most beautiful, wonderful girl in the whole world getting along? And the best-looking son a guy could want? Is Chad still getting bigger? I hope he's getting mean and keeps you really busy so you can't go out and hustle the boys. Not really, I don't think I could trust anybody more than I do you. I guess it's just because I know we're two of a kind, and we go along together better than any other couple there is. What do you think?

I really feel bad because I don't get to write you as much as I did in NCOC. They just don't give you time around here. At nights when we get off there's a bunch of guys running around and yelling and a guy just can't think. They don't provide you with desks or anything to write on. I think I've started four other letters and couldn't finish them because someone came up and said I was needed in the orderly room or one of the guys wanted to talk to me about his problems, or about talking to the First Sgt. to see if he could get a pass. You wouldn't believe some of the guys in my barracks. There's a couple of them that are getting out of the Army next week. One dude came up to me and told me he was afraid to go back out in the civilian world. He's been in the Army four years and has been to Germany once and Nam once. He was asking me what I thought of re-upping? I told him it was up to him, but they couldn't get me to re-up no way. We talked about how much more money he could make in civilian life and he said that he didn't know what he wanted to do. Boy, he's really mixed up, but he has decided to go back to civilian life and try to go to college. I hope he makes it.

Well enough of the Army life. Last night I got a pass so I guess what I did? Me and Sgt. Milhoan and Specialist 4 Colan went up to Waco, Texas in Colan's car, and went to a concert put on by the Blue Haze and the Iron Butterfly. Boy, the Butterfly was super fabulous. We picked up on some weed down there, and it is real super weed. I think I'm going to quit doping it so much. I really haven't had that much since I've been here, only twice in the week I've been here, but I'm not going to smoke it during the weekdays, when I smoke it it'll be on weekends.

Clellie, I really do miss you. I sure wish we could be together. Last night in Waco there were a lot of couples together, and I just wanted to be with you. The more I'm away from you, the more I realize that you are the only girl for me. I'm not afraid to admit how much I love you to anyone. I mean it.

I'd better go for now. I'll write to you every chance I get so don't get pissed off at me for not writing much. We're going out in the field the 21st for one week, so I probably won't write the whole week unless we get to come in for Thanksgiving. I love you, Clellie, and I hope you still and always will love me. You write soon.

Your very lonely loving husband,
Tony

P.S. I found out our Christmas vacation is only for five days. That's really a bummer. I hope I can get enough to get home.

Sgt. Tony Jolley
HHC 2/46 Inf. (Mech)
1st armor division
Fort Hood, Texas 76545

✉ *November 18, 1969* *10:15 PM*

Dear handsome hubby of mine,

How's everything been going for you? Have you received the package yet? Please tell me when you do so I will know how long it takes airmail. Tony, I love and miss you so much.

This check I was so positive that we would have $300 in the bank. Now the most we can hope for is $275. Makes me so mad. It cost $24 to fix my car. They put in a new battery cable and I had to have a new battery. The post was cracked on the other one. So $24 shot! I'm going to give up and sell that good for nothing. Now it's really missing bad. When I go to pay them tomorrow, I'm going to have them check to see if they crossed spark plug wires. It never was missing so awful! To top that off, Mom brought the car up to me and parked it in any meter zone without money so I got a ticket. On top of that, my kidneys are really acting up. I took Chad in for his shot and it made him somewhat sick. All in all it's been a great day. Anymore like them and I'll give up.

Work was really slow today. It goes so much faster when there's gobs to do.

I went into Penney's today and laid away a most beautiful baby stroller for Chad for Christmas. It's blue and it has a windbreaker. I put five dollars on it and I still owe $20. I know you'll love it. After Christmas I need to get him a mattress.

Guess who came into the store tonight? Polly Gibson. She smiled and said hi to me nice. However I'm still suspicious.

In about one month I'm going to put Chad on regular milk. It should cost me about the same as SMA has been.

Boy, this late shift really has been getting me down ugh!

Molly has a guy named Cliff living with her now. Today Opal and Daisy Day, and Cliff and Molly came over and Mom and them drank. Then she started acting off to the kids and made them all mad. Then she wonders why they don't mind her. She was bragging how she was supporting all six of us. None of us were on our own. Red's a little ticked because she got drunk. I don't blame him.

Well Hon, I guess I'll go for now. I miss you so very, very much, Tony! I do so bad want to be with you soon. I can't wait until Christmas, but the time goes so slow.

Your loving wife,
Clellie

P.S. Hugs and Kisses, etc.

November 19, 1969   **10:30 PM**

Hi Hon,

Boy, you sure are a great flatterer aren't you? I'm glad that you think I'm the best-looking, best-built, etc. girl there is. It had better stay that way too. Even when you get old and distinguished and I'm just plain old! Just think there's a whole world of sexy girls and you chose little ole me. I love you, Tony, and I will forever!

I was so very glad to receive your letter. My day went much smoother today. Work was slow but not bad. I'll try not to get irritated if I don't get a letter as often as I think I should. I do realize that you're very busy.

Nancy went to one class this morning and got three F's on her report card. She gave up and came home all upset so Mom's going to go to school tomorrow and see what the reasons are.

I took my car out to the place where it had been fixed and had it checked. He showed me where the wire from the distributor to the spark plug was cracked and so was the cap over the plug. He gave me a new wire. He told me that by rights I shouldn't have that safety sticker because the brakes need linings. I need a whole new clutch and all in all a complete overhaul. I asked him how much it would cost for an overhaul. He said that it'd be about $200 worth. He said I'd be better off getting a new car.

I saw Marie and Lance tonight. I don't know if they're back together now or not.

Honey, when do you think that you'll get to be home for Christmas? Do you want me to meet you in Salt Lake or somewhere else? Anywhere will be fine. I was so disappointed to hear you only get five days off. I wanted to cry but a few days is better than none! I love you and I want to be with you. I will quit the day before you get home because I've got stuff to get done. I need to get us a motel for that time.

How do you like listening to others' problems? I'll bet you really feel important. You are to me!

I want to quit work now (at Christmas) and be with Chad for a while. He's unsure about his mother. It's a draw between Mom, Alice, and I. It would kill me if he got more attached to Alice or Mom than me. It's important he knows I'm his mother, this way Mom, and Alice are with him more than I. I do want to work again next year about November so we'll have money for when you get home. Honey, please tell me, what you think.

I will close for now. Please come home for Christmas! I've counted on that so long.

All my love eternally,
Clellie

P.S. Hugs and Kisses, etc.

✉ **19 Nov 1969**

Dearest Clel,

How's everything there in Burley? How's the baby? Most of all oh how are you? You sent for that bodybuilder guide? Clellie, I don't care if you do all those silly exercises to build up your bust. I'm serious. The only thing I don't want you to do is lose more weight. Put some weight on if you can, but please don't lose anymore. I love your body the way it is. I thought you looked beautiful and perfect when we were in Salt Lake. Of course, maybe you could get more solid by exercises, but please don't worry about it. I love you no matter what.

I'm really glad for your mother and Red. I think the idea of your mom married to a guy like Red is real cool. I don't know him, but from the way you talk he must be a real nice guy. Do they get along pretty good? I sure hope they make it together. Tell them congratulations for me. (You've probably noticed my handwriting isn't very good. Well, I don't have a desk so I have to sit on my bed and use my knee.)

I got switched to a different section yesterday. They put me and three other sergeants with a ground surveillance section. In this section we use radars that pick up enemy movements. Over in Nam you set the radar sets out in front of your lines. When ole Charlie's try to sneak up on you at night, the radar will pick him up (most of the time). Then all you have to do is switch on your spotlights and shoot the little guy. Cool. Of course, I probably won't get that job in Nam. I'll still be recon.

We got another warning order for Nam today. Me and six other guys got warning orders so were supposed to start a two week RUN course (Republic Vietnam). It's every other day, so we go about our regular jobs on the days we're off. We start the 28th of November. That means I might leave here before the 10-week period is up.

They're really starting to screw up us NCOs about Christmas leaves. The captain down in S–3 said that while we were here on OJT we're not supposed to get any leaves. Boy, if that's true I'm going to be pissed off bad. If we do get leaves, we got two choices. We can take from 22 December till 26 December, or we can take from 29 December to 2 January. Which one do you want me to try for? I know it's not half the time I told you we'd get, but they're screwed up here at Hood. I'd like you to talk to Sue and ask her how much leave Spear is going to get out of Fort Carson? Would you please?

By the way, Clellie, that was really nice of you to write me so many letters. Today at mail call I got 12 letters. It was really cool.

That's too bad that Denny and Susan still have to be going through that divorce scene. I wish they could get back together, but I guess that'll never happen. What's this about Alice getting expelled from school? How long is she expelled? That really surprises me. I didn't think that would ever happen to Alice. So Ann is going with Danny Kloer? You know who he is don't you? He is that dude that's always hanging around with his brothers and cousins and they use to honk at my car quite a bit, remember?

I love you very much, Clellie. I don't know what I'm going to do for one whole year in Nam. I guess I'll just look forward to the day I'll be able to see you again.

Clellie, I wish right now we could be together getting ready for bed. I better close for now. I wish I could hold and kiss you and make love, but will have to wait I guess. Stay mine forever and love me always.

Your lonely restless husband,
Tony

I want you! I love you! I need you! Forever and ever!

Sgt. Tony Jolley
HHC 2/46 Inf. (Mech)
1st armor division
Fort Hood, Texas 76545

November 20, 1969   **11:00 PM**

Dear best-looking,

Sure do love you so very, very much. I can't wait to be with you. I miss you so very much.

Denny Carter came into the store tonight and asked for your address. Well I did it from memory. I goofed. I turned it around. I gave him 4/26 instead of 2/46, and I forgot to put Inf. I guess I'll have Mom call him at work and straighten it out. I'd like it to stay goofed up, but that's up to you. If you still want to chum with him I'll try and stay out of it. I really feel two-faced with him. He asked me if I was going to get some snow tires and I told him that I doubted it. I wasn't going to worry about it now. He told me he'd get me some and walked out. Honey, you're going to have to talk to him. I don't want to feel indebted to him in anyway. Do I really need snow tires?

Speaking about my car, it's in a bad way. It's really out of time. It shakes every time it misses now. You decide what I should do. I'll wait until you get home. It'll only be about five weeks from now so I'll wait. Honey, I realize that you have enough problems on your own without worrying about mine, you're so smart and I've depended on you for so long, it's hard to stop depending now.

Work was sort of slow today. We got the meat and the magazines in today. Do you know that we sell around 100 Playboys a month? Gobs. I'm getting to where it doesn't embarrass me when guys bring those magazines up to buy.

Chad is still growing. He is getting cuter all the time. Of course he's getting to look more and more like his handsome father. Chad hums when he's eating now. He's a born swimmer. Boy, put him on his stomach in the water and he really splashes. I get a bath in the process. He tries to crawl but he goes around in a circle still. He sits up by himself for about two minutes now.

Was that a dance or just a concert with Iron Butterfly? Did you enjoy yourself? How do you like Texas?

Honey, there's not any way that you could get a pass from Christmas Eve until the day after New Year's? I sure wish that you could. Could you try? What days will you be getting off? About when will you get home for your 30-day leave? Have you got your Thanksgiving package yet? If so when?

I guess I better close for now. Always remember I love you and need you so much.

Your loving lonely wife,
Clellie

P.S. Hugs and Kisses, etc.

November 21, 1969   **11:00 PM**

Hi Hon,

How's the greatest guy in the world today? I hope just fine.

I received your letter today, I was so happy to get it. It was so very sweet. I love you so much.

Guess what? A kid I used to have a crush on in the seventh grade was in the store tonight. I haven't seen him since the seventh grade. It was weird. He talked to me about three minutes. He's married and lives in California. It was really weird.

Work was such a drag today. I was so close to tears I couldn't hardly take it. You have to come home for Christmas. Please find out for sure. If you can't, I'm flying down so get a place if you can.

I've just been talking to Sue. I'm so near crying. She's going down with him Monday. She said that he doesn't get any time for Christmas for sure. It makes me so sick. If you don't…! Also I want you to find out this little bit. Here it is… Sue said one of the main reasons she's going down is because Matt wrote and told her that he'd been informed that starting after the first of the year all the guys that were going overseas will only get seven days leave prior to being shipped over. Please, Hon, find out about this and Christmas for me. If it's true you'd better be planning on finding a place for me because I'll get on a jet and fly down!

Guess what? On December 8 the Grass Roots will put on a concert in Twin Falls. How about that?

You asked me if we had a choice on when you'd come home for Christmas which I would like. It's up to you but I'd like you to be here for Christmas so 22 through 26.

Guess what? Nancy Graf and Allan Jolley like each other. Fancy that! They kissed! How about that?

I got that exerciser in the mail. I hope it helps, and I know you love me no matter what, but it makes me feel so undesirable to you. It's a sad deal when you shrink. I want you to look at me in my bra and panties and really desire me. I want to be perfect for you. By the way I'm trying to put on weight. Red teases me about him not getting enough to eat. He also kids me about having a new addition in September next year.

I talked to Harold Rausch's brother and wife. He's doing fine. I knew you'd enjoy 12 letters. I'm glad you liked them.

Alice was only expelled for about three days. Yes I remember Danny Kloer, but Ann goes with who she wants.

Well I guess I better close for now. I love you so very, very much.

Your loving lonely wife, Clellie
P.S. Hugs and Kisses, etc.

✉ *November 22, 1969*　　　　　　　　　　　　　　　　　　　*11:30 PM*

Hi Hon,

How's my best-looking, most intelligent, and best lover doing?

Just think maybe in one-month we will be crawling into bed, making love, and just being next to each other.

You know I remember how Flora and Susan didn't want me going with you. I would have really missed out on the most wonderful life if I would've listened to them.

There was a turkey race in town today. I was working so I missed out but I guess it was pretty neat. Work was fairly good.

Tonight at lunch when I came home I picked Chad up and he laughed and talked to me for about 30 minutes steady. I couldn't get a word in. His hair is coming in pretty fast now. He's so darn cute.

Denny dropped by tonight while I was home for lunch to show us a picture of Justin. I gave him your right address. Tony, you know I feel sorry for him. I really think he's disturbed. He acts like they just broke up for a little while. It's really hard to explain. I guess you'll have to listen to him and see what you think. I really think that it's a real bad deal but he did it.

Tony, you know if I thought I couldn't trust you I wouldn't be able to take it. We really do have a special kind of love. No one will ever be able to break it up. It's too solid! I'm so very pleased to be yours! Your touch is so special, so thrilling, even your kiss.

Susan came over after I got off work and we went to the Ponderosa for a piece of cake. Well they were out so we walked out and went over to Rupert to the A&W. Boy, that hamburger and fries were so scrumptious! Then we came home. Chad was over at Hope's. Tonight and last night I had to drag him out so he'd be watched.

What do you think about me cutting my hair? Do you want me to wait until you come home for Christmas or should I now? How about if I cut it to where it barely touches my shoulders?

Well I guess that I better close for now. Tony, I miss you so very, very much!

Your most loving wife,
Clellie

November 23, 1969   9:50 PM

Hi Hon,

How's everything been going for you? I hope just great. How was your week out away from everything?

Work was okay today. It was pretty busy. I had to work from 1PM until 9 PM, another day another dollar.

Molly had an epileptic fit last night at about 12:30 AM and ended up in the hospital. She was out drinking, and doing just what the doctor told her not to do. Chasing whiskey with beer nonetheless, her and Mom and got in an argument at 3:00 AM when they woke me up!

Boy, the veins in the back of my one legs looked pretty bad tonight. I'm so afraid that I'm going to have ugly veins all over the place.

Have you received my package yet? I'm curious how long it takes to get there by airmail. It cost $1 more to do it airmail.

Mom and Red think Ann's smoking grass. They say that four times they've seen her pupils dilated. I don't know. I wish there was some way I could find out. I really don't think I'd tell Mom if I knew. She lets Ann get away with a lot of stuff. Alice and Nancy really resent it too. I can't say as I blame them.

This morning I got up as usual and bathed Chad. I had to tug to get his undershirt on him. Finally when I did get it on I noticed that it hit him mid belly. Big kid! I guess I figured that he'd never grow out of his undershirts or something because I had never really thought about it before.
Needless to say I better buy him about five undershirts next paycheck.

I've done my bust exercises for two days now, and boy, I'll tell you it is hard wow! I may not have a firm bust but my arm should get pretty firm. I'll let you try it when you get home. Not that you need to be firmer or bigger but just so you can see.

I had the weirdest dream about you last night. I dreamt that when we got together I sexily unbuttoned your shirt (for some odd reason you didn't have an undershirt on), and much to my surprise you had about 20 long black hairs all over your chest. It was really weird!

Well I guess I had better close. I have to work at 9 AM and Chad's been waking me up at 6 AM lately. By the way our phone bill for us was eight dollars this time. That's really not so bad.

Your loving lonely wife,
Clellie

P.S. Hugs and Kisses, etc.

November 24, 1969   11:15 PM

Hi Hon,

You know I saw Sue leaving this morning and I wanted to cry so bad. I've been so close to tears all day. Right now she's with him and happy. He had a place for them and everything. Tony, I miss you so much.

What would you say to me maybe taking guitar lessons? I don't know whether I will or not but I'd like to.

I got up this morning and went out to start the car. No go. All day until this Cliff guy came over and fixed it wouldn't start. Needless to say I walked to work 15 minutes late, in the process no breakfast, and no lunch. Oh well I'm getting too fat now. Mom came and picked me up from work after he got it started. Boy, that car will be the death of me yet! I sure hope it starts tomorrow. I washed our bedding and Chad's. Mom and I went shopping for groceries. Naturally I've been voted the pie maker for Thanksgiving.

Have you decided what you want me to do about my hair yet?

Tonight I went upstairs and was in the process of looking through Ann's drawer to find my underpants when I came upon a bottle of Coors beer unopened. I didn't tell Mom. It's her business. It seems weird to me to walk into the room and see all three of them smoking. Ann has a friend staying here for a week named Ethel Hawn. Susan and Donna's little sister. She seems like a pretty nice girl.

Work went pretty fast today. I put the magazines away, the crackers away, took magazine inventory, ordered candy and tobacco. Boy, am I glad that tomorrow's my day off and so is Sunday. I need to give your address to your parents Sunday. Love and miss you SO very much!

Love eternally,
Clellie

P.S. Hugs and Kisses, etc.

November 25, 1969   **10:30 PM**

Hi Hon,

Well for a day off I sure worked. I went to town to mail another package to you. This one is for your birthday and our anniversary. It's not much but I hope you like it. I sent this early because I'd rather you get it early than late. I don't know how long it'll take to get to you but with the Christmas season getting closer I figured it'd be slower. I sent it airmail. Please don't open the little package until December 13th. Promise? Anyway I had to take the package back home, put it in different bigger box, and rewrap it before they would insure it.

I spend most of the day tending Chad though. He's so cute and getting to be quite a show off. Sort of takes after his father. Boy, does he ever love black licorice to suck on. Both him and I were black when he got through.

My car started today. Good thing. I'm so sick of it.

Say what do you think about Nancy and your brother going together?

If you get to come home for Christmas, should I wait to get us a small tree? I want to take quite a few pictures of us this Christmas.

I've got to buy Chad some warm sleepers. I think he's allergic to the ones I bought him. I think I'll wait until it gets cold to put them on him again. He might have just sweat a little and broke out. What do you think? I also need to get a record needle for our record player but I think I'll wait until you get home. What do you think?

This Cliff Hatch who's married to Molly took her out of this hospital and took her to Salt Lake to a special seizure clinic. I do hope that they find out what causes them.

I got a letter from Flora finally today. She said that she is doing just fine she's going out with a lot of nice guys but she hasn't found "the one" yet. I sure hope that she gets as lucky as I was. Of course she can't. She can only come close.

Tony, I want so much to be with you on our anniversary. We won't be together on our first or our second I guess we can celebrate it at Christmas. Auntie Em has that top of the wedding cake in her freezer and we're supposed to eat it on our first anniversary. I miss you so very, very much!

Your lonely wife,
Clellie

P.S. Hugs and Kisses, etc.

✉ **November 26, 1969** *10:30 PM*

Hi Hon,

I have to work tomorrow from 9 AM to 1 PM. Great holiday. But you probably had it rougher.

At work I had to put 43 cases of food away, seven cases of pop, magazines, and cigars. It really kept me busy. Then I came home and made two pumpkin pies and two cherry pies.

They're having the battle of the bands tonight. Alice went with Ethel Hawn. She's supposed to get home by 12 midnight. Ann couldn't go 'cause she didn't go to school. Allan was over tonight visiting Nancy so I gave him your address to take home to his mother.

This Dwayne character (a friend of Red and Mom's) checked my car over and he fixed my brake real good (adjusted it) and fixed it to run really good. Boy, am I glad. He said he would fix the clutch if I would buy a clutch disk. Mom does his washing and such. He's a bachelor of about 30. He sort of likes Hope but Hope doesn't dig him.

Steve got home tonight for Thanksgiving. He's staying with Roy I guess.

Boy, it sure has been cold here. However my car started right up this morning. I took Hope to work tonight. It takes quite a while for it to warm up.

Chad's doing just really great. He's getting spoiled more every single day.

Tony, I miss you and love you so very, very much.

All my love eternally,
Clellie

P.S. Hugs and Kisses, etc.

THANKSGIVING!

November 27, 1969 *10:55 PM*

Hi Hon,

Well I just got off the phone from talking to you. I love you so much.

Man, I'm not kidding, if you don't make it home for Christmas I don't know what I'll do. Honest this week will be all it takes for me to lose faith in everything. The Army is the crookedest, rottenest outfit I ever knew! Tony, I want to be with you so much. The Army has let me down so many times.

Well this Ethel that was staying with us and Loren Scofield ran away to Salt Lake, Mom has got the cops on it. Mom says that she'll let them sit it out in jail. It'll serve them right. The dumb girls.

Honey, I know you want me to work until the R&R and I know that I need to go get some money, but I also want to be a mother to Chad. I also want to get a different job because my boss gives me the real heebie-jeebies. I don't get enough time off to be with Chad. Do you realize that he still isn't crawling? Why? Because every minute I'm around him I want to hold him. No chance to crawl, also because everyone else has to hold him. No we won't forget about the R&R! I want to see Hawaii.

Tony, I'm so down because of that stupid Army. It seems so unfair that we can't be together. Sue gets to be with Matt.

Did you get into a lot of trouble for today?

Well I've got to be going. It's getting quite late and I work early tomorrow. I love you so very, very much, Tony.

Your loving wife,
Clellie

P.S. Hugs and Kisses, etc.

✉ **November 28, 1969** *10:30 PM*

Dear Good-looking,

Well I have simmered down a little. Say listen, Hon, please be careful or you may wind up in a stockade and more time added on. We only have one year and three months of this crap. Then we'll be happy together forever. I cannot help but count on Christmas. I have to hold onto that!

Ann and Red aren't getting along too great, but I guess things will get better.

I never told you how my Thanksgiving Day was. I went to work from 9 AM to 1 PM. I got home at 1:30 PM, changed Chad, trimmed Ann's hair, cut my bangs, and mashed potatoes. We had a real nice dinner…rolls, fruit salad, Jell-O salad, yams, cornbread dressing, three baked chickens, and pies. I spent the rest of the day taking care of Chad and keeping the kids off the phone.

Cora McCarthy came into Thriftway to see me. It was really nice to see her. She asked about you.

Bill's mother and his brother came into the store. They were looking for a gift for Bonnie's birthday. She asked about you.

Chad still is growing, the little pill. He's so darn cute. I'm really proud of him because he looks so much like you.

I talked to Susan tonight. She called her lawyer again to see what was holding things up. He told her that he figured they would make up. She told him to forget it and get it over with. She was tired of piddling around.

I guess I'm going to have Chad's picture taken again Monday. It costs $1.49 plus tax at Penney's for four wallet pictures. I decided to give one to your mom, one to mine, one to you, and one to me. How does that sound to you?

Ann's back with Billy Russell, and Nancy still likes Allan and vice versa. What do you think about them two? Alice likes some Curt guy.

Well I better close. It's bedtime and I have to get some beauty rest. It takes me half an hour to get the bed warm. Brrr it's cold. No skiing as of yet around here. I love you, Tony!

Your wife eternally, Clellie

P.S. Hugs and Kisses, etc.

November 29, 1969   *12:00 midnight*

Hi Hon,

How's the best-looking guy in the whole world? I love you, Tony, and I'm so proud of you. Boy, today was the longest day at work since I've been working. I got mad at Grant and talked pretty snotty to him. It shocked me so bad when I did. This girl came up to the cash register to buy something, she wanted me to see if we had the earrings that went to it so I was over asking Carol when Grant came up and in his not nice tone said "I sure would appreciate it if one of you would go to the cash register." I said snotty, "That's what I was doing and I just came over to ask Carol about the set." Boy, it shocked Carol, Zena, Grant, and me, anyway so he cussed Zena and Carol out about something. Awful.

I went to the Phillips 66 to get a gas cap for my car. It would've cost me $2.30 for the one like I was supposed to have for the car. I told him I didn't want an expensive one because it would just get swiped. Well he gave me an old one that fits it pretty snuggly. Thank goodness.

Susan and I went out tonight. We went to the show "Butch Cassidy and the Sundance Kid" with Paul Newman. It was really good, so funny, and yet sad, sort of like Bonnie and Clyde. Have you ever seen it? If you haven't and you get a chance to, go see it. You'll really dig it. Then we went out to the Ramada Inn to eat. Man it's so cool! Will have to stay there at least one night. You'll love it. I ran into your mother and Marie there. She really looks good in her blonde wig. She said to tell you she's sorry that she hasn't written but she's really been busy. I told them that you wouldn't get home for Christmas. Your mother said that it probably was because you got a letter from Andrew and you're trying to get to leave the same time as Andrew. I tried to tell her that the Army made you do as they want you to but I couldn't seem to change her mind. Oh well.

Susan asked me tonight what you think about me going to Provo with her to live. I told her that I would ask you. What do you think?

Allan was over visiting Nancy tonight, his mother didn't know that he was though.

I guess that I will close for tonight. Tony, I'll wait for you forever! I love you so much. Be good, Hon, and stay mine forever!

Yours eternally, Clellie

P.S. Hugs and Kisses, etc.

✉️ **December 1, 1969**   **10:10 PM**

Hi best-looking,

I love you so much! I received a Christmas card from Sue and Matt addressed to both of us today. I guess I'll dig out our old ones from last year and send a few out. What do you think?

Well the Army still owes me $60 for Chad before you became Sgt. Boy, I'm going to write letters and see if I can get it. You try too. I received the check today from the Army of $130.60, and I only got $50 from work. I wanted to get $100 in the bank but I don't think I'll quite make it. I want to put some down on Chad's stroller too and he needs plastic pants, food, T-shirts, and socks. The big ox!

Work wasn't too bad. Brenda and I got cussed out because we were sending people to the back! They tell us to get a check okayed so we send them back there for that. Oh well. Then Ginger and I got heck because we were low on $.10 bars. The Bell wholesale man hasn't been bringing us the bars we ordered so we're low.

Hon, don't you think I could come down in the car? It would take about two days. This friend of Mom and Red's is a mechanic and could tell me what he thought about it, don't you think? I called the airlines and it would cost me on Air West $132 roundtrip ticket to Killeen, Texas from Salt Lake. I figure for ticket and living for a month $400 would be enough. I just hope I'll have that much. What do you think? Tony, I really want to be with you so much! I want Chad with us too. We could probably find someone who would watch him when we want to go out alone, don't you think? What do they furnish in the hotel? Sheets, towels, and such? Did they have kitchens? Will I have to bring my dishes and pots and pans and such? I'll bring a scrub board so I can do some of Chad's washing in between washings.

Denny came into the store tonight and asked for your address again. He says he's mailing it tomorrow.

Is food cheaper at the commissary? If so, about how much?

Alice dyed her hair tonight. It's darker than mine. Can you believe it? It's something else. She wanted to go back to her natural color. No such luck. It went darker.

Nancy and Allan kiss and everything. Pretty good. I think they're young but I guess I'm fogey. Allan flipped her bra strap she told me and she told him not to do it again. I told her to knock them flat! You think I'm an old fogey too? Laugh it up cute boy!

Tony, I love and miss you so much. Please don't tell me I can't come! I want to be with you so much!! I try to be big and say I'm coming but if you don't want me to come then I won't! I need to work until the 15th because I need to give $20 to Mom for all these phone bills and pay $10 on Chad's stroller to get it out. It will only be about $65 or $70 more after all that's out of it. But it's a little more and I should barely have $400. Then when my check from the Army comes in January Mom can keep it here for us so we'll have some money here when we get back. What do you think?

Well I'll close for now! I love you so very, very much, Tony! I always will!! See you soon hopefully!

Your loving longing wife,
Clellie

P.S. Hugs and Kisses, etc.

✉ *December 2, 1969*　　　　　　　　　　　　　　　　　　　　*10:15 PM*

Hi Hon,

How are you getting along? Say have you received the package for your birthday and our anniversary yet? Did you eat the goodies for your birthday? Have you peeked at the present?

Well I bought a clutch disk for the car, only $14.50. I put $10 on Chad's stroller. I only owe $10 more and it'll be out so I'll get it on 15 December. I also have to get the plates for my car next check. If I'm lucky I'll have a little over $400 in the bank with my check on the 15th. I had to get Chad some socks, plastic pants, and undershirts. He better stop growing or else he'll go naked. Right now we have $378 in the bank. Not bad. Boy, I'm glad.

Here's $10 to have a nice time on. You deserve one. Except no girls you know.

I've been on the run all day with bills and such. Work was pretty good. My legs really ache tonight however. Oh this tobacco man (Young) came in today and I ordered some tobacco. I know he saw my wedding rings, but he asked me what I was doing tomorrow night and I automatically said, "I'm going home to my husband." He said, "Oh." Then he left. And this old guy about 45 thinks I'm so beautiful with beautiful eyes and he loves me he says. You told me to tell you everything so there you are.

Guess what I received in the mail today? A special invitation from the Woolworths store in Twin to come to a special sale for special people, look at people model clothes, and such, and a whole dinner for only $.77. I have to have my invitation to get in. I thought everyone got one, but no such thing. Not a one at the store got one. It was for tonight, but I had to work. How about that?

I'm not going to get a needle for the record player until we get home for leave. It will discourage anyone using it. Do you think I'm selfish?

Do you know what I want to learn? How to snow ski. If I remember right I told you that while you were gone in the Army I was going to learn how to ski better than you. Susan wants to learn too.

See you soon hopefully!

Your hopeful loving wife, Clellie

P.S. Hugs and Kisses, etc.

December 3, 1969 11:15 PM

Hi Hon,

How is everything with you today? I love you so very, very much.

Susan said that she had some relatives in Dallas and maybe she could drive down with me. I told her she could go without paying any gas. I don't know how things will turn out though. It's starting to snow in Salt Lake so I might have a pretty rough time by car without snow tread. What do you think?

Say is the hotel right in the town so we could walk if I don't bring my car? Do you know if there's another couple that has a baby that we can take turns tending so that we could go out alone once in a while? Could you get a ride back and forth from the Fort? Please try and see if you can. If I take a jet to Killeen, could you meet me? What do you think about bringing Chad? It would be good for you to get to know him, but I also want time with you alone. What do you think?

Work was pretty good today. I was told that only Grant was to do the thinking, not me. I ordered some pipes without his approval. I didn't know I needed to. Oh well.

I mailed Christmas cards to Matt and Sue, Bill and Bonnie, Luke and Stephanie, and Flora. Boy, I'm really getting good.

Well they were having trouble with the kids tonight and naturally yours truly is in the middle. It makes me so sick. I get one side from the kids, one from Red, and one from Mom. Really I have my own problems don't you agree? I'd rather just sit around and dwell on my own. I really am a miser you know. You'll see!

It cost five dollars for Chad's last shot. Quite a bit! I only expected three dollars but it ran more.

Well I better close, Hon! I love you so very, very much. See you soon hopefully!

Yours eternally,
Clellie

P.S. Hugs and Kisses, etc.

✉ *December 4, 1969*   *10:15 PM*

Hi Hon,

How's my greatest man doing? I can't wait to see you.

Work was okay today. I was sitting in the breakroom and Grant said, "Say Jimmy did you know that Clellie is a single girl now." I said, "I most certainly I am not. I'm a married woman." Grant said, "Can you prove it?" I said that I have a ring to prove it. He said, "Well anyone can buy a ring." I said that my husband was real and alive. He told me that he thought I was living in a daydream. I told him I wasn't but even if I was it was a pretty beautiful unreal one. Then I left. He really must think he's cute. I can see through that dirty old man's mind. He gives me the heebie-jeebies. After Mr. Peck and him, I think all bosses are a bunch of jerks.

I talked to this old guy tonight about the roads from here to Salt Lake. He said that they're just like ice. He said that he saw three wrecks. It's not so bad from Snowville to Salt Lake if you can make it to Snowville. It's hot here today. I guess that they're going to open Pomerelle next week.

My great uncle Claude died last week. They had his funeral in Arco today. He was one of my hillbilly relatives. He was a nice guy though. He died of cancer of the throat. At the last they had a tube running out of his throat so he could eat. He lived about six months longer than expected.

Do you realize our little boy is getting up there in months? Chad is five whole months old. Spoiled? Not Chad. Only reason he doesn't crawl yet is because he never has a chance to be on the floor. Someone's constantly holding him. I predict he'll be a great swimmer. In the tub he really tries to swim. He stands on the floor now if you hold his hands. He's so cute.

Well, Hon, I better go. I love you so very, very much! See you soon!

Yours eternally,
Clellie

P.S. Hugs and Kisses, etc.

✉ **4 Dec 1969**

Dear Clellie,

How's everything at home? Is Chad getting bigger and meaner still? I sure hope he's keeping you busy. Maybe he'll interfere with some of your hustling.

How are you, Clellie? Are you still the most beautiful and best-built girl in Idaho? I know you are, but I wanted to ask you anyway. I sure do miss you.

I sure wish I could get home for Christmas, but I don't think I'll make it. How about you coming down, Clellie? I want to find out just how much time I'll get off before you come down. If I'm going to be working overtime, I don't want you to come. It would be just a waste of time and money if that happens.

Clellie, I got to get back to work so I'll cut this letter short.

I wish we could be together. I'd like to run my hands up and down your body. I'd love to kiss and caress you. It's been a long time since you've touched me. I remember how in the car when I was driving you would start rubbing your hands on my leg. You almost drove me out of my mind, but I had to drive so I'd always speed up and find a place to park real quick.

Clellie, I want you very much and I always will. Please stay mine. I'll write you again as soon as I can.

Your loving husband,
Tony

✉ **December 5, 1969**   **10:50 PM**

Hi Hon,

How's the greatest man doing? I hope you're doing fine.

They're going to open Pomerelle tomorrow. It didn't snow all day today. It cleared up and melted what snow we had from yesterday.

Well I got some dry cleaning done today. I went to the do-it-yourself dry cleaners. I did that green dress and my parka. I got Chad a bumper pad for his crib because every morning his leg or arms always caught between the bars.

Work was pretty good today. No smart cracks from Grant. It got really busy from 9 PM until 10 PM. It took me until 10:10 PM to get out of there. I then took this girl to her car parked about 1½ blocks from Thriftway.

Chad's about 26 and three-quarter inches long and about 18 pounds he weighs. Husky little fellow, don't you agree?

Denny came into the store tonight and bought some cough drops. He told me he wrote you. Tony, maybe I'm being nosy but did he mention anything about his stepping out? Also does he seem to have plans for when you get home? You don't have to tell me if you don't want to. Just pretend I didn't mention it because I'm curious and I cross my heart and promise not to tell if you tell me.

I will readily admit that I was upset about no letter today. I realize that you warned me that you might not be able to write me, but I still almost cried. Couldn't you steal anytime at all to write so much as I love you? Do you still love me? Honey, I miss you so much and every day that goes by without a letter about kills me. I guess I'm not a very understanding wife, but I try. Please write.

This old guy told me tonight that he'd tell me a joke but I might hit him. I told him I probably would. He said, "Oh you don't like to hear them?" I told him nope. Pat me on my back.

Christmas will be so neat with you. Two more nights at this time I'll be able to make my plans. I'm so afraid in a way that you'll try to talk me out of it. Please don't. I've made so many plans and hopes and they've all turned out rotten. I love you so much and I want to be with you so very, very bad! Always love me.

Your loving wife, CLELLIE

P.S. Hugs and Kisses, etc.

December 6, 1969   10:45 PM

Hi Hon,

I love you so much and I'm so happy to get your letter. I was eight minutes late to work today because the mailman arrived with your letter just before I was going to leave so naturally I had to read it. I cussed you out last night because I had no letter and so today I get one. Teach me.

Work wasn't so bad today. It was really busy until about 6 PM. By then the roads were really slick and it was snowing pretty hard so it was pretty dead after that.

Chad's keeping me busy. Even if he didn't there's no one that is worth hustling because the only one I want to hustle is you.

How is the weather there? Is it cold? I guess skiing at Pomerelle was really good and powdery today. Say I hemmed up that brown dress with a high collar and long sleeves. Now it's about 5 inches above my knees. Short? Yes but sexy for you. What do you think?

Alice and Nancy stole some gloves at King's so Mom took them up today and made them pay for them. She also told me that she told them to keep an eye on them anytime they came into the store.

Tony, you're so ignorant but I like it. What I love was when you put your arm around me. Man it felt so groovy and it turned me on so fast, or when you could come close to touching me and stop.

Honey, I love you so much and I want to feel your touch and just be near you at night. Please let me come.

Your most loving wife,
Clellie

✉️ **December 7, 1969** **10:00 PM**

Hi Hon,

I sure do love you gobs and gobs!!! Mom and I got into another doozy. I've about had it. She tells me how immature I am. Pretty good. I'm sick of it!

Ann's going with Billy Russell again. He dropped out of school and he doesn't have a job. Ann and him went out last night at 6:30 PM. Well 8 PM rolled around here she was home. He went out with the guys. Boy, did I ever rib her for letting a guy do that! She still likes him though. He stood her up today too. Boy, she's ticked! He's playing his cards right though because he's not eating out of her hand. I still dislike him.

They're having a gas war in Rupert. At some places it's down to $.23 a gallon. Not bad.

Honey, do you think that the girls should be allowed to smoke here? I think if they're going to smoke they'll sneak if they have to. Am I wrong? That's what Mom and I were arguing about.

I sat home today waiting for you to call. What happened? Marie called three times wanting to know when I'd be over 'cause I had told them that I'd try to go over there today. Oh well I got all my sewing done and my washing. You didn't forget did you?

Tony, I love you so very, very much. I guess I'll close, Hon!

Your loving wife,
Clellie

P.S. I had this letter all written except for my name when you called! I love you, Tony, and I want to be with you so very, very much! I do want to come. Please don't tell me no! I would like to bring Chad with me too. He should be with us. It's up to you though. If I plan on staying until you come home he should be with us. What do you think? You're so special and I want to be with you! I would like to come as soon as possible much you think I should work until the 15th and leave the 16th to be with you. We'd have $100 more about. Whichever way you think would be the best.

Well I'll close again! I love you so very, very much!

Clellie

December 8, 1969   **10:30 PM**

Dear Tony,

Tomorrow is your birthday and I hope that you had a real nice one. Course there's not much chance of that in the Army. Just think you're a whole 21 years old. I hope you realize that we're getting ancient now.

I took my first birth control pill last night. This morning when I went to work, boy, I felt like I was pregnant again. UGH! Sick to my stomach bad! They say that they do that to you at first though so maybe I'll be okay after a few times of using them. They also are supposed to put weight on you. I sure hope that it doesn't.

Work was pretty good today. It went pretty fast. It didn't get real busy until about 3:00 PM. Everyone's trying to get their shopping done.

Angie Gibson and her mother were in the store yesterday.

Susan called me tonight. She wants to get on state aid I guess. We'll see if she does.

From what I hear (gossip) Butler's wife is having a real nice time playing around right here. She doesn't want to go to Germany anymore. I thought I waited on her yesterday but I wasn't sure. She was with some guy if it was. However, I'm not at all sure it was her.

At Twin Falls there is a concert with the Grass Roots. I didn't find out until today. I heard about it about the 15th of Nov. but I had forgotten about it until I heard it from Ann. I would have liked to see them. Oh well, doesn't hurt me to stay home I guess.

Allan gave Nancy a real cool necklace to be going steady. Oh by the way, you and Woods aren't related are you? I'd really like to know.

Hope is quitting at the office on the 13th of this month. She's really pretty sick of it.

Boy, the roads sure are slick. It snowed tonight for about 2 hours, but it was wet snow so it melted as it hit the roads.

Mom's going to start work at King's Friday. Alice's going to stay home that day with Chad so Hope won't have to try to feed him or anything like that. Next week I'll be on the late shift so I'll take him over to Hope's at about 1:30 PM and Ann will get him at about 4:00 PM. It won't be so bad next week. I'm quitting on the 21st or 22nd. This next check I have to pay $10 on Chad's stroller, take money out for gas, get my plates for my car, and put the rest in the bank. My next check will only be about $20 after they take all the taxes out.

Well it's about time that I hit the sack. I'm pretty tuckered out. I do love you, Tony, and I always will!
Love Eternally, Clellie
P.S. Hugs & Kisses etc.

✉ **December 9, 1969** *10:30 PM*

Hi Hon,

I love you so very, very much. I was so happy to hear from you. I'm so glad that you looked for a place. Tony, I want to be with you so much and I'm so excited.

You know I was pretty miserable yesterday because of being angry at you. I'm sorry, Hon. I was so completely let down when you told me that I couldn't come.

Have you gotten the money yet? How are things coming along? I'll give Grant notice that my last day will be the 21st. That way I'll work long enough to get the taxes from my first check paid off and be able to charge some Tampax, bc pills, and disposable diapers for the trip. I should still get about $10 out of it. Anyway, with this next check I want to pay $10 so I'll have Chad's stroller paid for and I need to pay Mom for the phone bills 'cause I couldn't stick her with it this time of the year.

I made plane reservations from Twin round trip for the 23rd. I'll leave at 8:20 AM from Twin and layover in Salt Lake on student stand-by. If I get out right away I'll be in Killeen at 4:10 PM. How's that? Will you be able to meet me? I sure hope so.

Sunday morning (if all goes well) I want to go to the Catholic Church with Chad for mass. The girls want to go too so…I want to go to the 11:00AM one I guess. Anyway call me before 11AM or after 12 noon sometime. I need to visit your folks. I haven't been to see them for quite some time.

Honey, we may not be rich when I get down there but we'll be together. Isn't that what counts or do you still think I'm being dumb?

I guess Red, Mom, and the girls are going up into the hills to get the Christmas tree this Saturday. How about that?

The girls bought Chad some booties and some more plastic pants. The ones I bought are too big and the old ones are tearing to bits. Sweet of them.

Mom's quite excited about her job at King's. She's nervous but excited. I'm really happy for her. It'll be good for her to get the experience. 'Sides, right now they need the money!

Well I guess I'll close for now! I'm so excited and I love you so much, Tony. It'll be so neat! Does it have a TV? Can you get a trailer? That would be our best bet. It's so neat and exciting. I miss you so much, Tony. I love you gobs and gobs.

Your loving admiring wife,
Clellie

P.S. Hugs & Kisses, etc.

December 10, 1969   *9:00 PM*

Hi Hon,

I'm so excited! I can't wait. I'm going to get me a scrub board to do quite a bit of the washing. That way it won't cost so much. I love you so very, very much!

Say is it really cold down there? Tell me about the average of the weather there. I'll bring an extra blanket so Chad can sleep on it at night, I can't wait!

My car has what is called a cold flood. It floods once it doesn't start and then it won't start again until it either gets pushed or gets warm. This is to say I walked to work today in 15° weather. Then at noon Susan came and I went to the bank and took out $150 in a cashier's check to you and sent it Air Mail. Then she brought me home. She had to leave so after lunch I walked back up to the store. After work it was snowing and Alice and I walked all the way home in the snow. Oh well! I'll walk tomorrow too I guess!

I broke the news to Grant that I was quitting. He simply told me that I couldn't. I told him that I could. He didn't want me to leave, too bad. I'm done on the 21st of this month. How's that?

I'll bet you'd never guess that I'm excited. It'll be so neat to be with you. It scares me to go to a new place but it bugs me worse not being there with you. We won't be rich but you're not rich now either so it won't be any different will it? Will you be able to get rides with other people back-and-forth? Will you meet me at the airport? Tony, I love you so very, very much! I can't wait to be with you.

Your loving excited wife,
Clellie

✉ **10 Dec 1969**

Dearest Beautiful Clellie (how's that?),

How is everything there? How's Chad getting along? Clellie, shouldn't Chad be at least crawling by now? If it's true that he doesn't have a chance to learn how to crawl you'd better tell the kids to let him alone on the floor once in a while so he can learn how.

Is everyone back there getting in the Christmas spirit? I sure wish I could come home for Christmas. Down here it doesn't even snow. It just keeps cold and windy. How much snow do they have on Pomerelle? Wouldn't it be cool if it was Saturday and we were loading up the car to go up skiing? It's been so long since I've skied that I've probably forgotten how.

Clellie, I'm really sorry about the other day when I hung up while you were crying. I couldn't sleep because I felt pretty bad about it. I really don't think we should hang up while we are mad at each other do you? Why, Clellie, do you have the feeling that I couldn't love you anymore? The only reason I would say you couldn't come down here is not because I don't love you it's because we couldn't find a place or we don't have the money. As long as we've been married and you still say I don't love you. It's kind of hard to understand.

Boy, that pisses me off what your boss said about living in a daydream. I guess when I get home we're going to have to walk in Thriftway together and you can show me who he is. I'd like to go up and hit the bastard in the face and ask him how that feels for being a daydream. He must really think he's a cool dude.

The CO said something to the effect that the young buck sergeants from Benning might get a Christmas leave now. If I did get a week's leave for Christmas, Clellie would you still want to come down, or would you want me to fly home? It's up to you.

Clellie it would be so neat to be with you right now. Just think we could lay next to each other all night. Anytime I wanted to I could reach over and feel your body. I think I could kiss and caress your body all night right now. Clellie, I love you forever. Remember that. I better close for now.

Your loving husband,
Tony

P.S. I want you! I need you!

Sgt. Tony Jolley
HHC 2/46 Inf. (Mech)
1st armor division
Fort Hood, Texas 76545

December 11, 1969   9:45 PM

Hi Hon,

How's everything with you? I sure hope you're great. I love you so much.

Susan called me tonight. Her sister Gay lost her baby at five months along. Sad. She's going to go and stay with her for a week to help her. She lost her water one day and the baby the next. It was a perfectly formed baby boy. They wanted a boy.

I went and helped Mom with her Christmas shopping Tuesday. I found a pair of boots I wanted. I really need to get some if I stay here with this weather. They cost around $17. Ugh! I'll wait! I also found this blue floor length robe. Mom bought Nancy, Alice, and Ann one. Then I showed her that blue beautiful floor length robe. Well she traded Alice's for that one. I about cried. Course it cost $14, but I wanted it so bad. I wanted to have a nice one for you. Oh well. I'll wait.

I got a new machine (cash register) at work. It's really neat. How's that for excitement? Mom's going to work at King's tomorrow.

I bought me and the girls a sundae tonight. I also gave Alice and Nancy $.50 a piece so they can go skating tomorrow.

It cost me one dollar to get the car started today. I walked to work before they got it started. This guy found two pieces that have fallen off my carburetor so it cost me another dollar for it. I took the clutch parts back because that guy can't put it on until after Christmas so I'll wait. I got around $15 back. $10 I took and got Chad's stroller out so we won't have to worry. Then one dollar for the part to be put on and the girls' money and sundaes.

I got a letter from Sue today. She's not working. Her and Matt are going to live off the government. They're doing great and happy together.

Mom called the airline. It won't cost anything for Chad as long as I hold him. I can take two huge bags, the equivalent of two RE footlockers or four bags. I think I can squeeze everything in three bags. If I weigh over then it cost me $2 per bag every time I make stops between here and Killeen. I can carry Chad's diaper bag on. So I'm not bringing a whole gob, the less the better!

Well it's getting pretty late. I'm so excited, Tony. I miss you so very, very much. I cannot wait until we're together again.

Love eternally,
Clellie

P.S. Hugs and Kisses, etc.

✉ **December 12, 1969**　　　　　　　　　　　　　　　　　　　　　　　　**9:00 PM**

Hi Hon,

I received your letter today and I was so happy and pleased to get them. You're the sweetest guy.

I've about decided to get the book 79 Park Ave. for when we're together. That's the only time I can read nasty books. What do you think?

Grant's kidding me about laying me off now, I just hope he's teasing. It kind of scares me.

Everyone seems to be in the Christmas spirit. It's hard for me to get into the spirit though when the biggest most important part of our family is in Texas. I want us together as soon as possible! I miss you and it's just not Christmas without you here.

I got a card from Bill and Bonnie yesterday, and Sophia Meyer. They say to say hi to you so hi!

Hon, don't worry about Chad. He is a smart little duffer. He just hasn't had many chances to learn to crawl. He'll probably learn to walk before he does crawl. Mom said some babies do. 'Sides I don't think Carter's baby started crawling till it was about seven months old. It wasn't crawling when you came home and it was six months old. Don't worry, give him time.

I'm not sure how much snow is on Pomerelle. From the way I gather there's not a whole lot yet. Tony, you're never going to forget how to ski, you're too good at it. I'd love so much to be going to Pomerelle. Course I don't know how to ski so you could ski alone (no girls!). I do want to learn however.

I don't like hanging up when we're angry at each other either. Course we were at a standstill. I felt one way and you felt the other. I felt so rotten afterwards. Sue had only $200 with her and she left. They are getting along fine. I love you so.

Hon, are you or aren't you getting a Christmas leave? I feel like I'm on a merry-go-round. I just get something going and get excited then I have to feel blue then I feel down and out and then I have to get excited over some other bit of hope. I feel so confused. I don't know what to plan on, to get gifts for the family or not etc. I'm sorry but the Army is getting me down. I would like very much to share both Christmas and New Year's together. We missed New Year's the first year of marriage and we will the third so I'd like to greet this New Year's together. I also realize that you'd like to come home for Christmas. Also we could be together for a sum total of two months if I flew down there. It's up to you. I can't decide. If you really want to be home for Christmas I couldn't deny you that, and I am afraid that I decided on the one you wouldn't want.

Your waiting loving wife, Clellie
P.S. Hugs and Kisses, etc.

✉ **December 13, 1969**   **10:10 PM**

Hi my most handsome man!

Happy 1st Anniversary! Just think of it, one whole year behind us. Only 49 more years and we will be celebrating our 50th. I can't wait! I'll love you as much as I do now. We have so many good years ahead of us, so much love and great happiness to share. We'll raise our 2 or 3 children and see our grandchildren. You'll look so distinguished and I'll look plain old. Oh well, that's the hazards of being a woman. You'll have girls 20 or 21 years old flocking all around you. Go ahead and laugh smart guy but you just wait! By the way, I should be six years older than you. Do you know why? 'Cause on the average women out live the men by about six years. I'll bet you can't guess why. Well, I'll tell you. We simply wear you out at night and you don't get the proper rest so you can't take it like we can.

Carrie Connor called tonight. They are doing real fine. They wanted to know when you'll be home and I told her to write me and I'd tell her as soon as I know. How's that? I asked her when Randy started to crawl. She said that he was really early to start. He was 6 months old and he walked at 8 or 9 months. So Chad's not so slow. He's learned he can scream, and boy, he sure lets you know that he knows how.

Work was so busy today. It was like a rat race. Mom said that they were really busy too. She really likes it though. We then went grocery shopping. Only spent $34. Wow! We're only having 2 kids, Chad and Jeanette. I baked a cake tonight.

Well I guess I'd better close. I can't wait until we're together, Tony. I'm going to love you up one side and then another.

Your loving wife,
Clellie

P.S. Hugs & Kisses, etc.!

✉ **December 14, 1969**　　　　　　　　　　　　　　　　　　　　　　　　　　9:30 PM

Hi Hon,

It was so neat to hear from you today. I loved talking to you. You're so cute when you get upset. I love it so much.

I sent you a lock of my hair. Great. Quite a bit off. Now I look even younger. Marie's hair is about 1 ½ inches longer than mine now. At least it won't get in your mouth or smother you.

I took Nancy and Chad over to your folks' place. Barry's no. 16 and the J's are the first to be called so he's as good as gone.

Your mother wants me to let her know as soon as I find out if you get to come home for Christmas. I told her that I would. So let me know soon.

I think that would be a groovy idea to have you fly home and both of us to drive to Texas together. I really would like it. Tony, I'd like anything that would let me be with you again. I miss you so much, and I'm wasting so much time staying here.

Red bought a tree today. He got it half flocked when he ran out. No place was open tonight so he didn't get it finished. I guess that they'll decorate it tomorrow night.

Guess what? One week from today will be my last day at work. I'm going to miss the money and the girls I work with but not Grant!

Honey, are we going to be able to be together for Christmas and New Year's both & no, you shouldn't go AWOL. I want to be with you for both of them.

Tony, have you found us a place yet? I sure hope so. I love you so very, very much! I want to be with you so bad. I guess I'd better close.

Your wife,
Clellie

December 15, 1969 11:30 PM

Hi good-looking,

How are things going for you this fine day?

Do you realize that there's only nine more days until Christmas?

Everyone loves my hair. They said that a flip flatters my face. So I'm glad that I did it. I'm sort of tired of real long hair anyway.

Work was pretty good today. Grant kept pointing at me and saying "that girl." It almost sounded like the beginnings of Marlo Thomas's shows.

Well we got the tree put up tonight. I must say it's the best-looking one that we've had in a long time! That's got all blue bulbs and all blue lights.

I got a present from Auntie Em. I peeked. It's pajamas! They'll keep me warm this winter without you.

It wasn't too busy at work today. It dragged! Five more days and I'll be done. In a way I'm sorry because I'll miss the money, and it helped the time go by. But I won't miss Grant and his smart mouth!

I wonder if Chad will even notice the pretty lights this year. He's so cute. Next year will be the best for him.

Did you know that Andrew only has about six more months in the service to go? I thought he was in for four years.

Well I guess that it's time for me to sign off for tonight. Only about seven or eight more days and we will be together again. I'm so excited.

Your loving wife,
Clellie

P.S. Hugs and Kisses, etc.

✉️ *December 16, 1969* *10:30 PM*

Hi good looking,

How's things going with you? I sure hope all's okay!

We got a nice card from the Blohms so I'm sending one to them.

I saw Dave Doutre yesterday. He came into the store. He lives in Oregon now. He dropped out of college. He said that he wasn't ready for it yet. He asked me how I liked marriage and I said I love it, except that you're in the Army. He was shocked when I told him that you were in the Army.

Tonight Grant and Morris spent 20 minutes talking to me about quitting. Grant said that he could give me a month off but not two. I never even asked him. I told him that I couldn't guarantee anything because I didn't know what we are going to do yet. He told me to let him know when we have decided. I told him that I still was going to keep my plans unless something comes up. He said that I was a hard worker and he hated to lose me. I don't know what will happen. As for now all I know is that I do want to be with you as soon and as much as possible. He told me that I wasn't being practical because it costs money to goof around for 60 days. I told him that I knew how much it costs and I have some money saved. Tony, all I really know is that I want to be with you so very, very much!

Chad was pretty cranky today. I think he's cutting teeth and it bugs him. It's taking him quite a little while. He still scratches his head. Makes me so darn mad. He is such a little doll though. He wants to eat everything we are eating now or he cries. He also loves attention. He's sucking his two fingers even through blankets so I slap his hand gently out of his mouth. He doesn't like that at all!

Well, Hon, I'll close. I love you, Tony, so very much! I miss you so much and I can't wait until we're together.

Your loving wife,
Clellie

December 17, 1969   *10:30 PM*

Hi ever so lovable,

Tony, I miss you gobs and I cannot wait until we can be together again.

We got a nice Christmas card from Bonnie Webster and Mr. and Mrs. Dale Conner. It was real good to hear from both of them. They told me to say hi to you so… hi.

Work was quite a drag today. I told them that you were coming home for about seven days and I wanted it off. Grant said okay but that he might need me for a couple hours on the 24th because the last day is real rough. I told him that I would see. What do you think about it? I wouldn't mind working about four hours during the day but not that night junk. I really don't want to work anytime you're home, he pretty well put it I do or else. So what do you think?

Ever since you called, Tony, I've been so excited. I love you so much and it'll be so neat. What do you think about staying at the Lamplighter here in Burley? Of course I guess we can decide on that when you get here.

Do you think that we should buy a big box of candy for each family or what?

Honey, I've got something to tell you about what happened tonight. It has shook me up so bad and it startled me so much I couldn't think. It's hard to tell you in a letter because I can't be there to calm you down. You see tonight after work I got in my car and was in the process of heading home when this train came bombing down the tracks. I waited for about three minutes when I realized someone was pounding on my car door. It was Greg from the store. I opened the passenger door and asked him what, and about that time the train was across the tracks so I drove to the place across from the Burger port and he said that he just thought he'd say hi and he was sorry he had scared me. I told him hi and asked where his friends were just as they drove up. He said goodbye and left. I think he was a little bombed. I'm going to tell him tomorrow but I don't want him to do that again. I will, Tony. I hate him because I hate anyone who does that when I'm married. Please, Tony, don't be angry. I know you are but please.

He loves his wife and he's expecting and he knows how much I love you and I think he thought he was being nice so I'll tell him. I wanted to tell you when I went to get you but I was afraid I might forget and end up writing to you later on to tell you.

I love you, Tony, and I will eternally!!

Your loving excited wife,
Clellie

P.S. Hugs and Kisses, etc.

✉ *December 18, 1969*   *10:25 PM*

Hi Hon,

I can't wait to kiss my big strong handsome Sgt. Tony! I'm so excited.

I guess I won't mail this till after you get back because it won't get to you in time, so by the time you get this it'll be ancient. However I know how much you like gobs of letters so I'll continue.

I never told you but after you called me Wednesday I called your mother to let her know and she was very pleased.

Well Sunday I work from 12 PM to 9 PM. What a drag!

I guess Grant has said that F word around two girls. Boy, he better not say it around me because I'll quit. I don't care. No one needs to say that word around girls.

Work wasn't too bad today. It still was a drag.

Chad's getting so cute! He sits right up next to me in the car and is just as content as can be. I get to where I hate to leave him with Hope or anyone more and more every day. He is so precious and he seems to change every day! He still scratches his head but he's a little doll. He stands up and holds onto my knees.

The time seems to be going so awfully slow! I kept thinking that today was Saturday. I sure wish it would hurry. I want to see you again so much! I love you, Tony, and I always will.

Your loving wife,
Clellie

P.S. Hugs and Kisses, etc.

OUR CHRISTMAS TOGETHER

A week home for Christmas was not near enough time but would have to hold me over until my leave before going to Nam. Clellie and I spent a wonderful week together and returning to Texas was nearly impossible. I realize how much I've missed and how fast time continues to pass when I'm not around. I am however grateful to be able to spend Chad's first Christmas at home and while I know he won't remember it, I will cherish this time in my heart.

✉ *December 28, 1969*   *11:00 PM*

Hi Handsome,

I love you so very much! Tony, I really wish that I could be with you now. If you could only feel the emptiness I feel now. Man, I walk up to the bedroom and I could cry. It seems so lonely to me. I dread going to bed. I keep thinking that in about 3 weeks we'll be together again, (I hope!).

We got home about 7:00 PM tonight. Your folks were really sweet to me. Say did you turn around and look at us before you got on board? I could barely see a guy in a uniform turn around. Was it you? It sort of looked like he gave a peace sign or a wave. 'Course you know me and my imagination. It was really cold up there on the watch deck. But I didn't mind. The thought of you just warmed me right up.

What happened with you? You know I should've had you call me tonight or tomorrow to let me know you got there okay. It worries me so bad for you to fly. I just like to know you're okay.

I called Susan tonight. We talked for a while about how nice it was to have you home, what we did, and how bad I dread going back to work. Ugh! I guess that she came over last night at about 7:30 PM to see me and go to the show, but guess what? I told her that I didn't wake you up because I wanted you to stay an extra day. Tony, I want you to know that I enjoyed this week and a day with you so fully. I love you so very, very much! I don't want you to ever hate me. I never want you to turn to anyone else for love 'cause I have a whole body full for you. You are so wonderful to me.

Tony, I love you so much! I miss you horribly! Only 2 more good-byes left and you will be home for good so Chad and I can hassle you.

Speaking of Chad, I got home tonight and took his temperature. 102 degrees. I'm kind of worried about him. We'll see how he's doing tomorrow.

Well I guess I'll close! I love you so much, Hon.

Your lonely loving wife,
Clellie

P.S. Hugs & Kisses etc.

December 29, 1969   *10:40 PM*

Hi Hon,

Well here's your hard-working wife writing to you.

I guess I go to work from 5 PM – 10:00 PM on New Year's Day. Groovy. Guess what? I got a bottle of Seven Winds cologne and $10 from Grant and Jean at work. Now I can go buy my skirt.

I just got through talking to Cathy Bowman whose husband is in Vietnam now. She went to the R&R in Hawaii. She hasn't worked at all and she has a baby. Her husband won't let her work. Anyway she said that it cost her $201 round trip to go to Hawaii from Portland. They spent about $400 over there. Not bad. I'd just like to sit home and wait for you. Lazy. Oh by the way her husband only got a 14-day leave and he was also due 35-40 days so now what? Will you still get the 30-day leave?

I got our sheets and Chad's washed today plus my ironing done.

Red and Mom went and bought a car today. It's a 1964 blue Oldsmobile. It's really nice. They let me drive it and I really like it. It's quiet and a smooth rider. Red also got a $.10 raise at work.

It sure bugs me not knowing what has happened to you. I've worried about it all day long. I was so dumb not to have you call and let me know what went on. It was dumb of you not to call…so there!

It's so lonely and miserable without you here, Tony. I really do hate it.

Chad still is quite sick. A lot of people are saying he probably is cutting teeth. It will make him get the sniffles, have a temperature, and feel rotten. I just don't know what it is.

Well, Hon, it's pretty late and I'm sort of bushed. I love you, Tony, and I miss you so very, very bad. Please hurry home and love me. I love you so.

Your loving wife eternally,
Clellie

P.S. Hugs and Kisses, etc.!!

✉ **December 30, 1969**   *10:05 PM*

Hi Hon,

Guess who's working at the store part-time? Elizabeth Belnap who is now Elizabeth Fillmore. She's 4 ½ month along. She married Grant's son. How's that?

Guess what we did at work today? Took inventory. I counted every candy bar, gum, cigar, pack of cigarettes, and cough drops. It sure was fun! (Ha Ha!) We have 11,332 pieces of 1-cent candy. I'm so tired I can hardly believe it.

Your mother called today and asked me if I heard anything from you, and I told her not yet. Boy, are you going to get beat by me! Then she asked me to pick up this game at work so I charged it out. It's normally $4.50. All toys are on ½ price so that would be $2.25. However Grant wants to get rid of them so this girl and I decided to charge me $1.00 for it so I charged it for $1. Anyway I'm not taking any money from your mom for it, I hope! You know how she is. I won't be getting a big check from work this time 'cause of the days off and all the taxes that is held out of this one. At the most I figure I'll get about $24. I hope I can get about $90 in bank with the Army check and mine. We only have $83 in the bank now. That's only enough to pay one month's rent, and a down payment on the lights.

Red told me to take the car to work when I came home for lunch. Man it's so neat. I really want a new car now. I think Red wants to pick you up in Salt Lake when you get there. If you can let me know about when you'll be there, I can ask him. Mom said he wants to 'cause he's never seen Salt Lake before.

Chad's feeling better today. He's got a runny nose and a little cough but he's better. We set him in his walker today and he moved it backwards one step. He tries to lean back and make it move. He doesn't quite understand that his feet have to make it budge. He's learning though. He's so cute.

Well I guess I'll be closing. I started my exercises again today. I miss you gobs and gobs.

Your loving wife,
Clellie

P.S. Hugs and Kisses, etc.!!

✉ **December 31, 1969**　　　　　　　　　　　　　　　　　　*10:15 PM*

Hi Hon,

Boy, I'll bet that you were having a very merry night tonight. I wish so much that I had had you call me at 12 o'clock midnight so we could bring in the New Year but I never even thought of it until tonight. Dumb little me.

I just barely got home from work. It was sort of busy. I did inventory again. I get so tired of counting everything. Thank goodness it only comes once a year.

Bonnie Webster came over today to see me but I was going to work. I saw Muriel Beckwith today in the store. Susan came over this morning. She had just got through seeing the doctor with Justin. Boy, he sure is a sickly kid. He's had one solid cold all winter. She said that she's had him in the doctor's office almost every day. Poor kid. She wanted to know if I wanted to do anything tonight. She sort of wanted to go to the dance at the steakhouse and I told her she ought to go do that. I didn't want to do anything. So she did. I sure hope she has a nice time. She needs to get out and mingle with some guys.

Man it's really cold here today. I about froze. It's sort of snowing too.

I do believe (cross your fingers) that Chad is going to have a tooth come through pretty soon. Maybe you'll see him with his first tooth. I can sort of feel the one or two that's trying to get through. They're on his bottom gum in the front. I'm so excited.

Guess what my New Year's resolution is? I want to always be the kind of wife and mother you and Chad deserve. I want to be more patient and more understanding. I love you.

Your loving lonely wife,
Clellie

P.S. Hugs and Kisses, etc.

January 1, 1970   **10:05 PM**

Hi Hon,

How's everything with you? I hope just fine. How's your new year starting out?

I shouldn't tell you this. Seeing as how you kept Natalie and Denny from me, I should not tell you. But I trust you enough to know you won't say anything to Denny if I don't want you to, which I don't. Last night Susan went to the New Year's Eve dance at the church with her brother. After the dance however she went to a party with a returned missionary named Blaine Cook. How about that? Now don't you dare tell Denny. I'm glad she's going out.

Well Ann pierced Nancy's ears today. I had to hold her hand. Talk about making me sick!

Last night Chad woke up at 11:30 PM so I got up and changed his diapers. There was not a thing wrong with him. We brought in the New Year together. I sure wish you would've called. I let him cry himself to sleep and then at 15 after 1 AM Ann and her girlfriend got home and turned on her record player so loud. Again I woke up. Mom and Red got home about 2 AM. Alice wasn't home yet. Again I was awake. Red went looking for her. About 3:45 AM she came in the door. We still haven't got the story straight. I got off work tonight and Amy brought me home. When I got here I found out that Alice and Ann packed their suitcases and are gone. No one knows where. They had it out with Mom and Red.

Hon, I like Red and all, but he is quite bossy to me even. Oh well!

I am so ticked off!! I walked to work again today! My car wouldn't start again! I was frozen. Any more like today and I'll quit! I'd like to really but money… money!

At the office last night there was a fight with some Mexicans. One guy got stabbed and Randy Jones got shot once in the stomach. He got up to go after them and they shot him again. He's okay though and so is the guy who got stabbed.

Well, Hon, it's that time again. I need so much beauty rest you know. I love you so much, Tony, and I always will.

Your admiring wife,
Clellie

P.S. Hugs and Kisses, etc.

✉ **January 2, 1970** *10:20 PM*

Dear handsome hubby,

Maybe 20 days from now we'll be together! (I hope!) This time seems to be going so slow.

Well I got the check from work and $23 is what I made after they took everything out ugh! I also got the $130 from you. After the phone bill, Mom, car, sheets, underclothes for me, stationery, and insurance I won't have a lot to put in the bank but I'll squeeze a lot.

Guess what? Chad has got to the point to where he doesn't want anyone to feed him at night except Mom or I. Even during the day when I am here he won't let Alice even feed him. Just me. I'm kind of glad in a way. It makes me feel good. One small thing worries me. He has an obsession with his fingers. He always has them in his mouth. You're going to have to do something about it when you get here. He's your son.

Hon, when you get here I want you to get the jumper cables from your dad or get me some because I need them with my car being like it is.

If I can I want to quit about June but it will be until September so I can be with you. I want to have about $800 in the bank for Hawaii. What do you think?

Boy, that show, "Funny Girl" must be fabulous. The last four nights it's been packed and lines outside. I won't get to see it though because the second show's at 9:30 PM and I don't get off until 10 PM. I want to try it anyway. If we can't, Susan, and I will go to the other show.

Well Ann and Alice went to see Rex the policeman and asked if they could be put in a foster home because of last night. She couldn't run to Dad any more so now it's the cops. I don't know what's going to happen. Alice and Ann talked Nancy into leaving too. They called me and told me. I told them that was up to them. I told Mom that she had been too liberal with them too. She said that she knew it. They might get sent to a home for girls in Twin. Anyway it serves them right. They're always throwing it out to Red that they bring $150 into this house so they can do what they want. Boy, Ann's got a lot to learn.

I guess I'll close for now. I love you, Tony, now and I will forever.

All my love eternally, Clellie

P.S. Hugs and Kisses, etc.

January 3, 1970   **12:45 AM**

Hi ever so handsome hubby,

Guess what? Our son is now six months old, one half year. Isn't that great? Guess what else? Chad stands up in his walker and sits down moving backwards. He's so cute. Tonight when I came home for lunch I was just going to leave to go back to work and I sat down to talk to him for a few minutes. Then I got up and headed for the door and he started crying. It's getting so hard for me to leave him anymore. Oh well only seven more months and I can quit for about five months.

Say, will I have to send your tax forms in for you or is it automatically done for you? On mine, who do I claim? Chad? I want to get it taken care of by about March but I'd like to know now.

I caused an accident today. I went uptown and came back. I was just about to pull in the driveway when it happened. This lady behind me had stopped for me but this guy came up and crash into her. Sad.

Well I spent the $23 from Thriftway and my $10 bonus today. I paid your insurance, and I bought a skirt, black-and-white, I have to buy a black scarf for it now, anyway a sexy bra, three sexy bloomers, a sheet for our bed, my slacks to get fixed, gas, and Chad's milk. Great. It went so fast. I also got a purple shirt with white buttons.

Say Hon, I told Mom I'd pay her $30 a month if she'd stay home with Chad and not work. It'd cost me $30 for a babysitter anyway plus the $25 I pay her so I'm saving $25. Susan and I went to the show "The Wrecking Crew" tonight after I got off work. Then we went to the Ramada for a sundae, delicious! We stayed there for about 45 minutes. Ann and Alice came in too. They talked to us for a few minutes.

I have to go to work tomorrow. I work from 11 AM to 7 PM ugh! Oh well, Sundays were always so boring. It's better to be out earning money than sitting on my bottom, don't you agree?

Hon, how come haven't I got a letter yet? I've been so worried and not a single word from you. Why? I thought you only have to work half a day Monday, Tuesday, and Wednesday.

Well I have to sign off for now. Hon, I love you so very much! I want to see you so bad.

Love eternally,
Clellie

P.S. Hugs and Kisses, etc.

✉ **3 Jan 1970**

Dearest Clellie,

How does Cpl. Jolley sound to you? I think it sounds pretty good. They haven't said much to me yet, but there is a rumor going around that all the ones that were late are going to get Article 15's. I really don't want to get busted, but I guess it doesn't really matter what I want, right?

Clellie, I'm sorry it took so long to write. I started to a couple of days ago, but something came up and I never got a chance. I've kind of been put on extra duty because there's a bunch of guys on restrictions and us NCOs that are back off of leaves have to keep them busy.

How is everything back in Burley? I already miss you, Clellie. I've been thinking of you very much since I got back. You know me and you can really be honest with one another. Can't we? I mean we've talked about if we could end in divorce and everything else. I don't know what you think about it, but I don't see how we could ever get a divorce. I just don't know what I would or could do without you.

Boy, I sure was bushed all day Monday. I didn't get back to the barracks till four in the morning. You know how they told me I would have to get a flight to Killeen when I got to Dallas? Well they didn't have any flights so I had to ride a bus…5 ½ hours on that damn thing.

Clellie, I haven't heard anything for sure when we'll get out of here. I just hope it's very soon. This letter is going to be short because I have to go. I love you very, very much and I'll try to write soon and more often. Clellie, I want you so bad and forever.

Your very lonely husband,
Tony

P.S. I love you! Send me some stamps.

Sgt. Tony Jolley
HHC 2/46 Inf. (Mech)
1st armor division
Fort Hood, Texas 76545

✉ **January 4, 1970**　　　　　　　　　　　　　　　　　　　　　　　　**9:30 PM**

Hi Hon,

How's everything with you now? Boy, am I ever angry with you! Ticked me off!! I'll tell you later.

Ann, Alice, and Nancy are home today. They had to come home or else. Alice and Nancy got in a fight tonight. In the process Nancy called Alice a "G.D. fcker." I sure was shocked! Poor innocent me. Evidently they call that to each other at school too!

Chad is so spoiled, and talk about a temper! He is so stubborn too! Tonight I just got in the door, and I was going to go past when he saw me. Alice was holding him and he started to whine and stretch his arms so I went over and picked him up and he was just fine. He's so cute.

I talk to Debbie Hall and she said that Staker will be home exactly one month from today.

Work was pretty good today. It was just busy enough to keep me busy. I worked from 11 AM to 7 PM. My legs really hurt today but that's okay.

This lady at work named Amy came up and asked me when you would be home. She needs to get a foot operation and Grant asked her if she'd wait until I get back. I told her that I wasn't sure when or for how long. I thought around 22 January for about 35 or 40 days. Please try to find out as soon as you can so I can let them know.

Now let's see I think that's all I have to tell you about my exciting days. Now are you ready for your Scotch blessing? Do you realize that it has been one week today at 3:40 PM when your plane left? In that week I have not heard one solitary word from you. Not a letter, not so much as the phone call, and I am so ticked off I could scream!!! You probably have a nice excuse, but I am not going to be at all understanding! I go to work all day come home and goof off with Chad but I still make time for you a letter. I've been at this one 45 minutes. I love to write you letters, Tony, because they bring you closer to me so it seems that I need and want your letters too. Please…I miss you and I'm worried sick about you. I don't know anything about you since you got back. I thought you might call me tonight but no such luck. Tony, I miss and love you so very, very much! Please write.

Your lonely loving wife, Clellie

P.S. Hugs and Kisses, etc.

✉ *January 5, 1970*   9:30 PM

Hi Hon,

I was so very, very pleased to get your letter today. I've been on pins and needles. You're so sweet. Do you know what else? I think that you're still the neatest, handsomest, and sweetest man that ever was! I love you, Tony, so very much!

Burley is just fine and so am I. Chad's doing real great too. All I think of is you. I've been taking my breaks in the makeup room since you left. One girl asked me where I was taking my breaks and I told her. She asked me why and I told her that I liked being alone. She told me that Grant doesn't like us taking breaks in there. It was for the customer's use. I'll just wait until he tells me anyway. If I'm in a rough mood I might tell him that I like it and I don't see what difference it makes. 'Sides half the time he has his businessmen down there and there's no room for any of us so us girls go to the makeup room. I'm really not worried.

Hey I want us always to be honest with each other. The only thing that bugged me was the fact that we argued and you were here for only a week. When we did, it scared me. Right now I can't see how we ever could. Tony, I couldn't get along without you. I love you so much! I need you so much! I depend on you.

Your picture was so good. You were so darn good-looking and I love you gobs and gobs. I'll always love you!

Your loving wife,
Clellie

✉ **5 Jan 1970**

Dearest Clellie,

How's everything back there? I haven't been busted yet, and maybe I won't, I don't really give a shit either. Is Chad's cold any better? I hope it is because that poor kid was miserable when I left.

How's the weather? Is it still snowing? Boy, I still can't figure out why I didn't go skiing while I was home. I guess we'll have to get together with Bill and Bonnie when I get home next time and go skiing.

Have you got any new threads yet, Clellie? I don't think I'll get any cowboy boots while I'm here because in the PX's they don't have the kind I want.

The way things are going here we might be here for the duration of time. We might not ever get home again. The group that is supposed to leave the 6th of January hasn't even started processing out yet. They're probably going to be late getting out and so are we. Of course we'll never know for sure when we're getting out, because it can change at any time. Don't worry though; I'll be home as soon as possible.

Clellie, I love you. We sure had some good times together when I was home didn't we? It was so good to have your warm body next to mine all night. Did you have a good time while I was home? I love and want you forever, Clellie, and I never want you to leave me. I think you and me were made for each other forever, don't you? I better go now.

Your husband forever,
Tony

P.S. When I got back the CO told me he couldn't make me shave my mustache, but he told me to trim it. I couldn't see that so I shaved it off. It might come in better now, but I doubt it. I might not try and grow it back.

I love you, Clellie!

Sgt. Tony Jolley
HHC 2/46 Inf. (Mech)
1st armor division
Fort Hood, Texas 76545

✉ **January 6, 1970**　　　　　　　　　　　　　　　　　　　　　*10:40 PM*

Hi Hon,

Guess what? Chad has cut his first two teeth! It's his two front bottom teeth. Cute. I hadn't felt his gums for about two days so I decided to feel them tonight. There they were just tiny little sharp things. It's so cute and I was so excited. After he moved that walker once, he hasn't done it since. Little spoiled baby.

Susan is moving pretty soon. She's going to live off the state aid, and they are going to pay her to go to college. I think it will be a really good deal. Don't you? If she'll just take full advantage of it.

Mom said that if we want to stay here for your leave then it'll be okay. She'll go places during the day or if we wanted her to babysit she would. That way we could save more money. We could also go stay in a motel over the weekends or go to Sun Valley one weekend. We could get a few groceries once in a while. What do you think? Are you still going to work? I asked Mom if she could hear the bed squeak or if the girls could, and she said that no she couldn't and the girls hadn't said anything. She told me to get a blanket or rug and use the floor. What do you think? If you would rather get a place it'll be okay! Do you know when you'll be home yet?

Well, Hon, I better be going for now. I love you so very, very much. Here are your stamps.

Your loving wife,
Clellie

P.S. Hugs and Kisses, etc.!!

January 7, 1970   9:00 PM

Hi Hon,

Everything's fine here except that I'm miserable without you here. I was so surprised and happy to get your letter today. Thank you so much.

Red was trying to start my car for me today and he looked in my trunk and found your battery charger and the cord with the light bulb. We used your battery charger to charge up my battery because I ran it down and the battery charger is sitting here in the kitchen. He wants to borrow the bulb under his car at nights so I said okay. I also need to get the battery cable from your dad because we need it. I wish you wouldn't have given it to him. I hate to go over and get it back from him. If I can hold out till you get home I'll let you get it back, this walking is for the birds. We're trying the dip stick in mine tonight. It's beginning to get 2° to 4° below zero at night here.

Last night after I left work Grant went up to Ginger and Linda and asked them what harebrained vacation I'm planning now. (As if he didn't know) oh I'm mad! Linda said none unless it was for Tony's leave. He asked when that would be and she said that even you didn't know yet. Today Grant left for Salt Lake to get an operation on his eye. He'll be back Monday. Breaks me up!

I took five dollars and bought Chad some new sleepers because he's outgrown the others. These are a little big but he'll grow.

No it's not snowing anymore. It's just cold!

Hon, save some money if you can so you can get a coat here. I want you to have one. Yes, I got some new threads that you heard about in one of my other letters by now. Is that enough threads for now? I haven't worn any of it yet.

I sure would like you to call me Sunday the 11th. Hint hint! I have that Sunday off. I want to go to your parents about 2 PM or 3 PM if I can so please try to call early. I don't know if you'll get this letter in time. I forgot to tell you last night, but I'll keep my fingers crossed.

Tony, while you were home I was so content and happy. We had fun just being together and goofing off! I'll always be yours. You're so special.

Your loving wife forever! Clellie

P.S. Hugs and Kisses, etc.

✉ **January 8, 1970**   *9:30 PM*

Hi Hon,

The dipstick worked real well in my car. I drove it to work.

Last night Chad woke me up at 6 AM. He was screaming bloody murder and it scared me so I picked him up and took him downstairs and checked his diapers and pants. No trouble with that. Boy, but he still was hollering and I realized that his hands were covered with the sleeves of his pajamas. I uncovered them and they promptly went in his mouth. He scolded me for about 15 minutes and then was sound asleep. Then he woke me up at 7 AM with the same problem. I could beat his little bottom.

Boy, work sure is slow now. It's such a drag. I don't like it real busy but I do like it busy enough.

You know I'm so awful as soon as I got your first letter I should've called your mother to let her know that you're okay. She was terribly worried about you too. I called tonight though and couldn't get hold of her but I got a hold of your father. He was pretty relieved to hear about it. I guess Andrew may not get to come home as soon as they thought. There was some sort of epidemic break out which killed quite a gob of people so they figure he may not be able to get out as soon as he hoped. They haven't heard from him one way or the other. They're just guessing.

Hon, you said in your letter that you shaved your mustache. Did you really? Tell me the truth or are you just trying to get a rise out of me? It's really up to you to shave it. I just hated to see it go. However I'd like to see you without it again.

I had to buy a watchband today or rather charged it out at Thriftway. It's pretty good but I didn't want to charge too much. I got Chad some milk too. How's that? It ticks me off. No money for the bank if I spend it all.

Well, Honey, I have to go for now. I love you so very, very much. I miss you so bad. You're so very, very special to me you know. You have been since the first time we were together. I knew that I had to cling to you. One side of me said that I should love an LDS boy, but the best side of me told me I'd be dumb to let you go. I would have been dumb too. I never could have found the kind of love I hold for you. You're so sweet, Tony, and so gentle with me which I love you more for.

All my love eternally!
Your loving wife,
Clellie

P.S. Hugs and Kisses, etc.

✉ **January 9, 1970**   **10:00 PM**

Hi my big masculine handsome one,

Boy, how's that for a starter? I love you, Tony. Maybe only 13 more days and we'll be together!

Work sure was a drag today. Well I about died. It was so slow. Nothing to do but walk the floor and that's so ugly.

My car's started real good lately. Boy, am I glad. This walking's for the birds.

It snowed all day today. It was a pretty wet snow so it's pretty rotten and sloshy. All it needs to do now is freeze and the roads will be great.

Carrie and Dale must be down again because she called today while I was at work. She wanted to know if you were still here and said that she would call me tomorrow. I should call her but I'm so lazy because I came home, took care of Chad, checked my oil, and put the dipstick in. I didn't even change my uniform until I took a bath one hour ago. I really am lazy after work.

Like I said I'm lazy. I did my exercises for about one week and here I've gone one whole week without. Even if I do them every other day they're supposed to help so I'll get busy again.

Red started to work at the saw mill for $2.50 an hour. Well the river froze so poor guy worked one whole day and hasn't been able to since. He gets his first check on the 25th.

Hon, I heard that they're only keeping the guys over in Nam 11 months instead of 12. How true is this? Even at 12 months you'll be home in February of next year. And you could get out the last of December. So you could go to college, couldn't you?

Your loving wife,
Clellie

P.S. Hugs and Kisses, etc.

✉ *January 10, 1970*   *10:10 PM*

Hi handsome,

Well work was boring again. It gets to be quite a drag. I try to keep busy but there's only so much that I can do. I sure am glad that I don't have to work tomorrow. Everyone left Nancy today alone with Chad. She called me at work at 20 after 4 PM and I could hear Chad screaming his lungs out. She couldn't get him to be quiet nor could she feed him. I was so upset I about went home. This is only the third time they've done this and every time Nancy calls me upset and I get upset. It ticks me off. Works bad enough without that garbage. After I got off, I was heading to my car and who did I see coming out of the Calico Cat? None other than Red, and Mom. I don't mind them going out, but why couldn't they wait until 5 PM? Red borrowed a dollar from me for gas so he can get his $15 from his last job. Do you realize that's all they have to live on until the 25th? I have a feeling that they're going to want to borrow some money. We'll see. However I told Mom that I do need all the money I can have for when you get home.

Last night Mom and I were talking about Warren Dudley. She was going to let Alice ride with him, Jed Kloer, and Lauren but didn't. Anyway I told her that Dudley only thinks of one thing and I told her what you told me that day Dudley called here and you answered. She said that she wouldn't tell them but you should for their own good. I agree. What do you think?

Susan's moved to Twin. She starts college Monday. How about that?

I saw Carrie and Dale today. They came into the store. Dale's grandmother died and her funeral was today. I told them that I heard from Bill and Bonnie that Dale was laid off. They said no that he had a job until at least June there. They also said that they hadn't seen Bonnie and Bill since last summer. I said that her mother was to have told Bonnie. Carrie said that her mother talked to Bonnie about three months ago and at that time they were worried about it. So see I was right.

Well, Hon, I have to go now. I miss you so much! I wish you were here with me now!

Your lonely loving wife,
Clellie

P.S. Hugs and Kisses, etc.

✉ **January 11, 1970** 9:45 PM

Hi Hon,

How was your day today? I'm so ticked off because you haven't called yet. I've paced the floor and everything.

Well I've spent my day off cleaning. I should have went to visit your folks but no such luck. Oh well. Chad's been really cranky today. He's trying to cut one of his top front teeth, and boy, does it ever bug him. I felt so sorry for him.

Mom and Red went to Twin to see Aunt Jane who's in the hospital. She had an operation on her gallbladder. She's feeling okay now

Well here it is 25 to 11 PM and I just got off the phone with you. I miss you, Tony, so much. I want to be with you. I've been so counting on you coming home on the 22nd. It's such a rotten deal. I want you to be here now and I can't tell the Army what to do can I?

Well I start on late shift tomorrow. Ugh! I'm beginning to really hate that ugly job anyway.

Tony, it was so neat to talk to you. You sounded so neat as usual. I can't wait until you come home.

Ann said that everyone knows you and Barry too. She said that everyone tells her that they know you and think you are really cool. All the Kloers know you.

Last night I bought Alice, Nancy, and me some fries and sundaes. Then I spent a nice evening alone. This girl at work, Brenda who's divorced, wanted to get together and go have a Coke. I told her that Susan and I were planning on going to the show so she said okay.

Chad is eating one jar of vegetables a day and 1 jar of fruit. How about that? He's so cute. He's getting more and more hair. Do you want me to get it cut when it gets long? He still doesn't have any hair on the side and very little on the top, but he's doing pretty good.

I guess I'll close for now my husband. I don't know how I'll get along six or seven months without seeing you or talking to you.

Your loving lonely wife,
Clellie

P.S. Hugs and Kisses, etc.

✉️ **January 12, 1970**   *10:15 PM*

Hi Hon,

Do you know what I think? I think that you know when you're coming home, and do you know what else I think? It's around the 23rd or 24th and if it is I'm going to bust you in the mouth. (Not too hard, then I'll kiss it a lot to make it better.)

I got another letter from Sue Spear. She said that they'll be coming around the 22nd or 23rd. She said that they had a poor but nice Christmas. At least they're together!

Do you realize that on the 16th you'll have been in Ft. Hood exactly 10 weeks so you should be home by the 24th? Tony, I miss you so much! Thank heavens we have almost one year behind us. I'm so happy that it's not just beginning. Maybe you'll be home for New Year's next year.

Work was a drag except better than last week. I plan on working only until first of June I hope. Then Mom wants to get a job so I don't want to get another job until maybe Christmas to get a few presents. I have the whole year planned.

I haven't heard from Susan since last week. I hope that school's going to be okay for her.

Man I'm dying to learn how to ski. I want to so bad, but I can't get a chance to go. Thursday is ladies day and we get lessons at a special price. Oh well maybe next year, I hope so. I'll feel so dumb if I'm the only one in our family who can't ski. Chad's going to be an athlete. Skiing, swimming, horseman, and a charmer just like his dad! The best in everything he does, like his dad. I sure hope so. I'd be so proud and happy.

I saw Marlynn Woods tonight. You know she really doesn't look like a Woods does she?

Hey when you get home I'd like to take off to Sun Valley for a weekend just you and me. What do you think? I want some time completely alone with you. (I prefer all the time.)

Well I better go. Hon, I love you so much. I will forever and ever.

Your loving waiting wife,
Clellie

P.S. Hugs and Kisses, etc.

12 Jan 1970

Dearest Clellie,

I thought this card was cute so I bought it just for you. I've been pretty busy lately and I haven't had a chance to write you a letter. I thought this card with a letter on it might be sufficient enough communication to hold you until I can write a formal letter.

Clellie, in a letter I received today you used the word F--C-K twice. I don't like that. It doesn't sound like you. I'm not mad or anything, but it just doesn't sound like you.

I love you very much, Clellie. I just can't seem to get used to being without you. I miss you so much I can hardly stand it. Do you still love me as much as you used to? I sure hope so. It would be so neat to have you here so I could hold and caress you. I love you so much. I know I'm the luckiest guy in the world, because I have you for my very own. Clellie, I love and miss you very much. Please stay mine forever and ever.

Your very lonely husband,
Tony

P.S. I love you!

✉ **January 13, 1970** **10:15 PM**

Hi Hon,

How are you doing this fair night? I sure hope you're just fine.

One year and one month we have been married. How does that sound? We keep it up and will beat Susan and Denny's marriage. I guess that wasn't very nice was it? We're just lucky. That is… I'm just lucky because I got you. I'll trust you forever! Well until you tease me again.

It's been raining here off and on for almost 3 days.

Listen if you find out by Sunday when you'll be coming home call me. I work from 1 PM to 9 PM Sunday.

I guess that we should stay here for that month. We can go to the motels for the weekends. I'll get a check from the Army on the first so will be okay. What do you want to do when you get home?

I have to get some Numbs It I guess for Chad's gums. He's having such problems with them hurting him. He's cranky all the time and spoiled rotten!

Hon, I love you so very, very much! I always will. Damn I can't imagine life without you. I miss you so terribly much now. Be good, Hon, and stay mine.

Your loving wife,
Clellie

P.S. Hugs & kisses etc.

January 14, 1970   **10:30 PM**

Hi handsome hubby,

I received your card today and I thought that it was so darling. Thank you so much. I love you gobs and gobs. I still better get one more letter.

I'm sorry that I said those nasty words in the letter. I was just telling you quotes. Now you know how I feel when you say those ignorant words. Oh and please don't call me a b---- anymore. When you get home I never want to hear that from you again in reference of me please. It really hurts and bugs me.

Work was a drag as usual but it went by okay.

Well Nancy might as well face it. She's flunked. Straight F's again.

Speaking of school. Guess who is resigning as principal? You're right… Mr. Ingersoll. He probably couldn't hack the new dress system. Girls can wear slacks and pant dress. Boys can have their hair sort of long and sideburns. How about that?

I got home tonight and washed my hair, and got it put up. It's been such an exciting day. It seems all that I get done is watch Chad a little, sleep, and go to work. What a drag. Speaking of Chad. He's getting to where he moves that little stroller backwards pretty regular now. He's so cute. He knows it too.

I cannot wait until I can quit work. These walls are a sight. Man I've never seen it so dirty. I hate for you to have to come home to such a dirty place, but maybe you won't notice it.

Tony, I love you more than I used to. My love for you seems to just keep expanding. I don't know how but I seem to be finding deeper love and respect for you. Maybe I'm finally growing. I'm still spoiled and selfish when it comes to you. I miss you so terribly much, Tony.

Your loving lonely lucky wife,
Clellie

P.S. Hugs and Kisses, etc.

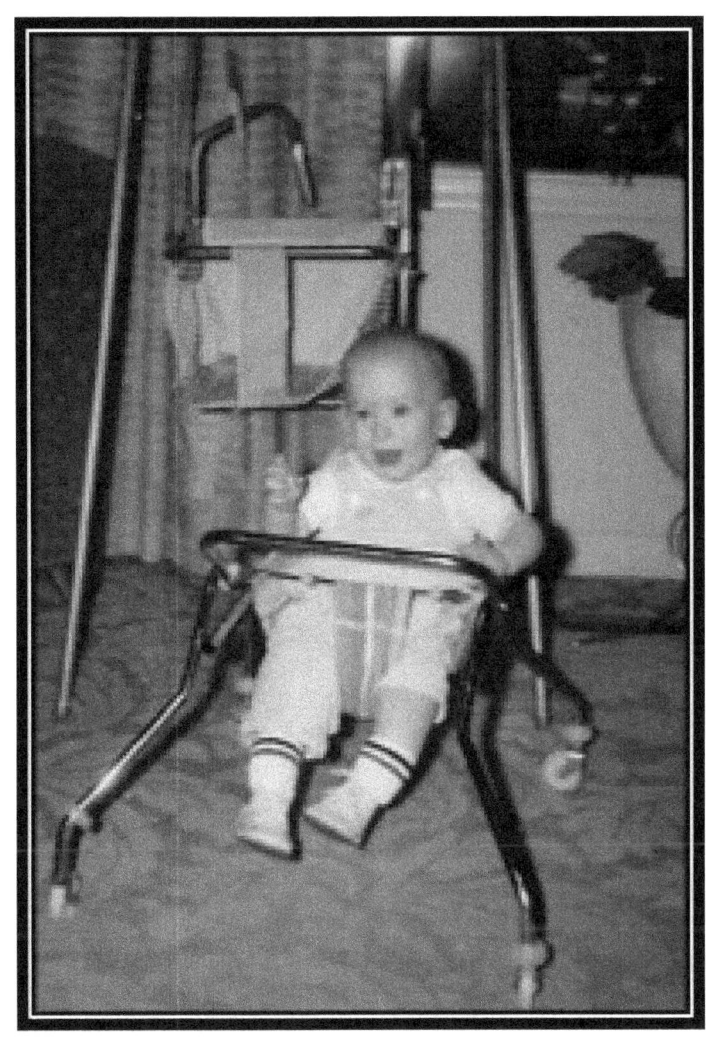

✉ **14 Jan 1970**

Dearest Clellie,

How is the most beautiful, charming, and the most perfect person in the whole world? I hope you are fine. Is Chad still cutting teeth? I was really happy to hear that he cut two of them already. Man I won't be able to recognize him by the time I get home if he keeps cutting them.

You told me a couple of letters ago that Red looked in the trunk of your car and found the battery charger and stuff. What you should do is get that extension cord and hook up the electric dipstick and leave it in your car overnight. That way it will start in the morning. Don't go losing or loaning any of that stuff to anyone though. Clellie, also call Dad and tell him that you need the jumper cables, and he'll give them to you. You don't have to be afraid to ask him because the only reason I let him use them is because someone stole his and his battery was shot. Now he doesn't need them because I bought him a brand-new battery. So ask him for them. If you use that dipstick in your car be sure and check the oil real often, because the heat from the dipstick will evaporate some of the oil so you better check it quite often.

Well I decided to let my mustache grow back. I started at Sunday and it isn't doing too good. It might look a little bit better than the last one though.

Have you decided whether or not we are going to stay at your house or rent an apartment? It wouldn't really make a difference to me; it's up to you.

Do you think Alice and Ann will get sent to that school for girls in Twin before I come home? I believe it would be just like living alone. I don't mean I wouldn't want to stay there if they were there though, like I said it's up to you. You ought to check and see how cheap you could get a nice furnished apartment for.

Clellie, I don't know yet how soon I'll be leaving here. I know the soonest we could get out of here would be 30 January, but might not get out of here until the 20th of February neither. I think though it will be around 30 January.

I sure wish I could come home right now though. We could play around and could touch each other anytime we want. I love you very much, Clellie, but I have to go. I'll write again soon. Goodbye for now.

Your husband,
Tony

Sgt. Tony Jolley
HHC 2/46 Inf. (Mech)
1st armor division
Fort Hood, Texas 76545

✉ **January 15, 1970**　　　　　　　　　　　　　　　　　　　　　　　**10:20 PM**

Hi Hon,

How have you been doing?

Local news from Ore-Ida! Some 20 guys got fired last night. They worked in the warehouse. Well it seems that they were all making money on the side selling the products on their own. One was a foreman even. It seems that Ore-Ida hired a private detective to work there and got all their names. How about that?

There was about three old duffers came into Thriftway about 65-75. Anyway they were betting each other about my age. One said 15, the other 16, and the other 21 because I was married and have a boy. How about that?

I was reading in The Look about homosexuals. They reclassify them as transsexuals. There's been about 50 operations to transform sexes. Man anymore you'd never know if you're marrying a real man or woman or a fake one. It's really weird. I feel sorry for them.

Well, Hon, I better go for now. I love you so very, very much. I can't wait until you get home. I miss you so very, very much!

Buckets and gobs of love,
Clellie

P.S. Hugs and Kisses, etc.

✉ **January 16, 1970**   *10:40 PM*

Hi Hon,

I was happy to get your letter today. I wanted to cry so bad. Honey, I hate this not knowing when you'll be home. I miss you so much and your letter was so sweet.

Tipper, Nancy's dog, has the beginnings of distemper. It's so sad. The veterinarian said that they thought they had caught it in time. He has convulsions and everything. Makes me sick. He had one tonight after I got home. Nancy just got cleaned up. It's sickening.

We've always leveled with each other right? I know I've already told you that you could go out so I can't back out of it now. I know I'll cry though because I want you for myself alone. I'm going to tell you how I feel so please don't be angry with me. Please! I won't mind you going with Andrew and your dad. I understand that really. However I don't trust Denny. To me he's a sign of danger. I like him, Honey, but he's single now and he might try a few things that married guys don't do. I trust you but not Denny. Also I don't want you to go in any bars without me. I know of too many marriages going to pot because of it. You see, Tony, I'm changing some of my views. I can't help it. Tony, I realize that I'll lose you by my views now or if I let you go to bars some other dish will grab you. I guess I shouldn't discuss this in a letter because I can tell I'm not explaining myself and you're getting ticked so we'll not worry about it until you get home. Please try to understand me. It's probably just my mood.

I found out today that Alice's been going behind my back while I'm on the late shift and wearing your shirts. I cussed her out. I was so ticked.

If I knew when you were going to be home I'd try to find us a place to live by ourselves, but until I know I'll just forget it. I think it would be better. What do you think?

The girls will be here now. They're back for good. And I love you and I hope you still love me. I was going to tear up this letter and write a different one but this is the mood I'm in now and you know me and my moods. Do you still love me?

Yours eternally,
Clellie

P.S. Hugs and Kisses, etc.

✉ *January 17, 1970* *10:10 PM*

Hi Hon,

How's everything going for you? I hope just great. I love you.

Right now I feel rotten. I have an ugly headache, and my kidney is really having fits now. Maybe I'm a hypochondriac.

Dale and Carrie were down today. They think Chad is a doll but so big. Dale got a new car, 1966 GTO maroon color. How about that? Four on the floor, and white interior, I told him that we'd have to go out in it while you're home. He said, "What do you mean we? Only Tony and I are going out." I said, "Nope, all of us." And then we laughed. They want to know when you're coming home so they can make plans to be down here so I told them that I'd let them know when I find out.

Work was such a bore today. It was so tiring

Nancy's dog has to be put to sleep. It's really sad. I told her to save her money till she had enough to pay for the shots and we'll get her another dog.

Chad is such a doll. He's getting to look and act less like a baby and more like a little boy. He's getting more hair too! Thank heavens. It's sort of a light brown.

Well, Hon, I better close for now. I love you so much, Tony, and I miss you gobs and gobs. Be good and stay mine forever!

All my love eternally,
Clellie

P.S. Hugs and Kisses, etc.

✉ **January 18, 1970** 9:45 PM

Hi Hon,

How's my greatest guy that ever was? I miss you so much. I want you to come home so bad!

I got so sick at work today that I about came home but I couldn't afford to. I have to work at least seven days to pay the taxes and I have about $20. I think I'm getting the flu. Great.

I saw Denise tonight. She came into the store. She quit her job. She said that they just couldn't see eye to eye so... she really looks nice!

No school tomorrow for Minidoka County because of the roads. It's been like Oregon here as far as rain. How about that?

I guess Pomerelle really is snowed in. Someone came in the store tonight and said that it is so deep up at Pomerelle that they had to walk down to get to the ski lodge. How about that?

David O McKay the president of the Mormon Church died last night. It's kinda sad.

Work was pretty good today. It ran in a steady stream just like I like it. I still can't wait until the last of May so I can quit. I want to take Chad outside and swimming too. (Maybe) speaking of Chad. He's doing really great. Spoiled but great.

Gossip... Ann said that they hear Natalie Johnson has a V.D. I don't know how true that is neither does she. I saw her pretty close up and she is uglier than she used to be honest. She asked Alice what I thought about her going with Denny and Alice told her that she didn't know. I told Alice that if she asks again, tell her I think it stinks.

Well Hon! I guess I'll close for tonight. I wish so much that you were here with me! I miss you so much, Tony.

Your loving lonely wife,
Clellie

P.S. Hugs and Kisses, etc.

✉ **January 19, 1970** **8:45 PM**

Hi Hon,

Chad is doing great. He was kind of unhappy today but that's all.

Roger McCall and Joyce Conklin got a divorce. How about that?

I had Hope trim my hair an inch. It's grown so fast.

Work was okay today. I kept myself fairly busy.

Say call me Sunday. I don't have to work. However I want to go see your parents and show Chad to the McCarthys. So call me before 1 PM or after 5:30 PM. Speaking of your folks they still haven't heard anything from Andrew yet. Have you?

Some things have been missing from the makeup room so I decided not to take my breaks in there anymore because I don't want to be blamed. Today I waited until Linda got off break and waited for a few minutes to go on break because Greg usually takes his breaks with Linda or Gail. I went down there and he was still there. I said hi, he said hi, then I proceeded to read my magazine. Well he apologized about that night that he came up to my car, said he was loaded or else he would never have done it. I told him it was passed that he should've thought and that I tell you everything so naturally I told you about it. You weren't too happy about it and neither was I. I also told Greg that I told you I wouldn't take breaks with him so I'm not. I told him that I didn't want to have you worried about anything 'cause I think that you are the greatest and no one could ever beat you. You're too special. He told me it was neat the way I feel about you, and said again he was sorry again and said he was going to go back to work and left. Oh, Honey, I hope you're not angry with me but I have to tell him how it is. I thought I'd wait till you got home to tell you because letters are no good for explaining, but I wanted to let you know because I promised I'd tell you everything. Tony, I love you so much and I always will. Please call me on Sunday.

Your loving wife,
Clellie

P.S. Hugs and Kisses, etc.

✉ **19 Jan 1970**

Dearest lovely Clellie,

How's that for a starter? Man I sure do miss you. How's Chad and everyone else doing? I hope everything is real good with everyone especially you.

Did you get that cool card I sent you the first part of this week yet? Kind of cute.

Wow it sure is cold down here. It's about 12° outside. It even hailed today. The cold here is different than Idaho though. The humidity and wind make it seem like it's 15° below zero. No matter what you wear the wind goes right through it.

I'm starting to grow my mustache again. It'll be a week old tomorrow. It doesn't look like shit, but I thought you sounded like you didn't like the idea of me shaving it off without asking you. I decided I'll grow it back until I get home again. And you can decide whether I should shave it or not. (Of course if it looks real bad I'll shave it off the day before I come home.)

Clellie, we still haven't heard anything about when we're leaving. We probably won't get out of here for at least two weeks. The groups that got here three weeks before us got held up, and they're not leaving till Tuesday. They had to stay in action for two weeks, so we'll probably be here two weeks longer than we expected. I hope not, but we'll probably have to.

I'm glad Spear's getting home on time for his leave. Like I told you before I always get the screwed-up places to get stationed. It would have been so neat if I could have got stationed at Fort Carson and you could've come to live with me. If that would have happened I wouldn't care if they ever gave me a leave. They could've left me there for the rest of my time in the service.

You know, Clellie, I've been reading this book on ESP. It tells how you can call spirits, and all about the spirit world. There's another guy in the barracks that really believes in it. He has told me of some of his experiences and wow after reading this book (endorsed by about three great psychiatrists) I believe it too. We're going to go up in my room one of these nights and then we're going to try and see if we can in anyway communicate with someone in the spirit world.

Well, Clellie, I guess I better go for now. Clellie, I love you. Please don't get mad or upset if it takes me a little longer to get home. That just means when Spear has to say goodbye to Sue, you and I will have a couple more days together. I want to be with you so bad, Clellie. I miss you next to me in bed, but most of all I miss your kindness and sweetness. You're such a sweet and lovely woman. You know that don't you, Clellie? Of course you do. I'll be home as soon as I can, Clellie. I love you now and forever.

Your loving husband,
Tony

Sgt. Tony Jolley
HHC 2/46 Inf. (Mech)
1st armor division
Fort Hood, Texas 76545

January 20, 1970   **8:20 PM**

Hi Hon,

How's things going with you these days?

Well we now have $222 in the bank. However I might end up withdrawing four or $5 before 2 February because I stupidly forgot to save any out for gas or Chad's milk. To my name on me I have the total of $4. If I'm really, really careful I might be able to make it till then on that amount but I doubt it. Oh well. I forgot to get Chad a baby book too. However I did pay the doctor off and Mom got the phone bill yesterday so I paid her. It was up until 27 January. Guess how much? $26.10. Can you believe it? I about died. Oh well it's paid off and it was well worth it. I got to talk to the greatest guy on earth for it!

Boy, you wouldn't believe the weather we've had here for the past three days. It's just like spring outside. So nice and warm except today is the first day so far that it hasn't rained. School at Minico was called off today too because of rain.

Chad sure can fight with those bottom teeth of his. Wow! He still hasn't cut anymore yet though.

I haven't seen or heard from Susan for about two weeks now. I sure hope that she's getting along okay. I haven't seen Denny either but about twice with Natalie. She has his class ring again. According to her they're getting married when she finishes school!

Honey, don't forget to call Sunday before 1 PM or after 6 PM.

Boy, I was so busy today. I got all of our bedding and sheets washed (blankets and all), baked a German chocolate cake, and went to town to pay bills. One day off is rotten. There's too much to get done.

Well, Hon, I have to be closing for tonight. I love you so much. I got a whole roll of film today so when you get home I want to use it on you.

Love eternally,
Clellie

P.S. Hugs and Kisses, etc.

 *January 20, 1970*

Hi Hon,

I thought that this was so darling so I got it. I hope you like it.

The weather here is just great. It's just like spring here. It's so neat. I love you, Tony, with all my heart! Hurry home.

Love forever,
Clellie

January 21, 1970   **10:00 PM**

Hi my handsome man,

I love you with all my heart! Have you gotten my card yet? It was cute and yet so true.

The weather is the same here it's still raining, nice. However it has been said that Pomerelle has more snow on it now than it ever has! Hardly anyone can make it up.

I'm glad you're growing your mustache again! I bet it looks great. You better not shave it until I pass my judgment. If I don't like it, I'll tell you then you can decide what you want to do.

Honey, I was so very, very pleased to get your letter. If I wouldn't have gotten one today I think I'd of cried! What bugs me is the fact that I don't know when to expect you. It frustrates me awful.

Man, work was a drag. I kept hoping the time would hurry by so I could get home to see if I got your letter.

It worries me, Tony, about your monkeying around with spirits. I'd rather you don't. I think it's evil! Really go ahead and laugh at me! So I'm from the Middle Ages. You can't say that spirit stuff is of God! Just think in 20 years Chad will be doing the same stuff.

I never told you but about 2 ½ weeks ago Red backed into a truck at a garage with the new car. Well you can guess. What was once a nice new car is now a nice new car with a hole in the trunk.

I better go for tonight. I love you so much. Hurry home! And call Sunday the 25th.

Your loving lonely wife,
Clellie

P.S. Hugs and Kisses, etc.

✉ **January 22, 1970** **9:20 PM**

Hi Hon,

I love you so much. You should see my calendar. Today was my big hope day! I was hoping that you'd be home today. I have a calendar in our bedroom and I cross every single day off as they go by. Sometimes I get over anxious and crossed 2 days off ahead of time. I want you so very, very much!

If you promise not to tell anyone I'll tell you something that happened about two nights ago. Ann was over to Sarah Grace's home when Warren Dudley came over and grabbed her up and took her to his house with Lauren. I guess he tried to rape her. She was so shook up. He called her a bunch of dirty names because he couldn't. Promise me you won't let her know I told you. Yes I think she's had experiences now or he wouldn't have thought he could right?

Well I got a whole bunch of Valentine candy in today, also got in the magazines, tobacco, and candy bars, plus we got a whole bunch of stationery. Boy, if you don't think I was running all over the place.

There's a job in a bank open, and an office job in a plant. I don't dare try for them now because you'll be home pretty soon and I hate to ask for a month off the first week. Oh well I'm only working till the last of May.

It's still been raining here. It's supposed to keep until this Sunday coming up. Which reminds me, when you come home I want you to fix my blinkers. My horn honks when I use my blinkers. Also it blinks wrong. Sometimes it blinks the opposite way.

I dread trying to get dishes, pots and pans out of those boxes. I told you I should've marked them. Maybe we can scrounge up enough things here. We'll just have to wait and see.

Hon, I love you so much. I can't wait until we can be together for a whole month. I'm so excited.

Your loving wife,
Clellie

P.S. Hugs and Kisses, etc.

✉ **22 Jan 1970**

Dear Clellie,

How is my beautiful wife and our most handsome boy today? I sure hope everything is alright. Man I can't believe how much I miss you and Chad. (Of course I think I miss you the most. It's just natural though because I know you better than I do Chad.)

I had guard yesterday and last night so I get a half a day off today. There's no better way to spend a day then with someone you love so I decided to write. Wow aren't I getting poetic? Of course I'm still waiting for my head to clear up. I just got up and it's early.

Wow, Clellie, I'm kind of pissed off you know. What's this shit about you'll let me go out with Andrew and Dad, but not with Carter? For one thing both Andrew and Dad have a completely different bag than I do. I thought we agreed to at least one or two nights a week I could go out. I know you don't trust Denny and I don't blame you. Don't you think that I have the right to say yes or no when I'm with Carter? It sounds like you think he's going to gag and hogtie me and make me do whatever he wants to do. You know that's pretty ridiculous. I can tell him what I want to do and he'll do it. I know. I know Carter goes out with girls now, but I'll tell him the nights we go out together we have to both be girl-less. No women, all right? Enough of that then!

Clellie, we still haven't heard when we're getting out of here, the guys that have been here three weeks longer than us just left yesterday. So we could possibly be here two or three more weeks. You know though that as soon as I can get out of here I'll be on my way home to the only girl I could ever love. The only person in the world I couldn't possibly do without.

Are we going to get an apartment, or live at your house, Clellie? In your letters you don't sound like you're quite sure. It doesn't really matter to me, but if we have the money it would be nice to rent out an apartment.

Clellie, no matter what we do when I'm home on leave I know we will have a beautiful time. We can really have fun together you know. We have a few little quarrels, but I don't think we would love each other if we didn't quarrel once in a while.

I'd better go for now, Clellie. I love and miss you very much and can't wait to get back home to you. Oh I want you so bad. Love me a lot and forever.

Your loving husband,
Tony

Sgt. Tony Jolley
HHC 2/46 Inf. (Mech)
1st armor division
Fort Hood, Texas 76545

📧 **January 23, 1970** *1:00 AM*

Hi Hon,

Well how's my great man doing? Galen Staker will be home around February 3 so Denise said tonight.

Susan came home tonight so we decided to go to the show in Rupert which was good. It was "Undefeated." There were two shows, one at 7:30 PM and one at 9:30 PM. Well I didn't want to leave till Chad was in bed so at 15 to 9 PM I went over and got her. After the show we went to the Ramada Inn and split a hamburger and we had a salad. Then I took her home and we chatted. You remember Brenda Reeves? Well she got married and moved to California. Recently they got a divorce and now she's going to college too. She has a 16-month-old baby. I think it's so sad anymore. Everyone's split up. We saw Luke and Stephanie at the show. They're still as chunky as ever. Susan's going back to Twin tomorrow, but may be back Sunday. She really digs college. She said the only hang-up is that everyone's younger than her except a very few. Oh well, it'll do her good.

At work we got more Valentine candy in.

Chad eats donuts now and bread. Oh and he has one bad habit. He has to eat anything he sees you eat. He likes to play with flower arrangements and stuff, and cries if he can't. He's not spoiled at all. He's fascinated at anyone who smokes and he bites. He is getting to be a big man.

Well, Hon, tomorrow's another working day so I guess I'll close. Tony, I'll love you forever!

Your loving wife eternally,
Clellie

P.S. Hugs and Kisses, etc.

January 24, 1970　　　　　　　　　　　　　　　　　　　　**10:00 PM**

Dear handsome hubby,

How is everything going today? Right now it's raining again. It was such a beautiful sunshiny day until about noon then the rain began again.

I got carried away at the store. I charged out $8 worth of stuff. Two dollars on the stationery, a big baby book for Chad, some milk, Kotex, and baby lotion. Shame, shame. I guess my check won't be too big but it'll be okay.

Now about your letter. I was so pleased to get it and I love you, but you had a touchy subject which ticked me off. Here it goes… as far as you taking two or three nights a week while you're home. This is completely up to you. I cannot and will not pin you down to me. However I'm not going to be pleasant about it! Fair warning. If you want to spend half your time with your buddies and half with me, it's your time. I mean it's up to you. I never told you two or three nights a week. You asked me if you could do it without getting me all huffy and I told you that you couldn't then you said we'd wait and decide when you get home. Evidently you've made up your mind. Also as far as Denny I told you that you could go with him and I meant it. If he's your friend it's okay. He's nice. Just when Natalie pulls up beside you guys one night, you can't tell me he's going to tell her to get lost. She'll want to pull over and talk. Tony, I'm sorry about the way I feel. I trust you, Tony, but not Denny and Natalie. The way I see it is if you love me like you say then you'd want me around as much as possible. We're going to be apart a whole year. I mean two or three nights a week is a pretty big deal, don't you think? You say that your dad and Andrew have a completely different bag. Well don't we? I don't smoke pot. Is that why I don't fit your scene? I'm sorry about this and man I can see that you're steamed but so was I when that part in your letter hit me. I want us to get this straightened out but a letter is not clear enough. It gets us both ticked off. Please I'm sorry I started it but we have to get it straightened up now or when you get home we'll be ticked off all the time. Tell me, Tony, you still love me even if we are not seeing eye to eye. I love you, and I know I'm selfish. Also I'm so upset about this delay. I want you home now! I miss you so bad!

Yes, I want to get an apartment of our own. We'll get one too. Honey, quarrels get things aired out so it's all right once in a while. I love you and I don't want any quarrels when you come home. I want to be happy and have this time for happy memories. Please try and understand me and don't resent me. If I didn't love you I wouldn't be arguing with you about you leaving me at nights. I'm sorry I'm so rotten!

Hon, I better close for now. Tears seem to flow constantly anymore. I'm so afraid! I need you desperately. Please never leave me!

Your loving wife,
Clellie

✉ **January 25, 1970**　　　　　　　　　　　　　　　　　　　**9:30 PM**

Hi Hon,

How's everything going with you? I miss you so much and I'm so excited. It was so neat to talk to you!

Say do you want us to pick you up in Salt Lake? I told Barry to tell your mom to be prepared in case we go get you there. I'd really rather 'cause I'll have an extra 4 hours. Call me when you find out what time you'll be there. In case your mom can't (which I know she'd be happy to) then I'll see about Mom and their car.

I went over to your folks' place today and guess what? No one was there except Barry, Leon, & Allan. I guess it was your grandmother's birthday so they were gone. I told Barry to tell them when to expect you. Faith McCarthy was gone too so my day was spent at home except I visited with Hope for a ½ hour.

Susan called me today. She's going back to Twin. Her & Brenda went to the Ville last night and went by the Inn Club but didn't go in. She said that she's heard that The Alley is the liveliest place. She seems to be having a nice time there. I'm glad. I hope she meets a real nice guy. The only thing that bugs me is maybe she's going to go with Brenda a lot and get a little wild. I can't see her doing that though. I know one thing, Tony. If I lost you I'd either go really wild or stay at home all the time. I couldn't take losing you ever. I love you too much!

Well last night Red came home and Mom stayed up at the bar. Finally after I wrote you a letter he went up and got her. Hon, she was drunk and swinging her coat at Red cutting his face with the zipper and shoving him. It's hard to explain but a flash of the time she was going to hit Dad with the sweeper went through my mind and I ran and stopped her from hitting him. Then I came in the kitchen and sat down with Nancy and Alice when all of a sudden she came and slugged me in the face and said, "You think all men are so great and trust them." Well my lip was bleeding, and I was enraged! She won't slug me ever! I tore into her, hit her face, and she grabbed my hair, and I grabbed hers. Red pulled her away. Nancy was hitting her telling her not to ever hit me again. I got her away. This morning Mom apologized and when I washed my hair quite a bit fell out. Honey I feel sorry about it, but I won't let her hit me just 'cause she's drunk. Do you think I'm awful? I shouldn't hit her but man I just snapped when she hit me.

Marie and Lance are back together since about 2 weeks ago. They are living near the school in Paul.

Well, Hon, I guess that I'll close for now. I love you so much and I will forever.

Love Forever, Clellie

P.S. Hugs and Kisses, etc.

Home on Leave

From January 26th to March 9th I was home on a very welcome leave with Clellie and Chad prior to shipping to Nam. It was a great time spent with my family. We made the most of our time together and made every moment count. It was harder than ever to leave my wife and son, but I had to do what I knew had to be done.

LEAVING FOR NAM

11 Mar 1970

Dearest Clellie,

I thought I would write and let you know that I'm doing fine. I got into Oakland about 12:00 noon the same day I left you. By the time that night rolled around I had been processed in and had my jungle fatigues and boots issued. We have to wear jungle fatigues until we leave this place. We can't wear civilian clothes or nothing. We even had to turn in our class A's.

Guess what I got today? Guess what I got today? You're right an Article 15. Out of 200 guys that reported in yesterday 139 got Article 15's. They charged me $50. How do you like that? I didn't get busted though because the CO said since my record was good he wouldn't bust me, I really wouldn't care though. Since we're late reporting in, we have to wait on a standby status before getting shipped to Nam. I really don't know when I'll leave, but it will probably be by tomorrow. I'm commander of the guard right now. It's not a bad job but I could sure use some sleep. There are two other guys from Ft. Hood here and they told me that gross Bob and the rest of the guys in our group shipped out Monday. These two guys reported in Saturday so I guess I was about the last one to report in.

You know I've told about 4 guys here about my dog tags and they keep telling me to wait until I get to a different station and they'll check us out for proper ID cards, and dog tags. If they don't correct these dog tags I'll mess the blood type up so you can't tell what it says, and they'll have to look on my ID card for the blood type if I get hurt.

Clellie, I love you so very much. Saying goodbye to you this time was the hardest thing I think I've ever had to do, man I'm not kidding ya. If I hadn't got out that door when I did, I would have cracked up. I already miss you so much. I don't know how I'll be able to go a year without you. Just think though, after this year is up, that's it!

Well Clellie, I'd better close for now. I was debating on calling you, but I just thought it would make things harder. I don't know though I want to hear your voice so bad I can hardly stand it.

I love you, Clellie, and I always will. I could never do anything to hurt you, Clellie, because it would be like hurting myself. I love you now and forever.

Your very loving lonely husband, Tony

P.S. I'll send you my address as soon as I get it.

P.P.S. I love you, Clellie

P.P.P.S. The return address on the letter is not my real return address. I just had to put it on to send the letter. I love you.

Sgt. Tony Jolley
Oakland, California

✉ **19 Mar 1970** **Postcard**

Hello Clellie,

Well here's that big bird that's flying me across the big pond to the land of sunshine.

It took us about 5 ½ hours to fly to Honolulu and now are engaged in a 10-hour flight to Okinawa.

Clellie, I mainly wrote this letter to let you know that I'm fine. Don't worry about me. I'll be okay. We'll be in Vietnam in about 12 more hours.

I love you very much, and I'll write as soon and as often as possible.

Love ya always,
Tony

✉ **23 Mar 1970**

Dearest Clellie,

Here I am in a land of the sunshine. I got here Saturday, that's Friday in the world. That's because you lose a day coming over here, in fact you lose about 27 hours.

How are you, Clellie? I miss you so much. How's Chad and the rest of the clan? I would have written a couple of days ago, but they keep you pretty busy at the 90th replacement company.

Right now I'm sitting at the Bien Hoa airport waiting for a flight to Cu Chi. I've got orders for the 25th infantry division. I probably won't have a return address for another week or so.

Man the weather down here is unbelievable. I'm way down in South Vietnam, and it is hot and sticky. Last night it was kind of moist, and I almost got eaten alive by mosquitoes. Wow wouldn't that be a bummer if I got malaria before I was even in the country for a month.

I guess Bien Hoa was under mortar attack the day before I got here, luckily nothing very serious.

When I got here and had my first look at Vietnam it seemed real strange. They had big sandbag bunkers and wire obstacles all over the place. The people I've met down here so far are kind of cool. They have Vietnamese people working everywhere at the 90th replacement center. I'll have to admit too, some of these little girls are really cute, but nothing like you though, Clellie. I can't help comparing some of these girls to you and believe me, Clellie, there's just no match for you. I've only been gone a week I'm just thinking of the times we had together while I was home makes me miss you all the more.

I can't wait to get a letter from you, Clellie. Tell how work is going in your letter. I think if you're getting too much BS from your boss you should quit and get a job at King's or something.

Remember I told you I would send you some money as soon as I got to Oakland? Well I haven't got paid yet. I probably won't get paid for another week either.

Clellie, I have to close for now because it's about time for the plane to leave. I'll write to you as soon as I can. I love you very, very, very much, Clellie, and I always will. Keep loving me too if it's at all possible.

You probably wouldn't want to claim me right now I'm so sweaty and grubby, but I still love you. I can't wait until this is all over and we can be together forever. Stay mine, Clellie.

Your loving lonely husband,
Tony

P.S. I want you forever because I love you!

Sgt. Tony Jolley
Bien Hoa, Vietnam

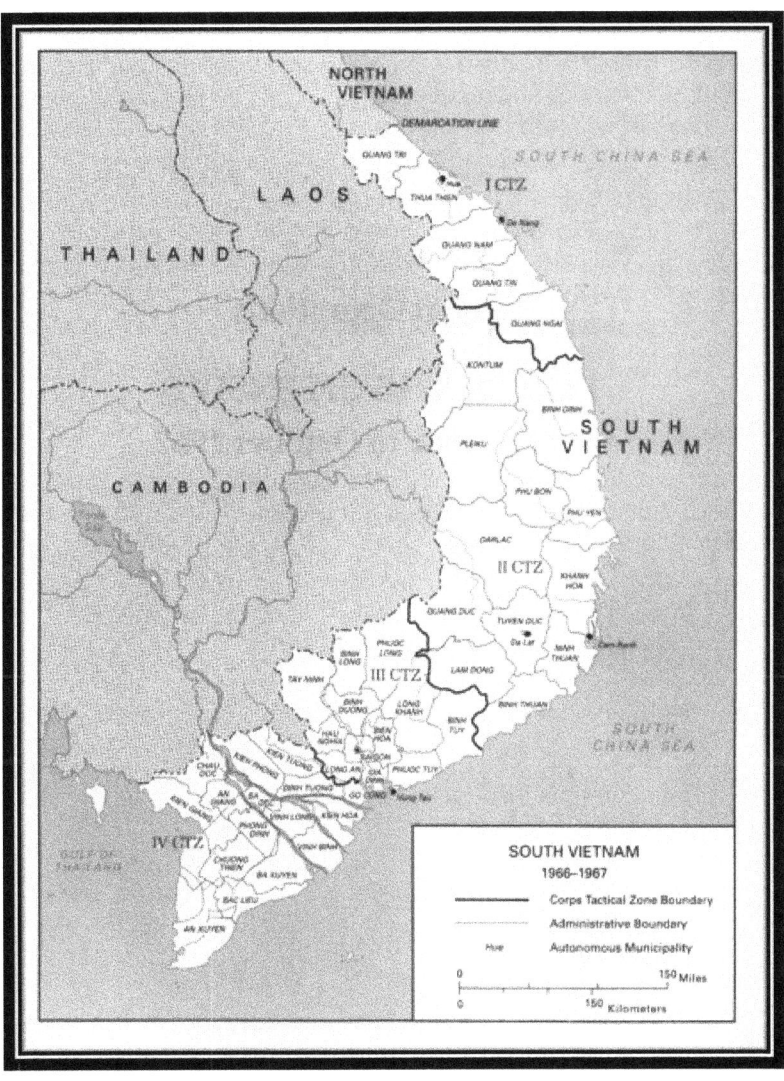

✉ **27 Mar 1970**

Dear Clellie,

You realize don't you, that I love you more than is imaginable by the human mind? How's that? Dramatic? But it's true!

How's everything back in the world? How's Chad? Most of all how is the world's most adorable creature? (Wow, Clellie, I miss you so much.)

Well I finally got it, my return address that is. It looks like I got a leg unit, but I expected it all the time. The only thing that pisses me off is that they split all of us NCO's up. I'm the only one out of the 104th company that's going to the 3rd or the 22nd, their area of operation is up at Tay Ninh (rocket city). There's supposed to be some shit going on up there. I guess I'll find out for myself in about three days though. Don't worry about me, Clellie, I'll be perfectly alright.

By the way you know how Nixon's talking about the big drawback of American troops? Well the first division is pulling out of Nam by the 14th of next month. But guess what? Out of 18,000 men, 246 of them are going home. This is no bullshit. All the others are getting assigned to other units. The ones with 10½ months in country get to go home. There's all kinds of guys in the first getting assigned all over the 25th A.O.

Clellie, I love you very much and I always will. I just think of the way you looked next to me in bed. So good, but yet so soft and innocent. Never forget me, Clellie, please.

I better go for now. I have to go to jungle training now. Three more days and I'll be heading up to where the action is. I love you very much, Clellie. Write all the time. Gobs and gobs.

Your lonely husband,
Tony

I want you!

Sgt. Tony Jolley
Co. E. 3rd Bn 22 Inf.
APOSF 96385

✉ **28 Mar 1970**

Dear Clellie,

I sure do miss you. How is everything at home?

I don't have much time to write you, but I said I'd write you when I could. This will probably be about that last letter I'll be able to write for a while because I'm heading to Tay Ninh in the morning. I'll probably be kept busy for a few days.

Clellie, they finally paid me yesterday for February and March so I sent $400 home to you. I have about $40 left for the next 1½ months so I might have to have you send me some before May, but I doubt it. If you need any of the $400, use it. Put the rest of it in my account for the first savings on our new car.

I'm going to try to send from $150-$200 every month after this plus the $150 you should be getting. I looked in my finance records and they took out $150 to send to you. If you don't get the $150 this next check, take it down to the bank and have a photograph made of it. Then send the copy to whoever you wrote before about the allotments. Also Clellie, please tell me in a letter when you get the $400. Well enough about money.

Wow it's hotter than hell over here. For the last four days it's been from 114° to 136°. How about that? I'm drinking about 2 gallons of water a day, and hardly eating a thing.

I'm pretty unsure about going out in the field, but the sooner I get out there the sooner I find out what's going on. The way it sounds there might be a little going on up there, but it's not known how much.

Clellie, when you get the chance find out from Sue what kind of a job Spear got over here. Maybe he got a job he wanted. I don't really think recon is going to be too bad though if you keep your shit together over here. I hope I get an outfit with some good men, and I won't have to worry about coming home.

Tell me what's going on when you write. Tell me who you meet, and things that you think I would like to know. It's so far away over here that it really gives me a hollow feeling inside. I try not to think of how things are going in the world, but I can't help it. I especially think of you. If anyone makes a pass at you, or asks you out tell me about it. I won't get mad at you, but I'll kill the sob when I see him.

Clellie, I love you very much. I don't want to write the things I'd like to be able to do to you, because I miss you just that much more. I love you now and forever, Clellie. Lots of love.

Your lonely husband,
Tony

I love you!

Sgt. Tony Jolley
Co. E. 3rd Bn 22 Inf.
APOSF 96385

✉ **1 Apr 1970**

Dear Clellie,

How's everything back there? I hope you're doing good. I hope you missed me a lot too because I miss you so much I can hardly stand it. Is Chad getting along okay?

Man I'm really bushed. Five days ago we went out on a four-day bushmaster. We had to hump the first two nights, and then we would hide in the jungle during the days. At night would work out into an open area and set up night ambushes. The first day of our mission we came under contact. We didn't have any casualties, but we called in artillery on Charles. That made his shit really weak too. Oh to get back on the subject. After our four-day bushmaster, we were supposed to get to sleep last night. We got in about 6 o'clock last night I was supposed to be able to sleep until noon today then we go on another Eagle flight. Well about 1 o'clock in the morning Charles was firing mortars in here so we had to go out and try to locate him. It's 10 o'clock in the morning now and we just got in. Then at about 1 o'clock this afternoon we go on an Eagle flight. So I guess I won't get too much sleep today. Maybe time will go faster though.

Clellie, it's been over three weeks since I saw you last and I haven't gotten any mail. I know it isn't your fault, but it seems like the damn Army could hurry up the mail little.

Did you get all the other letters I wrote you? How about that $400?

Clearly the year I'm going to have to spend here is going to seem like an eternity. It already seems like it's been so long since I've been home.

Well how was work? Is your boss giving you any static? If he is tell him to go to hell and quit. You could get a job anywhere you like.

Is there any news on when Andrew will get home for sure? When you get my address, give it to my mom and Marie. I probably won't have much time to write them now. I barely find time to write you. Tell Marie she can forget about me getting her those things she wanted. The closest I get to civilization is when we go into the base camp to get clean clothes. Maybe one night every two weeks we might get to get drunk.

Clellie, I will close for now, but I'll write the next possible chance I get. Oh before I forget. Clellie, send me some 126mm film. It is impossible to get over here, and some flashbulbs like yours. I'd like to take some pictures. Clellie, I love, love, love you. Love me too.

Your loving husband,
Tony

I love you!

Sgt. Tony Jolley
Co. E. 3rd Bn 22 Inf.
APOSF 96385

✉ **3 Apr 1970**

Dear Clellie,

How's everything going back in the world? I hope everything is fine. Is the most charming and beautiful girl still waiting for me? I sure hope so. If she wasn't waiting I wouldn't have a thing to come back to. I'd just spend the duration of my time over here.

Well I've had some pretty exciting things happen since I got over here. A couple of things about made me sick though. The things that made me sick was the other night a guy in recon got shot in the head, and another one got hit in the leg. The worst thing about it though was it was friendly fire that hit him. Then yesterday we were coming back off a mission and we came on a truck that had wrecked. There were two GIs that were smashed and killed. The good thing I saw was when the choppers were flying us back in. We saw a bunch of GIs just outside the wire. When we landed we went over and looked at what was going on. Some gooks tried to get in the wire, and they got four of them. When I saw their bodies it kind of shocked me 'cause they were all torn up. Then I kind of felt better because the next night, and every night since they've been hitting us with mortars. Last night seven guys got really screwed up. Two of them were killed.

So tomorrow we, recon, have to go out and try to find the mortar tubes. Eight of us are going out. We'll probably get contact and maybe get a body count.

You know that's all that matters over here, we only want a body count. Kill gooks. I'm getting used to the idea.

Clellie, I wish you would send me that film I asked for because I can't get it over here. I'd like to get some pictures. Especially some while I'm on those choppers, also of some of the guys.

I miss you very much. You know you're the only person I could care for. At nights I get very lonely for you. I'll be sitting out on the night ambush every time it comes my turn to pull watch, I sit there and think of you. I have to keep alert but I still find time to think of you. It seems like a person would be scared, I am in a way, but I got two good things going for me. One, the guys I'm with really know their shit. Two, I have the best family in the world to come back to.

You and Chad, what more could a guy ask for. I don't want anything more. I love, Clellie, now and forever.

Your lonely loving husband,
Tony

I need you forever!

Sgt. Tony Jolley
Co. E. 3rd Bn 22 Inf.
APOSF 96385

✉ **7 Apr 1970**   **5:00 PM**

Hello beautiful wife,

How is everything? How are you and Chad? Man I sure do miss you both. Especially you.

What's this you said in your last letter about me looking like a little boy? That's what I think, you ought to write our congressman and tell him he shouldn't send boys to fight a man's war. Ha ha.

I decided to write and answer some of your questions. Yes I'm in the 25th infantry. No you don't have to put it on the address. Tay Ninh is about 125 miles from Bien Hoa. Yes, I'm in recon, and it's the best outfit in the battalion. There's only 25 men in the platoon, and they have the highest body counts of any line company in the battalion. That's compared to a 160-man line company. How's that?

Spear's battalion is down in the southern end of our AO. I think they're stationed at Cu Chi or Bearcat. They're both good places to be, because they're fairly secure areas. Ask Sue where for sure he's stationed. If he's stationed at Cu Chi, he's really got it licked. That's where Lilly got stationed and he wrote me and told me they hardly ever go out. If they go out they don't even stay out overnight.

Here at Tay Ninh we have a big mountain that sticks up 3000 feet. It's called Nuy Ba Dien (Black Virgin Mountain). We have relay outfits on top, and we're at the bottom and in between the top and bottom is all VC. We're supposed to go up pretty soon, and most of the guys that have been up before say they won't go again. Every time we try to get Charlie out we get our asses kicked. They bombed it and everything, but there are so many caves and they're so deep that Charlie goes in them and comes out at night to raise hell. I'll probably see how it is pretty quick. The 1st Calvary is in this area and about a week ago they ran into a regiment size VC force. About 40 GIs were killed and many wounded. Recon almost had to go out and try to keep progress on their movement, but they needed us to secure a FSB for two days. Man we were all relieved. These guys don't like to go on missions like that, but they will. I'm kind of getting used to the idea too.

When we're not in the field we have jeep missions we go on. Man that's a hell of a lot better than humping too. We have two 60s, one 30 Cal, and one 50 Cal mounted on the jeeps and we can really kick ass. I'll take some pictures if you'll send that film and flashbulbs.

Clellie, I don't want to worry you, because Nam isn't as bad as you think. Especially when you're over here. You just get used to it. I'm not used to it yet, and it's about killing me.

I love you very much and I want you to love me as much as I love you.

I have to close for now because we're going on a night ambush in about an hour and I have to get squared away. I want you to know I'm not going to be able to save your letters. Out in the field we have limited space and aren't allowed to keep anything identifying our lives back home. Every couple days we have to destroy personal letters and such. I do appreciate hearing from you though and want you to continue to send letters and care packages. Hearing from you is one of the only things that keeps me going and I would have a hard time finding the will to make it through another damn day without knowing you and Chad are back home waiting for me.

Clellie, I love and want you forever. Love me always.

Your loving husband,
Tony

P.S. Don't worry about my dog tags. They're squared away. I love you!!

Sgt. Tony Jolley
Co. E. 3rd Bn 22 Inf.
APOSF 96385

✉ **10 Apr 1970**

Dearest Clellie,

How is the most beautiful creature on earth? Also how was our good-looking young Chad doing? I hope everything is all right.

Everything is going okay here. Cambodia is kicking all the VC out of there and pushing him right into us. See the Cambodian border's only about 10 miles from here. The Cambodians are pushing Charlie right into our AO. We have two companies in our battalion out there now. They have a blocking force setup and they're trying to knock off Charlie as he comes out of Cambodia.

This war is already making me so sick I don't even like to write or talk about it.

The clipping I'm sending you is out of a military paper. The part about the 25th infantry I have circled is part of the forces coming from Cambodia. Recon got 10 or 11 of those 32 kills with only one casualty. We are in for a day's rest. Tonight we're going on a night ambush. At six in the morning we are coming back and then choppers are flying us to a landing zone about 1 mile from the border of Cambodia. We're supposed to stay out there five days and set up night ambushes. Maybe we'll get another body count.

Clellie, when I tell you what's going on I think it sounds worse than it really is. I think from now on I'll just write as little as possible about what's happening over here. I don't want to be telling you a bunch of war stories and having you worry when there really isn't that much to worry about. Well that's enough for that.

About R&R, if I get a 90-day drop for college, I don't think we should take the R&R. I want to wait until my seventh or eighth month before I take it. If I get the drop I would only have a month left over here anyway. What do you think? Do you think I should try for the drop? I can't see how Spear is doing it. Spending all that money just for himself and then taking the drop anyway. If I go on any R&R though it will be to Hawaii to meet you.

Clellie, I have to go for now. I love you very much. I want to be with you so much. I wish this damn war was over and I could come home to you. Take care of yourself and stay just like you are now. Never change or let your love for me change. I love you now and forever.

Your loving husband,
Tony

I love you!

P.S. I received your package and it was very nice. Thanks so much. You're so thoughtful. I love you very much, Clellie.

P.P.S. Thank Alice for the letter. I'll try to write her one.

I want and miss you!

Sgt. Tony Jolley
Co. E. 3rd Bn 22 Inf.
APOSF 96385

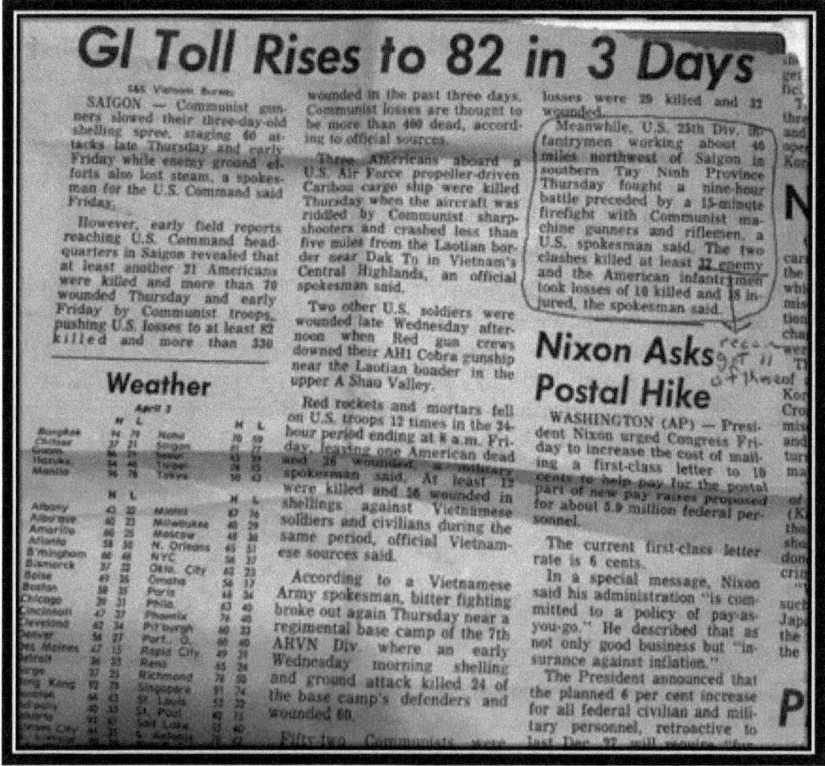

✉ **18 Apr 1970**

My lovely Clellie,

How is everything? Does the most charming and beautiful girl in the world still love me? How's our son?

Clellie, I can't understand why you said you haven't heard from me in two weeks. I haven't got a letter from you for four days. I usually write one every three or four days though, Clellie. Except for this letter. That's because I've been into a minesweeping and demolition school. Then recon had a three-day bushmaster. We just got back this morning.

We got rained on the other night. I slept in the rain and mud. I was so tired though I didn't give a damn. I better get used to it, because in another couple of weeks the monsoons will be here. That will be five months of living in water. I sure hate to see it come.

We had a little bit of action. We found where the bunker complexes were old Charles was shooting mortars at Tay Ninh base camp. We blew it sky-high with hand frags and Claymores.

We're not going to get much rest this time, because at 3 o'clock we go out on a twilight sweep. Then tomorrow we go on a 4 to 6-day field mission. So I might not be able to write to you for a while. I only write very few letters in the field because we're usually moving. You once told me in a letter not to write to you while I'm on guard. I have news for you. First of all, I'm usually too damn scared, and second, it's too dark to see.

At times like this when I can write home things seem to be better. When I'm out in the field though it's different. You're humping during the day, right? You think back to what people are doing back in the world. You're sweating and working your ass off. Taking a chance on getting your shit blown away and there's not a person back in the world that knows or cares what you're doing over here. Except for maybe your really close loved ones.

Clellie, I'm so lucky to have you for my own. You're the most charming person a guy could ever want to meet. I don't worry about you waiting for me ever. I know the guys might ask you out, but I don't feel I ever have to worry about you stepping out. I sure hope not anyway.

I better close for now. When you write me from now on make your letters a lot longer. Don't tell me all about the problems around the house, just tell me about yourself and how you love me.

Your lonely husband,
Tony

I love you, Miss Clellie!

Sgt. Tony Jolley
Co. E. 3rd Bn 22 Inf.
APOSF 96385

✉ **23 April 1970**

My Clellie,

What's been happening back in the world lately? How are you and Chad doing? I hope everything is all right.

I just got off a four-day mission. The first day we saw 3 VC and we blew their shit away. That's the first time I've aimed through my rifle at a human body and shot. I could have hit one too. It felt pretty cool. I'm kind of getting used to the way things are over here.

I met a couple of sergeants from the same outfit Spear's in. They're stationed at Dau Tieng. He told me they don't have any contact up there. They used to be at Cu Chi. You know where they're thinking of moving now? You're right, they might move here to Tay Ninh. This dude was saying he sure doesn't want to come here, because he heard about all the shit that happens here.

Clellie, you asked me about what type of film I used. I told you in one of the first letters I wrote. It's a 126mm film for an instamatic 100 camera. I want colored film. No I didn't buy a camera. I gave a kid $3 for this camera at Long Binh. He never paid me back so I kept the camera.

I got a letter from Mom and I wrote back. About 3 weeks ago I got a letter from Ann from Pocatello. I've never had a chance to answer her letter though. If you see her tell her I thought the letter was nice and to keep on writing. I'll try to answer her soon. How come no letters from Marie or anyone?

Send that film as soon as you can and as much as you can. Then you can send it in your care packages.

Clellie, if I started sending a little bit of weed home in my letters, would you save it in a plastic bag or something? You ask me how the weed is over here. It's really great. It messes your head up and you can get it anywhere. I don't smoke out in the field, but when we get in for a day's rest I set my head.

Clellie, I wish I could make you understand how much I love you. While I'm over here, whatever I do it's for you and Chad. I only hope it's meant that we will be together again. Clellie, I love you very, very much forever and ever. Stay mine.

Your lonely husband, Tony
I love you!

I want you! So bad

Sgt. Jolley
Co E 3rd Bn 22 Inf.
APO SF 96385

```
VUB213 SYA146 SS4692 SY MA439 HO  XV CWT
FOR 12 EXTRA
PAX WASHINGTON DC 23 750P EST
MRS CLELLIE M JOLLEY, REPORT DELIVERY DONT PHONE CHECK
DLY CHGS ABOVE 25 CTS
358 OVERLAND BURLEY IDAHO
THE SECRETARY OF THE ARMY HAS ASKED ME TO INFORM YOU
THAT YOUR HUSBAND SERGEANT ANTHONY JOLLEY, WAS SLIGHTLY
WOUNDED IN ACTION IN VIETNAM ON 24 APRIL 1970 BY FRAGMENTS
WHILE ON A COMBAT OPERATION WHEN A BOOBY TRAP DETONATED.
HE RECEIVED WOUNDS TO

                   UTIXYN RIGHT ARM AND RIGHT
LEG. HE WAS TREATED AND HOSPITALIZED IN VIETNAM.
ADDRESS MAIL TO HIM AT THE HOSPITAL MAIL SECTION, APO
SAN FRANCISCO 96347. SINCE HE IS NOT REPEAT NOT SERIOUSLY
WOUNDED NO FURTHER REPORTS WILL BE FURNISHED
    KENNETH G WICKHAM MAJOR GENERAL USA P-115-98 THE
ADJUTANT GENERAL DEPT OF THE ARMY WASHINGTON DC
(BT).
644P-PST APR 23 70


RECD 8:00 PM MST TKB
```

Jolley Suffers Wounds From Mine Explosion

Sgt. Anthony Jolley of the 21st Infantry Division suffered serious wounds from an explosion of a mine near the Cambodian border on April 24.

He is now convalescing in the military hospital at Cam Rahn Bay, Vietnam.

In a War Department telegram to his wife Clellia and parents who reside in Burley, it said Sgt. Jolley's wounds were incurred as a platoon of infantrymen were moving toward a boat which was being loaded on a nearby river near the border. A soldier in the rear of Jolley stepped on the mine and it exploded causing serious injury to three other soldiers, one of whom may lose a leg and one lost an eye.

Sgt. Jolley suffered shrapnel bursts into his hip, calf and back.

Mrs. Jolley and infant son, Chad, reside in Burley.

Sgt. Jolley's parents, Mr. and Mrs. Wayne Jolley, have two other sons in the service. Sgt. Dee Jolley is with the Air Force in London while Mike Jolley is scheduled to enter the Army on May 12 as an enlistment candidate from Cassia County.

SGT. ANTHONY JOLLEY

✉ 28 Apr 1970

Dearest Clellie,

I miss and love you very much. How is everything back there? How are you and Chad?

Well I don't know whether you've been notified or not yet, but about three days ago, I got hit. Don't worry though; it's not all that bad.

I would've written sooner, but they've kept me pretty doped up. I've also been lying flat on my stomach for three days.

I'll tell you how it happened. First of all there was eight of us hit by a booby trap. Four of us were hospitalized and the other three besides me are going back to the world. So I guess I'm pretty lucky.

We were loading on boats to go down the river near the Cambodian border. The guy behind me tripped the booby trap and eight of us were hit. Red, the guy behind me, will probably lose part of his right leg, Doc lost his eye, and Davidson got shrapnel all over the front of him and his belly. They're all going home. The other four guys received minor wounds and were sent back to the company area.

I'm now in Long Binh hospital. I've got three fairly large pieces of shrapnel in my left hip and left cheek of my ass. My worst one is a large piece in the back of my right calf. I also have a few small pieces in my right arm and the side of my face. When I was out in the field it looked pretty bad but now it's not so bad.

I'll have some scars but you don't mind, do you? I'll have about a three inch scar across the back of my leg, also a small one on the side of my face and about three large ones on my left hip and down.

What really bugged me was they left the wounds open for three days and kept cleaning them so I wouldn't get an infection. I still might get an infection too.

They're going to send me to Japan or Cam Rahn Bay for a month or so. I told them I'd just rather stay in Vietnam at Cam Rahn Bay so I could draw combat pay so they'll probably send me there.

I'll be out of the field for a month or so anyway. When I get back I really want to get some gooks bad. Red was one of the best men in my squad, and Davidson had only been in the country less than a month.

Clellie, I'll write you again in a day or so. I'll leave here tomorrow so don't send anything to the address on this letter.

I love you very much, Clellie, and I always will. Write you again soon. Don't worry about me. I'll be okay. Stay mine forever. I'll always love and need you.

Your lonely sore husband,
Tony

I love and want you badly!

P.S. I just found out I have to use my regular address so disregard what I said about not writing to this address. Understand? I hope so!

Sgt. Tony Jolley
Co. E. 3rd Bn 22 Inf.
APOSF 96385

✉ **30 April 1970**

Dear Clellie,

Well here I am in Cam Rahn Bay. Wow it's real nice. You don't even know there's a war going on here. It's located on the beach and the water is beautiful, crystal clear. I only have one hang-up. I can't go swimming. My stitches are still in. They say I'll be here for about a month, but I'm trying to leave sooner.

The doctor said I'm advancing better than he thought I would. I'm limping around a little bit more every day. I'd like to rest up here for about 2 or 3 weeks then go back to my unit. I feel like a goldbricker, only been in country 2 months and already shamming.

My wounds aren't really too bad, but they are deep. One piece of shrapnel almost hit my pelvic bone, from the inside out. Also the calf on my right leg might be a little deformed with a scar, but you won't mind if I have ugly legs will you, Clellie? I sure hope not.

Well how is everything at home? How are you and Chad? I sure do miss you. I wish so bad I could be with you. It's been over a week since I got hit and since I got any letters from you. They told me to tell you to keep writing to my regular address until and they would send the mail to me. That way when I go back the mail will automatically stop coming here and I get the letters right there. Clellie, what I want you to do is this though, after you get this letter, send the next 4 or 5 letters you write directly to the address on this envelope. Then start sending the others to the regular address. Also send Ann's address in one of those letters. I have more time to write so I should answer her letter. It's only been over a month since I got it.

I love you so much. When I got hit I realized it could have been worse. I might even have lost you forever. I wish I could be at home, but somebody's got to do this bullshit over here, and I'm going to do my damnedest to get a couple of gooks for Doc and Red.

I'd better close for now. They're going to send me down to physical therapy to learn some new exercises.

Clellie, I'll always love you forever. Love me always.

Your lonely loving husband,
Tony

I love and want you forever!

Sgt. Tony Jolley
6th Conv. Center
Cam Rahn Bay
APO SF 96392

3 May 1970

My dear lovely Clellie,

How was the most beautiful creature on earth? I sure wish I was there to see for myself.

Today I feel pretty good. I got stoned last night, and I have a better outlook on things for a while. Man all the patients down here have weed. It's all over the place. This is really a good place to blow it too, because it's a real secure area.

The doctor looked at me yesterday and said I might have a little trouble getting around for a while. I told him I was already walking quite a bit and he was surprised. He told me to take it easy until I got the stitches out, or I might end up tearing them loose.

I have a feeling that my right calf will pull a little when I walk. They had to cut some of the dead muscle out on the inside and it pulls when I walk.

Clellie, I sent you a card for Mother's Day. I tried to find one that said for my wife on Mother's Day, but they just didn't have any. Have a very pleasant Mother's Day. This will be the last Mother's Day that we will be away from each other.

I'm sending a picture that was taken by a dude that was with the Colonel when he came to see me. The guy standing to the side of my bed is the big Colonel himself.

They informed me that I was being put in for a Purple Heart and a Bronze Star with a V for valor. How's that? It don't mean nothing really. The only reason I'm getting the Bronze Star it's because I put dressings on Red's arm and leg when we got hit. There's really nothing else I could do. When the booby trap when off, Red landed on my legs. When I tried to get him off I saw how bad he was hit, and helped him. Three or four other guys helped too.

Clellie, you do realize that I love you more than anything else in the world don't you? I do.

If it wasn't for you I would have avoided the draft and left the country. I really have it luckier than most guys over here. When I go home I have the most wonderful girl in the world waiting for me, also a son that any man would be proud to have.

Clellie, I need you forever. If you ever leave me, don't expect to see me come back. I'll stay over here for the duration of the war. Always love me, Clellie, please!

Your lonely husband,
Tony

P.S. Only send about two or three letters strictly to this address. I love you! I need you!

Sgt. Tony Jolley
6th Conv Ctr.
APOSF 96392

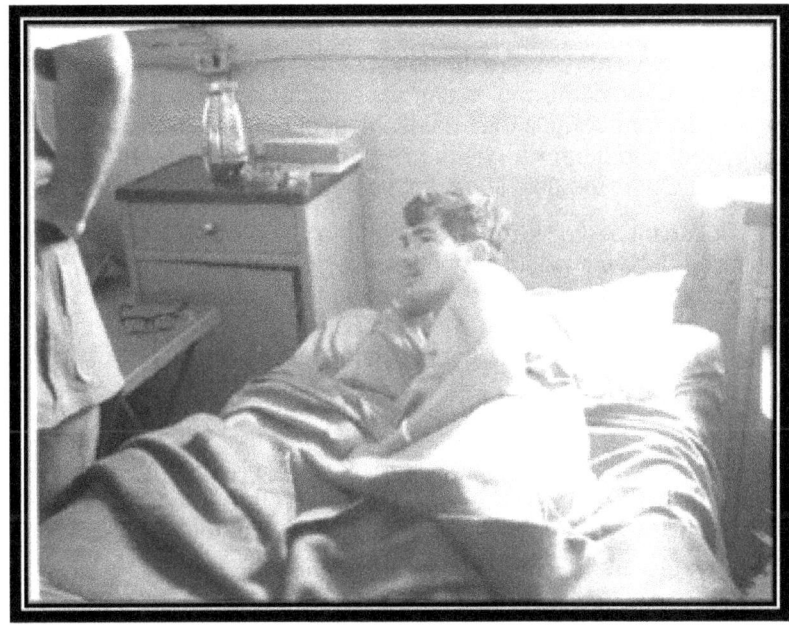

✉ **5 May 1970**

My lovely Clellie,

I sure do miss you! It seems like this being separated is never going to end.

How are you and Chad? How is everything going back in the world? Has anyone tried to hustle you at work yet? How about uptown? If anyone whistles or honks at you, or asks you to load you'd better tell them you have a husband in Vietnam who is a tough infantryman. Tell them he's been humping in the jungles just for you, and he might not take it very kindly them getting fresh with you. Wow, don't I sound tough? It must be all these war stories I've heard going to my head.

I feel all right today. I've been walking around quite a bit lately. I wish they would take the stitches out. I might get them out Thursday though.

As soon as possible I'm going to try and get the doctor to let me go back to my unit. You wouldn't believe how surprised he is that I'm already walking as much as I am. He keeps asking me if I'm sore and stiff, but I tell him just a little.

Some of the guys here are really pathetic. They have clerks and drivers and shit that have hemorrhoids and appendicitis and these guys are telling the doctor about all their pains. Most of the legs that are here for wounds want to get back to their units because down here they have too many lifers. Out in the field lifers don't screw around with you.

Clellie, doesn't it seem like such a long time since we've kissed? I was just thinking of how it would be to kiss you right on the mouth. I haven't even puckered up to kiss since I left you at the Burley airport. I've probably forgotten how. It's really kind of a silly thing to talk about anyway. You haven't kissed anyone since I left, have you?

Clellie, wouldn't it be neat to be already in Hawaii on our R&R? Laying on the beach, you in a real sexy bikini. I can almost see you now. Lying beside me on your stomach I'd be leaning up on one elbow looking at your shapely hips and legs. Man if I saw you right now I doubt if I could control myself! I can't wait until then. Another five months is all we have to wait.

I love you and miss you very much, Clellie, one of these days we'll be together forever right? Well I'll close for now. Always love me.

Your lonely loving husband,
Tony

P.S. Tell someone at home to write me. I love and want you! I miss you! I need you!

Sgt. Tony Jolley
6th Conv. Ctr.
APOSF 96392

✉ **6 May 1970**

My lovely lady,

Man I'll bet you're surprised that you're getting all these letters. I'm now sending a letter just about every day. I sure wish my unit would send me my mail. It's been almost 2 weeks since I've had a letter. I sure hope nobody died or anything; because the way the Army's screwing with my mail I'd never know.

Wow I'm getting sick as hell of this place. There are so many lifers around here it stinks. These lifers trying to tell you how it is and they've never even seen the field. They've probably never seen a live gook with a weapon neither. The only gooks they see are old mamasan's that clean their hooch.

The only thing I like about down here is the beach. You wouldn't believe how crystal clear the water is. It's also just the right temperature, I've taken my shoes off and felt it, and it's nice. I can't wait to get the stitches out. Then maybe I'll have a day or so to go in before I ship back to my unit.

Clellie, you'd better just send all your letters to my regular address, because I might get out of here sooner than I expected. I'm going to talk to the doctor tomorrow and rap like hell for him to let me go get my stitches out. Like I said I don't dig lifers. I can hear my unit is moving into Cambodia anyway, and I wouldn't want to miss out on that. There are a lot of gooks over there. Ha ha! Not really. We've already been on a couple of long-range recon patrols over there, enough of Vietnam.

How's everything with everybody back there, Clellie? How's Chad? How's Ann getting along? I sure wish I had her address so I can answer that letter of hers. Are her and Wageman going to get married? Is Alice still going with Kloer? How about little sweet-tempered Nancy May? I hope everything is fine.

Clellie, would you be interested in getting some china and silverware? I have this PACEX catalog that has all kinds of stuff in it. It even has some dolls that maybe we could get Marie. If you're interested let me know and I'll send it to you. I'll let you pick out the china and silverware and I'll see if I can get it. Pick three choices in case I can't get your number one choice. I don't care how expensive it is either.

I better close for now. I love and miss you very much. If only we could be together, but it won't be too much longer. I want you to be mine forever and ever, Clellie. Never leave me. I wouldn't know what to do without you. Clellie, I'll love you no matter what happens. If you only love me that will be all I ever want.

Your loving lonely husband,
Tony

I love and I need you forever!

Sgt. Tony Jolley
6th Conv. Ctr.
APOSF 96385

✉ **8 May 1970**

My dearest wife,

I love you so much! I sure wish this was all over and we were together.

How is everything back home? It's still the same over here. You really made my day today. I just received about eight letters in the mail. All of them from you except one from Carter.

What's this about Ann going with Terry Wageman? I really can't believe that. It sounds kind of funny to me, but you never know, it might work out real good. Who's to say? Right? Right. The way it sounds in your letters it sounds like Red has moved out of the house. Is that right? Tell your mother when I get out of Nam, if she's divorced Red, I'm going to kick her ass. I sincerely think he's done a lot for her and the kids. All she's done in return is treat him like shit. You can tell her I said so too. In fact I want you to tell her. Maybe I ought to write her a letter and cuss her out. Also that Molly moving in about makes me sick. Piss on it. When I get back we won't even have to be around it.

I also got a letter from one of the guys in my squad. He told me they've really been hitting some shit over in Cambodia. He told me our new lieutenant was saying that he wished I was back to take over that second squad again. He got there about three weeks before I was hit. I guess I'll have to get back soon. I've had enough rest for a while.

I'm feeling pretty good today. The only thing wrong is one of the wounds on my ass isn't healing for shit. One piece hit me about right on the spot that makes contact with whatever you're sitting on. So it just isn't healing.

Clellie, you don't realize how good it was to hear from you. You asked me about the college drop. If I'm going to get it, you'd have to get everything ready as soon as you could. If you could dig it so can I. Only one thing, if Barry hasn't got orders by then I would just as soon stay over here for three more months than have him sent here for a year. What do you think?

I love you so very much, Clellie. We were really made for each other. Love me forever and ever, Clellie!

Your lonely husband,
Tony

P.S. Have you seen much of Carter lately? I love you, Clellie!

Sgt. Tony Jolley
6th Conv. Ctr.
APOSF 96392

✉ **9 May 1970**

What's happening my beautiful wife?

Do you still love me? How much? You'd better love me more than is imaginable. I sure do love and miss you.

How is everything in the world? Are you and Chad still waiting for me? I sure hope so.

Guess what? I just got two more letters today, both from you. You ask me how the olives were. They were good. You don't have to send me anymore socks though or beans. Send me bacon rinds in bags, and corn chips, and Jiffy pop. Also canned fruit in the real small cans.

Clellie, in this one letter you said you pay your mother $28 for groceries, and another $30. I thought that's what the $30 was for in the first place. That means you're giving her $60 a month. That's ridiculous, Clellie! Why don't you just support the whole goddamn house? Then everyone could just sit at home and let me and you support them. Wow that really pisses me off. If that's the way you want it though go right ahead. Why don't you live with Mom or Marie? It wouldn't cost you hardly a thing, and you'd always have something to eat. Well hell just do your thing.

Clellie, I still haven't gotten the letter in which you wrote me when and how you found out I was hit. Did the Army notify you, or was that letter I wrote you the first you knew about it. Tell me.

Clellie, I love you so much. I've been completely stoned ever since I got here. Somebody's always asking me to go down on the beach. We end up staying down there all day just smoking. I'm already getting sick of Vietnam.

I've talked to a lot of guys, and for the first seven or eight months of their tour they've never seen a gook. I've been here two months and I've seen beaucoup gooks, and even got hit. I think it's time I went home. I'm seeing too much shit. Our whole platoon is.

Well Clellie, I have to split. I love you dearly. I wish we could be together now. When I see you, I'm going to embrace you and I'm never going to let go. You'll just have to spend the rest of your life in my arms. I want you so bad. If only I could have what I want! Love me always, Clellie!

Your very lonely husband,
Tony

P.S. I love and need you bad!

Sgt. Tony Jolley
6th Conv. Ctr.
APOSF 96392

✉ **11 May 1970**

My lovely Clel,

Here I am writing you another letter. I've written so much lately I'm probably sounding like a broken record.

How is everything at home? Is Chad still good-looking and growing like ever? Are you feeling okay?

Clellie, I got a letter from you with a funny address on it. From now on just use my regular infantry address. Also you said Vicki's husband is tracing me. Man if that clerk bastard traces me here and starts asking me a bunch of questions I'll hit him. Not really, Clellie, but I know you've got my letters by now so settle down. I appreciate you being worried about me, that's one of the reasons I love you like I do, but I'm alright.

I got my stitches out two days ago. I tried to get the doctor to let me go, but he said a couple of the wounds are slightly infected, and didn't close up right. He's going to keep me here for a while longer. I hope not too long, maybe just a couple of days.

I'm sending you the lid of one of the packs of film I got here. The camera is a Kodak Instamatic 100. The film is 126mm. I want exactly the same film as this with one exception. I want color instead of black-and-white. If they don't have it at Thriftway, I'm sure they have it at Rexall. Please send it ASAP.

Clellie, how did everyone find out about me getting hit? They didn't put it in the paper, did they? How did Mr. and Mrs. West find out? Clellie, don't tell anyone more than those who ask you or heard about it. The rumor will probably go around that I got killed. You know how rumors are.

I love you, Clellie. I never thought I would or could love anyone as much as I do you. We really have a good thing going.

When I get home, do you think Chad will know who I am? I guess even if he doesn't you can't blame him. He's still too young to really know what's going on. I hope he never has to see anything like what's going on over here.

I want you bad, Clellie. It would be so cool to be able to get into those sheets off your bed and wait for you to join me. I'd be nude like I was asleep but when you got in bed I'd grab you from behind and you know the rest. Just always remember, Clellie, I love you and want you forever.

Your loving husband,
Tony

P.S. I love you! I need you!

Sgt. Tony Jolley
6th Conv. Ctr.
APOSF 96392

✉ **15 May 1970**

My lovely lady,

Wow it sure is lonely without you. How is everything back in the world? How are Chad and your sisters? I hope everything is okay.

Guess what? I talked to the Doc and he's finally going to let me go tomorrow. It's about time. I'm about going nuts around here.

I got a letter from Bill yesterday, so I think I'll write him back today.

Yesterday down on the beach we were getting stoned. I took a swim, and when I came back, some guy had accidentally sat on my tripping glasses and busted them all to hell. What a bummer! Do you think I should try to get some more? If I sent them home you could get them fixed, couldn't you? Oh well, I'll probably try and get a new lens put in here.

Clellie, I hope you've been sending all your letters to my regular address. Don't send them to the hospital section anymore. It takes them longer to get here than the mail that goes through my unit.

I think it's going to be kind of cool to get back out in the bush. I'll probably be ready to take it easy though after a couple of missions. Our whole unit is in Cambodia. They say we're supposed to pull out June 30. I'll bet money that recon is in there for six more months.

I love you so much, Clellie. Don't worry about me. I'm coming home just for you if it's meant to be. If not, there's nothing we can do about it, but our love will last for all eternity. We'll love each other as long as there's matter that exists. Right? Right.

I'd better go for now. I'll write you when I get back to my unit. I love and miss you very much. Please love me forever too.

Your lonely loving husband,
Tony

P.S. I love you very much!!!

Sgt. Tony Jolley
Co. E. 3rd Bn 22 Inf.
APOSF 96385

ENTERING CAMBODIA

✉ **27 May 1970**   **Cambodia**

My dearest Clellie,

I love you! I'm so sorry I haven't written you. It's been over a week since I last wrote you. We moved into Cambodia the day after I got back to my unit. We've been in the field ever since. We never get back to a base camp lately so I didn't have time to write. This is the first time they've dropped paper and soap and things in to us. I'm sitting against a tree right now, and it's hot and dirty so please excuse the writing and dirt, but it's the best I can do.

I also finally got a big load of mail from you and Mom. It was so nice to read letters from home. I love you so much and you mean the world to me.

How is everything at home? How's Chad? Is he growing a lot? I hope he's mean as hell.

You asked me if I made a tape recording for the world. To my knowledge I didn't. I don't know who those people heard on the radio, but it wasn't me.

So Vicki's husband is a lifer? I can't believe he re-upped like that. If he goes to OCS, that means he'll probably be infantry when he comes back over. She's really going to have a lonely life if he stays in the Army. I don't think he should have re-upped unless he got her okay because she's going to have to live with the Army as much as he is.

Over here in Cambodia, we're really kicking ass. It's really the only way to try and end this war. Will probably be here until about the 20th so don't expect too many letters. Tomorrow we're flying in on choppers to a suspected VC headquarters base camp. We're going to work with two other companies, because there are beaucoup gooks.

Clellie, tell Mom I'm out in the field all the time and thank her for the letters. I probably won't have too much time to write until we clear out of Cambodia. I hope you understand about me not writing and don't worry about me because I'm all right.

We've got about eight guys in recon screwed up since we got here, but we've got a tremendous body count. I'm seeing a lot of action and I'm glad. I'm feeling in good condition except my leg gets tired sometimes while we're humping. Well another month and we might go back to Vietnam with a good body count and get some rest and hot meals.

Clellie, I love you so much. Don't worry about me because I want to get back to you so bad, no damn gook is going to get me. They have their chance to put me out of action, and they muffed it. I love you more than is possible. I've been away from you for so long, but when we get together it'll be forever. Clellie, love me as much as I do you forever. That's all I ask.

Your loving husband,
Tony

P.S. I received your film. Thank you so much. I had it sent back to Tai Ninh because I didn't bring my camera out in the field.

I love you! I want you! I need you!

Sgt. Tony Jolley
Co. E. 3rd Bn 22 Inf.
APOSF 96385

✉ 29 May 1970

My lovely wife,

I just got a little more time to write you. I wouldn't have got this time, but one of our vehicles got shot up today and we stopped for repairs.

Clellie, don't get pissed off. I know I haven't been writing lately, but I swear we don't have time. We've been in the field over two weeks and we have another month to go.

How is everything back home? Are you and Chad still waiting for me? I love you both so very much. I only wish I could be home with you. That's where I should be.

Recon's spending a lot of time in our jeeps. We're driving around these Cambodian dirt trails, and they're using us for everything. They call us to do a lot of things because we can move real fast and hit old Charles hard. In the last five missions we've been on we got hit six times. How's that? We had one dude killed and three wounded with about 20 enemy killed.

Today we came on a French mansion. The French have a big rubber plantation down here, but they moved out when we moved in. I got a picture of it if my film doesn't get wet before we go back to Tai Ninh.

I got a letter from Dale today and I'm going to try and write him a letter after this one but it's getting kind of dark.

Clellie, I love you so much. From now on I'm not going to write about him. Wait till we get to Hawaii, or when I get home and I'll tell you all about it because certain things happen and they might sound worse than they actually are.

Wow Clellie, I wish I could hold you, kiss you, and caress your beautiful body. It's been so long!

I have to go for now. I'll write you ASAP! Please keep loving me because I love you so much.

Your loving husband,
Tony

P.S. What's this about Andrew coming over here? He doesn't have to if he doesn't want to. He probably wants to get the extra money. He should have a fairly secure job

I love you! I need you!

Sgt. Tony Jolley
Co. E. 3rd Bn 22 Inf.
APOSF 96385

✉ **6 Jun 1970**

My beautiful wife,

Do you miss me? Are you and that darling son still waiting for me? How's everything at home? Well enough for the questions.

Clellie, I'm really sorry that I haven't written. I know I told you I wouldn't be able to write too often, but we have less time than ever to write! There's a rumor that recon is going to pull out of Cambodia back to Vietnam. There's supposed to be a big buildup of VC over there so we really don't know what to expect. Guess what though? You know where Spear was stationed? That's where we're going to go for about two or three weeks so we might have it pretty nice for a while. I hear there's very little action there, that also means Spear must have gone into Cambodia. It's a good thing he wasn't in our AO.

We also got out of Cambodia for another reason. I shouldn't even write this, but we almost all got our shit blown away. We were getting ambushed everyday towards the end, twice a day a couple of days. The last time we got ambushed 18 of us and recon were ambushed by a couple of company size units. The only thing that saved us was that Charlie sprung the ambush too soon.

We got three guys killed and two wounded very bad. The two that lived are both going back to the world. Our first lieutenant, and two squad leaders were killed. Sgt. McDaniels was really close to me. I knew them all so well. It really got me. Our 60 gunner got hit so I took the gun. If we didn't call in gunships (choppers), they would have surrounded us. Needless to say I was scared shitless. I couldn't let go of that 60. I was firing ammo as fast as it would fire. The lieutenant was hit in the head by a RPG. We couldn't even find his head. From the waist up he was completely blown away. Really made me sick. Also one of the other sergeants was a dude from Utah. He was also married and had a kid. He never swore or drank or smoked. He was a Mormon. He was on a mission in Europe too. He was a real squared-away guy.

Clellie, I really feel low. I just want to get away from all this and everyone. I have to collect my thoughts. I chased a gook down and shot him after we swept the area, it was too thick and it was getting dark so we have to get out of the area. I wish I could have found him. I would have spit in his face and kicked his head in. It made me feel a little better after that until that night. You can be so close to the person and the next moment they are gone forever.

Clellie, I'm only sure of one thing. I love you so much that it's almost unbearable over here. I'll go out in the field and I'll kill every gook I can. I'll do my job and try to keep myself and my men together so maybe the rest of us can go home. We really got it bad here in Cambodia, but maybe it'll be better when we go back to Nam in a couple of days until we go back to Tai Ninh, then the shit will probably fly again.

Clellie, it's getting dark and I have to close. I try to make the letters a little longer than usual, because I can't write as often. Don't worry about me, I'm depressed at the moment but it will pass as all things do.

I love you, Clellie, and I can't wait to be with you on R&R. Always love me as much as I do you.

Your loving husband,
Tony

I love you!

P.S. Maybe I can write more when I get to the new AO.

Sgt. Tony Jolley
Co. E. 3rd Bn 22 Inf.
APOSF 96385

Minnert on LT.
Gays jeep after
got blown up.

Cam.

✉ **11 Jun 1970**

Dearest Clellie,

How is everything at home? How are you and Chad? I'll bet the weather is getting pretty nice about now. I sure wish I was there so we could go swimming together and stuff.

Well, we finally made it to our new AO (Area of Operation). I think it's the same place Spear was at. We're spending quite a bit of time in the field, so I still don't have much time to write you. I'll write as often as I can though.

So far it doesn't look like too bad of an AO. I would just as soon spend the rest of my time over here without seeing another gook. I've already seen enough and have lost too many close friends.

Clellie, have you written Twin Falls College about me getting registered? Maybe you ought to go rap to one of the counselors about it. I was also thinking about taking a R&R about the middle of September. What do you think?

I'm sending you a picture that was taken of me down at Cam Rahn Bay on the beach. That's a jay in my mouth and on the left side of me on the towel there's a small plastic bag of more jays. How do you like my shaved right leg? The wound is on the back side, but they shaved the entire leg.

Clellie, I know you get upset and worried when I don't write for a while, but please don't. If I don't write, it's because I'm in the field and can't, but I will when I get the chance.

I got a letter from Barry today. He went to Fort Lewis, Washington. I'm glad he didn't get Fort Ord. He said that they were going to start Basic Sunday. He also told me to send him some weed so I just might.

Clellie, I love you so much. I wouldn't know what to do without you. I can't wait to see you in Hawaii. You say we'll be in bed most of the time, and you're right. We still have to go a few places maybe. I might even get me a couple of tailor-made suits for Hawaii.

Clellie, I have to go for now. Please love me forever. I'll always love you.

Your loving husband,
Tony

P.S. Is ole Ann very fat?

I love you, Clellie! I love and want you!

Sgt. Tony Jolley
Co. E. 3rd Bn 22 Inf.
APOSF 96385

16 Jun 1970

My beautiful Clellie,

How is everything back in the world? Do you and Chad still love me? I sure love you both.

I'm sending the pictures you sent to me back. I'm sorry some of them are ruined, but get some more made from the negatives. I'm also sending you a picture of me. It was taken right before I got hit. I was really stoned. All those rolls of film you sent me got soaked so I don't know if they'll turn out. I hope they do.

Clellie, you should be getting $560 in a Treasury check. I know your birthday is the 22nd so you can spend some of it on clothes or something. I'd like to at least send you a card, but I've been in the field so long I don't have a chance to get anything.

We're humping quite a bit now. We never get to do anything but walk. We're in for a day and tomorrow we go on a 4-day bush.

Clellie, see what you can do about paying the bill to the paper. They keep sending me the bill to enclose the money, but all they got over here is that funny money. So see what you can do about it.

I got a letter from Barry and when I get off the next bush I'm going to try and send him some weed; also I'm going to try and send some to you to save for me.

What do you think about getting R&R in the middle of September? Try and see what you can do about that college drop. Barry says he is going to volunteer for Nam. Actually it's a good time to come over because things are going to quiet down a bit after we pull out of Cambodia. They say Recon has seen more action just in Cambodia than a line company sees in an entire year, so I really feel like I'm ready to come home. I hope Barry doesn't get infantry or he would be crazy to come over here, but I think he wants to do his own thing, just like I did.

Clellie, the only thing I look forward to is R&R, and then when I get to come home for good. I've been too close too many times to getting snuffed out and deprived of coming home.

I love you forever and I always will. I can't wait to be able to hold and kiss you and touch your body only the way true love permits it to happen.

I love you, Clellie, now and forever.

Your lonely husband,
Tony

I need you forever!

Sgt. Tony Jolley
Co. E. 3rd Bn 22 Inf.
APOSF 96385

 **19 Jun 1970**

Dear Clellie,

We came in early, but we have to go back out in a couple of hours. I got a hold of a bunch of grass from mamasan yesterday, so I'm sending some home. I sent it already. It'll come in a tape holder so please keep it for me. Get a big plastic bag 'cause I'm sending more. If it don't make it before this letter. Write me and let me know. Also let me know if you got that $560 in a Treasury check.

How are you and Chad doing? I still love you both very much. Especially you! Are you bringing Chad to Hawaii? If you leave him home, who's going to tend him?

The other day I also sent some to Barry's address. I told him not to volunteer for Nam if he gets infantry. I told him anything else wouldn't be so bad but don't go infantry, even if that's what I dig. I think it's the only way to go.

Clellie, please love me forever. If you get any letters with funny addresses on it, it's still me. I'm just sending it so maybe I won't get caught, if anyone asks you if you know anyone in Vietnam tell them no.

I have to go. We'll be leaving pretty soon now. I'll love you forever you know that? See about the college drop, and I might be home in 6 months.

I need you, Clellie. It would be so neat to touch your body and caress you. I could just fondle your body all night. Then we would make love for 2 days. I have to go for now so please never leave me.

Your loving husband,
Tony

P.S. I need & want & love you!

Sgt. Tony Jolley
Co. E. 3rd Bn 22 Inf.
APOSF 96385

✉ **23 Jun 1970**

My Dearest beautiful Wife,

How is the world treating you and Chad? Are you still waiting for me? I sure hope so.

Well this new AO we're in is a pretty good one. I'm pretty sure it's the same one Spear was in. I lost a real good point man the other day. I had Keith walking point and he hit a booby trap. He got dusted off and he's going back to the world.

My leg got infected and I had to go on sick call. The doctor told me to stay back a few missions, but I had to take my squad on an ambush patrol that night so I didn't give it much rest. We really have to hump our ass off here, that's why my leg's been giving me trouble.

Clellie, I'm so sick of this war, but I still want to kill gooks. The other day we received fire from a gook in the rice paddies. Me and Swiger (one of my close dudes in my squad) ran after the gook shooting our ass off. When I get shot at something in me snaps and all I think of is to protect my men and kill. It's afterwards that I think of what I did then I get scared.

I love you so much. It'll be so cool to make tender love to you. I want to squeeze you so bad. Just to lay next to your nude body in a big bed. Do you want me to bring my hammock? And we'll make love in it?

Clellie, I always love you. Love me too. I can't wait for all of this shit to be over.

Your loving husband,
Tony

P.S. I need & want you!

Sgt. Tony Jolley
Co. E. 3rd Bn 22 Inf.
APOSF 96385

Swiger

Cambodia

✉ **26 Jun 1970**

Hi Hon,

How's everything back in the world?

I got about a week's back mail today and it was real good to hear from you. I've been real busy lately. You are now married to the second in command of the 3/22 infantry recon platoon. I have two squads of men now. I've been taking one squad out each night for AP's. That means that I go out every night of the week and I rotate my squads. It's a little extra work, but I get to do it my own way. I'm getting a bunch of new guys and my squads, and you wouldn't believe how they rely on a person when they're in a leadership position.

You mention something about Bill Cosby's record "Forgotten" I've heard it. It's a real nice record too.

I'm sending you these pictures of me. Notice I shaved my mustache and sideburns. I was really stoned that day so was the guys. The names are on the box. You want me to send a couple of headbands home so we could wear them when I get out?

Clellie, I'm going to have to cut it short because I have a meeting at six.

I love you now and always, Clellie. I'll write soon. Stay mine please!

Your lonely husband,
Tony

I love you! It's still raining!

P.S. Clellie, just save all these pictures and we'll put them in a photo album together.

I miss and I need you!

Sgt. Tony Jolley
Co. E. 3rd Bn 22 Inf.
APOSF 96385

✉ **6 Jul 1970**

My beautiful Clellie,

Well we finally made it in from the field last night. We get a day off. We don't have to go out again until tomorrow.

How is everything back home? It's been about a week since I got any mail from anyone. I have a different APO again. It's APOSF 96225.

This rainy season is really getting to me. I've got jungle rot all over my feet and legs and back. I also lost all my tan, because we are continually wet and in the field.

The picture I'm sending you was taken last night in our bunker. We had just got in, took a shower, and put on clean clothes. How do you like the towel and orange paint? It brightens things up. We stole the orange paint from the MP's. We also have red polka dots and blueprints on the walls, but you can't see them. You can also see I got my tripping glasses fixed. I sent them to Saigon, and they did a pretty good job of fixing them. We also were smoking and got really messed up. Has any of that grass I sent to you got there yet? Clellie, if any more is sent it will be addressed to me. I don't even want you to open the tape cases up. Just put them in a bag. Maybe you could bring a little to Hawaii because they really check the GIs.

A couple of guys got busted the other day. One of them was Swiger (the guy in the picture) the other one was Wilburn. They're both good friends of mine. I'm testifying that they weren't smoking.

Clellie, I sure do love you. I wish we could be together now. The way you live over here makes you forget certain things back in the world. Everyone over here is a lot more like animals. Especially when we're out in field. I know I've changed a lot, but I really don't know in what ways. I guess I'll have to wait until we get together again.

Love me forever, Clellie, because I'll love you. I wish I could fondle you and make love to you. I can't wait to hold your lovely body next to mine. I can't even write about it, I get too horny. I'll always love you, Clellie.

Your lonely husband,
Tony

I love you!

P.S. Clellie, the reason for not opening the grass is in case they trace it and follow it. You won't get busted. I love you so much, Clellie Jolley!

P.P.S. Send me pictures of you! Sexy ones!

Sgt. Tony Jolley
Co. E. 3rd Bn 22 Inf.
APOSF 96385

✉ **12 Jul 1970**

Dearest Clellie,

How is everything at home? How is Chad? Most of all how is the most beautiful and wonderful girl in the whole world? I sure do miss you.

Clellie, how come you don't write me every day anymore. I'm hardly getting a letter a week. I'm not pissed off yet, because I don't know for sure whether it's you not writing, or if it's the Army screwing up the mail. I don't even know if you got the weed yet. Also you mentioned something about Allan in your Fourth of July letter, and I don't even know who you're talking about. If something is going on back home with you let me know. Please tell me next letter if you write every day or not. You'd better write!

Clellie, did you want me to get the suitcases? You'd better go down to the PX at Mountain Home because I never get in where I can buy them anymore.

I got a letter from you 4 July. The last letter I got before was dated June 28. Tell me what's going on.

Things around here are starting to get hot. The gooks are coming out of hiding and starting to hit us pretty regular. We got one gook one day and another one the next so that's not bad at all.

I've got a couple of rolls of film of the guys and the place we stayed when we came in out of the field in Cambodia. It ain't much, but what can you expect from the Army. We stayed here for one and a half months. How do you like it? I'll send the rest in different envelopes.

Clellie, we won't be able to go on R&R until October because I don't have enough time in country. That's when we were going to go anyway, right? Also I got a letter of acceptance for CSI, so I'm going to see if that's all they need to get my early out. Don't count on the early out though because they're supposed to be cutting the drops way down.

I love you very much. Do you still love me? I can't wait until we get together. I'm going to caress and feel your body till my fingertips wear off. Every time I see you I'm going to start feeling you over and kiss you and make love.

Love me forever, Clellie. We can really have a groovy thing when I get out. I want to make love to you!

Your lonely horny husband,
Tony

P.S. Send more film! I love you! I need you!

Sgt. Tony Jolley
Co. E. 3rd Bn 22 Inf.
APOSF 96225

 **19 Jul 1970**

My lovely Clellie,

I sure do miss you. How is everything at home? How's Chad? It's okay if you don't bring him on R&R. It'll be kind of cool just the two of us making love and doing our thing.

I really don't know what clothes for you to bring of mine. I guess my bell bottoms and Levi's and sandals and shoes. Bring some shorts, (undershorts) because I don't have any, I don't wear them over here. I was going to get some threads over here, but I'm not kidding I never get the chance to get anything.

Wow we were on a pretty hairy mission. We found a great big bunker complex and had to blow it. You wouldn't believe the size of this complex. It had big kitchens and could hold maybe from 150 to 200 gooks.

Do you think I should grow my mustache for R&R or not? I might start growing it around September. I did tell you that it wouldn't be until October 15 or so before we go on R&R. Our clerk said I'd have a better chance to get it then.

You keep asking me about my leg. Don't worry about it. It's okay. You can hardly tell I got hit there compared to what it used to look like. It's all right though so don't worry about it.
What's this shit about me liking Angie? What do you mean I used to like her? Tell me who the person is that informed you I liked her, and I'll see what I can do about it when I get home.

I want you to tell me how many tape cartridges you got in the mail. It sounds like you just got one and I sent you two. I might start sending letters home with grass in each one. If you get one with my name on it, and an unknown return address just take the center tape up part and throw it in with the tapes.

I love you very, very much, Clellie. I can hardly wait to be with you again. It's been a long time since we've even kissed. Do you know that? I can't wait to hold and kiss and caress you. Wow, it's really going to be cool. Clellie, I have to go for now. Always love me. I'll always love you.

Your lonely husband,
Tony

I need and want you!

Sgt. Tony Jolley
Co. E. 3rd Bn 22 Inf.
APOSF 96225

✉ **26 Jul 1970**

Dearest Clellie,

Today is the day I finally made it back to the base camp. How is everything back there? For the last 3 to 4 days we've been on the jeeps because the gooks are starting to hit the convoys around here. We've been hit five times in the last four days. Last night they almost got my jeep's number. We were riding last jeep in the formation. The gooks let the whole convoy go by and blew the ambush on my jeep. They shot an RPG at us, and it hit 30 meters from the jeep. Then my gunners 60 jammed on him. Luckily no one was hurt.

We got a new lieutenant now, and he's pretty good. I met him in Cu Chi when I first came in country. That means also I'm just a squad leader again, and it sure feels good. All the guys in my squad wanted to form the same squad I had before so I still have the same guys, and they're still the best squad in recon.

You asked me if I ever received Jimmy's or your mother's letter? No, I never did get them. What address did they use?

I'm going to try and get the R&R for sure in October. I can't put in for it until 60 days prior.

I don't know whether that school drop is going to come through or not.

Clellie, I cannot wait until the day we can be together. It'll be so neat to get in a big bed with sheets on it, especially with you. Also I want you to wash my back while I take a bath. All we'll have to do all day long is anything we dig. At nights we can make love any place we can find.

I hear Honolulu is real cool and it'll be especially cool because you'll be there. I love you, Clellie, very much and I always will. Please be mine. I need, want, and love you!

Your loving husband,
Tony

Sgt. Tony Jolley
Co. E. 3rd Bn 22 Inf.
APOSF 96225

✉ **2 Aug 1970**

My beautiful Clellie,

Here it is. I just got paid $180. It really pissed me off. I thought I would get a lot more than that. They took some back money and partial pays out. I'll try and send some money home later on in the month. I'm going to try to send $200 home and have enough money over here for the rest of the month.

Clellie, are you putting every other check from the government in my account, or are you putting them all in your account? It doesn't matter I guess, it just seems like we should have more money saved up.

I can't remember what kind of clothes I have, Clellie, so just bring the clothes of mine that you like.

Yes, I've received both packages you sent. I got the little pipe and really dig it. You wouldn't believe all the grass that goes through that little bowl, just one thing, the stem got busted off. I still use it though.

In your last letter you said that Susan said she knew that Carter stepped out on her while she was pregnant. She doesn't realize how very wrong she is. I know for a fact that he didn't. He thought the world of her then. He would never have done it. I think when he started stepping out on her was when she really came down on the dope and told him to stop. There I answered your question.

I'm going to send a few more tapes home, Clellie. Let me know as soon as you get them. Is anyone asking you about the grass? Does Ann or your other sisters know about it? Don't let anyone know about the deal other than the people who already do know about it.

Clellie, does Vicky know that I smoke dope? I don't really know why I asked, she just seems like the kind of chick that would really freak out if she knew that.

I have to go for now, Clellie. I have to set my head today so I'll be in condition to hit the field tomorrow. Always love me as much as I do you. I love you now and always.

Your loving husband,
Tony

I love you, Clellie!

Sgt. Tony Jolley
Co. E. 3rd Bn 22 Inf.
APOSF 96225

✉ **6 Aug 1970**

Dearest Clellie,

I sure do wish this whole mess was over and we were together again. I miss and love you so much.

So Chad is really growing? It would really be cool if I could see him. I really can't remember what he looks like hardly. I want you to send some pictures of you and Chad. I want some good ones of you in your swimming suit and with Chad. Buy some film today, take the pictures, and get them off as soon as possible. I also want you to start getting a good tan. I'm not very dark at all, but I'm a little bit tanned anyway.

I guess all the American troops are leaving Tai Ninh. The ARVM's are talking it over. I guess I'll never have to go back there. I kinda wish I could get out of here though, because the gooks are starting to get close. The other day they hit another convoy and in a matter of five minutes killed three GIs and had run out of the area before we got there. They run out of the area now because they know recon's gun jeeps will be there in a matter of minutes. Recon has really got a name in this area because of all the shit we do. We've still got the highest body count in the whole battalion too. This AO is as good as any though, because if you're going to get it, it doesn't matter where you're at you'll get it. Well enough of this war shit.

Clellie, I put in for R&R 5 October. How's that? Like you said the later we go the less time we'll have after the R&R. It'll be so nice to get on R&R. Just to touch interests you? It'll be so neat to make love. If you're half as horny as me, it's going to take only about one minute to go off. Are you doing your exercises? I'm glad you lost that little stomach, but I'll have it back when we get on R&R, because all the love we'll be making you'll start eating like a horse. Not really, ha ha!

Clellie, I love you so very much. Are you really looking forward to R&R? It's going to be really cool. You're going to love Honolulu. We're also going to have to see as much as we can. You said you wanted to spend most of our time in bed, but we don't have to. We can still make love wherever we want. We'll just make love wherever we're at. I want to make love on the beach at night. Clellie, I love you now and always. Please love me forever.

Your loving horny husband,
Tony

P.S. Don't forget the pictures.

Sgt. Tony Jolley
Co. E. 3rd Bn 22 Inf.
APOSF 96225

✉ **12 Aug 1970**

Dearest Clellie,

I love you so very much. How is everything back in the world? Are you and Chad still waiting for me, Clellie?

I'm writing you this short letter, Clellie, to let you know that I am changing units. There's an opening on the mountain (Nui Ba Den) and the CO put me in for it. It's a good chance for a real job. It's not an office job, but I won't be humping as much I don't think. All the guys I knew in recon when I first came in country are either wounded and sent home, killed, or have gone back to the world anyway. The only one left is Swiger and he goes home in 10 days. I figured I might as well go, because it might mean a better job or at least a change. The CO (Captain) thinks I've seen enough. (Wow ain't that a laugh! How about the guys that got killed? They must've seen too much.) Like I said though I think a change would be good. I hear up there they see gooks down lower on the mountain, and they just lay in their bunkers and shoot at them. The only time they hump is on short recon missions. All the new guys want me to stay, but I don't feel like seeing any more of them fcked up.

Clellie, that sounds like I'm really down, but believe me it's a better job and it might mean a better chance of making it back to you. I feel I've seen enough, and that's it. I don't want to see anymore. I don't know what would happen if I did.

Clellie, have you got those tapes yet? I sent another with this letter so you should get three altogether if you get them all.

Also Clellie, don't send any more letters after you get this letter to this address. I'll send you my new address as soon as I get it.

I better go for now. I can't wait until R&R to be with you. If time goes to slow up there, I'm coming back to recon. I'll love you now and always, Clellie!

Love you always,
Tony

I need you, Clellie Jolley!

Sgt. Tony Jolley
Co. E. 3rd Bn 22 Inf.
APOSF 96225

✉ **22 Aug 1970**

My Beautiful Clellie,

I sure do love you. Time is really going slow. How is everything back there? I hope everything is all right.

Guess what? I just got back from Saigon. When I came here to Cu Chi to get my stuff before going on the mountain, I met this dude and he's ready to ETS so we split to Saigon for three days. I've never been to Saigon before so I decided it was about time I saw some of the good parts of this country. On the way back we went to Cam Rahn Bay on the beach. I'm a couple of days AWOL, but it doesn't mean anything. All I have to do is say I had trouble clearing my other unit. I guess I'll be heading up there tomorrow. Wow I couldn't believe how some of the guys in the Army really got it made. We stayed with these heads that have a place right in the middle of Saigon. We really got super stoned. It was really nice to get out of the field for a while.

I put in for R&R for 5 October. I might have trouble getting it back now that I've changed units, but I shouldn't. You asked me when I put in for it in one of your last letters. So Vicky's husband got them a hooch maid? You don't have to worry about me getting one of them, because the places I've been stationed at they won't come to them.

The new address is on the envelope, but it might be changed when I get up there.

I love you, Clellie. I wish we could be together now. I can't wait to hold you and make love to you. Hawaii is really going to be cool. I can't wait. Well I better go for now. Always love me. I need you!

Your lonely husband,
Tony

Sgt. Tony Jolley
HHC 1st Bde 25th Inf. Div.
Nui Ba Den Prov. Co.
APOSF 96268

 **23 Aug 1970**   **Written on an envelope**

Dear Clellie,

I couldn't find any paper, but I just wanted you to know that the APO is still 96225 so don't send anything to that other APO. I love you very much, Clellie Jolley. You're all I ever want.

Love you,
Tony

Sgt. Tony Jolley
HHC 1st Bde 25th Inf. Div.
Nui Ba Den Prov. Co.
APOSF 96225

✉ **29 Aug 1970**

Dearest Clellie,

I sure could dig being with you and Chad right now. Time sure seems to be dragging by.

Is everything all right at home? I sure hope so. You do know that I put in for R&R the 5th of October right?

Well I'm on the mountain. It's pretty nice up here, except the clouds are always fogging the place over. I've lost about all my tan again. I'm the radar sergeant. It's not too bad at all. During the night we run the radar, if we catch movement I call in mortar rounds on him then in the morning I take my section on a sweep of the area to see if we got anything. That's when we'll get ambushed if we do. The other day we got sniper fire and it was too damn close. I'd kind of like to go back to recon, but it's a little safer up here. It's not a real job by a long ways, but it's pretty safe. At least I got a bunker to sleep in and I'm not sleeping on the ground.

There's only one thing about this job. That is I'll be here until I ETS, and I won't be able to get a real job because they need men up here and it's hard to get them to stay. The main reason is because we're way up here all by ourselves, and nobody could get to us in time if we got overrun. But there's a very slim chance of old Charles overrunning this place because of our defense. We only have 18 bunkers guarding the place, but we have wire and Claymore and booby-traps and everything out there. The only way we can get resupplied is by choppers; there are no roads or nothing leading up here it's just too damn steep. The only other way to get up is by foot. Well enough of that. I'll send you some pictures of the place and also the view on a clear day. Send me beaucoup film, Clellie, because I really want to take a lot of pictures. Also send me some flash cubes.

Tell Alice that was really great of her to write. I'll answer her if I get a chance. How come she broke up with that Kloer kid?

Clellie, guess what? I sure do love you. It's really great the way love can make a guy feel. I can't wait until R&R. We're really going to have a great time. It'll be so good to just be with you. We won't even know the war's going on. I love, love, love you now and forever. I can't wait until you're next to me in bed where I can do anything I want and we can make love again like we used to. Well I better go for now. Love me always, Clellie!

Your lonely husband,
Tony

I need you, Clellie!

Sgt. Tony Jolley
HHC 1st Bde 25th Inf. Div.
Nui Ba Den Prov. Co.
APOSF 96225

✉ **12 Sept 1970**

Dearest Beautiful Clellie,

How is everything back in the world? Are you and Chad still waiting for me? I sure hope so!

Clellie, I really do love you, and you know something else? I will love you forever. I'm sorry I haven't written for quite a while, but I haven't been in one place long enough to write. For the last week and a half I've been up and down this mountain trying to get my radar fixed. (Of course I haven't been walking up and down the mountain, because the only way up here it is by chopper.)

I thought I would answer some of your questions. I don't want you to put the weed in a pouch. I don't even want you to open the tape holder. Bring one tape holder as it is. If you want to buy a wig, it's all right with me. It's also okay with me if you get a mixed drink on the plane. I would recommend a Bloody Mary or a Tom Collins. They'll only let you have two drinks on the entire flight though. The Reef Hotel sounds like a good place to stay at also. If we don't like it we can always move out.

I want to ask you a question now. Who is Reed the pharmacist? It seems like you're always saying what a cool guy he is, and how you can't wait until he came back. I wasn't going to mention it, but you brought him up in numerous letters.

I've got enclosed in this letter a copy of my R&R orders. You should have already gotten some from the Army, but I'll explain them like you asked me to. Send this copy back to me if you received yours. I might need it. First of all, Clellie, I'm sorry we didn't get it on 5 October. The R&R is for 18 October. The part I have underlined in the bottom left hand corner is the estimated time of arrival in Hawaii, which is 1330 (1:30 PM) 18 Oct 70 the R&R ends on the 24 Oct 70. That's about all there is to it. I hope you can understand it now. If not just let me know what else you want to know. It won't be so bad to go on the 18th; it's just that much closer to my ETS date.

Clellie, I love you so much. I'm really looking forward to R&R. I can't wait to be able to hold your warm smooth body next to mine. I'm really kind of scared in a way. I don't know how I'm going to act. I hope everything goes all right. Remember Clellie, sometimes I can't write the words to tell you how much I love you, but I do so much. Love me too!

Your lonely husband,
Tony

P.S. I need and want you, Clellie! Where's my pictures?

P.P.S. Clellie, send me a box with fudge and brownies and goodies. I really get hungry in this high-altitude. Also I sent $320 home this month. I lost some money last month, but I almost made up for it this month because I only got paid $240. I love you!

Sgt. Tony Jolley
HHC 1st Bde 25th Inf. Div.
Nui Ba Den Prov. Co.
APOSF 96225

✉ **16 Sept 1970**

My Dearest Clellie,

I'll bet you're really surprised to get this letter so soon after the last one. I found some time and decided I'd like to spend it talking to you.

How is everything back there? I love both you and Chad, but I wish you'd hurry and send me those pictures you were going to. How about my homemade fudge and brownies? Are you going to send them to me? Don't send them in a coffee can because by the time they get here they are really bent up and in bad shape. Also Clellie, could you send me some batteries to my camera? It's a Kodak Instamatic 100! (Wow! Gimme gimme ha ha!)

We spotted some movement the last couple of nights on radar so the CO asked me what I thought of taking out a squad-sized element after dark to observe the area. So about 3 o'clock this afternoon I'm taking 10 guys out and we're going to observe the area until about 10 or 11 tonight. Just like the good ole days.

Yes, Clellie, I've been receiving your mail. I usually get it four or five letters at a time. Have you been writing every day? The postmarks are usually all screwed up. I received all 13 letters and two packages.

About the hooch maid, the reason I won't get one is not only because they're not up here. I've been places where I could have had one, but I have you so why mess things up by doing that? Right? Right!

If you can find a good deal on skis, boots, and poles do it. Tell them that you want to ski, and ask them to help you pick them out because stores like Michael Mark should do it. Also if you want to go with Sue go ahead. It's all right by me.

How does it feel to be off work? What do you do to keep yourself busy? Seriously I know there's a hell of a lot to do.

I'm really sorry about the R&R, Clellie. According to the last letters I received from you, you really didn't want to put it off. It's not really that much longer, and it's less time we'll have to be apart when we leave. Let me have that copy of the orders back as soon as you can, because I have to turn it in to the orderly room so they know I'm going.

Well Clellie, I really have to go. I can't wait until Hawaii. How much money are you bringing? We really don't need any.

I love you, Clellie. It's going to be so cool to crawl into bed with you and feel that hot little body of yours next to me. We can do anything we want. We have to have breakfast brought up to us in bed. Right? I'm really looking forward to it. I love you now and always.

Your lonely loving husband,
Tony

I love you! I need you!

Sgt. Tony Jolley
HHC 1st Bde 25th Inf. Div.
Nui Ba Den Prov. Co.
APOSF 96225

✉ **23 Sept 1970**

Dear Clellie,

How is everything back home? I received your package a couple of days ago. I also received the pictures of you and Chad. Why did you scribble on the picture of you in the swimsuit? Wow your hair is really super long. I dig Ashley's glasses. Yes, I think it would be okay for you to get a vest with stringy things on it.

Clellie, you really sound depressed about not getting any of my mail. I've been writing every chance I get. I can't understand why you haven't received my letters yet. You also have another tape coming. Let me know as soon as you receive it. Don't open it. Just put it with the rest of them. You ask me why I didn't write anything with the money orders. That's simply because I didn't send them. I turned in a self-addressed envelope and the money to the mail clerk and he went below and got the money orders and sent them to you. That's why I didn't write even "I love you!"

When you send a box with the homemade goodies and such could you send some zigzag rolling papers (two or three packs), and another one of those miniature pipes? A friend of mine wanted one of the pipes so I would really dig it if you could send them.

I'm really sorry about the R&R date. I can't understand why they gave me it at such a late time compared to what I asked for. I hope you can switch those reservations for the appropriate time instead of the date you said you made them for.

Use that set of orders I sent you to get your plane reservations. I hope nothing screws up. Are you still going to bring one of the tapes full of dew? Make sure you bring one that is addressed to me, and is unopened. I hope you keep all that stuff well-hidden so nobody messes around with it too.

I sure hope nothing goes wrong. I don't care about those bruises you got either. All I want is you. That sounds like a nasty spill you took. So please take it easy. I started growing my mustache again about a week ago. So if you don't like it I'll shave it off. I'm also white again because the clouds are always up here in the rainy season. I can't wait until the dry season and the sun.

Clellie, I love you very, very much. I don't know what I would do without you. I can't wait to see you again. I really don't know how I'm going to act. It'll be such a switch from being here. I feel kind of nervous anyway. I love you now and always, Clellie. Love me no matter what.

Your lonely husband,
Tony

I need you!

Sgt. Tony Jolley
HHC 1st Bde 25th Inf. Div.
Nui Ba Den Prov. Co.
APOSF 96225

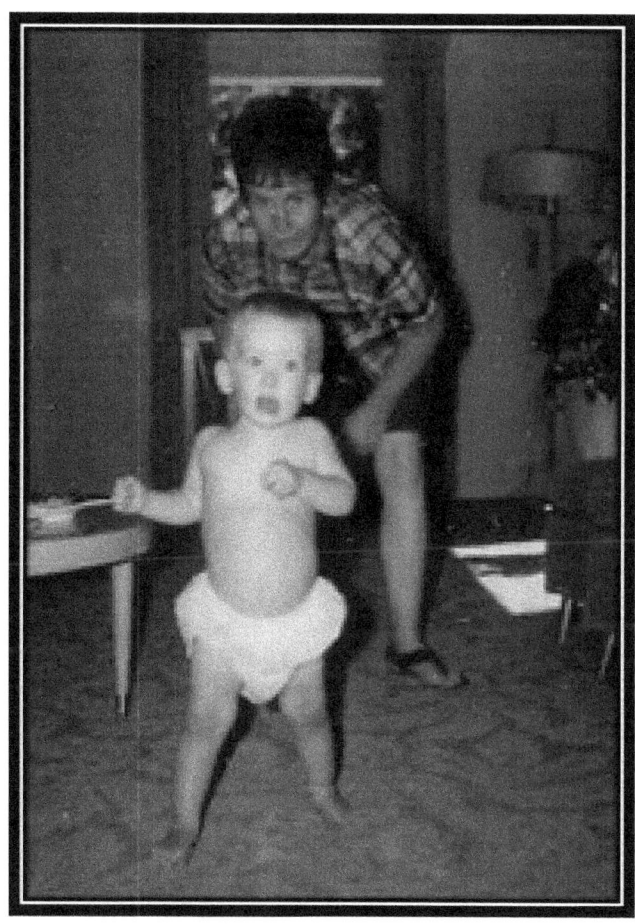

✉ **27 Sept 1970**

Dearest beautiful Clellie,

Here it is, another Sunday in Vietnam. The days are all the same, and you wouldn't even know it was supposed to be a special day.

How is everything with you? Have you received all my letters? Clellie, don't get so upset when you don't hear from me for a while. Sometimes I just don't have a chance to write. No matter how long you have to wait for a letter you know I'll still love you. Our love is too great to be spoiled so easily. You and Susan sound like you're really having a good time. About the ski equipment if you want you can go ahead and buy the whole outfit. It would be better that way. If I decide to get new equipment, I'll just sell my old ones for what I can get and buy a new outfit.

Have you got the orders for R&R that I sent you yet? I sure hope so. The 18th really isn't that far off now. From today it's only 21 more days. Just think 21 more days and we'll be together again. When we get together, and I act different than I used to, let me know in what ways. I know I've changed, but I don't really know how. I think we'll both probably have to be patient with one another. I can't wait to see you again, but in a way I'm kind of unsure how to act.

Guess what, Clellie? I might get a real job finally. I'm not sure, but there was a job opening up in Dau Tieng in about two weeks. I might have a chance at it, but the CO asked me to stay here. It's not bad up here, but it's still considered being in the field, and as much gook movement as we've been picking up lately, I'd like to get the job even if I have to put up with the lifers. All I know is I want to come home and I don't want to get messed up. I've seen too many people already get killed and messed up. I just don't want to see anymore.

Have you heard where Andrew's supposed to be stationed? How about Barry? Is he going to stay out of Nam by saying he has a brother over here?

Clellie, do you still love me? I'll always love, want, and need you so please don't lose faith in me. It seems like such a short time until R&R now. I hope everything turns out just right. It's got to, or I don't know what will happen. I'll love you now and always so always love me too.

I love you.
Tony

I need and love you, Clellie!

Sgt. Tony Jolley
HHC 1st Bde 25th Inf. Div.
Nui Ba Den Prov. Co.
APOSF 96225

 **1 Oct 1970**   **17 days to R&R**

Dearest Clellie,

I'm sure glad you finally got the orders for Hawaii. I thought you were going to go crazy waiting for them. Really you've got to try and relax, and not worry so much about things like that. You know that I would try anything possible to get that R&R right? I want it as much, if not more, than you do. I really think it's going to take a little time to get use to each other though. I've been working on my language, because it's three times worse than you have ever heard it. I'll try real hard to keep from offending you, but I just don't know.

How is Chad and everyone back there in the world? I kind of wish in a way we could bring Chad, but it would be better to leave him at home. If we brought him we wouldn't be able to do a damn thing. It won't be too long and I'll be able to see both of you for good.

Hey that's really great about Ann's baby! You know I never even realized she was that far along. Congratulate her, and tell her I'm expecting a great big "It's a boy" cigar in the mail. If I can get down within a week or so I'll send her a dozen red roses. What do you think? We'll be late, but better than never. Also send me some pictures of the baby.

Clellie, what's this about only bringing $400 to Hawaii? I thought you were going to look at these catalogs and pick some china and silverware. I have the books and order blanks. They have some nice things too. Really I think you should bring about $500 or $600. What were you going to do with the rest anyway? If we have it left you can always take it back with you. Didn't you save $800?

About the car, Clellie, keep it running good, because we'll have to use it for a while after I get home too.

Could you get me a pair of Levi's bellbottoms, and maybe a pair of semi-dress flares? Maybe a shirt to match the dress ones too. It be cheaper than buying them in Hawaii. The size would be 30 waist and 30 inseam or 29 inseam. You can use the Army check for it.

Well, Clellie, we don't have long at all now until we're together. It's really going to be cool.

I hope you don't find me any different than I was. I might seem different at first maybe, but it'll probably take a little time. Piss on it! I'm not going to worry about it. Don't you either.

I have to go now, Clellie. I love you now and forever no matter what happens. Always love me too. I'll see you soon in Hawaii.

Tony

P.S. Are you going to party the night before I get there? And after I leave?

Sgt. Tony Jolley
HHC 1st Bde 25th Inf. Div.
Nui Ba Den Prov. Co.
APOSF 96225

6 Oct 1970 card

Clellie,

Well, Clellie, just about time for R&R. I thought this card is good for the way I feel right now.

It's been a long time since I last saw you. I'm really looking forward to seeing you. 12 days and we'll be together. I love you, Clellie.

Love always,
Tony

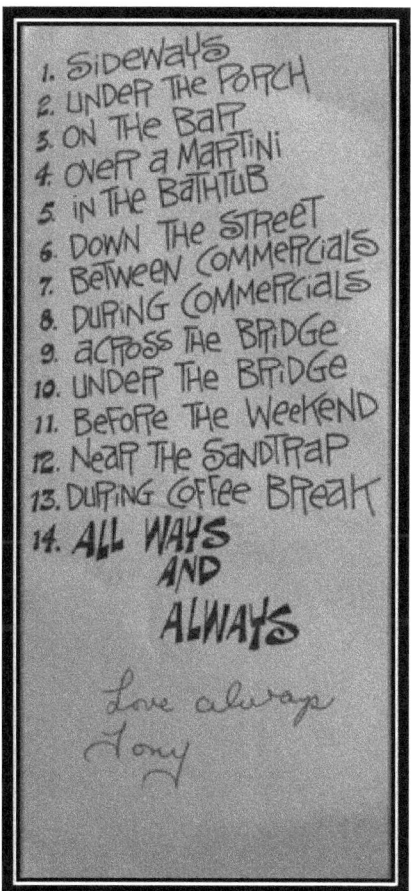

✉ **8 Oct 1970**

Dearest Clellie,

I received a couple of letters and the package you sent me a couple of days ago. Wow that fudge and brownies tasted great. They got here in real good shape too. Everyone on the mountain that had some really liked them. That is definitely what I want in the care packages from now on, if it's okay with you.

How is everyone there doing? How was Ann's baby? I'd still like to see some pictures if you could send them. Does Chad like the baby? Has Wageman come to see him yet? If he comes tell him he can send me a cigar. What is going to happen? Are they going to get married or what? They'll probably work things out between them if everyone else would stay out of it.

About me finding someone to write to Susan. I don't really think I know any return missionaries up here. I know some real cool guys, but they're not Mormons. They're great people just the same. I don't really think she could be happy with someone like that anyway. Have you heard anything about Carter? Is he really going to give Taylor an engagement ring? If he does it's up to him. Who knows maybe he really digs the chick, and they could make a good go at it. I only hope Susan can do the same.

R&R is coming up real soon now, Clellie. It'll be great to hold you in my arms and be able to talk to you, and sleep with you. It'll be real great. Do you want to go to the beach much? How's your tan coming? Mine's about gone. It's been so cloudy up here I've lost it all. You're still bringing the dew aren't you? You can smoke too. I'd kind of like to see you stoned. We'll get stoned, and walk on the beach at three in the morning. I can't wait to make love. I'll be kind of shy though. Ha ha! I'm kind of worried how I'm going to act, but I'm sure it's just because I'm excited about the R&R finally getting through.

I better go for now. Love me always, Clellie. That's all I ask. I can't wait to see you again.

Love, Tony

P.S. 10 more days and we'll be doing our thing in Hawaii!

I love you so much Clellie!

Sgt. Tony Jolley
HHC 1st Bde 25th Inf. Div.
Nui Ba Den Prov. Co.
APOSF 96225

HAWAII AND RETURNING HOME

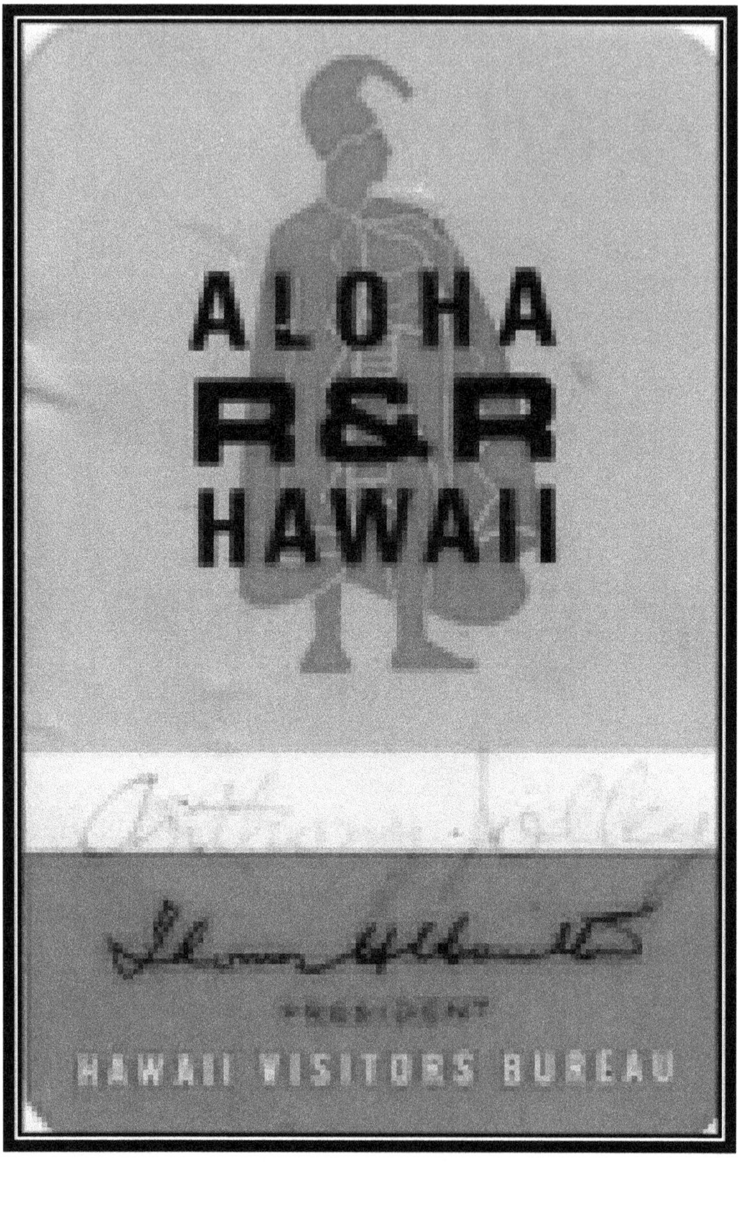
ALOHA
R&R
HAWAII
PRESIDENT
HAWAII VISITORS BUREAU

Two Ladies Return From Hawaiian Trip

Mrs. Vicki Steffen and Mrs. Clellie Jolley recently returned from Waikiki Beach, Hawaii, after having spent a week with their husbands who were on R and R leave.

Sp/5 David Steffen is with the Americal Division Artillery at Chu Lai, Vietnam.

Sgt. Tony Jolley is with the 25th Infantry Division out of Tay Ninh, Vietnam.

✉ **29 Oct 1970**

Dearest Clellie,

Well here I am back on top of the mountain. It was fogged in again so it took me longer to get up here than I expected. I got up here late yesterday. Well do you still love me? Did you meet anyone in Hawaii after I left? How is Chad? I'll bet he sure missed you while you were away.

If you want that china and silverware, or whatever you want just send the picture of what you want. They have a new catalog out so the numbers have changed. Send me the picture and I'll pick it out of the new catalog. If you want the stuff send for it fast because I got another thing to tell you. Guess what? All American troops on top of this mountain have to be off by 15 November. That means I'll probably go back to my old unit. That also means that they'll probably send me back out in the field. I sure hope not. Well anyway if you want that stuff send the pictures as soon as possible because I don't know where I'll be in another two weeks. I knew something like this would happen. I don't know what I'll do. I know I don't think I should have to go in the field again, but they'll probably send most of us back to the field because they won't have any other openings. Well to hell with it, I'm not going to worry until it happens.

Clellie, it was so good being on R&R with you. I hated so much to have to come back here. It was so nice to be able to touch and hold you. The last few days we got along a lot better too.

It's going to be so nice to be back with you forever. Love me forever, Clellie, and I will you too. Right after the 15th if you don't get mail for a while don't worry, because I'll be changing units and won't have my address. I sure hope this doesn't mess up my early out. I love you, Clellie, forever.

Tony

I love you!

Sgt. Tony Jolley
HHC 1st Bde 25th Inf. Div.
Nui Ba Den Prov. Co.
APOSF 96225

✉ **3 Nov 1970**

Beautiful Clellie,

Well R&R is over, all we have to wait for now is the next time I come home, it'll be for good. I love you very much, Clellie, and I always will.

I sent a letter about five or six days ago. I forgot if I told you that I did buy a doll. I sent it airmail to you. I also saw a real nice 400 day clock. I found out I can order it through Pacex, so let me know if you want one. Look at the ones in your catalog and send me the one you want.

How is Chad? I'll bet he really missed you. I'm really getting anxious to see him. I'm so lucky to have you, Clellie, and also a son like Chad. I hope he's not too spoiled when I get home.

Well, Clellie, I might just as well tell you the good news. I just got my school drop today. I have 58 days left in the Army. How does that sound? I leave Nam and the Army on 31 December or 1st of January. It sure feels good to have it almost all over.

We have to leave the mountain in about 10 days. Watch me have to go back to the field. I sure hope not, but at least I'm finally getting short. I don't know what's going to happen, but some lifer better not get me messed up or I'm going to be pissed. I'm too short for that shit.

Did everybody ask you how R&R was? Did you tell them we spent most of the time in bed diddling? It's true you know, but we still saw a lot of things. I sure have no complaints. I was sore for two days after I left. How about you? Were you still sore? Man what am I talking about this stuff for? It's bad enough over here now without you. I can't wait to get home.

Did you ever check and see how many tapes we have? We should have five. I might send some more just before I come home.

Wow ever since I've been back up here we've had clouds, wind, and rain. That Typhoon that hit Da Nang caused 60 mph winds up here. It blew our antennas down and tore the roof off our mess hall. I'm sure glad we are going because as soon as it clears up there's going to be a lot of rebuilding.

Clellie, I have to go for now. I love you now and always. I can't wait to get back home. I'm so sick of Vietnam. When I do it'll be just you, Chad, and me.

Love you always,

Tony

I need you, Clellie!

Sgt. Tony Jolley
HHC 1st Bde 25th Inf. Div.
Nui Ba Den Prov. Co.
APOSF 96225

✉ **6 Nov 1970**

My Charming Clellie,

How is everything with you and Chad today? I miss you both very much, especially you, Clellie. I sure wish this shit would end and I could get back to the world with you.

Guess what? Well about four days ago the radar equipment had to go down, because we're pulling off the mountain. So I got reassigned to the bunker life. I'm now bunker com on bunker 14. How's that? I won't be long though 'cause we're pulling off soon. We are all packed and ready to go. We are eating c rations now too. Supposedly we'll be off by the 10th now. I still don't know where I'm going. Probably back to my old unit. I don't care though because I'm short! Only 55 more days left!

Clellie about wanting to know what medals I'm getting. I don't want you putting anything else about me in the paper. I don't even want you to put in when I'm coming home. I've had enough put in that damn paper. I just don't want anything else put in the paper.

Well do you still think about R&R? It seems like it took so long to get here, and it went too fast. I really had a good time there, Clellie, and it was mostly due to you being there. I sure wish we were back there. Of course I'm coming home for good the next time.

I'll be sending another tape, and maybe a couple of packages, Clellie. I got my carving back so I still might send it. I'd sure like to have it home. It's a nice little weapon. I might not buy that stereo equipment. If you don't want me to buy it, tell me so. I was going to buy it for both of us so if you don't want to let me know. How about just a reel to reel tape stereo for $283? Then I could bring or send the rest of the money home for a down payment on a cabinet stereo. You dig?

Clellie, I better go now I can hardly write without messing up. I guess it's about time to hit the sack. You might not get another letter for a while, but don't let it worry you. I'll take a while to find where I'm going, or my address.

I love you so very much, Clellie. I always will too. You know that? Well I'll write as soon as possible. Can't wait to be able to hold and love you again. I really miss you. Always love me too.

I love you,
Tony

Sgt. Tony Jolley
HHC 1st Bde 25th Inf. Div.
Nui Ba Den Prov. Co.
APOSF 96225

 **19 Nov 1970**

Dearest Clellie,

Well here I am in Cu Chi again. I'm waiting for the convoy to get here to take me to Bien Hoa. I'm getting transferred to the first Cavalry. I don't know my exact address so I'm using my old one.

We left the mountain on the 14th, and this is the first chance I've had to write. I don't know what they'll do with me, but I don't care. I only have 45 days left anyway.

How is everything back home? Do you still love me? I haven't got any mail from you for over a week. I probably won't get it for quite a while either. I don't even see how they reassigned me. Anyone with under 60 days was supposed to go home with the 25th on 10 December. I guess I'm just not lucky enough. I'm in a different div. now so it's too late to do anything about it.

They gave me that leave for the 20th of this month. That's tomorrow though and I'll be still reporting and processing in to the first Cavalry, so I don't know if they'll let me take it. I have orders to go. Also I'm short on money, and I don't think I'll have enough. I'd like to go in a way, but I'll be with you in a little over 40 days. I love you so much, Clellie. It'll be real nice to get back there with you and Chad.

Clellie, I have to go for now. It's a short letter that we should be leaving real soon. I'll write you again as soon as I find out my new address.

I wish we were together now, Clellie. It won't be too long at all now, and we will. I love you now and always.

Love, Tony

P.S. Wait till you get my new address before you send any more letters.

Sgt. Tony Jolley
HHC 1st Bde 25th Inf. Div.
Nui Ba Den Prov. Co.
APOSF 96225

✉ **22 Nov 1970**

Dearest Clellie,

Well it finally looks like I got a rear job. It's really a bummer getting assigned to a new unit with only 39 days left though. It feels good to start getting short. Just think a little over a month and I'll be home for good. You do realize though that I'm supposed to go to school? If I don't and they find out, they can pull me back into the Army. Whatever, I'm not going to worry about it!

Clellie, I'm not sure what I want to do when I get back. I really shouldn't take the drop, but I don't think I can take much more of this over here. If I knew I would get a rear job like this in the end, I would have turned down the drop. Of course then I wouldn't have got it. You probably want to know what it is. Well I don't know. I just got here and they haven't decided what to do with me. I hope I don't get stuck inside all the time. I could dig a job where I could be outside in the sun. I've lost about all the tan I had from Hawaii, and I'd like to get it back.

If my letters don't make much sense, Clellie, just ignore them. I feel like my intelligence level has dropped 50 points since I came over here, and as you know I can't afford that right? Right! I just feel mixed up. I don't know what I want to do when I get home. I hope the hell people don't start hassling me about what they think I should do, because I can work it out myself (with your help of course) but I just need some time. Well enough of that.

How is everything at home? I hope everyone is fine. I haven't got a letter now for quite a while. I probably won't get one for still another while yet to. I sure wish I would get some soon.

I really don't have much more to say because nothing is really happening. I'll let you know what I get assigned to when they let me know. I think I'm going to shave for a couple more days. They've already told me to cut my sideburns and hair, I can put up with the lifers for 39 days. It's better than humping again.

I love you now and always, Clellie. No matter what happens always remember that. I can't wait to be with you again. I wish just me and you and Chad could split somewhere and live without the big hassle in the world. I know I'll always want you, I just hope you'll always want me.

Love you always,
Tony

I love you!

Sgt. Tony Jolley
HHC 1st Cav. Div. Rear
Bein Hoa Army base
APOSF 96490

✉ **2 Dec 1970**

Dearest Clellie,

I sure do miss you. I still haven't heard from you since about 13 November. Looks like the Army is still up to form as usual, and screwing up people's minds. How is everyone, Clellie?

I know I haven't written for a while, but there's really not too much happening here. I don't know what's going on in my mind. I want to come back to the world, but I've lived such a simple life over here for so long I don't know what to expect. The only thing I'm still sure of back there is that I still love you, Clellie. Don't think I'm writing like this because I'm stoned or something. I haven't done any dope for two days, so I'm really down. Not really down, but time has gone so slow over here that I can hardly remember how it was back in the world. The way the news is people are screwing up everything. Seems like they're trying to turn the states into a big machine, and have the people in them working as a bigger organization. When I get back, Clellie, I don't want to be in that organization. I want to be an individual, and lead a separate life away from that organization. But to do that would be to live outside society, and I have a responsibility to you and Chad so that's no good either. I don't know what to do. I'll just have to wait and see what happens. If you don't understand what I'm saying, Clellie, it's just because it's hard to put in words what I mean. Like I said before the only thing I'm sure about is I still love you. It's a good thing we did get married before I came over here. If it wasn't for that I don't think that old hometown of ours would ever see me again, not for very long anyway. On the other hand, maybe I could find myself in a place like that.

If you don't get much mail for me until I get home don't worry about it. My feelings for you will never change so don't think it's something you said or done. I'm trying to get my head together and this place never has anything happening. I'll be home in 30 days and we'll be able to talk to each other, and that's not really that far off. Even though it seems to be.

Clellie, always love me. Don't worry about anything I have said because the Army's had me in a rut for almost 2 years, and it's going to take a while to get out that's all.

I can't wait until I'm with you again, forever the next time too. I'll always love you, Clellie, so love me too.

Your loving husband,
Tony

I love you!

Sgt. Tony Jolley
HHC 1st Cav. Div. Rear
Bein Hoa Army base
APOSF 96490

✉ **12 Dec 1970**

Dear Clellie,

Well here it is the 12th already. 19 more days, and I'll be home for good. Are you glad it's all over with? I can't wait to be home with you again. I don't know how I'm going to like going right into school though.

How is everything at home? Hope everyone is okay. Clellie don't expect me home for Christmas, because I already have my orders to go home, and I don't leave now until the 31st. We'll have our own Christmas when I get there. I don't want you to save any presents though. Just have a nice Christmas, and when I get home me and you and Chad will have another one.

Are you mad at me for taking so long to write? I hope not. I think about you all the time, but it just don't seem like I have time to write.

Nam is really hot during the days now. It gets up to about 110°, and it really beats down. Right now it's about 7:30 PM and the sun is just starting to set. It's really beautiful. I didn't know Vietnam could be this peaceful. I can see how a lot of people spend their time over here in the rear like this, and think Nam isn't really that bad. Of course I had a lot of good moments in the field, but here you feel a little safer.

I got all your letters, Clellie, and it was really cool to hear from you. I went from 13 November to 8 December without a letter. It really seems like a long time. I'm glad I got them though.

You asked me if I ever went with Armen. No I never did. Back about in the ninth grade or eighth I think she showed me and someone else her house. I don't know where we should live, Clellie, it's up to you. I just don't know what we're going to do.

I love you, Clellie, and I always will. Remember when we said goodbye in Hawaii. It seemed like I had forever to go over here. Now it's almost all gone.

Are you glad you waited for me, or have you maybe met someone else you think you could dig more? I hope it's still me. I might be kind of simple, but my love for you is extra special and it's very real. I always love you so please do me too. See you in titi.

Tony

I love you, Clellie!

Sgt. Tony Jolley
HHC 1st Cav. Div. Rear
Bein Hoa Army base
APOSF 96490

✉ 20 Dec 1970

Dearest Clellie,

How is everything at home? By the time you get this letter it'll probably be about Christmas. I want to wish you and Chad a very good Christmas, Clellie. I really wish I could be there with you, but I'll be home in just a little bit.

So Andrew and Barry are home now? That's cool! I sure hope I get to see them, but they'll probably be gone when I get home. Tell them to stay a few days longer, Clellie. I should be home the first or the second at the latest. They don't have any balls if they can't be a couple of days late. I did it, ha ha!

Well now that you've met Andrew, do you still think he's the dreamboat you had imagined? I'm just kidding. What do you think of him? Does he smoke dew or anything? I'd sure like to get home before he leaves, and I could turn them both on to some good dew.

Clellie, I'm going to give you Swiger's stateside address. I want you to write a letter asking him to send us his address at Fort Carson to our address there (your mother's). Also thank him for me for sending that ripple and incense. Tell him when I'm getting home, and ask him the date he's getting out of the Army. I don't have time to write because I'll be going all the way to the rear at Long Binh day after tomorrow. This will be my last letter to you to Clellie. The address is:

Eddie Swiger
R route
Ohio

I should only have about three days left when you get this letter. I should leave Nam the 31st and be home the first.

I still don't know about school. Maybe I just won't go. I'd kind of like to go to Pocatello. I really don't think I could dig going to Twin.

Clellie, I love you very much, and I always will. Nam has done us both some good. There are some parts I'm really going to have to forget. I know you'll help just being there. I'll always love you Clellie, so don't think there is any way I'll leave you as long as you want me. Always love me too.

Love, Tony

P.S. I love you!

Sgt. Tony Jolley
HHC 1st Cav. Div. Rear
Bein Hoa Army base
APOSF 96490

FREEDOM!

The friends I met in Nam were the best comrades any soldier could have found; they were very strong-headed men, a lot like me. I met Kershaw who was from Pocatello. We both came home from Vietnam. I'd go visit him and he would come to visit me. After about 6 months being home, Kershaw was driving on a curvy road and ran off it and was killed. I couldn't understand why after going through Vietnam he came home and then was killed.

I also met Gleason who had a desk job, but volunteered to join my Recon group. He was a good friend of Eddie Swiger who was also in my command. When we got home, Gleason hooked us up on a three-way phone conversation which was unheard of at that time, but Gleason was so smart and was working in New York. He arranged for us all to talk together. Within 1 year, he overdosed on heroin and passed. It was so sad and unbelievable because none of us were ever into heroin. It was a damn shame! Gleason was a good man.

Me and my old bud Eddie still communicate once in a while. He lives in Ohio. Clellie and I met with him and his girlfriend in Portland about 11 years after we returned. I could tell how much he thought of me because I saved his life. He would always say, "It was because of Tony I came home."

It seemed almost worse coming home than going to Nam. When I got the letter saying I was going home it was a damn shame. I wanted to stay till the end; of course I didn't know there was only four more years left. I felt I had let my comrades down, my friends, my team.

I returned home in January of '71. The trip from the Boise Airport back to Burley was horrible. Old food, eggs, rocks, bits of metal, and a lot of shit were tossed at me both in and out of the car. My Clellie could only look at me with sadness, and my boy Chad looked at me with so much confusion.

When I got home I went upstairs, ripped off my uniform, and threw it away. I set my Purple Heart and Bronze Star medals on the dresser, took a shower, and just cried.

They never tell you when you're heading into war what you need to know. I figure it must be because they wouldn't be able to get anyone to stay if they knew the truth. Early on I was so excited to serve my two years and get on with my life; little did I realize how much those two years would impact the rest of my days.

Things got better over the next 47 years. My wife and I were blessed with twin girls. As years went on I worked, and the kids grew up and had kids of their own. After all I've been through I can say, I lived my life to the fullest. I have a good family and good friends. I've lost some and won some along the way.

As I come to the end of my time on Earth, I look back on a life well lived. I think about those times long ago. I reflect on the loss, the senselessness of it all, and the wisdom that can only come from age. I'm not sure why we have to go through all the stuff that we do, but maybe one day it will all make sense. Maybe one day, when I'm reunited with my old friends, I will be able to rest in the peace of knowing I did the best I could. Until then I will live the best life I have to live and love like tomorrow is never promised.

~THE END~

ABOUT THE AUTHOR

Denise Jolley is a passionate storyteller.

After many decades of customer service-related work, Denise discovered her passion of sharing the stories of her family, friends, and customers. To honor not only the people but their stories, Denise shares every story with integrity, honesty, and respect.

Stay Mine Forever: Letters from Nam is her first published book, but not her last.

Upon becoming an empty-nester, Denise and her husband, Chad, relocated to Arizona from La Grande, Oregon. Together they share seven amazing children and enjoy time spent with them. Other favorite activities include vacationing in new and exciting places, visiting family and friends, and being active in their church.

www.ingramcontent.com/pod-product-compliance
Lightning Source LLC
Chambersburg PA
CBHW050847160426
43194CB00011B/2056